PERSPECTIVES

ON
SPIRIT
BAPTISM

PERSPECTIVES
ON
SPIRIT
BAPTISM

FIVE VIEWS

RALPH DEL COLLE
H. RAY DUNNING
LARRY HART
STANLEY M. HORTON
WALTER C. KAISER, JR.

EDITED BY
CHAD OWEN BRAND

BROADMAN
&HOLMAN
PUBLISHERS

NASHVILLE, TENNESSEE

Published by Broadman & Holman Publishers
Nashville, Tennessee

Dewey Decimal Classification: 234.12
Subject Heading: BAPTISM IN THE HOLY SPIRIT \
SPIRITUAL GIFTS \ HOLY SPIRIT

1 2 3 4 5 6 7 8 9 10   10 09 08 07 06 05 04

*This volume is affectionately dedicated to
Tashia, Chad, and Cassandra.*

*You have contributed to my sanctification
(in more ways than one),
and I love you more than my very life.*

Contents

Contributors

Chad Owen Brand, Ph.D.
Associate Professor of Christian Theology
The Southern Baptist Theological Seminary
Associate Dean for Biblical and Theological Studies
Boyce College
Louisville, KY
> Chad Brand is editor of *Perspectives on Church Government: Five Views on Polity,* as well as the *Holman Illustrated Bible Dictionary.*

Ralph Del Colle, Ph.D.
Associate Professor of Theology
Marquette University
Milwaukee, WI
> Dr. Del Colle is author of *Christ and the Spirit: Spirit-Christology in Trinitarian Perspective,* published by Oxford University Press. He is one of the premiere figures in Catholic charismatic renewal today.

H. Ray Dunning, Ph.D.
Professor Emeritus of Theology
Trevecca Nazarene University
Nashville, TN

Dr. Dunning is author of a widely used systematic theology in the Wesleyan tradition, *Grace, Faith and Holiness,* published in 1988. It is an excellent work of scholarship.

Larry D. Hart, Ph.D.
Professor of Theology
School of Theology and Missions
Oral Roberts University
Tulsa, OK

Professor Hart has written *Truth Aflame: A Balanced Theology for Evangelicals and Charismatics,* the second edition of which is published by Zondervan. His work has been a model of dialogue between charismatics and evangelicals.

Stanley Monroe Horton, Th.D.
Distinguished Professor of Bible and Theology, Emeritus
The Assemblies of God Theological Seminary
Springfield, MO

One of the premiere theologians in the Assemblies of God, Dr. Horton is author of many books, including *What the Bible Says about the Holy Spirit.*

Walter C. Kaiser Jr., Ph.D.
President, and Colman M. Mockler Distinguished Professor
of Old Testament
Gordon-Conwell Theological Seminary
S. Hamilton, MA

Professor Kaiser is a prolific author, with such works as *Toward an Old Testament Theology* and *A History of Israel: From the Bronze Age through the Jewish Wars.* He is a leader in theological education and Christian renewal in America today.

Preface

Like most important books, this one has been longer in the making than it has been in the typing, and I am confident that each of the writers who has contributed to this volume could say the same thing. For me it represents a stage in a long process of knowing and understanding the Holy Spirit of God, as well as coming to grips with a biblical doctrine of spirituality. One side of my family is deeply rooted in the Church of God of Prophecy. My father grew up with the impression that A. J. Tomlinson was seated just a little to the right of Jesus in the heavenly court. I still recall some rather interesting revival services from my early childhood years and am grateful for that legacy in the lives of some family members, though I have not followed in those footsteps. During my college years I came under the influence of a resurgent Keswick spirituality in my church in Denver, Colorado. A saintly Welsh lady in my church, Lucy Esch, was on personal terms with some of the English Keswick teachers, such as Norman Grubb. Her godly influence and profound prayer ministry led me to drink deeply from the wells of this brand of spirituality. In addition, my pastor, Carey Miller, often invited some of the best of the "Baptist Keswick" teachers of the mid-seventies into our pulpit—Jack Taylor, Manley Beasley, Jim Hylton, and Peter Lord. Some of these men would later move consciously into Charismatic renewal and away from their "deeper-life" roots, but I learned much from them, even if eventually I found the Keswick model to be biblically wanting. In the years that followed, personal issues and theological interest drove me more and more to investigate the nature of biblical spirituality, a major component of which is an understanding of the nature of Spirit baptism. Hence, this book.

I owe a debt to several persons who have made major contributions to this volume. First, I want to thank the contributors. These are all devout Christian scholars who love the Lord and have much more in common than they do in opposition. They have worked diligently and cooperatively with an editor (me) who has sometimes been demanding. I am grateful for their spirit and pray that God will use the fruit of their labors for his kingdom.

Second, I am grateful to the editorial staff at Broadman & Holman Publishers. They kindly extended the deadline when difficulties arose, and they have offered excellent editorial assistance throughout the process. Pride of place goes to Leonard Goss, who is editing this entire Perspectives series and who has been helpful since the first day he downloaded this proposal. Also, John Landers has helped with suggestions along the way. I want also to thank Timothy Grubbs at B&H. I first mentioned the idea for this series to him, and he has been an encourager from that day forward as the volumes have begun to take shape. He is a good friend and a firm supporter.

I have to thank, third, my colleagues at The Southern Baptist Theological Seminary and Boyce College. President Albert Mohler, Seminary Dean Russell Moore, and our new dean at Boyce, James Scroggins, have all urged me on and provided moral support in the midst of full teaching and administrative loads. Their contribution has been enormous. The seminary also provided a one-semester sabbatical in the spring of 2003, which helped this volume to see the light of day. My colleagues in the theology department, Bruce Ware, Stephen Wellum, and Gregg Allison, have all shown much interest in the project, and my dear friends Charles Draper, Mark McClellan, Ted Cabal, and Jerry Johnson helped tremendously by constantly "bugging me" about the book. Professors Tom Schreiner and Bruce Ware also helped me define the nature of this volume in conversations I had with them two years ago.

I am also very grateful to three Ph.D. students at the Southern Baptist Theological Seminary who worked very hard and at short notice to prepare the indexes for this volume. Travis Kerns, Brian Walls, and Heath Rickmond willingly stepped up to the plate to take on the tedious task that makes this volume more usable. I thank them (and their wives!) from the bottom of my heart.

Several persons have been my dialogue partners over the years in the area of pneumatology. I joined the Society of Pentecostal Studies in the early 1990s, and the members have been accommodating of an "outsider," as I have presented papers in their annual conferences. At these events I met two contributors to this volume, Larry Hart and Ralph Del Colle. I have also been privileged to make acquaintance with William Faupel, for many years the secretary to the society, and he encouraged me to participate at every level, despite my not being a Pentecostal. Pride of place as coresearcher of both doctrine and spiritual life, though, goes to my friend Tom Pratt. He and I began research on a different, though similar, project many years ago. Some of what was begun there bears fruit in this volume, though certainly not all.

Every writer (or editor) knows deep down that the only reason he can pursue the task of publishing is that there are people around him who make his life easy and simple enough to make that happen. In my life that task goes to my family, my wife, and our children. My wife Tina does double duty as homemaker in our house and as my secretary at the office. So for her there is double the work and, sometimes, double the frustration. But she endures it as a soldier of Christ. No man could ask for a more loving and dedicated wife. And she is beautiful to boot! I am also deeply grateful to our children, Tashia, Chad, and Cassandra. All three endured doctoral studies with me, including that dreaded nemesis that most of them did not understand at the time—the dissertation! They have also been willing to sacrifice time with me on occasions as I was hacking away at the computer on some new project. There is no way I can adequately thank them for their patience and willingness to let Dad do his work, but I would like to dedicate this volume to them, in prayer that the Spirit of God who is discussed in this volume will fill their lives with all good things in the years to come.

The Holy Spirit and Spirit Baptism in Today's Church

CHAD OWEN BRAND

This is a book on Spirit baptism. Why is such a book important? The Bible speaks about the baptism in the Spirit as an aspect of the work of the Spirit in the lives of believers. Several questions come immediately into play when we ponder this issue. First, we might wonder about the relationship of such an experience to Christian initiation—to what we as Evangelicals call "conversion." Second, we might probe the relationship of Spirit baptism to spirituality in general. How does this experience with the Spirit relate to the believer's everyday existence? Third, how can believers with differing views on Spirit baptism relate to one another? Will this cause divisions between them, or can they abide together as brothers and sisters in Christ? These are important questions. They may not all be answered within these pages, but clues to solving these dilemmas will be found here.

In this Introduction I would like to address two issues related to the questions being raised in contemporary conversations about the Spirit, both of which have some bearing on the question of Spirit baptism. First, I will speak to the question of the continued existence of the miraculous in the postapostolic church. That has a bearing at least in part because of the Pentecostals' claim that Spirit baptism today is evidenced by a miraculous sign—speaking in tongues. Second, I will address the matter of the relationship of the Spirit to the Word. Historically, many different groups have polarized over this very issue, and the conversation plays a role in the current debate. Then I will give a brief representation of the various interpretations of Spirit baptism in Christian history as a prelude to the debate between the five authors of this volume.

The Holy Spirit and Miracles in the Early Church

The early church was Charismatic. Paul and Peter both spoke of the free and abundant exercise of spiritual gifts (1 Cor. 12–14; Rom. 12:9–13; 1 Pet. 4:7–11) in the church, gifts that were essentially the representation and outworking of ministries among all believers, not merely the "clergy." The early church father Clement of Rome noted that early Christians set out "in the assurance of the Spirit" to carry out these ministries.[1] This Charismatic dimension continued on into the second century. But some have argued that the miraculous phenomena, or the sign gifts, ceased soon after the death of the apostles.

Benjamin Breckenridge Warfield launched a major academic broadside against Holiness theology and healing practices and the claim that miracles or sign gifts are present in the church today. He argued that all modern claims to miracles were *de facto* spurious because the miracle-working stage of the church's existence "belonged . . . exclusively to the Apostolic age. . . . [Miracles] were part of the credentials of the Apostles as the authoritative agents of God in founding the church. Their function thus confined them to distinctively the Apostolic Church, and they necessarily passed away with it."[2] Warfield supported his hypothesis by an analysis of the purpose of miracle in the Bible (especially the New Testament) and a lengthy treatment on aretology and enthusiasm in the history of the church. He concluded that miracle reports in the post-Apostolic period are either spurious (or at least highly questionable) or associated with groups and theologies which are clearly heterodoxical (such as medieval Catholicism and the French Prophets), infected with theological viruses of an anthropocentric nature (such as the Methodist Holiness Movement[3]), or often completely alien to the true faith (such as Christian Science).[4]

Warfield's argument has been extraordinarily influential in the last century.[5] It has not gone unchallenged, however. Both planks (i.e., the biblical[6] and the historical[7]) in the Warfield hypothesis have been vigorously assaulted, especially in the last twenty-five years.[8] Both of these matters are complex, and a thorough analysis of them is a prerequisite to any theology of the Charismatic in the church's present existence. The biblical question does not, however, come into the purview of this present analysis in any direct way.[9] The historical question does.

Did miracles pass away at the closing of the Apostolic Age? Any answer to that will depend, in part, on a definition of the word *miracle*.[10] This chapter will examine evidence from the extant writings of several of the Fathers who took note of miraculous activity in their day. It will look specifically for mention of healing, glossalalia,[11] prophetic utterances,[12] resuscitations, and other paranormal spiritual phenomena that could be understood as "miraculous."

In general, the early church was a vibrant, spiritually charged movement that swept the empire with a new message of hope. A Notre Dame professor states it thus: "The church experienced a time of great vitality during the two hundred years after the apostolic period. Starting from small bands of Christians, usually centered in the big cities, it grew to a vast spiritual fellowship reaching into nearly every corner of the Roman Empire."[13] It spread in spite of the disfavor and eventual proscription of the authorities, and its advance was marked by testimonies of wondrous things being wrought in the name of Christ.

Early in the second century, there is evidence that the church was concerned about spiritual gifts in general and prophecy in particular. Ignatius encouraged Polycarp to "ask for invisible things so that they may be made manifest to you in order that you may lack nothing and abound with all spiritual gifts."[14] Ignatius may have believed himself to possess prophetic gifts as well. In his letter to the Philadelphians he wrote, "But the Spirit made an announcement to me, saying as follows: Do nothing without the bishop; keep your bodies as the temples of God; love unity; avoid divisions."[15]

The author of *The Shepherd of Hermas* apparently saw himself as a prophet as well. He made repeated claims to be the recipient of divine visions.[16] He also indicated that there were tests that should be administered to evaluate the trustworthiness of a prophet. "By his life you test the man that has the divine Spirit. . . . You have before you the life of both kinds of prophets. By his deeds and life test, then, the man who says he is inspired."[17] He further said of the function of the prophet, "So whenever the man who has the divine Spirit comes into an assembly of righteous men . . . and a prayer is made . . . then the angel of the prophetic spirit which is assigned to him fills the man, and that man, having been filled by the holy Spirit, speaks to the group as the Lord wills."[18]

Justin Martyr was the first to enumerate a variety of spiritual gifts, but he made mention specifically of gifts of utterance and gifts of healing.[19] Later in the same writing he indicates that the "prophetical gifts" that were given to Jesus and the apostles "remain with us, even to the present time."[20] Justin also claims that exorcisms were known both to him and to the Roman Christians.[21] He does not, however, elaborate on the gifts of healing or foreknowledge, as to whether they were in existence *in any great measure* in his day.[22]

In the final decades of the second century a Charismatic-type movement arose in Phrygia called, after its chief exponent, Montanism.[23] There is serious difference of opinion as to whether the Montanists were "orthodox."[24] There is no question, however, as to the attitude the Montanists had toward the churches of the day. They considered the churches to be immoral and spiritually sterile.[25] In their opinion, the early church was marked by vibrant power, and, when it was at its best, by moral purity. They perceived the church in their own day to be slipping into moral decline while it gradually succumbed to a hierarchicalism that had no precedent in the New Testament.[26] "The conquering power of the Spirit seemed to be dying out. How would the Church be kept pure? A clergy with authority seemed the only way."[27]

The Montanist "Charismatic" emphasis was primarily, perhaps exclusively, verbal. Montanus and his followers saw themselves as prophets of the "latter rain."[28] Theirs was a prophetic gift, "incited by the spirit of frenzy."[29] Some have seen in this movement the first verifiable expression of subapostolic tongues-speech.[30] This conclusion certainly is possible and perhaps even likely, but it is not irrefutable.[31]

Irenaeus of Lyons discussed the gifts of the Spirit several times in *Against Heresies*. Irenaeus developed his views in response to the Montanist challenge, but he does not seem to have been as reactionary as one might expect.[32] He did speak of false prophets,[33] but this is likely a reference to the kind of prophecy exercised by Marcus, the gnostic magician.[34] Irenaeus believed that prophetic gifts originated with God.[35] The bestowal of prophetic gifts, as is the case with all gifts, is a result of the sovereign activity of the Lord.[36] Though spiritual gifts, and especially prophecy, are partial, yet they will remain with the church until the Second Advent.[37] Thus, prophecy and tongues were intended by God to remain in the church through history.[38] Healing is also a part of the permanent possession of the church. "It is not possible to name the number of gifts which the Church, [scattered] throughout the whole world, has received from God."[39] Irenaeus does not record any specific healings performed in his time but is clearly convinced that healing power is still the possession of the church.[40]

Hippolytus of Rome addressed the issue of healing by laymen in the church.[41] This passage speaks of someone receiving the gift of healing and of that reception being announced by a revelation. The text is not clear at every point, but there does at least seem to be a parallel between this and the teaching of Paul in 1 Corinthians 12:8. If so, it is evidence that the charism of healing was at least expected to belong to the ministry of the church in the early third century.[42]

Origen apparently believed the gift of healing was still available:
And some give evidence of their having received through this faith a marvelous power by the cures which they perform, invoking no other name over those who need their help than that of the God of all things, and of Jesus, along with a mention of His history. For by these means we too have seen many persons freed from grievous calamities, and from the distractions of mind, and madness, and countless other ills, which could be cured neither by men nor devils.[43]
He argued that the gifts of the Spirit are granted only to Christians, and not all Christians at that, but only to those who were deemed

worthy.[44] Origen knew many Christians who had performed exorcisms.[45] He likewise believed the gift of prophecy to be active and powerful in the church of his day. The true prophet was one who possessed clear vision and could therefore declare the profundities of the Christian faith in lucid language. This was in contrast to the Pythian priestesses who fell into frenzies and lost consciousness in their prophesyings.[46]

The Cappadocians were quite interested in divine healing. Gregory Nazianzus related two incidents of healing in the life of Basil. As Basil was about to be exiled, he was recalled to pray for the emperor's ailing son. He prayed, and the boy made a remarkable recovery but later died. Later, an ailing Bishop Eusebius called for him to pray at his bedside. Basil complied, and Eusebius was restored, never again questioning the power of God in Basil's life.[47]

Gregory also relates that his own sister Gorgonia was once dragged by a team of mules and injured so severely the family was sure she would die. But the church prayed, and she was healed. In later years this same sister was once so severely ill with fever that there was little hope. But in the night she went into the church and took some of the reserved sacrament and knelt at the altar, crying out that she would not relent until she was made whole. After rubbing the sacramental wafer on her body, she felt refreshed, and did indeed soon recover.[48]

The early church was marked by a vibrant spirit, as well as by the manifestation of the power of God in prophecy and healing. It appears that there was a significant diminution of the frequency of miracles from the time of the apostles into the subapostolic period, but they were not eliminated completely. The Warfield hypothesis—that the true charismata ceased with the death of the disciples of the apostles—is in need of revision, at the very least. But he seems to have been correct on one point: the miracles of the church from the third century on had begun to take on superstitious characteristics not found in biblical accounts. Still, the question of the continuance of the miraculous charismata is a live and open issue for debate today.[49]

Word and Spirit in Historical Context

One of the most enduring challenges in theological understanding and indeed in Christian living is to establish an appropriate

INTRODUCTION — 7

relationship between Word (Scripture) and Spirit (or the experience of God in one's life). Furthermore, Christians have to face the question of the role of language (word) as an adequate conveyor of truth. Is language up to the task of speaking meaningfully and appropriately about God, or ought believers to look more to subjective encounter or intuition as the only real means of appropriating the benefits of Christian faith?

How can language speak adequately about God and truth? In some sense, this problem has ancient roots. Christian mystics taught that "God transcends the purview of our perception and imagination and therefore cannot really be known conceptually."[50] Gregory of Nyssa contended that "concepts create idols, only wonder comprehends anything."[51] Thomas Aquinas, on the other hand, maintained that believers could know something of God by seeing the similarity between God and his creatures in the midst of an even greater dissimilarity. For Thomas, analogy was a middle way between univocity (literal knowledge) and equivocity (uncertain knowledge).[52]

Donald Bloesch joins with Aquinas in advocating a *tertia via* concerning the knowledge of God. He alleges that in the modern context some American Evangelicals—specifically, Carl Henry, Ronald Nash, E. J. Carnell, and Gordon Clark—contend for a univocal knowledge of God.[53] On the other end of the spectrum are theologians who regard human language as wholly inadequate for contributing any real knowledge of God. Karl Jaspers and Fritz Buri view words as mere ciphers of transcendence, pleading that God cannot be objectified.[54] Tillich, echoing the mystical impulse, maintained that humanity can have a symbolic awareness of God, but both theoretical and direct knowledge of God are an impossibility since there is a "God above God" who is the ground of being but is not himself a Person.[55] Feminist theologians "generally call us to construct a new language about God based on consciousness of a holocentric world—in which every aspect of reality is seen as part of an organic whole."[56] Sallie McFague urges that humans can have only intimations of transcendence that can, at most, be apprehended by use of metaphor.[57] Metaphors, for her, "underscore by their multiplicity and lack of fit the unknowability of God."[58] Hermeneutical theory must include a paradigm for a linguistic reconstruction of biblical images for God.[59] Even Pannenberg maintains that human language about God is little more than equivocal and must wait for its fulfillment until the eschaton, when both equivocity and analogy are transcended.[60]

Karl Barth followed Aquinas in affirming an analogical relation between God and humanity but rejected Aquinas's natural theology. For Barth, the truth of human speech about God lay not in analogical relationships but in God's free act of condescension to humanity's weakness and imperfection.[61] Thomas F. Torrance takes a similar approach: "theological language and theological statements participate sacramentally in the mystery of Christ as the Truth."[62] Torrance warns against mystics and evidentialists who speak of a noncognitive and nonconceptual language about God. "There can be no knowledge of God . . . which is not basically conceptual at its root."[63] Human language will certainly not capture God in all his essence, but human concepts are determined by divine revelation "under the creative impact of the speech of God" and "are grounded beyond themselves in the *ratio veritatis* of the divine Being."[64]

In line with the mystical tradition, some important figures in the history of the church have opted for immediate inspiration of the Spirit over against knowledge of God through his Word. The Radical Reformers during the Reformation included many who were orthodox and who affirmed the importance of both Word and Spirit. But certain "inspirationists" among them virtually rejected the Word in favor of Spirit. Thomas Müntzer, for example, contended that the Holy Spirit had told him to participate in the Peasants' Revolt of 1525. He fired off a tract against Martin Luther, who had been his mentor, for not supporting the peasants' cause. Müntzer called Luther "Dr. Pussyfoot" and "Dr. Liar," and Luther reacted by denouncing the rebels in *Against the Murderous and Thieving Hordes of Peasants.*[65]

Some of the inspirationists contrasted the "inner word" with the "outer word" and opted for the former. Once a colleague of Luther's, Karlstadt later wrote, "As far as I am concerned, I do not need the outward witness. I want to have the testimony of the Spirit within me, as it was promised by Christ."[66] Luther replied that Karlstadt believed himself to have "devoured the Holy Spirit, feathers and all."[67] Müntzer argued that the Bible has only a preparatory role. The outward Word must be abandoned in favor of the inner.[68] Sebastian Franck rejected all external religious observances, such as baptism and the eucharist, in favor of an inner experience of Christ. "He was convinced that there is in each man a divine element which is the source of all spiritual life."[69] Hans Denck rejected water baptism in favor of Spirit baptism, opted for the inner Spirit as opposed to the biblical text, and argued that all external forms of religious observance were to be rejected. This polarization toward the Spirit and against the Word can be multiplied many times over in movements such as the Catharii, the Friends, the French Prophets, and various other radical groups that have cropped up, especially since the Reformation.[70]

In this volume, all of the authors attempt to give full credit to both Word and Spirit. In addition, all of the writers here believe that there are both cognitive/intellectual and pneumatic/experiential components to the process of theological construction. The differences are in the mix, on both issues. In other words, all of the traditions represented here are probably closer to the center within their respective traditions rather than on the fringe. The fringe might be represented on the one side by those who consider it apostasy to use anything other than the KJV, while in the more pneumatic traditions it would be something like the Manifested Sons movement or the advocates of Word/Faith theology.[71] The authors of this volume give place to both Word and Spirit, but the reader will have to decide the degree to which each writer has done so appropriately.

A Typology of Spirit Baptism

This volume presents five models for understanding Spirit baptism. It is not an exhaustive exposition, though it is representative. It is not exhaustive since there are nuanced differences within the various traditions. In one way or another, the major positions are represented here. But before launching into the essays, it might be helpful for the reader to survey the key models that have been proposed.

Though there was no conscientious theological reflection on Spirit baptism as such before the nineteenth century, various traditions interpreted the gift of the Spirit differently, both as to the manner of the giving and the timing. One ought not to be surprised at the delay in developing a consistent Pneumatology, but one must never forget that the absence of the doctrine did not mean the absence of the experience of the Spirit. "Long before the Spirit was a theme of doctrine, He was a fact in the experience of the community."[72] Developing Catholicism, as Professor Del Colle notes in his chapter in this volume, saw the Spirit as being given in the sacrament of confirmation, though that gift was, in reality, an extension of baptismal grace. Representatives of the Catholic tradition held in common their conviction that the Spirit was given in the sacraments of the church, but they were divided over the question of whether there was one anointing or two.[73] This understanding of the Spirit given in the sacraments is suggested by the *Shepherd of Hermas,* who contends that believers must come through water to be made alive by the Spirit, and that water is then the "seal" of their salvation.[74] Ralph Del Colle ably wends his way through the complexities of sacramental interpretations in this present volume.

Several Puritan divines concluded that the baptism in the Spirit constituted a sealing by the Spirit which produced assurance of salvation. Thomas Goodwin, for example, connects the passages in the book of Acts where the Spirit is poured out with the promise of the gift of the Spirit in John 14–16, and with Paul's comment on being sealed by the Spirit in Ephesians 1:13. He suggests that in all of these cases the recipients were regenerate, that is, they had been born of the Spirit. Still, they are all receiving a spiritual ablution that has a profound and obviously life-changing effect on them. The result is that all those who receive it are persuaded in their hearts that they will surely be granted their final inheritance in salvation.[75] D. Martyn Lloyd-Jones, a prominent English pastor and theologian in the twentieth century, also advocated the view that Spirit baptism constituted a subsequent experience of being sealed by the Spirit.[76] None of the writers in this volume take quite this position, but Larry Hart's dimensional approach in some manner includes this element.

John Fletcher took John Wesley's twofold pattern of salvation and perfection and posited a two-stage process of salvation and sanctification and interpreted the second stage as Spirit baptism. He called on sanctified people to "enter into the full dispensation of the Spirit" and to be "baptized with the Holy Ghost."[77] Fletcher argued that Spirit baptism was sanctification, and he saw this as an identifiable experience following conversion. He further noted that not all Christians had this experience, but that it was available to all, and that one who had been so baptized "would prophesy out of the fullness of his heart."[78] This interpretation would set a standard followed by such Holiness leaders as Phineas Bresee, A. B. Simpson, Benjamin Irwin, and Asa Mahan.[79] Charles Finney would likewise affirm this understanding of Spirit baptism, and Phoebe Palmer would integrate it with her "altar theology," an approach to sanctification that circumvented some of the detailed procedures advocated by other Holiness teachers.[80] In this present book, Ray Dunning defends the position held by John Wesley over against the Holiness teachers who altered his position in nineteenth-century Methodism, and in so doing he presents a critique of the Holiness interpretation.

The late nineteenth century witnessed the rise of another spiritual life movement that was more closely identified with Reformed theology than was the case with the Wesleyan Holiness tradition. The town of Keswick, in England, began in 1875 to be the site of an annual conference on the theology and practice of the Christian life.[81] The theological interpretation of the spiritual life that is associated with this trend is thus known as "Keswick theology." In some sense that title is a misnomer, for the Keswick "teachers" often held divergent views on many things, especially in the area of ecclesiology. But they have held broadly similar interpretations of the Christian experience. Among the intellectual architects of this theology, Bishop H. C. G. Moule articulated a Keswick interpretation of Romans that has become virtual "orthodoxy" for the movement.[82] Popular early advocates included F. B. Meyer, Andrew Murray, R. A. Torrey, Hannah Whitall Smith, A. J. Gordon, and D. L. Moody.[83] More recent advocates include Watchman Nee, Major Ian Thomas, and Alan Redpath.[84] Though Keswick advocates argue for a genuine reception of the Spirit at salvation, they contend that Christians are not generally delivered from the power of sin at this time. This deliverance awaits a subsequent "baptism" or "filling" of the Spirit that gives one power over sin.[85] After this baptism one can live a virtually spontaneous Christian life with power for service and power over sin. This results from a fundamental shift taking place in the heart that transforms character and produces a kind of spontaneous Christian experience.[86]

Pentecostalism arose as an identifiable movement in the Azusa Street Revival in Los Angeles in 1906. But there had been earlier rumblings. Most notable was the experience at Charles Fox Parham's Bible college in Topeka, Kansas, in January 1901, where first Agnes Ozman and then others in the college experienced "spirit baptism with the evidence of tongues."[87] In the Azusa Street mission from 1906 to 1909, under the guidance of William Seymour, thousands came to have the experience of tongues, and many others were converted to the Christian faith. Large numbers were from other parts of the United States and from foreign countries. They took their testimony back to their home churches, and in many cases the new experience broke out in these new places, so spreading the movement internationally in a few short years.

As time passed and leaders such as Frank Bartleman, William Durham, E. N. Bell, Gaston Cashwell, and A. H. Argue began to reflect and eventually to write on the new movement, the conviction settled in that tongues was both an initial evidence of Spirit baptism and a spiritual gift. All Christians would not have the gift of tongues, but all Spirit-baptized Christians would definitely speak in tongues as initial evidence.[88] In the early days there were divergent opinions among Wesleyan Pentecostals as to the place of sanctification as an identifiable experience in light of the new perspective on Spirit baptism with tongues. Some held to a three-stage process of salvation, sanctification, and then Spirit baptism. Methodist Asbury Lowery contended that since Christ was holy and yet sought and received an anointing from the Spirit, so Christians today must also be saved, sanctified (as an identifiable second experience of grace), and only then can they be Spirit baptized for empowerment.[89]

Eventually, though, most Pentecostals would drop sanctification as an identifiable encounter, and opt for a two-stage understanding of salvation and Spirit baptism with the evidence of tongues as the biblical model. Stanley Horton ably defends the traditional Pentecostal interpretation of tongues as initial evidence of Spirit baptism in this book. That is not, though, the end of the story. Pentecostals today are embroiled in a debate over whether Paul's theology of Spirit baptism is the same as Luke's. Roger Stronstad raised this question a few years ago, and William and

Robert Menzies have recently offered their opinion that Luke and Paul are not in full accord.[90]

Dennis Bennett was pastor of a large Episcopalian congregation in Los Angeles in 1960. He began to meet for Bible study with some young couples in his church. Their studies eventually brought them to a Pentecostal experience, and Dennis Bennett began to speak in tongues.[91] Pastor Bennett informed his congregation in April 1960 and was subsequently fired from his position, though he was called to pastor a congregation in Seattle shortly thereafter.[92] Within months many people from mainline denominations were experiencing neo-Pentecostal renewal. At first their experiences followed the pattern of traditional Pentecostalism—Spirit baptism with the evidence of tongues. Two things happened. First, most of these people did not leave their denominations but stayed, often sharing their new perspective with others in their churches. Second, over time the new "Charismatics" began to shed some of the Pentecostal trappings, including the iron-clad necessity of speaking in tongues as initial evidence.[93] Further, as the Charismatic movement further developed, many of its leaders called into question the whole issue of Spirit baptism as subsequent to conversion.[94] It is safe to say today that Charismatics do not have a unified set of convictions of the timing of Spirit baptism, nor on the evidence for its having occurred.[95] Larry Hart's essay in this volume will make clear that there are various ways to formulate this position in the current discussion.

The final approach is one that goes back, in some ways, to Augustine and his notion that Christians receive the full benefits of salvation at regeneration. This insight was not applied to the question of the timing of Spirit baptism until that issue came under dispute in the last 200 years. In response to the rise of Pentecostal and Charismatic movements, Reformed scholars have addressed this question intensely, especially in the last half-century. John Stott, Richard Gaffin, Frederick Dale Bruner, and James D. G. Dunn have written works that are considered by many Evangelicals to be standard responses to the claims of both sacramentalists and advocates of a two-stage process of salvation.[96] Though they differ with one another in some respects (Gaffin argues that the experience of Spirit baptism is not identifiable by the recipient, while Dunn claims it is),[97] they hold in common that Spirit baptism happens at conversion-initiation, and that Paul's theology of Spirit baptism is the same as that of Luke. This position is represented by Walter Kaiser's essay in the present book.

Conclusion

Let the reader decide. These essays are offered to you for your instruction and edification. One's view of Spirit baptism may not be a hill on which to die. But certainly there are important issues here: the nature of spirituality, how one relates to the Holy Spirit at different stages of life, what graces are available to believers at any one time, the role of spiritual gifts, and whether speaking in tongues is a normative sign of Spirit baptism. I know one thing: you are in for a treat in reading these essays. I am grateful to God for bringing together such a remarkable, thoughtful, spiritual group of writers to set forth these ideas. May God bless these chapters for the furtherance of his kingdom and the uplifting of his body, the church.

CHAPTER 1

The Baptism in the Holy Spirit as the Promise of the Father: A Reformed Perspective

WALTER C. KAISER JR.

Many mark the initiation of the modern discussions on the baptism of the Holy Spirit with the publication of James Dunn's doctoral dissertation in 1970 by SCM Press in the United Kingdom and the later publication by Westminster Press in 1977 in America. But an earlier pamphlet by John R. W. Stott, entitled "The Baptism and Fullness of the Holy Spirit," was printed by InterVarsity Press in 1964 from an address given by Stott at the Islington Clerical Conference on January 7, 1964. Thus for four decades now, this discussion has occupied the hearts and minds of a good number of Evangelicals and Pentecostal scholars and believers.

Stott began by making three introductory points.[1] First, God's purpose for our lives is to be found in Scripture and not in experience. Second, the purpose of God should be determined from the *didactic* parts of Scripture, which inform and command us on what is to be appropriated, rather than from the historical parts [such as the book of Acts], which merely *describe* what happened to others. His third point was that our motive in seeking God's purpose is practical and personal and not academic or controversial.

Stott then offered three major propositions.[2] First, "The fullness of the Holy Spirit is one of the distinctive blessings of the new age (2 Cor. 3:8)." Second, "The fullness of the Holy Spirit is not only a distinctive blessing of the new age, but a universal blessing." Finally, "The fullness of the Holy Spirit . . . is also a continuous blessing, to be continuously and increasingly appropriated."

Dunn, on the other hand, engaged the particular doctrine of Pentecostalism that baptism in the Spirit is a distinct act separate from becoming a Christian and is Charismatic in nature. For Dunn a number of questions need to be raised: First, is baptism in the Holy Spirit to be separated from conversion-initiation?[3] Second, is Spirit baptism something essentially different from becoming a Christian and, therefore, as a result some may have been Christians for years but never have been baptized by the Spirit?[4] Third, is possession of the Holy Spirit the primary factor in determining who is and who is not a Christian (Rom. 8:9, 14)?[5] Should the order in this text be emphasized? *Namely,* "If anyone does not have the Spirit of Christ, he [or she] does not belong to Christ." Dunn says, "It is 'having the Spirit' which defines and determines someone as being 'of Christ'; it was by receiving the Spirit that one became a Christian."[6]

Thus there are the questions as to the *timing* of the baptism of the Holy Spirit and the *nature* of the Spirit's empowerment. While the typical Reformed position maintains that the baptism in the Spirit is received at the time of one's conversion, Holiness and Pentecostal Christians are just as certain that Scripture speaks of a special empowerment that comes subsequent to the moment of conversion. Moreover, these two ways of conceptualizing the receiving of the Holy Spirit tend to emphasize different biblical statements: the former depends more on the didactic passages in the apostle Paul while the latter group tends to stress the narrative texts found in Acts.

The Promise of the Father: The Holy Spirit

In the grand divine design of the all-embracing promise-plan of God for the whole Bible, the gift of the Holy Spirit was one of the features of that promise doctrine. For example, Jesus taught the startled eleven disciples assembled in the room after Jesus' resurrection, "I am going to send you *what my Father has promised*;

but stay in the city until you have been clothed with power from on high" (Luke 24:49, emphasis mine). That command was repeated again in Acts 1:4–5: "Do not leave Jerusalem, but wait for *the gift my Father promised,* which you have heard me speak about. For John baptized with water, but in a few days you will be baptized with the Holy Spirit" (emphasis mine).

And so it happened just as the Lord had said on the day of Pentecost, just a few days after the time indicated in Acts 1:4–5. Peter declared: "[Jesus] has received *from the Father the promised Holy Spirit* and has poured out what you now see and hear" (Acts 2:33, emphasis mine). No wonder, then, that Peter preached so vigorously on the day of Pentecost: "Repent and be baptized, every one of you, in the name of Jesus Christ for the forgiveness of your sins. And you will receive the gift of the Holy Spirit. *The promise* is for you and your children and for all who are far off—for all whom the Lord our God will call" (Acts 2:38–39, emphasis mine).

The apostle Paul does not see it any other way either. He preached to the Galatians that they too could receive the promised Holy Spirit by faith: "[Christ] redeemed us in order that the blessing given to Abraham might come to the Gentiles through Christ Jesus, so that by faith we might receive the *promise of the Spirit*" (Gal. 3:14, emphasis mine).

But where had this promise been declared originally? When and where had it been given birth as a promise before it was now to become a realized reality? If it is connected, as we believe it is, as part of that unifying plan of God[7] that stretches from Genesis 3:15 to the book of Revelation, where, to whom, and for what purpose, had that promise of the Father about the coming of the Holy Spirit been announced in those Old Testament times?

Even though reference is made often to the fact that the prophets of the Old Testament received what they wrote by and through the Holy Spirit (Num. 11:16–17, 25–29; 2 Sam. 23:2; 2 Chron. 15:1–7; Ezek. 2:2; Mic. 3:8), and Moses even longed for the day when *all* God's people would experience the Spirit more fully (Num. 11:29), there was a building expectation in the Old Testament about a promised coming of the Holy Spirit.

If the prophet Joel is correctly placed in the ninth century BC,[8] then Joel 2:28–29 may have been one of the earliest of these promises from the Father. In the new age to come, Joel saw a day when

God would "pour out [his] Spirit upon *all flesh*" (emphasis mine). The universalism expressed here was not one that came irrespective of one's inward heart preparation for receiving the Spirit, but it was without distinction of sex, age, race, or rank on all who did believe. Both sons and daughters, young men and old men, men servants and maid servants, and even "all who are far off" (i.e., even on all Gentiles, as this euphemistic circumlocution adds by avoiding the use of what seems to be the politically incorrect term of that day: "Gentiles," Acts 2:39), as Peter emphasized at Pentecost as he preached on this same text from Joel 2:28–32. Jew, Gentile, male, female, young, and old were to be included in this new downpour of the Holy Spirit.[9]

Later on, in the eighth century BC, the prophet Isaiah announced that our Heavenly Father would "pour out water on the thirsty land, and streams on the dry ground; [he would] pour out [his] Spirit on [Israel's] offspring, and [his] blessing on [their] descendants" (Isa. 44:3). The act of "pouring" and the water metaphors of "streams" and "water on the thirsty land" as well as the "dry ground" would connect easily with the parallel water figure of "baptism" after John the Baptist's and Jesus' day. God's "servant" would have God's "Spirit on him [and her]" (Isa. 43:1) just as Isaiah 59:21 noted God's "Spirit [was] on [Isaiah]." Moreover, God's "servant" was preeminently the promised one, the Messiah; but it also, by virtue of the view of that day that we today call "corporate solidarity," included all who also put their faith in the Man of Promise who was to come, God's Servant, Jesus.[10]

In the days of the sixth-century BC exile in Babylon, Ezekiel received the same promise from the Father. As part of the new covenant that Jeremiah had promised (Jer. 31:31–34), here in Ezekiel 36:26–27, God had announced that he would "give a new heart and put a new spirit in [believers]," and this implantation of God's Spirit in each person would move them to follow God's decrees and help them to be "careful to keep [his] laws" (Ezek. 36:27). The promise was repeated in Ezekiel 37:14: "I will put my Spirit in you and you will live." One more time Ezekiel predicted that "[God] will no longer hide [his] face from them, for [he] will pour out [his] Spirit on the house of Israel" (Ezek. 39:29). Notice the allusion to a mighty downpour of his Spirit once again in this last text. The image of the Holy Spirit was that of water; only here it was also connected with a supersaturating abundance that was likened to a veritable downpour, just as the prophet Joel had emphasized in Joel 2:28–29!

While many have been satisfied to associate the Spirit's work in the Old Testament to the Spirit's help in the prophet's reception of revelation and others to the Spirit's purifying his people from their sin, there is more to the Spirit's work in the Old Testament than just these two important functions. I have argued this case elsewhere.[11] The Old Testament also looked forward to a day when the Holy Spirit would be poured out on all who believed in a special way. But this in no way diminished the importance of the work in individual believers in the Old Testament.

Therefore, we conclude that the Holy Spirit's outpouring in the new age was clearly predicted in the Old Testament; it went beyond what he had done in the Old Testament. Even though this specification in the promise doctrine of the outpouring to the Holy Spirit is not *directly* connected with the overall promise-plan given to Eve, Shem and Abraham, Isaac and Jacob, "This mode of conception and of diction, once established, would maintain itself. But the reference to the ancient record is *real,* whether direct or indirect."[12]

The Seven New Testament Teaching Passages

Six of the seven passages that directly refer to the "baptism of/in/with/by[13] the Holy Spirit" contrast John the Baptist's baptism by water with Jesus' future baptism in the Holy Spirit.[14] The seventh one is from the apostle Paul in 1 Corinthians 12:13. However, all seven are identical in the use of the preposition *en,* "in, with."

John the Baptist marks the end of the old order. It is he who predicts that the Messiah, who will come after him, will baptize with more than water; Jesus will baptize with the Holy Spirit and fire.[15] John R. W. Stott[16] notes that the three Synoptic evangelists all use a simple future ("he will baptize"), but the fourth Gospel uses a present participle in John 1:33 ("this is he who *baptizes* with the Holy Spirit," emphasis mine), which indicates a timelessness in the announced action. This accords nicely with the parallel present participle in John 1:29 ("Behold, the Lamb of God, who *takes away* the sin of the world" ESV). Thus the two great works of Messiah, brought together by the prophets in the Old Testament, are not separated in the New Testament: Jesus' work involves the removal of sin and a bestowal of the Holy Spirit. But how closely in time and action are they connected? That question we must still explore.

One way of understanding these seven verses is to note that the four in the Gospels all look forward to a time when the baptism of the Holy Spirit will take place. By the time we get to Acts 1:5, the fifth of the seven verses, this forecasted event is only a "few days" off. In the sixth verse, Acts 11:16, Peter applies John the Baptist's quote to explain what has just happened to the Gentile Cornelius; thus, the "few days" noted earlier in the book of Acts had already expired. In a similar manner, the seventh verse gives a Pauline retrospective interpretation of what it meant to be baptized with the Holy Spirit in 1 Corinthians 12:13. Before Paul treats the subject of the diversity of spiritual gifts, he wanted to stress the fact of the *unity* of the Spirit in writing of the oneness of the body of Christ. This unity happened in the past, for now instead of talking about a future baptism of the Holy Spirit, Paul notes that somewhere between the "few days" our Lord talked about just prior to his ascension into heaven (c. AD 30) and his writing of 1 Corinthians (c. AD 55), the baptism of the Holy Spirit had occurred. It may be diagrammed in this manner:

"will"___>"will"___>"will"____>"will"____>"in a few days"____> <"were baptized."

This, unfortunately, did not settle the debate, for some argued that the first six verses referred to the "baptism *in* or *with* the Holy Spirit," whereas 1 Corinthians 12:13 referred to "baptism *by* the [Holy] Spirit" into the body of Christ. Paul's use, it is claimed, is something totally different from what the other six verses are claiming. However, the Greek expression (*en*) is exactly the same in all seven instances; the only difference is that the adjective "*Holy*" occurs in the first six passages and "*one* Spirit" in the seventh passage, the one in Paul. If it is said that Holy Spirit in Paul's Corinthians passage is the subject, that is, the baptizer, in what element then are these Corinthians baptized? A baptism metaphor demands that an element be specified; otherwise it could not be called a baptism. The most natural assumption is that Paul is alluding to the words of John the Baptist and the words of Jesus just before his ascension, hence the use of the metaphor of baptism.

Care must be taken to note that the verb in all four Gospels is *active* with Christ as the subject ("he will baptize," "this is he who baptizes"). But in Acts 1:5, Acts 11:16, and 1 Corinthians 12:13, the verb is *passive* ("you shall be baptized," "we were all baptized"), and the subject drops out in favor of either the *objects* of the baptism or the *one* Spirit in which we were baptized. This is a key distinction, for as we have already indicated, there can be no baptism metaphor if the Holy Spirit is made the subject or baptizer with the result that the *element* with which he baptizes is left unstated. Moreover, this fits the parallel in 1 Corinthians 12:13 where it is also the Holy Spirit of which we are made *to drink*. The element of drinking must be none other than the Holy Spirit, just as in John 7:37 we are "made to drink" of Christ.

So, as John the Baptist baptized "in/with" water (Greek, *en*), by the same analogy there is a baptism "in/with"[17] (Greek, *en*) the Holy Spirit. The preposition is the same in both cases, so no distinction should be sought on the basis of a translation distinction such as "in" or "by."[18] This baptism and drinking, as Paul urges, was not randomly experienced, but Paul is at pains to emphasize that "we . . . all" have shared in this drinking and baptism, meaning all who have believed. The two terms of drinking and being baptized are used as equivalent expressions that all Christians experience. What is more, the timing of this universal Christian experience took place in the past, for both verbs ("were baptized," and "were given to drink") are Greek aorist tense verbs that point to a single act in the past (1 Cor. 12:13).

As John R. W. Stott noted, "In every kind of baptism (of water, blood, fire, Spirit) there are four parts."[19] Therefore, God is the *subject,* or the baptizer, in all of the baptisms. The *object* upon whom the baptism is being performed is the one being baptized. The *element* of the baptism is either the water, as in John's baptism, fire, or as is the case here, the Holy Spirit. Finally, there is the purpose for which the baptism takes place: an expression of repentance, judgment, or being united into the one body of Christ.

Is Luke-Acts Baptism to Be Distinguished from Pauline Baptism?

Is there more diversity in the New Testament than what James Dunn[20] or we have noted so far? Does Luke in Luke-Acts speak of a baptism of power for service, while Paul refers to the soteriological work of the Spirit?[21] And does Luke provide more room for "a second work of grace" subsequent to conversion, an outpouring of the Holy Spirit on a person separate from that person's initiation into the faith, i.e., his or her conversion? Is this Lukan gift of the Spirit an empowering gift distinct from a salvation gift? In the past, Dunn's argument, though much appreciated by Pentecostal scholars,[22] was criticized especially for his alleged reading of Luke-Acts with Pauline eyeglasses.

The break in the debate over favoring Paul over Luke-Acts (because Paul was theological and Luke-Acts was merely historical and descriptive), in the minds of many, came in Roger Stronstad's seminal work entitled *The Charismatic Theology of St. Luke* (1984). He argued that Luke was just as good a theologian as he was a historian. The difference, according to Stronstad, was that Luke had "a Charismatic rather than a soteriological theology of the Spirit."[23] If Stronstad was correct, then former Evangelical perspectives on the Holy Spirit had to be revised, wherein Luke's witness to the Spirit must be placed alongside, even if in a subordinate position to Paul's more theological witness to the Spirit. On Stronstad's reading of Luke, then, in contradistinction to what many Evangelicals had claimed, Luke did not relate the Spirit to salvation but to a new source of power subsequent to salvation. Luke viewed the Spirit exclusively in Charismatic terms.[24] The Evangelical line, Stronstad believed, was to say that Luke and Paul had the same theology but with a different emphasis: Both related the gift of the Holy Spirit to salvation, but Luke emphasized the vocational purpose of the Spirit's role in preparing and equipping the church for service and for her mission. But the Pentecostal scholars saw the Holy Spirit in Luke not necessarily as one who is brought into relation with our salvation or sanctification but as one with a third dimension, power for service.

The most hotly contested passage of all in this debate of the Luke-Acts emphasis was Acts 8:4–25. In the Pentecostal way of emphasizing elements of the text, here the Samaritans believed the preaching of Philip and were baptized (v. 12), but they did not receive the Spirit *until later* (vv. 15–17, especially v. 16, "because the Holy Spirit *had not yet come* upon any of them; they had simply been baptized into the name of the Lord Jesus," emphasis mine). What, then, can be said for those Evangelicals who contend that the reception of the Spirit is linked in time and theology with conversion in this situation? Was this case really an exception that proved the point? Did this case necessitate the withholding of the Spirit until the apostles from Jerusalem could come?

There seems to be little doubt that in Luke's treatment of the Spirit it is characteristically the Spirit's work to inspire prophecy and empower for witness. Where the dispute lies, however, is this: Is that all that the Spirit does in Luke-Acts, as many Pentecostal scholars argue? Surely R. P. Menzies's claim goes too far when he says, "Luke does not view the gift of the Spirit as a necessary element in conversion."[25] Not all Pentecostals agreed with Menzies's assessment, for J. B. Shelton affirmed, "Luke is not averse to associating the Holy Spirit with conversion."[26] Nevertheless, Luke, according to that view, argued for the Spirit's work subsequent to and separate from one's salvation experience.

Few have put forth as strenuous an argument for Luke's associating the Spirit with initiation into the faith, i.e., conversion, as James D. G. Dunn.[27] Dunn considered three important sets of texts: (1) Luke 1:35, 46–55; (2) Acts 2:38–39; and (3) Acts 10:43–48; 11:14–18; 15:7–9, that were alleged to set forth a different connection with the Spirit's work from the Pauline conclusion, especially in 1 Corinthians 12:13.

Dunn argued, in the same order as the sets of text are noted here, that Mary's saying, "The Holy Spirit will come upon me," is not an event of inspiration *subsequent* to the impregnation referred to in the scriptural line that follows it, as R. P. Menzies wanted to see it, but Luke 1:35, 46–55 spoke to a "life-effecting function of the Spirit and not at all simply the inspiration of a particular utterance."[28]

In the second text, the "gift of the Holy Spirit," along with the "promise," clearly connected the two parts of the Joel prophecy: the pouring out of the Spirit and the calling on the name of the Lord for salvation (Joel 2:28–32). Surely there is a soteriological connection here!

In the third set of texts, "*While* Peter was still speaking these words" (Acts 10:43–44, emphasis mine) about the promise of forgiveness of sins for all who believed in Jesus," the Holy Spirit fell on those who heard this message. The fact that they "heard this message" reminds us that the word to *hear* in this context has its Semitic background that means more than receiving audible sounds; it also means to act appropriately based on what is heard. It is similar to the Hebrew expression "to remember," which also involves more than merely a calling to mind certain facts, but it also means *to act* appropriately on the basis of those facts. Thus, when the Lord "remembered" Hannah, she became pregnant (1 Sam. 1:19). Likewise, when the Lord "hears" the cries of his people, he does more than respond by saying something like, "Hello, may I help you?" It means he also acted on behalf of those who cried out to him for relief! Therefore, the hearers in that same moment also believed on Jesus as their Lord and Savior! Peter, the previously reluctant preacher to these Gentiles, now inquires out loud, since these have received the Holy Spirit, how could they be refused Christian baptism (Acts 10:47)? Accordingly, the Jewish believers who had accompanied Peter on this revolutionary Gentile mission were asked, despite all natural racial prejudices, how could these Gentiles, to whom God had so obviously already given of his Spirit, be refused acceptance (by water baptism) into their number?

The order of the Spirit's work and the experience of believing salvation is no different in Acts 11:14–15. Once again it happened in the same way: "*As* [Peter] began to speak, the Holy Spirit came on them as he had come on [the disciples] at the beginning" (emphasis mine). It is difficult to claim, in the face of evidence like this, that Luke did not associate the Spirit's work with salvation. But in contradistinction to the apostle Paul, who did make such a connection, Luke, so the argument goes, *only* argues here for a Spirit of prophecy and power for the service of witnessing. Such a claim clearly seems to omit some of the key evidence in Acts.

As if to clinch the point, Acts 15:7–9 observes that *as* the word was preached and a call for a response of belief was issued, there came a "giving of the Holy Spirit" (v. 8) and the "purify[ing of] their hearts by faith" (v. 9). Would it not be fair to say that they came in that order? However, one would have thought that the cleansing and purifying of the heart would have preceded the gift of the Holy Spirit, if the argument that there is a second work of grace subsequent to salvation and sanctification was what is being advocated here, as many Pentecostals read the text. But the two works of the Holy Spirit are synonymous or complementary.[29]

What Is the Biblical Precedent
for Using Historical Precedent for Doctrine?

As already noted, Stott had proposed in his 1964 book on *The Baptism and the Fullness of the Holy Spirit* that the "revelation of the purpose of God in Scripture should be sought in its *didactic, rather than in its historical* parts."[30] He clarified this a bit in his 1976 second edition by protesting that he was not saying that narrative passages have no value. Instead, he affirmed, "What I am saying is that what is descriptive is valuable only in so far as it is interpreted by what is didactic."

Earlier Evangelicals had used a similar approach known as the Analogy of Faith. In my view, this rule is best used in forming a Systematic Theology rather than as an exegetical tool, for it assumes that the required exegetical work has been completed and that we are now ready to collect all the passages that deal with similar subjects and group them into systematic arrangements for the sake of gaining a comprehensive overview of the subjects at hand.[31]

Gordon Fee, himself Pentecostal in viewpoint, surprised all in the volume he wrote with Douglas Stuart on *How to Read the Bible for All Its Worth* by saying in his chapter on "Acts—The Problem of Historical Precedence" this: "Our assumption, along with many others, is that *unless Scripture explicitly tells us we must do something, what is merely narrated or described can never function in a normative way.*"[32]

A decade later several strong reactions to the Ramm/Stott/Fee problem of historical precedence appeared. First, Grant Osborne responded in 1991 in his book on hermeneutics and the section on narrative. He scolded:

> Moreover, I also oppose the current tendency to deny the theological dimension on the grounds that narrative is indirect rather than direct. This ignores the results of redaction criticism, which has demonstrated that biblical narrative is indeed theological at the core and seeks to guide the reader to relive the truth encapsulated in the story. Narrative is not as direct as didactic material, but it does have a theological point and expects the reader to interact with that message. My argument is that biblical

narrative is in some ways even better than the teaching applied to similar situations in the lives of the people.[33] This was followed in 1993 with another hermeneutics textbook by the three Denver Seminary professors, William Klein, Craig Blomberg, and Robert Hubbard. They addressed the same topic saying: "We have already stated that narrative often teaches more indirectly than didactic literature without becoming any less normative. Thus, we reject Fee and Stuart's highlighted maxim that 'unless Scripture explicitly tells us we must do something, what is merely narrated or described can never function in a normative way.'"[34]

The points argued by both the preceding books are fair and helpful on the main points they make. Fee, however, pressed his argument even further. How do Pentecostals propose to distinguish what is normative from what is merely descriptive? If historical precedent is "to have normative value, [it] must be related to intent."[35] Pentecostals must show, Fee demanded, that Luke really intended his narratives in Luke-Acts to establish a precedent for the future; otherwise, perhaps we should still choose church officers by casting lots, and we should encourage all believers to sell all their possessions and give it all to the church. We cannot simply pick and choose what we wish to do and jettison the rest! Moreover, is any aspect of what is narrated understood as an interim situation and not to be applied in all its detail? For example, was the Samaritan period of waiting for the apostles to arrive a *normative* feature to be observed by all later generations? What then would be the modern equivalent of waiting for the apostles to arrive? Or did this have something to do with the fact that the Samaritans were so despised that the stamp of the apostles was necessary to shut down any future criticism that Samaritans need not apply for the graces thought to be experienced here—at least according to the possible prejudiced racial views of some Jews?

Fee added another argument to those already noted. Pentecostals tend to use biblical analogies as arguments for biblical precedent. Thus, to point to Jesus' experience at the Jordan River as a subsequent event to his miraculous birth by the Holy Spirit, or to the disciples' experience at Pentecost subsequent to the breathing on them by the Holy Spirit in John 20:22, was problematical. Fee warned that it is unusual to demonstrate from biblical analogies such as these that the biblical text was also being intentional and giving us thereby a biblical precedent—at least in every case! Moreover, since the events described above about Jesus and the disciples came before the day of Pentecost, are we still confident that the argument for continuity overrides the argument for discontinuity between the two ages on this point?

Despite the advances in the hermeneutical debate about the legitimate use of narrative in theological construction, that would not be the end of the discussion, for normativity and intentionality still had to be demonstrated from the text. Moreover, the unevenness of the evidence was likewise to factor in, for even if the Samaritans in Acts 8 and the Ephesians in Acts 18 point to subsequence in the baptism in the Holy Spirit, Acts 10 with Cornelius's house cannot be used to show subsequence! Intention of the biblical writer was still a key factor that could not merely be assumed on theological or experiential grounds but had to be established on exegetical and biblical theology grounds.

While we have referred earlier to Roger Stronstad's 1984 work on Luke, already in 1970, I. Howard Marshall had published his magisterial work entitled *Luke: Historian and Theologian.*[36] Marshall's thesis was that not only could Luke be trusted as a careful and accurate recorder of history; he also wrote history with a theological agenda in mind. As a result, Evangelical scholars began to treat the Synoptic Gospels for more than mere historical facts; they now treated the Gospels as history with a theological purpose.[37]

There is little doubt that this opened new windows for conversation between Pentecostals and Evangelicals. Pentecostals had usually placed their stress on Luke-Acts as being distinct from Paul and his association of the baptism in the Holy Spirit with conversion and one's incorporation into the whole body of Christ. In this way the key issues shifted from arguments about the Analogy of Faith to issues of exegesis and the use of Luke's narratives for theology.

Stronstad set the case on a new footing for Charismatics in his work *The Charismatic Theology of St. Luke.* As already noted, he argued that Luke has "a Charismatic rather than a soteriological theology of the Spirit."[38] Evangelicals responded, as we have argued above, that Luke is similar to Paul in that he did relate the gift of the Spirit to salvation, but he did also emphasize the Spirit's role in equipping the church for the mission God had given it in this world. Thus, the slogan for Evangelicals in this Luke-Paul debate became "same theology, different emphasis."

But Pentecostals and many Third Wave[39] Christians felt that this slogan undermined the entire biblical basis for any Pentecostal theology.[40] They protested that Luke viewed the gift of the Spirit *exclusively* in Charismatic terms; it had a distinctive theology of the Spirit.

Besides offering a detailed exegesis of the passages that Charismatics think are definitive in the debate (Luke 11:13; Acts 8:4–25; 18:24–19:7), they have responded to two commonly held Evangelical assumptions that they believe have inhibited their Evangelical brothers and sisters from seeing how distinctive Luke's pneumatology really is. These assumptions are: (1) given the inspiration of the Bible, all authors must speak with one voice and share the same theological perspective on every topic; and (2) given the fact that Luke traveled with the apostle Paul, it is difficult to see how Luke's doctrine of the Holy Spirit could be different from Paul's.

The rejoinder to the first assumption was this: While the Scriptures as a whole are harmonious, this does not rule out theological differences that exist "in harmonious development rather than irreconcilable contradictions."[41]

Surely, in principle, that is a perfectly acceptable standard that equally embraces a high view of inspiration and inerrancy. But it does not address the issue of linking a technical term such as "baptized in the Holy Spirit," which appears in seven passages, with other works of the Holy Spirit in other passages! Here is where the transfer takes place and where there must be evidence to support the fact that every Lukan instance of the Spirit's work is equal to that of the baptism in the Holy Spirit. Or to put the question another way, is the filling, indwelling, sealing, and giving of the Holy Spirit in any or all instances equal to the teaching passages on the baptizing in the Holy Spirit? Remember, the debate centers on the traditional Pentecostal definition that "the baptism of the Holy Spirit is primarily an empowerment for service and that the initial physical evidence is speaking in tongues."[42] The mistake of including all the references to the Spirit in the discussion of the Spirit's baptism is seen also in the incorrect gathering of Pauline texts in a similar but an eisegetical manner. Thus the collection of texts for the baptism of the Spirit that groups as one and the same all Pauline texts on a believer's cleansing (Rom. 15:16; 1 Cor. 6:11), or one's righteousness (Rom. 2:29; 8:1–17; 14:17; Gal. 5:5, 16–26), and intimate fellowship with God (Rom. 8:14–17; Gal. 4:6), as well as power for mission (Rom. 15:18–19; Phil. 1:18–19), can only result in a confusion of the case.[43] This is the method of the analogy of faith gone to seed! It cannot help us in determining what is meant by being "baptized in the Holy Spirit."

On the second assumption, it is true there is no evidence that Luke had access to or was acquainted with any of Paul's letters. But such an admission does not mean that God, the Revelator, could not have been aware of what he was revealing to Paul! If Luke was present and summarized some of Paul's preaching, he may well have caught the germs of the same thoughts that Paul later put into his letters. To say that Paul's earlier preaching did not contain any traces of his soteriological pneumatology is itself either an argument from silence or one that ultimately will need to argue for Pauline dependency, rather than divine dependency, for revelation. No Pentecostal I know wishes to go in that direction.

We conclude that Luke does have a different emphasis in his doctrine of the power the Holy Spirit gives to believers, but we do not think that that work of the Holy Spirit can be linked to the promise of the Father about the baptizing in the Holy Spirit and fire. Those are separate topics that have incorrectly been linked by way of the approach of "an analogy of faith"[44] rather than by way of solid exegesis.

Are Tongues the Initial Physical Sign of Spirit Baptism?

"The chief distinctive and *sine qua non* of the Pentecostal movement is its doctrine that 'an enduement with power' called 'the baptism in the Holy Spirit' is described in Scripture and is available to all believers who seek it."[45] However, it must also be conceded that this "hallmark of Pentecostalism" runs into a major problem. As Larry Hurtado correctly observes, "The question of what constitutes 'the initial evidence' of a person having received the 'baptism in the Spirit' simply is not raised in the New Testament."[46] Not even Luke takes up this question, nor do the other biblical writers. Hurtado does not think this renders the doctrine invalid, even if we cannot show anywhere that this was the primary intent of the author of a scriptural text or one of his teaching intentions! Experience, he allows, can fill in the needed evidence here!

What about Paul's statement in 1 Corinthians 12:30, "Do all speak in tongues?" Donald Carson[47] argues on the basis of this text that the expected answer was no. Thus, we should not expect all believers to have the gift of *glossolalia*. Paul's point seemed to be that God distributed the gifts as he was pleased to do so without everyone demanding that all that the other believers had should be replicated in all believers' possessions.

It is true that Paul did say in a generalist way that "I would like every one of you to speak in tongues" (1 Cor. 14:5), but that also seems to give away the case, for apparently not every believer did have the gift of tongues. The retort is that 1 Corinthians 12:29 also asks, "Are all prophets?" And Paul seems to say in 1 Corinthians 14:31, "For you can all prophesy." However, that quote leaves out the rest of the verse and what appears in the context to be the point: "For you can all prophesy *in turn* so that everyone may be instructed and encouraged" (v. 31 again, emphasis mine). The suggestion that the reference in 1 Corinthians 12:30 is limited to *public* use of the tongue, while the use of the tongue gift in chapter 14 focuses on the private manifestation of this gift is interesting but not altogether demonstrable.

So, if Scripture does not directly teach, or the biblical authors' primary intention is not to teach, tongues as the initial physical sign of the baptism in the Spirit, why does Pentecostalism insist on its presence in this manner? The answer is that it is based on inferential theology, not on the explicit teaching of the text. Moreover, the initial physical evidence is a fairly recent theological formulation. It stands, its advocates argue, in the process of the same doctrinal development first observed in the New Testament, which is now continued in the twentieth and twenty-first centuries of our Lord.

The case that has not been made, therefore, is whether this gift of tongues is given to all believers and whether it accompanies the baptism of the Holy Spirit. Paul seems to say that an assortment of gifts is given out freely by God, but not every believer's set of gifts matches his neighbor's. God has done this deliberately so that the body of Christ might experience its interdependence within the body. One part needs the other part in order to be complete.

A Second Work of Grace?

Believers in the Wesleyan, Holiness, and Pentecostal traditions have usually held that there is a "second work of God's grace" that comes after one has been converted. Some in these circles refer to this "second work" as "sanctification," while others refer to it as the "baptism of the Holy Spirit." If the "baptism of the Holy Spirit" is separated from one's sanctification, then *three* works of grace, not two, are called for in this scheme of things. Most Reformed and many Puritan traditions view all of this as happening at conversion.

We have laid the case in the preceding sections of this chapter for a view that seems to favor aspects of the Reformed or Puritan tradition. The reason we have favored one work of grace in the conversion, the initiation of sanctification, and the baptism of the Holy Spirit is because the term itself, "baptism in the Holy Spirit," as used in the seven contexts where it appears, all refer to what happens at one's initiation into the faith at the time of conversion. It does not seem possible to have the Gospels, then Paul, and finally Luke, all use the term "baptized in the Holy Spirit" in distinctive and separate ways, especially since all of the references relate to the ancient promise found in the Old Testament that came from our Heavenly Father about what he would do in the new age.

How then shall we define the technical term "baptized in the Holy Spirit"? We believe it is best to go with Paul's inspired statement of purpose in 1 Corinthians 12:13 that this baptism was the initial work of God of incorporating all believers, first at Pentecost, then at Samaria, and again at Caesarea, into one unified body of Christ in the Holy Spirit. Thereafter, all who believed, at the time of their conversion, were brought by God in the Holy Spirit to join this body and to be part of this one body that is called the believing church of Jesus Christ.

But what of the work of the Holy Spirit that speaks of empowerment, sealing, filling, or the gift of the Holy Spirit? Surely in one or more of these expressions there must still be a hope for a "second work of grace," is there not? It will appear from the texts that follow that the judgment of D. A. Carson was correct: "Although

I find no biblical support for a second-blessing theology, I do find support for a second-, third-, fourth-, or fifth-blessing theology."[48]

To state the case, first of all, the "sealing" of the Spirit in Ephesians 1:13 cannot be located, as some have hoped, separate and subsequent to our salvation. To argue from the grammar of a past tense here would be to lose the force of the context where, a few verses later (Eph. 1:19–20), Paul used the same construction to speak of how God raised Jesus from the dead. As Craig Keener said so aptly, "[The raising] cannot imply subsequence, because if it did, it would mean that God exerted his mighty power in Christ *after* resurrecting him, rather than by resurrecting him."[49] Moreover, Keener continued, this "seal" of the Holy Spirit is "an earnest," or a "down payment" validating our future inheritance when our bodies are redeemed (Eph. 1:13–14; 4:30). Again, if the sealing is subsequent and after our conversion, then our conversion alone is inadequate to grant us a future place in the kingdom of God!

It is also clear that the Holy Spirit always comes as a "gift," not as one whom we have in some way earned or prayed through in order to get. He is "received" by faith, not by any works or deeds of righteousness (Gal. 3:2).

Can those who have been converted speak only technically of the work of the Spirit in the past? No! There is a continuous supply of the Holy Spirit for all believers (Phil. 1:19). We are taught to "keep on being filled with the Holy Spirit" in Ephesians 5:18.[50] The verb is passive in voice, present in tense, and imperative in mood. Accordingly, God calls us to a *continuous* supply of his Holy Spirit rather than to a single event that is a single crisis in this act of infilling of the Spirit. The element of filling is the Holy Spirit, for the Greek preposition that follows (Greek *en*) only indicates the element of the filling. Thus, it is the Holy Spirit that fills believers so there is no need for physical or material dependencies on stimulants, such as strong wine, that may turn out only to be depressants. This command to "keep on being filled with the Holy Spirit" is followed by four participles in verses 19–21: *namely,* speaking, singing, thanking, and submitting. These four participles either express the results of being filled or the means that the Holy Spirit continually uses to fill believers with himself.

Consequently, there is a work of the Holy Spirit that comes after salvation. It is the "filling" of the Holy Spirit. He is described as coming on "all" in Acts 2:4; 4:31; and on the disciples in Acts 13:52. But he also came upon Peter (Acts 4:8) and Saul/Paul (Acts 13:9) with great empowerment to speak God's word boldly to the amazement of all who witnessed it.

But what about that one other passage that is often raised as being troublesome for those who link the baptism of the Holy Spirit with one's initiation into the faith? It is Acts 19, which speaks of "some disciples" (19:1), who, when asked, "Did you receive the Holy Spirit when you believed?" (19:2), answered negatively. In fact, they did not even know if there was a Holy Spirit! (19:2).

Does this not suggest, however, that even though some may already be "disciples," that there is a "second blessing" that is accompanied by special signs of the Spirit? Usually the word *disciples* refers to believers elsewhere in Acts (9:10, 36; 16:1), but these "disciples" knew only of John's baptism and had not yet heard of the Holy Spirit (19:2–3). Therefore, Luke may only mean that these were disciples of John rather than believers in Jesus. When Paul told them that John's baptism was a baptism of repentance (19:4) and urged them to believe in the One who came after him, they believed and "were baptized into the name of the Lord Jesus" (19:5). But it is verse 6 that presents the most difficulties, for "when Paul placed his hands on them, the Holy Spirit came on them, and they spoke in tongues and prophesied." Surely this is a case for a subsequent second work of grace, argue some.

But as some have observed, does not the question as to whether they received the Holy Spirit indicate that the expected answer was that it was *normal* to receive the Spirit *when* one first believed? However, does not the question also say it is *possible* to believe without receiving the Holy Spirit?[51] We respond to this rebuttal that if it is possible, then what is our new definition of a Christian (Is this it: one who believes but who does not yet have the Holy Spirit within?) and, more importantly, can we attribute such a definition to Luke? If the new definition is one who has believed and been baptized but has not yet received the Holy Spirit, where can we point in Luke-Acts to show that that is exactly what Luke would affirm? And would that not contradict Paul in Romans 8:9, 14?

Can we show in Acts 19:1–7 that these twelve Ephesian "disciples," who later believed after Paul's preaching, were baptized, and who had Paul's hands placed on them as they received the Holy Spirit, did not receive the Holy Spirit at the same time as their believing, rather than in a separate and subsequent action? If they were merely disciples of John who may have earlier left Palestine before Pentecost and were not in contact with any Christians or their message about Jesus, was not Paul's opening question a probing one to determine if they indeed were actually believers in Christ? And given the terse and concise way that Luke reports their conversion, baptism, and reception of the Holy Spirit, is it possible to attribute an intended sequence here in 19:4–6? I doubt it. Others, however, may come to the opposite conclusion. Then the issue will be whether we build our theology on the exceptional cases or take our clue from the more repeated and theologically explained contexts.

Baptism in the Spirit and the Fruit of the Spirit

The work of the Holy Spirit continues to transform the new believer in ways that are in marked contrast with his or her former lifestyle. Paul pointed to such a radical transformation in Galatians 5:24, "Those who belong to Christ Jesus have crucified the sinful nature with its passions and desires." The evidence of such a divine work can be seen in the fruit that is produced, as Galatians 5:22–23 puts it: "But the fruit of the Spirit is love, joy, peace, patience, kindness, goodness, faithfulness, gentleness and self-control. Against such things there is no law."

But what, then, is the relationship between the baptism in the Holy Spirit and the fruit of the Spirit? Or, to state the same thing differently, is there any connection between baptism in the Holy Spirit and a believer's maturation and growth in sanctification?

Typically, the Holiness, Pentecostal, and Charismatic position links Spirit baptism and Holiness or Christian maturity. For example, as William and Robert Menzies point out, the *Full Life Study Bible* in its article on "baptism in the Holy Spirit" states that this baptism results in "enhanced sensitivity to sin," "a greater seeking after righteousness which conforms to Christ," and "a deeper awareness of the judgment of God against all ungodliness."[52] But the Menzies think this is an incorrect association of the Spirit baptism with holiness of life and Christian maturity. In their view it confuses Paul's language about the fruit of the Spirit and being "filled with the Spirit" (Eph. 5:18) with Luke's language of Pentecost (Acts 1:8; 2:17–18).[53] For the Menzies, Luke described a

> powerful experience of the Spirit that is now available to every believer" that "initiates a believer into the prophetic dimension of the Spirit's power." As the source of prophetic inspiration, the Spirit inspires bold witness for Christ, especially in the face of opposition, and guides and encourages the church in its mission (Acts 1:8; 2:17–18; 4:31; 9:31). . . . Luke does not present the Spirit as a soteriological agent, nor does he describe the Spirit as the direct source of ethical transformation. Spirit-baptism in the Lukan sense, then, cannot be linked with holiness or Christian maturity.[54]

We agree that Spirit baptism is a separate work of the Holy Spirit from the fruit of the Spirit or the filling of the Spirit. As we have already argued, the Holy Spirit's baptism is that work, which first came for the Jews at Pentecost in Acts 2, the Samaritans in Acts 8, and the Gentiles in Acts 10, and then for all subsequent believers when they experience new birth in Christ, that incorporates all who believe into one body of Christ so that we all drink of one Spirit. In that sense, then, the two works of the Spirit are correctly separated by William and Robert Menzies. But to argue that Luke and Paul speak of two dimensions of the Holy Spirit so that one is power for prophetic inspiration (Luke) and the other is soteriological (Paul) is to erect barriers where they do not exist.

The major line of demarcation in our two positions, that are otherwise so closely related, is that Luke's work of the Spirit is placed outside of the salvation process and made to be a separate use of the same term that Paul shares with Luke, *namely,* being "baptized in the Holy Spirit."

On the other hand, the Menzies are accurate and most pastoral when they warn their fellow Pentecostals that the concept that "Spirit-baptism necessarily leads to greater holiness sounds remarkably similar to the sort of claims that Paul sought to counter in the church at Corinth."[55] This, as many similar emphases in other parts of Christendom, can lead to an unwarranted and unacceptable elitism that raises all sorts of undesirable problems in the church.

The conclusion we come to is this: each believer, subsequent to the three "Pentecosts" mentioned in the book of Acts, is automatically placed in the body of Christ and made to drink/participate in the Holy Spirit by being "baptized in the Holy Spirit." It is this same Holy Spirit who also is available to "fill" believers and who produces the "fruit of the Spirit" in those who walk by faith and obedience to their Lord.

Conclusion

Nothing we have written ought to lead the reader to conclude that this writer therefore takes a cessationist point of view with regards to the supernatural gifts. First Corinthians 13:8–12 cannot be used to make that case, as some have tried to do in the past. Our concern has strictly been with the phrase "baptism in the Holy Spirit." Of course, the noun phrase "baptism in the Holy Spirit" actually does *not* occur in the New Testament; it is only the verbal phrase, either in the active voice ("baptizes in the Holy Spirit," John 1:33) or the future tense ("he will baptize in the Holy Spirit," Matt. 3:11; Mark 1:8; Luke 3:16) or in the passive voice of the future tense ("will be baptized in the Holy Spirit," Acts 1:5; 11:16) or in the passive voice of the past tense ("were baptized in one Spirit," 1 Cor. 12:13). But these seven texts must be determinative in our search for a proper explanation of what is involved in this term.

But there is more: this distinctive work did not come out of the blue, nor was it suddenly invented in early New Testament times; it had its origins in the ancient promise-plan of the Father. That promise mentioned in Acts 1:4; 2:33, and 39 was part and parcel of the Abrahamic-Davidic-New Covenant (cf. Acts 7:17; 13:23; 26:6), which mirrored the declaration that God had made early on in time that his plan for the future was a promise that included many specifications, the Holy Spirit being one of the key items in that plan.

We conclude then, that Spirit reception is part of Christian initiation. It refers more properly to those, who at Pentecost, Samaria, and Caesarea, and to all who subsequently believed on Jesus, were incorporated by God, in the Holy Spirit, into one spiritual body of Christ, regardless of all other distinctions, be they of gender, color, age, denomination, nationality, or one's status in society. To have

God's Spirit is to believe (Rom. 8:9, 14). The baptism of the Holy Spirit is a distinctive blessing of the new age in which all believers are made to participate and drink of the Holy Spirit so that they form one unified body in Christ despite all the denominational or other labels believers may wear.

However, it continued to be possible for all believers to be filled with the Holy Spirit and empowered for specific tasks at specific times. He could increasingly be appropriated in such a manner that "rivers of living water" continuously flow out of the Christian's inner being to the glory of God and the blessing of the church and a waiting world (John 7:37–39).

Responses to Walter C. Kaiser Jr.'s Reformed Perspective

Response by Stanley M. Horton

I appreciate Walter Kaiser's scholarship and have used his *Toward an Old Testament Theology* as a textbook in my teaching at the Assemblies of God Theological Seminary. His exposition of God's promise-plan is important. Because I am an alumnus of Gordon Divinity School (now Gordon-Conwell Theological Seminary), I am glad he is the current president. I have enjoyed his writings and his communications from the Seminary.

Walter Kaiser is clearly well acquainted with the literature from both the Evangelical and Pentecostal positions. It is true that most Evangelicals tend to emphasize the didactic passage, and Pentecostals emphasize the Acts text. He says that Luke surely did not disagree with Paul. This causes him to take Paul as the one through whom we must interpret Luke. My contention is that Paul's letters were written to believers who were already baptized in the Spirit. He was dealing with problems that are similar to some of the problems we face in our Pentecostal churches. Thus, he does not give attention to the initial receiving of Spirit baptism. Pentecostals spend a great deal of time studying and teaching what Paul has to say about spiritual gifts and holy living. Most recognize also that all believers have the Spirit and that there can and should be many "refillings." But they see that Luke in Acts is the primary source for understanding the initial reception of Spirit baptism.

We also agree that the Old Testament, and especially Joel 2:28–29, "look forward to a day when the Holy Spirit would be poured out on all believers"; though I take it that it is an outpouring distinct from and subsequent to the Spirit's work in regeneration. Kaiser's discussion of Roger Stronstad's *The Charismatic Theology of St. Luke* gives a brief summary of Stronstad's arguments. I recommend that both Evangelicals and Pentecostals make a closer study of his work. Stronstad is one of the best of the younger Pentecostal scholars.

Kaiser gives much more attention to Dunn's arguments, which I believe Pentecostals have answered to their satisfaction. Then in dealing with the question of the biblical precedent for using historical precedent for doctrine, he draws attention to Gordon Fee and Douglas Stuart's *How to Read the Bible for All Its Worth*. I was asked to use that book in teaching a hermeneutics class in Singapore. I was disappointed in both writers, but especially in Gordon Fee. My copy of the book is full of markings where I had to take issue with the authors. Acts 2:4 is not a matter of mere analogy. It is part of a distinct fulfillment of prophecy that is an important part of the plan of God.

Kaiser believes the case has not been made whether the gift of tongues is given to all believers and whether it accompanies the baptism in the Holy Spirit. He rejects the idea of a second, definite work of grace. He also takes it that the disciples in Acts 19:1 were more likely disciples of John, and if there was subsequence, it was an exceptional case. That would make Acts 2:4 an exceptional case as well. I see that those who were filled on the Day of Pentecost were already believers. In my commentary on Acts (2001), I noted that, like Apollos, they must have known about Jesus but did not know that the age of the Spirit with its promised mighty outpouring had come. No Jew would have meant that they had never heard of the existence of the Holy Spirit. Several ancient manuscripts do read, "We have not even heard if any are receiving the Holy Spirit."

I am glad Kaiser is not a cessationist with respect to spiritual gifts and that he recognizes that "it continued to be possible for all believers to be filled with the Holy Spirit and empowered for specific tasks at specific times." May all of us have "rivers of living water" flowing out of our inner beings.

Response by H. Ray Dunning

My general response to Professor Kaiser's incisive exegetical paper is a simple "Amen." His analyses basically concur with those of John Wesley regarding "baptism with the Holy Spirit." However, I would add a few observations on the matter of subsequence. As I note in my response to Del Colle, it is easy to lump the Wesleyan and Pentecostal theologies together on this issue because in the American Holiness Movement, there was a near perfect coalescence of views, except on the issue of tongues-speaking. John Wesley himself approached the matter in a distinctively different way that is more convincing to me.

The assumption that informs these remarks, consistent I believe with the history of classical Christian theology, is the inseparable relation between the work of the Holy Spirit (regardless of what terminology is used) and sanctification. With this stipulation in mind, it should be noted that there are two forms of "subsequence." One is *theological* and the other is *chronological*.

The debate that culminated with the Protestant Reformation focused on the theological order of justification and sanctification with the outcome being, following Luther, that justification preceded sanctification as these metaphors related to our acceptance by God. Granted my Protestant lenses, I cannot see how one could read the Pauline material in the New Testament and come to any other conclusion than that. Even though, as Professor Kaiser suggests, sanctification begins at the moment of Christian initiation, one must make a theological distinction in the *ordo salutis*. Wesleyans have normally done this by saying that justification and sanctification are chronologically simultaneous but sanctification is theologically subsequent.

The issue of chronological subsequence is more complex and hence more controversial. It became one of the burning issues during the Holiness revivals of the nineteenth and early twentieth centuries. Advocates of the "second blessing" combed the Scriptures for resources to demonstrate their experience of a "second" encounter, which they called "entire sanctification." As noted in my essay in this volume, the experiences in the book of Acts provided the most clear-cut examples when interpreted in a certain way. This is doubtless why these advocates of a "deeper life" clung so tenaciously to the identification of the "baptism with the Holy Spirit" with "entire sanctification."

John Wesley took a significantly different approach to the matter. Defining "entire sanctification" in scriptural terms as "loving God with one's whole heart, soul, mind and strength," he discovered through wide experience of his converts that none arrived at this level of spiritual attainment at the time of their initial conversion. Those who did experience this level of grace, he further found, did so in a moment sometime later and generally after a period of growth and development. This led him to conclude that sanctification (in its broader meaning of renewing persons in the image of God) was both gradual and instantaneous. Simply put, he derived the content of the "deeper life" from Scripture and the structure of it from experience.

Using this method, Wesley approached the subject of the structure of Christian experience with considerable diffidence. He would clearly allow the possibility of "entire sanctification" to occur at the moment of one's conversion, provided the understanding and preparation were present. Hence, one could say that subsequence was the normal pattern but not the norm to which everyone must conform. With a wider poll of individual experience, Wesley would more than likely subsume his understanding of how it unfolded under William James's rubric of a "variety of religious experience." His central concern was always the content, the renewal of persons in the image of God, which, in a word, was Christlikeness. The work of the Holy Spirit in the believer's life was always toward actualizing this ideal, however it unfolded.

Response by Ralph Del Colle

Although Walter Kaiser's Evangelical account of Spirit baptism emerges from conversation with Pentecostals, it is not irrelevant to a Catholic view of the matter. Before responding to him, I will first comment on the significance of the Evangelical tradition in its own reception of the doctrine of Spirit baptism. More accurately, I pose a query.

Merrill F. Unger in his book *The Baptism & Gifts of the Holy Spirit* begins his reflections by giving an account of "the baptism of the Spirit in Charismatic Christianity," the title of his first chapter.[56] His rendering is a critical one, intended to correct the

Pentecostal/Charismatic notion that Spirit baptism is an event in the believer's life subsequent to conversion/initiation. He also notes that Pentecostalism gained support for their doctrine from "a number of prominent Evangelicals of the late nineteenth and early twentieth century," including such notables as "F. B. Meyer, A. J. Gordon, A. B. Simpson, Andrew Murray, and most significant of all, R. A. Torrey."[57] One could mention D. L. Moody as well. The corrective denies that Spirit baptism endows the believer with power for life and witness subsequent to conversion. Rather, the doctrine of Spirit baptism is an immersion by the agency of the Holy Spirit into the body of Christ, basically the theological position argued by Kaiser. My query, a genuine one, follows.

Is the Evangelical appropriation and definition of Spirit baptism an identifiable doctrine prior to the challenge posed by a two-stage or three-stage construal of the work of the Holy Spirit? Or is it simply a clarification of the biblical reference to being baptized with the Holy Spirit in light of the Pentecostal challenge? Of course, Pentecostals were not the first to present a definitive pneumatological event subsequent to conversion. Unger's reference to prominent Evangelicals complements the nineteenth-century Wesleyan appropriation of the doctrine as a subsequent work of entire sanctification, whether it was termed the second blessing or Spirit baptism. One may also reference the Puritan or Reformed Sealers as a proto-version of the two-stage theory. Why the query?

If there was no operative doctrine of Spirit baptism among Evangelicals prior to the Wesleyan and Pentecostal doctrines of Spirit baptism, then how might we measure the theological import of its present identification as a doctrine in Evangelical theology? I ask this, for as I argue in my essay, Catholic positions on Spirit baptism emerged directly out of the Catholic Charismatic reception of the classical Pentecostal doctrine. While this is not entirely determinative of a Catholic understanding of Spirit baptism, it does seem that it is the specifically Wesleyan and Pentecostal doctrine of subsequence that evokes both the Catholic reception and the Evangelical correction of the doctrine.

I raise these issues not in order to diminish the weight of the doctrine as stated by Kaiser and other Evangelicals, or to suggest that we are involved in some sort of theological artifice. Rather, the reception or correction may indeed help clarify the pneumatological dimensions of the Christian life in our various theological and ecclesial traditions.

In Kaiser's essay Spirit baptism raises a number of substantial theological issues that have informed the Evangelical/Pentecostal conversation on the matter. The theological definition of the doctrine entails choices in regard to both theological method and the theology of grace. I begin with theological method.

Kaiser distinguishes between the didactic and narrative uses of Scripture, an old saw in the Evangelical/Pentecostal debate. Even though many Evangelicals argue that doctrine can only be determined by the didactic parts of Scripture (his reference to John Stott in this regard), Kaiser is more amenable to the theological import of scriptural narrative. In fact, the exegetical work required to define the meaning of Spirit baptism should not be short-changed by a premature use of the analogy of faith more appropriate for systematic theology. Nevertheless, on the grounds of exegetical and biblical theology alone, including criteria of intentionality and normativity, the Pentecostal interpretation of Spirit baptism ("being baptized in the Holy Spirit") as a subsequent (to conversion) empowerment for service with tongues as initial physical evidence are all denied. This is not to deny that progress has been made on exegetical grounds in regard, for example, to the acknowledgement of the distinctive theology of the Spirit (with its emphasis on power) in Luke-Acts, an argument often employed by Pentecostals.

Kaiser's implied comments about the relationship between the analogy of faith and exegesis are worth pondering. True, Norbert Baumert (representative of one of the two dominant Catholic positions on Spirit baptism) is fairly insistent that the exegetical interpretation of Spirit baptism is not identical with either the Pentecostal or Charismatic use of the term. On exegetical grounds then majority Catholic theological opinion—there is no official Catholic doctrine on the matter—would agree that the biblical "being baptized with/in the Holy Spirit" is not identical to Pentecostal/Charismatic usage as an event subsequent to conversion/initiation. This also holds true for the majority Catholic Charismatic position that identifies Spirit baptism as experienced in the renewal with the release or appropriation by faith of the outpouring of the Spirit given in the grace of the sacraments of initiation.

Having said this, I still would probe Kaiser's position in regard to the relationship between exegesis and biblical theology on the one hand and the analogy of faith for the construction of Christian doctrine on the other. Can it really be established that there is a biblical doctrine of Spirit baptism that has to do with being "incorporated by God, in the Holy Spirit, into one spiritual body of Christ"? It is based largely on 1 Corinthians 12:13 as the interpretative lens for the other passages on Spirit baptism and underscores the pneumatological (and ecclesial!) aspects of the blessings of the new age.

My query is not so much a matter of the particulars that in large part I agree with. Namely, the outpouring of the Holy Spirit embraces both the soteriological and empowering dimensions of the Spirit's work, constitutes the ecclesial reality of the Christian life (although as a Catholic I am dissatisfied with the notion of the *spiritual* body of Christ if that means that sacramentality is not being considered), and that this event is associated with Christian initiation. Does all this mean, however, that the "doctrine of Spirit baptism" then occupies a place in the *ordo salutis,* for example, as it seems to in some evangelical accounts? This is implicitly the case in Kaiser's essay where he distinguishes between Spirit baptism and the infilling(s) of the Spirit. If so, how does one arrive at such a position—only by biblical exegesis, or also by the analogy of faith?

Catholics, of course, reserve doctrinal definition to the magisterium of the church. This does not deny that the faith, the *depositum fidei,* as contained in sacred Scripture and tradition is entrusted to the whole church (*CCC* 84). But it is to affirm that the authority to define the faith is reserved to the magisterium who consider the Word of God (under which it stands) in light of the "content and unity of the whole Scripture" (*CCC* 112), the "living Tradition of the whole Church" (*CCC* 113), and the analogy of faith defined as "the coherence of the truths of faith among themselves and within the whole plan of Revelation" (*CCC* 114). It is perhaps my bias as systematic theologian combined with being Catholic that wants to situate Spirit baptism within the larger dogmatic domain in relation to the doctrines of the church (rather than so-called "Bible doctrines" if that was ever implied).

In the end such is not the case regarding Spirit baptism relative to Catholic dogma, meaning it has not emerged as another Catholic doctrine such as the Immaculate Conception of the Blessed Virgin Mary. It can only register as theological understandings at this point. Perhaps it was the best pastoral approach to allow various opinions to coexist while attempting to discern and promote a Catholic reception of the Pentecostal doctrine, or more accurately the Pentecostal experience.

As I seek to demonstrate in my essay in this volume, the Catholic reception was not theologically innocent. A two-stage *ordo salutis* could not violate the sacramental integrity of Catholic ecclesiology and the theology of grace. Is such the case with the Evangelical reception? To suggest an Evangelical reception (rather than mere correction) may seem surprising. However, apart from the most polemical anti-Pentecostal tractates, many Evangelical expositions of Spirit baptism, even in their correction of the two-stage *ordo salutis,* attempt to accentuate a proper understanding of the work of the Holy Spirit along with a pneumatological praxis (in other words, a spirituality). Kaiser's essay is an example of this, refusing to disassociate the soteriological from empowerment, emphasizing the pneumatological basis for incorporation into Christ and his body, while allowing for ongoing infillings of the Spirit that transforms (by the fruit of the Spirit) as well as empowers. The theological aspiration, despite differences from Pentecostals over subsequence and gifts, is nothing less than the fullness of the Holy Spirit.

Response by Larry Hart

Evangelicals have served faithfully over the years as the theological watchdogs of the church. Thoroughly committed to biblical authority and bent on careful exegesis, they have provided sterling leadership and sound theological scholarship. Now that Pentecostals and Charismatics have joined their ranks, they have also provided sage theological perspective for this burgeoning new wing of the larger Evangelical movement. Dr. Kaiser, as a proven leader in this family of the faith, has rendered both institutional and scholarly guidance in the crucial decades in which Evangelicalism gradually took the reigns of leadership in mainline American Christianity. His Evangelical instinct to demonstrate the *unity* of the teachings of the Bible is evident in his presentation here and serves to strengthen his argument.

Theologically, preserving the unity of the work of the Holy Spirit in general and Spirit baptism in particular is a legitimate and worthy goal. But there are different ways to go about doing this. Dr. Kaiser, in typical Reformed fashion, has chosen to treat Spirit baptism as a doctrinal rubric with a requisite unified significance. Another approach would be to treat Spirit baptism as a flexible *metaphor* with varied uses among the New Testament writers, resulting in a broader, yet still unified, conception. In any event, as even Dr. Kaiser's treatment of the Acts narratives demonstrates, it is difficult to fit neatly the mysterious workings of the Holy Spirit into our given theological categories. This is probably one reason New Testament scholars, for example, are sometimes impatient with systematic theologians, who are seeking to codify the Bible's teachings. As a leading Old Testament scholar, Dr. Kaiser, however, has less difficulty discerning doctrine in narrative passages than perhaps his New Testament counterparts. His analysis is careful, nuanced, and fair. His starting point, however, as previously indicated, has determined his ending point and consequent rejection of Pentecostal/Charismatic insights.

One of the most important contributions of the Reformed tradition so ably represented here is the Christ-centered and ecclesiological orientation it defends. Spirit baptism is a Christ-oriented reality; he is the baptizer. And it also relates directly to the corporate life of the church and is not just an individualized experience. We are brought by the Spirit of Christ into his one body to the glory of God. The genius of Reformed theology lies precisely here: it is thoroughly Trinitarian and thoroughly doxological! It demonstrates the unity of the faith perhaps better than any other tradition.

Dr. Kaiser is no cessationist, but his theological conclusions on this subject fit neatly into cessationist theology. Why? Because the specifically *Charismatic* dimension of Spirit baptism has been tacitly ignored. And is not that the exact point being raised by the Pentecostal/Charismatic tradition? All Christian experience is *Charismatic*; that is, its source is to be found in the gracious workings of God's Spirit. But it is easy to identify, in both Testaments, Charismatic activity that transcends the norm. It is the

Pentecostals of the twentieth century who brought back the signs and wonders of Acts to the church (God did, through them). Acts describes tongues speaking and prophetic utterances in association with Spirit baptism. Have these ceased now? Dr. Kaiser's theology has no specific answer, but the implication could clearly be that these phenomena, in association with Spirit baptism, are no longer important. Actually, to be fair to Dr. Kaiser, the theological framework he provides here has plenty of room, as it stands, for all legitimate Charismatic activity in the contemporary church, including speaking in tongues and prophecy. But the specific questions related to Spirit baptism still need to be answered.

Nonetheless, Dr. Kaiser and I have come to similar conclusions in terms of the ongoing nature of the Spirit-filled, Spirit-led Christian life ("many fillings"). Both of us recommend referring to continuing empowerment as *infillings,* my recommendation issuing as much from pragmatic grounds, since I also argue that Pentecostals and Charismatics can make the case for an empowerment concept of Spirit baptism (with Luke). There is much common ground upon which we all can build at least a broad consensus.[58]

In practical terms there are problems on every side. All of us know that there are both spiritual catatonics and silly charismaniacs among us who make life difficult for all. Attitudes of superiority are evident on all sides as well. But my sympathies are still with the Pentecostals, who simply will not allow us to substitute tidy doctrine for Pentecostal power. Dr. Kaiser does not do this, but many in the tradition he represents do. Perhaps in the future, leading biblical scholars such as James D. G. Dunn, in New Testament scholarship, and Dr. Kaiser, in Old Testament scholarship, could focus more on the specifically Charismatic elements of Spirit baptism in Acts and their implications for present-day experience of Spirit baptism. In the meantime we should all be able to find unity in Paul's words to those feisty Corinthian Christians: "For in one Spirit we were all baptized into one body—Jews or Greeks, slaves or free—and all were made to drink of one Spirit" (1 Cor. 12:13 ESV).

CHAPTER 2

Spirit Baptism: A Pentecostal Perspective

STANLEY M. HORTON

Introduction

Pentecostals have always understood Spirit baptism[1] "as the coming of God's Spirit into the believer's life in a very focused way."[2] Down through church history there were occasional incidents of Pentecostal experiences.[3] Some affected churches. Others were simply the experiences of individuals. My grandmother, Clara "Daisy," was the daughter of Dr. Heman Howes Sanford, an ordained Baptist minister and professor of Greek and Latin at Syracuse University. About 1880, after finishing the course at the University, she became president of the New York State combined Christian Endeavor Societies. On one occasion she was invited to speak to the women of a Baptist church in Erie, Pennsylvania. When she arose, she "felt an unusual move of the Holy Spirit and began to speak in a language she had never learned. Then the Spirit gave her an interpretation that was all Scripture and fitted together to form a message. The women wanted to know what that funny foreign language was,"[4] but she didn't know, nor did she fully understand this. But when she was alone, she would often pray in tongues.

Please do not close your mind when I speak of experience. Spirit baptism is an observable and intensely personal experience, not just a doctrine.[5] I remember the first time I met Dr. Gordon Clark, then professor of philosophy at Butler University in Indiana. I expressed appreciation about some of the things he had written. But when I told him I am Pentecostal, he said, "Oh, I don't want to have anything to do with that. That's experience, and experience can only lead you astray. All I want is the Word." He could not seem to understand that New Testament believers learned more about the Spirit and the Word as they experienced Spirit baptism and the Spirit's power and gifts.

Experience given by the Holy Spirit can make a difference in one's understanding of the Scripture. I heard a friend of my father named Butler, from England, tell how when Smith Wigglesworth, the British evangelist, had his first big tent meeting in Vancouver, BC, Canada, he went to Brother Wigglesworth and asked if it might be possible to receive the baptism in the Holy Spirit with the evidence of the mighty rushing wind. Wigglesworth could have explained that the signs of the appearance of fire and the sound of wind preceded and were not part of the Pentecostal outpouring of the Spirit nor were they repeated.[6] However, speaking in other tongues was repeated, and in Acts 10 is clearly the evidence of receiving the baptism. But he didn't. Instead, he said, "why don't you go into the prayer tent and ask the Lord about it." As Brother Butler prayed, a wind actually picked him up and laid him down at the other end of the tent. Brother Butler thought, "I must get up and tell people I have received the baptism in the Spirit with the sign of the mighty rushing wind." But he could not get up. He felt as if he was nailed to the floor. Then he began speaking in tongues. He had no doubts after that about tongues being the initial outward evidence of the baptism in the Holy Spirit.

An Episcopal minister in Springfield, Missouri, told a group of us of the unbelief promoted by his seminary

studies. He was reading books such as *Honest to God* [by
J. A. T. Robinson (Philadelphia, Pa.: Westminster, 1963)]
to try to find some excuse to stay in the ministry. The
Episcopal funeral service included reading 1 Thess.
4:13–18 [For the Lord himself will come down from
heaven, with a loud command, with the voice of the
archangel and with the trumpet call of God, and the dead
in Christ will rise first. After that, we who are still alive
and are left will be caught up together with them in the
clouds to meet the Lord in the air.]. He did not believe it,
so he would mumble it rapidly, hoping no one would
understand what he was saying. Finally, he decided to
leave the ministry. But the very day he did so, someone
invited him to a prayer meeting where they loved him to
Jesus. He found real salvation and received the baptism
in the Holy Spirit. Now he loves to talk about the coming
of the Lord.

In Youngstown, Ohio, another Episcopal minister told
me the Old Testament professors in his seminary were
the antisupernaturalists. He said he was glad he had
taken only one Old Testament course, because now that
he had been baptized in the Holy Spirit he had that much
less to unlearn.[7]

The Pentecostal Revival

Jesus compared the Holy Spirit to the outpouring of rivers of
living water "not poured out at random over the whole country-
side, but through lives that are yielded to Jesus Christ" (John
7:37–39).[8] The outpouring of the Spirit that is now often called
"Classic Pentecostalism" began with the study of the Word of God
and prevailing prayer that was inspired by the Word. In a day when
theological liberals were spreading skeptical views of the Bible,
many Bible believers were searching the Scriptures, seeking to
know more about the work of the Holy Spirit. Several streams
contributed to the twentieth-century Pentecostal Revival. Most
important was the Wesleyan Holiness emphasis on a distinct,
instantaneous crisis experience of sanctification as "a second work
of grace," coming after conversion.

Others who helped to prepare the way included Adoniram Judson Gordon, whose books, *The Holy Spirit in Missions* and *The Twofold Life,* stirred interest in the work of the Holy Spirit. The Keswick Higher Life Movement proclaimed that "fullness of the Spirit" is part of normal Christian life and fillings of the Spirit provide victorious living in the midst of the sin and temptations of the world. A few German scholars, such as Hermann Gunkel and R. Pesch even recognized tongues as strikingly characteristic of the Holy Spirit's work and his witness of the kingdom of God.[9]

Then at Moody Bible Institute in Chicago, Reuben Archer Torrey and Dwight L. Moody taught that receiving the Holy Spirit was an empowering experience able to help in evangelizing the world. I learned of this first through my grandparents. After my grandfather, Elmer Kirk Fisher, graduated from a college in Ohio, he went to Moody Bible Institute to prepare for ministry. There he met and later married Clara "Daisy" Sanford. On one occasion Torrey and Moody lined up the students and, following the example of Peter and John at Samaria (Acts 8:17), proceeded down the row, placing their hands on each student and saying, "Receive ye the Holy Ghost." This encouraged their interest in the Holy Spirit.[10] Clara Daisy, however, had a great interest already, having attended Keswick conferences earlier at Chatauqua, New York.

A new development came in 1900 at Bethel Bible School in Topeka, Kansas. In a room "dedicated to the Lord as a Prayer Tower," the students prayed in three-hour watches. "Day and night, ceaseless intercession ascended to God."[11] Students there became convinced by their study of God's Word that baptism in the Spirit "would always be evidenced by speaking in tongues."[12] On January 1, 1901, the Holy Spirit fell on one of the students with the evidence of speaking in tongues. After several received the experience, the school's principal, Charles Parham, a former Methodist minister, took the message with "its distinctive hermeneutic, theology, and apologetics"[13] to El Dorado Springs, Missouri, and then to Houston, Texas. There, a black man, William J. Seymour, accepted Parham's "Apostolic Faith" message and took it to Los Angeles, California. "On Monday, April 9, 1906, Seymour and seven others received the Spirit baptism."[14]

Soon Seymour began daily meetings in an abandoned Methodist Church at 312 Azusa Street that could hold about nine hundred persons. The result was a Pentecostal explosion with huge crowds of all kinds of people coming to morning, afternoon, and night services, sometimes lasting until the next morning. Many who came to make fun stayed to pray. Outstanding conversions took place. "By 1908, only two years later, the surging movement had taken root in over 50 nations."[15] Stronstad identifies this in Lukan terms as an "outpouring of the Spirit of prophecy" that "restores the immediacy of God's presence to his people . . . worship gains a dynamism and a vitality . . . there is a new hunger for the Word of God . . . and . . . the Spirit restores . . . empowering in witness."[16]

Los Angeles was the fastest growing city in America. People were coming from all over the world. Many churches as well as independent and Holiness missions were praying for revival.[17] Among them was Joseph Smale, pastor of the First Baptist Church who visited the Welsh revival and took part of his congregation to form the "New Testament Church." Smale's church helped spread the message of the restoration of Pentecostal power.

One example was my grandfather, Elmer K. Fisher. He was pastor of the First Baptist Church in Glendale, California. In 1906 he began a series of sermons on the Holy Spirit. His deacons said they didn't like the excitement this was causing. They told him, "It's all right to preach on courage or on Daniel, but soft-pedal this message about the Spirit." Fisher resigned and went to Smale's New Testament Church. Mrs. Seymour came there and told how the Holy Spirit had been outpoured according to Acts 2:4. My grandfather said he knew something was missing in his experience and Acts 2:4 was the key. That Sunday, he and a number of others received the Pentecostal baptism with the evidence of speaking in tongues.

When he took his wife, Clara, to the Azusa Street Mission, she said, "I already have this." They replied, "You couldn't have, you're a Baptist." She didn't argue. She just knelt down and began to pray. Soon she was speaking in tongues, and a man from Norway told her she was speaking in Norwegian. My mother knelt to seek the baptism, and in ten minutes she was speaking in tongues. A black woman from one of the French-speaking islands told her she was speaking in French. There was enough of that to let them know that what they were experiencing was a restoration of the experience of the book of Acts. Some did jump to the wrong conclusion that the gift of tongues would enable them to preach the gospel in foreign lands without learning their languages. My mother knew three couples personally who believed this and went overseas. They were disappointed, of course. The Great Commission was to make disciples. That means knowing and teaching the people—in their own language. No one was converted on the Day of Pentecost by the tongues that were glorifying God. It took Peter's anointed, prophetic teaching to bring them to the place of repentance and faith.

Soon those who received the Pentecostal baptism were carrying the news in all directions. A great revival broke out in the Christian and Missionary Alliance Bible School in Nyack, New York. Though their leaders did not continue to accept speaking in tongues as the evidence, a number of their students who received the baptism in the Spirit there later became leaders in the Assemblies of God. One of them was William I. Evans, dean of Central Bible College in Springfield, Missouri. He often told his students how he sought the baptism in the Spirit at Nyack and would experience holy laughter. Then one of their faculty members told him he needed to take a further step of faith and receive the baptism with the evidence of speaking in tongues.

Early in the Pentecostal revival, the question of the initial physical evidence became controversial. One of the first to write in its defense was my grandfather, Elmer Fisher. In an article "Stand for the Bible Evidence," he wrote:

> We have found the Holy Spirit endorses those who stand for the Bible evidence. The evidence that is given us in the Word of God will stand. The evidence of the full Pentecostal baptism in the Holy Ghost and fire, according to Acts 2:4, is that they "Spake in other tongues as the Spirit gave them utterance." Also in Acts 10:44–48 when the Spirit was poured out upon the Gentile converts in the house of Cornelius, the Jews who came from Joppa with Peter knew that the Holy Ghost had been given to them "For (or because) they heard them speak with tongues and magnify God." Again in Acts 19:6 while Paul laid his hands upon the twelve disciples at Ephesus, "The

Holy Ghost came upon them and they spake with tongues and prophesied."

In the Samaritan revival (Acts 8:16–17) the speaking in tongues is not mentioned, but we know that there was an outward sign of some kind for when Simon saw it, he offered money that he might receive the same power to bestow the gift.[18] If there is one thing that Satan fights more than another and tries to counterfeit, it is the speaking in tongues which is the utterance of the Holy Spirit.

Remember, beloved, it is not the gift of tongues, but only that speaking in tongues which is the utterance of the Holy Ghost, is the evidence of the baptism. When the Spirit of God has gotten such full possession of you that He can use your tongue to utter His own words in another language then you have the baptism in the Holy Ghost. If the Spirit has obtained such full possession there must also be love in the heart, also the other fruits of the Spirit are manifest. He is always the same; and it is impossible to get the fullness of God without getting love and graces also. Let us be careful not to confound the speaking in tongues which is the utterance of the Holy Ghost (this the evidence of our baptism) with the gift of tongue.

But beloved don't allow any of the counterfeits of the Devil or the failures of men to cause you to lower the standard of the Word of God that those who receive the full baptism of the Holy Ghost will speak in tongues as the Spirit gives utterance always.[19]

"As wonderful as the outpouring of the Spirit was [on the Day of Pentecost], not everyone accepted it. [So] it is understandable [that] there are those who reject the present-day revival."[20] One of the groups that did accept the message was the Church of God in Christ, led by Charles Mason. Mason's ministry reached both blacks and whites. "Between 1907 and 1914, numerous white ministers sought credentials from Mason's Church of God in Christ."[21] Some of these later joined the Assemblies of God.

Partly because the major denominations rejected the Pentecostal message, many who were Spirit-filled sought fellowship, and numerous Pentecostal denominations eventually came into being.[22] Two hundred forty of them in 170 countries today are Holiness (Wesleyan, Methodistic), "teaching a three-crises experience (conversion, sanctification, baptism in the Spirit)" and include the Church of God, Cleveland, Tennessee. Three hundred ninety of them in 210 countries are Baptistic (teaching a "two-crisis experience," conversion, baptism in the Spirit) and include the Assemblies of God.[23] Since I am a member of the Assemblies of God, I shall tell the story primarily from that point of view.

In the spring of 1914, a group of Pentecostal ministers from seventeen states and two foreign countries met at the Grand Opera House in Hot Springs, Arkansas. They formed the General Council of the Assemblies of God with a view of providing ministerial training and supporting world missions. The outpouring of the Holy Spirit made them feel a new sense of the imminence of the Christ's return and a new urgency for the spreading of the gospel to the entire world.

At a later General Council, October 2–7, 1916, they approved "A Statement of Fundamental Truths" as a basis of fellowship. The first statement, "The Scriptures Inspired," was basic. Numbers 5–6 dealt with Spirit baptism:

5. The Promise of the Father

All believers are entitled to, and should ardently expect, and earnestly seek the promise of the Father, the baptism in the Holy Ghost and fire, according to the command of our Lord Jesus Christ. This was the normal experience of all in the early Christian Church. With it comes the enduement of power for life and service, the bestowment of the gifts and their uses in the work of the ministry. Luke 24:49; Acts 1:4; 1:8; 1 Cor. 12:1–31.

6. The Full Confirmation of the Baptism in the Holy Ghost

The full consummation of the baptism of believers in the Holy Ghost and fire, is indicated by the initial sign of speaking in tongues, as the Spirit of God gives utterance. Acts 2:4. This wonderful experience is distinct from and subsequent to the experience of the new birth. Acts 10:44–46; 11:14–16; 15:8–9.[24]

This Statement of Fundamental Truths was modified and clarified in 1961 as points 7 and 8:

7. The Baptism in the Holy Ghost

All believers are entitled to and should ardently expect and earnestly seek the promise of the Father, the baptism in the Holy Ghost and fire, according to the command of our Lord Jesus Christ. This was the normal experience of all in the early Christian church. With it comes the enduement of power for life and service, the bestowment of the gifts and their uses in the work of the ministry (Luke 24:49; Acts 1:4,8; 1 Cor. 12:1–31). This experience is distinct from and subsequent to the experience of the new birth (Acts 8:12–17; 10:44–46; 11:114–16; 15:8–9). With the baptism in the Holy Ghost come such experiences as an overflowing fullness of the Spirit (John 7:37–39; Acts 4:8), a deepened reverence for God (Acts 2:43; Heb. 12:28), an intensified consecration to God and dedication to His work (Acts 2:42), and a more active love for Christ, for His Word and for the lost (Mark 15:20).[25]

8. The Initial Physical Evidence of the Baptism in the Holy Ghost

The baptism of believers in the Holy Ghost is witnessed by the initial physical sign of speaking with other tongues as the Spirit of God gives them utterance (Acts 2:4). The speaking in tongues in this instance is the same in essence as the gift of tongues (1 Cor. 12:4–10, 28), but different in purpose and use.[26]

Clearly the Assemblies of God (as well as other classical Pentecostals) recognize two important truths about Spirit baptism: (1) it is an experience that follows conversion, and (2) it is evidenced by speaking in tongues. Luke gives us accounts of Spirit baptism in five passages of the book of Acts: 2:1–41; 8:4–25; 9:1–19; 10:1–11:18; 19:1–7. Let us examine each passage, first to see if the experience of Spirit baptism was subsequent to conversion, second to see what part speaking in tongues had.

In doing this, we are accepting Luke as both a historian and a theologian. Sir William Ramsay started out believing the book of Acts was written in the middle of the second century AD. His research convinced him that Acts fits the historical and geographical situation of the first century. Some still question this, however, I. Howard Marshall writes, "Nevertheless, the basic point made by Ramsay can still be defended and indeed stands beyond doubt."[27]

Many, even some Pentecostals, take Acts as only history and reject Acts as grounds for theology or doctrine.

They overlook the fact that the Bible does not give us history to satisfy our historical curiosity but rather to teach truth. Even the Epistles refer to both Old and New Testament history in order to teach doctrine or theology. When Paul wanted to explain justification by faith in Romans 4, he went back to the history of Abraham in Genesis. When he wanted to show what God's grace can do, he went back to the history of David. Acts does more than give a mere transition, or "shifting of gears," between the Gospels and the Epistles. It provides a background to the Epistles and is necessary for a better understanding of the truths they teach.[28]

Marshall also points out that "modern research has emphasized that he [Luke] was a theologian."[29] Luke uses history "to present divine truth"[30] with Jesus as the center and the advancement of the church's mission by the power and guidance of the Holy Spirit as an important theme. Thus, Wagner calls Acts "a training manual for modern Christians."[31] Stronstad points out that "spiritual experience . . . gives the interpreter of relevant Biblical texts an experiential presupposition which transcends the rational or cognitive presuppositions of scientific exegesis, and, furthermore, results in an understanding, empathy, and sensitivity to the text."[32] This is true of saving faith. It is also true of Spirit baptism. Actually, we need both traditional Protestant hermeneutics and Pentecostal presuppositions.[33]

Spirit Baptism Is a Distinct Experience Subsequent to Conversion

The Day of Pentecost

To see if the disciples were already converted, let us go back first to Luke 22:20. Jesus gave a cup to his disciples saying, "This cup is the new covenant in my blood." Hebrews 9:11–29 makes clear that the new covenant was put into effect by the death of

Christ and the shedding of his blood. Hebrews 10:10 adds, "We have been made holy through the sacrifice of the body of Jesus Christ once for all." During the forty days after his resurrection, Jesus restored the apostles and other followers into a right relation with him and commissioned them to "go and make disciples of all nations, baptizing them in the name of the Father and of the Son and of the Holy Spirit, and teaching them to obey everything I have commanded you" (Matt. 28:19–20). By this we can see that those Jesus left behind were already the new covenant body, the church.

In the days that followed, the 120 in the upper room gathered together as a united body of believers waiting for the promised baptism in the Holy Spirit. During this time Peter recognized that Judas had lost his place of leadership and that the Psalms prophesied that another should take his place. So Matthias was selected to be one of the twelve apostles (Acts 1:12–26; cf. Acts 6:2). The recognition of the need for leadership further indicated that the 120 were already a united body, already the church.[34] What they were waiting for was not the birthday of the church but the promise of the Father, the empowering of the church by the Holy Spirit (Luke 24:45–49; Acts 1:4–5). What Peter says in Acts 11:17 further confirms that the 120 were already believers when the Spirit fell on them (see below).

During that time of waiting, Luke shows the 120 "all joined together in prayer" (Acts 1:14). "Praying for the Spirit serves as a prelude to Acts. Receiving the Spirit, then comes through prayer, and this is especially the case in Acts 2. . . . In the parables following the Lord's Prayer in Luke, there is a suggestion that it may take much prayer, persistent prayer, to receive the Spirit. This further supports that this does not refer to the Spirit's work in regeneration, for, when Jesus gives life at salvation, one does not have to 'persist.' This encouragement to persist dovetails with Jesus' exhortation to the disciples in Acts 1:4 not to leave Jerusalem until they receive the Spirit."[35]

To prepare them, God surprised them with two signs (Acts 2:2–3). First, a sudden "sound like the blowing of a violent wind came from heaven and filled the whole house where they were sitting." Wind in the Old Testament accompanied divine manifestations, as when God spoke to Job out of a storm (Job 38:1; 40:6), when a wind dried out a path through the Reed Sea (Exod. 14:21), or when the Spirit moved on Ezekiel (37:9–10, 14). They would remember too how Jesus spoke of wind, referring to the Holy Spirit (John 3:8). "The sound of the wind indicated to those present that God was about to manifest himself in a special way. That it was the sound a wind with carrying power would make also spoke of the empowering Jesus promised in Acts 1:8, an empowering for service."[36]

The second sign had the appearance of flames over the entire 120 that then were distributed with a single tongue of flame over the head of each person. "There was, of course, no actual fire, and no one was burned. But fire and light were common symbols of the divine presence, as in the case of the burning bush that Moses saw (Exod. 3:2), and also the Lord's appearance in fire on Mount Sinai after the people of Israel accepted the old covenant (19:18). The Spirit coming in power charred the ropes that bound Samson (Judg. 15:14). The 'fire of the Lord' burned up Elijah's sacrifice and even the stones of the altar and the soil (1 Kings 18:38). Fire is also connected with the Old Testament prophecies of the outpouring of the Spirit in Isaiah, Ezekiel, Joel, and Zechariah. Tongues also indicated speech—the fiery, powerful, prophetic witness that the Holy Spirit would give.

Some suppose these tongues constituted a baptism of fire bringing cleansing and fulfilling John the Baptist's prophecy. However, the hearts and minds of the 120 were already open to the resurrected Christ, already cleansed, already filled with praise and joy (Luke 24:52–53), already responsive to the Spirit-inspired Word (Acts 1:16), already in one accord. Rather than cleansing or judgment, the fire here signified God's acceptance of the Church body as the new temple, or sanctuary, of the Holy Spirit (1 Cor. 3:16: Eph. 2:21–22). Then when the single flames rested on the heads of each individual, it signified accepting them as also being temples of the Spirit (1 Cor. 6:19). Thus, the Bible makes clear that the Church was already in existence before the Pentecostal baptism. . . . It is important to notice that these signs preceded the Pentecostal baptism, or gift of the Spirit. They were not part of it, nor were they repeated on other occasions when the Spirit was outpoured. Peter, for example, identified the filling of the Gentile believers at the house of Cornelius with Jesus' promise that they would be baptized in the spirit, calling it the "same [Gk. *isen*, 'identical'] gift" (Acts 11:17; cf. 10:44–47). But the wind and fire were not present. They seem to have been needed only once.[37]

In the Old Testament only a few selected individuals were filled with the Spirit. Then after four hundred years of silence, there was an outburst of prophecy on the part of six people—John the Baptist, Mary the mother of Jesus, Elizabeth, Zechariah, Simeon, and Anna—that "was the *arrabon*, that is, the promise or pledge of the fulfillment of Moses' earnest desire that all of God's people would be prophets [Num. 11:29]."[38] But on the Day of Pentecost, something new was about to take place. "All of them [the 120 believers] were filled with the Holy Spirit" (2:4). Kee suggests that only the twelve apostles were filled.[39] Luke, however, lists more than twelve languages, and the list is not necessarily complete. It may have been representative or may be that these were the ones who spoke out about what they heard. The Jews were scattered in many more countries than those Luke mentions. They came on pilgrimages from all directions so there were probably more than 100,000 of them in Jerusalem at this time.

Then Peter, quoting Joel, includes Joel's mention of sons and daughters. No doubt, all 120, as well as the 3,000 who also believed that day, were filled with the Spirit. That is, they had "a full, satisfying experience." Some try to make a distinction between being baptized in the Holy Spirit and being filled. Actually, the Bible uses a variety of terms. It was also a pouring out of the Spirit as Joel prophesied (Acts 2:17–18:33); a receiving (and active taking) of a gift (Acts 2:38); a falling upon (Acts 8:16; 10:44; 11:15); a pouring out of the gift (Acts 10:45); and a coming upon. With this variety of terms, it is impossible to suppose that the baptism is any different from the filling.

"Remember, too, that since the Holy Spirit is a Person, we are talking about an experience that brings a relationship. Each term brings out some aspect of the Pentecostal experience, and no one term can bring out all the aspects of that experience."[40] Thus, those who receive the Pentecostal experience today can say they are both filled with and baptized in the Spirit. Jesus, the exalted Lord of the church, received from the Father the promised Holy Spirit for distribution. He poured it out on the believers on the Day of Pentecost. And the crowd saw and heard them "declaring the wonders of God in our own tongues" (Acts 2:11).[41] Jesus still pours out the Holy Spirit on believers with the same initial evidence of speaking in tongues (2:33; 2:4). *I find no proof for this in these 2 verses*

By recognizing this distinct experience of Spirit baptism, we are not diminishing the work of the Holy Spirit in the new birth. "Furthermore, responsible Pentecostals have always taught that one is indwelt by the Spirit at the time of conversion (Rom. 8:9; 1 Cor. 6:19)."[42] But Pentecostals and other Charismatics[43] agree *"this deeper experience of the Holy Spirit in no way refutes or denies any experience the Christian may have had before. It simply opens unto us a whole new realm of spiritual possibilities."*[44] *"We need to receive the supernatural power of the Holy Spirit in our lives and our ministries to the greatest extent possible in order to serve God well in our world."*[45] Let us not eliminate a miracle-working God from our Christianity.

The Samaritan Believers

When Philip preached in Samaria, his proclamation of Christ and the miraculous signs, deliverances, and healings brought great joy. The result was they "believed Philip as he preached the good news of the kingdom of God and the name of Jesus Christ," then "they were baptized, both men and women" (Acts 8:6–8, 13). Not until after that did the apostles in Jerusalem respond to the Samaritans' acceptance of God's word and send Peter and John to them. Peter and John then prayed for these believers "that they might receive the Holy Spirit." Probably to encourage their faith they "placed their hands on them and they received the Holy Spirit" (8:14–17). Again it is clear that Philip recognized them as believers and baptized them in water some time before their Spirit baptism.

This presents a difficulty to those who hold that everything is received with water baptism. Some suppose the Holy Spirit should have been received and the deficiency was corrected as soon as possible. But it is impossible to explain why there should be such a deficiency on that basis. Others suppose the faith of the Samaritans was not real, or was not saving faith until Peter and John came and prayed. However, Philip was a man full of the Spirit and wisdom. He most certainly would have had enough discernment and wisdom not to baptize people before they truly believed in Jesus.

Others suggest that perhaps Philip did not preach the full gospel to them. Since the Samaritans were on the other side of the fence, perhaps his prejudice kept him from telling the Samaritans of all the benefits that Christ as Savior and Baptizer offers to the believer. However, this idea is not borne out by what we find in Acts. The disciples were not able to withhold part of the message. They said, "We cannot but speak the things which we have seen and heard" (Acts 4:20). Philip preached the Word, preached Christ (8:4, 5). The Samaritans believed what Philip preached concerning the kingdom (rule) of God and the name (authority) of Jesus. These things are often associated with the promise of the Holy Spirit. Philip must have included the exaltation of Jesus to the throne and the promise of the Father.

The problem seems to be on the side of the Samaritans. Now, they realized that they had been wrong, not only about the deception of Simon the sorcerer, but also about their Samaritan doctrines. Perhaps, humbled, they found it difficult to express the next step of faith. When Jesus found faith expressed simply on the basis of His Word, He called it great faith, and things happened (Matthew 8:10). When faith rose above hindrances and testing, Jesus called it great faith, and things happened (Matthew 15:28). But when faith was weak, He did not destroy what there was: He helped it, sometimes by laying on His hands. So the people did receive (were receiving, kept receiving) the Spirit as the Apostles went to each of them and placed their hands on them.[46]

Their experience was unusual and identifiable—"a strong argument in favor of the doctrine of subsequence."[47]

The Apostle Paul

When the light from heaven flashed around Saul of Tarsus and he fell to the ground, he would know from his Old Testament studies that this was a divine manifestation. So when Jesus said, "Why do you persecute me?" he answered, "Who are you, Lord?"— and he meant *divine Lord.*

Then, when Jesus said, "I am Jesus, whom you are persecuting," it must have brought the truth of the gospel to him. He had heard Stephen's speech. We can be sure that the other Christians whom he persecuted had been faithful witnesses as well. So he was ready to go to Damascus and wait for what he would be told he must do (Acts 9:6). That he did so shows he was already accepting Jesus as divine Lord and Savior.

At the house of Judas on Straight Street, he prayed and God sent Ananias to him. When Ananias went to the house, he addressed him as "Brother Saul." Before in his response to the Lord, he had referred to Saul as "this man" (9:13). But when the Lord explained that Saul was his chosen instrument, Ananias accepted Saul as a believing brother. So he told Saul, "The Lord— Jesus . . . has sent me so that you may see again and be filled with the Holy Spirit" (9:17). Though Luke only draws attention to the healing in the following verse, we can be sure that Paul was also baptized in the Holy Spirit. Titus 3:6–7 indicates this also by saying that the Holy Spirit was "poured out on us [both Paul and Titus] abundantly through Jesus Christ our Savior." That is, Jesus was already their Savior and then became their baptizer, pouring out the Spirit on them.

We can see, too, that Paul was indeed filled with the Spirit when Ananias prayed for him. Paul did not leave Damascus. Instead, immediately "he began to preach in the synagogues that Jesus is the Son of God." In fact he "grew more and more powerful and baffled the Jews living in Damascus by proving that Jesus is the Christ" (9:20, 22). Luke's emphasis on the power and effectiveness of Paul's preaching shows that the Holy Spirit had made a difference, and the power was the power of the Holy Spirit, as Jesus promised in Acts 1:8.[48] Furthermore, in Paul's case the Holy Spirit was poured out on him as an individual—contrary to some who say Spirit baptism was to incorporate groups into the church.[49]

The Gentile Believers

When Peter spoke to the believers in Jerusalem about the experience of the Gentiles in the house of Cornelius, he said: "As

I began to speak, the Holy Spirit came on them as he had come on us at the beginning. Then I remembered what the Lord had said: 'John baptized with water, but you will be baptized with the Holy Spirit.' So if God gave them the same gift as us, who believed in the Lord Jesus Christ, who was I to think I could oppose God?" (Acts 11:15–17).

From this it is important to notice two things: (1) What these Gentiles received was a baptism in the Holy Spirit, just like the baptism the 120 received on the Day of Pentecost. (2) The phrase "who believed" (Greek: *pisteusasin,* "having believed") is an aorist active participle, which shows that these Gentiles were already believers, just as the 120 were when the Holy Spirit fell on them.[50]

Going back to chapter 10, we see that Cornelius and all his family were "devout and God-fearing" (10:2). God sent him an angel who told him his "prayers and gifts to the poor had come as a memorial offering before God," and he was to send for Peter.

When Peter came and spoke to a large gathering of Roman relatives and friends, he not only explained that "God does not show favoritism but accepts people from every nation who fear him and do what is right," he went on to say something significant about what the people already knew: "*You know* the message God sent to the people of Israel, telling the good news of peace through Jesus Christ who is Lord of all. *You know* what has happened throughout Judea, beginning in Galilee after the baptism that John preached— how God anointed Jesus of Nazareth with the Holy Spirit and power, and how he went around doing good and healing all who were under the power of the devil, because God was with him" (10:36–38).

Clearly these Gentile God-fearers knew the gospel. Since they knew about the baptism that John preached and how Jesus was anointed with the Holy Spirit and power, they must have known what John said about Jesus as the One who would baptize in the Holy Spirit. As Paul told King Agrippa, "these things" were "not done in a corner" (26:26).

Cornelius knew the gospel and knew about the Holy Spirit. Merrill C. Tenney, a Baptist professor, told a New Testament Introduction class that I was in at Gordon Divinity School that he believed Cornelius was already a believer in Jesus and wanted to receive Spirit baptism. But because the Spirit-filled believers were all Jews, his prayers (10:4, 31) were about whether he should become a proselyte to Judaism in order to receive Spirit baptism. It took Peter's vision of chapter 10 to make him ready to say "God does not show favoritism" (10:34–35). With this in mind, it should not be so amazing to us that as Peter continued to review the message of the gospel, these Gentiles already knew the Holy Spirit came on all of them (10:45)—though it did amaze Peter and the six Jewish witnesses he brought with him.

Furthermore, God through the angel prepared the heart of Cornelius to accept Peter's message. When he gathered in his relatives and friends, he must have prepared them also, so their hearts were open to receive Peter's message and the baptism in the Holy Spirit. Even if some of them were not already believers,

it took only a split second for them to believe and be saved. It took only another moment to receive the outpouring, which Peter saw as a baptism in the Spirit. Thus, though their conversion and baptism in the Spirit were not separated by a long period of time, <u>there is no reason why they could not have been distinct events.</u>

Peter at the Jerusalem Council (Acts 15:8) also indicates that the gift of the Spirit was God's way of bearing witness to them. This surely implies they were already converted. Their baptism in the Spirit thus witnessed to the fact that they were already believers. Acts 15:9 does mention the fact that God purified their hearts by faith. But the purpose of Peter in mentioning it last is not to indicate the time it happened, but to give it emphasis. The point at issue in Acts 15:9 was primarily the question of whether Gentiles had to keep the Law and be circumcised, so Peter is not simply rehearsing what happened.

Others suppose Acts 10:47 means water was needed to complete the experience. Again, their hearts were purified by faith, not water (Acts 15:9). Water baptism here was both a recognition by the Church that God had accepted these Gentiles, as well as a testimony to the world that they had indeed become members of the Church.[51]

Notice, too, that Peter did not ask them to repent. Their very presence and desire to hear Peter showed they had repentant, believing hearts.[52]

Marshall also points out that "E. Schweizer correctly notes that in the end Luke was not too concerned with water baptism as the necessary means to the bestowal of the Spirit. He is more concerned to stress the importance of faith (always) and prayer (often) as the appropriate attitudes of men."[53]

The Ephesian Disciples

On Paul's second missionary journey, he came to Ephesus. There he found about twelve disciples (Acts 19:7). Wherever Luke mentions disciples without qualifications in the book of Acts, he always means disciples of Jesus who followed him and believed in him.[54] Like Apollos, they must have known the facts about Jesus (18:25)[55] but needed further instruction. It is possible also, as archaeological discoveries show, that they might well have had parts of Mark's Gospel.[56]

Though Paul sensed there was something lacking in their experience, he did not question the fact that they were believers, nor did he ask them to repent. In fact, he recognized that they did believe. The question he asked shows rather that they lacked the freedom and spontaneity in worship that always characterized Spirit-filled believers. The fact that he asked the question also shows that Paul recognized that there could be a separation between saving faith and the experience of receiving the Holy Spirit.

Modern versions generally translate "since ye believed" (v. 2, KJV) as "*when* you believed." But this translation is based on their theological presuppositions. The Greek is literally, "Having believed, did you receive?" "Having believed" (*pisteusantes*) is a Greek aorist (past) participle. "Did you receive" (*elabete*) is the main verb, also in the aorist. But the fact that they are both in the aorist is not significant here. The fact that the participle "having believed" is in the past is what is important, for the tense of the participle normally shows its relation to the main verb. Because this participle is in the past, this normally means that its action precedes the action of the main verb. That is why the King James translators, as good Greek scholars, translated the participle, "since ye believed." They wanted to bring out that the believing must take place before the receiving. This also brings out the fact that the baptism in the Spirit is a distinct experience following conversion.[57]

One writer, James D. G. Dunn, claims that we who say that the aorist participle here means its action precedes that of the main verse are only showing that we (as well as the King James translators) have a poor grasp of Greek grammar. Dunn, however, contradicts himself by admitting that the aorist participle usually does indicate action that precedes that of the main verb.[58]

Dunn gives no examples of Luke's use. Rather, he refers to "answered and said" as a chief example. But this is from a Hebrew idiom and does not apply here. Some others he mentions seem to be coincidental, such as Hebrews 7:27: "He sacrificed for their sins once for all when he offered himself." Also, Matthew 27:4, "I have sinned, . . . for I have betrayed innocent blood." But this is not parallel to 19:2. "The sin is defined as betrayal. It hardly seems that receiving the Spirit is being defined as believing in Acts 19:2, especially since other passages indicate the receiving to involve definite outpouring of the Spirit."[59]

Many other passages in the New Testament do show that the action of the aorist participle normally precedes the action of an aorist main verb. One is: *"Having fallen asleep in Christ, they perished"* (1 Cor. 15:18). That is, after they fell asleep they perished if Jesus did not rise from the dead. Another example is Matthew 22:25. Speaking of seven brothers, the Sadducees said of the first, *"Having married a wife, he died."* Obviously, even though the King James Version translates this, *"when* he had married a wife," it does not mean the marrying and the dying were the same thing, or even that they happened at the same time. They were distinct events and the marrying clearly preceded the dying, probably by some time.

Other examples can be found in Acts 5:10, "Having carried her [Sapphira] out, they buried her"; Acts 13:51, "Having shaken the dust off their feet, they came to Iconium"; Acts 16:6, "And they went through the Phrygian and Galatian region, having been forbidden by the Spirit to speak the Word in Asia"; Acts 16:24, "having received the orders, he threw them into the inner prison." In these cases and many more the action of the participle clearly precedes the action of the main verb.

The disciples' reply, "No, we have not even heard that there is a Holy Spirit," may be translated, *"But we have not even heard if the Holy Spirit is."* The meaning, however, does not seem to be that they had never heard of the existence of the Holy Spirit. What godly Jew or interested Gentile would or could have been so ignorant? It is more likely that the phrase compares with John 7:39. There, the condensed phrase *"It was not yet Spirit"* means that the age of the Spirit with its promised mighty outpouring had not yet come.

From this we see that these disciples were really saying they had not heard about Pentecost or the availability of the baptism in the Holy Spirit. In fact, several ancient manuscripts and versions of the New Testament actually read, "We have not even heard if any are receiving the Holy Spirit."[60] Obviously, they had not been taught about this when they were converted.[61]

Furthermore, since they had been baptized with John's baptism, they must have known what John said about Jesus as the Baptizer in the Holy Spirit—so important that it is found in all four Gospels (Matt. 3:11; Mark 1:8; Luke 3:16; John 1:33).

Notice also that it was after they heard Paul and after they were baptized into the name of the Lord Jesus that Paul placed his hands on them and they were Spirit-baptized with the initial outward evidence of speaking in tongues. It should be observed also that the placing of hands was not to bring them salvation, nor is there any evidence that it was to ordain them to some office.

Other Significant Passages

Paul's epistles have little to say about receiving Spirit baptism since it was something the first-century believers had already experienced. However, a few passages are important. One of them is 2 Corinthians 1:21–22: "Now it is God who makes both us and you stand firm in Christ. He anointed us, set his seal of ownership on us, and put his Spirit in our hearts as a deposit, guaranteeing what is to come" (see also 5:5). Ephesians 1:13 is emphatic: "Having believed, you were marked in him with a seal, the promised Holy Spirit." Later Paul adds, "Do not grieve the Holy Spirit of God, with whom you were sealed for the day of redemption" (4:30). The words "deposit" and "seal" are important.

Deposit really means "first installment." That is, Spirit baptism is "an actual part of the inheritance, and is the guarantee of what we shall receive in larger measure later. . . . The seal is related to the thought of 1 John 3:2. Though we are already sons of God, there is no outward glory yet. We still have these dying bodies with all their limitations. We still have many of the difficulties, problems, and sorrows common to man. But we have a present possession of the Spirit which is the seal giving us assurance we are God's children and that our hope will not disappoint us (Rom. 5:5)."[62]

We are not to suppose that the seal means "protection, safety, or security. . . . Nor does the Greek imply here the kind of sealing that is done when food is sealed in a jar or tin can to protect it from contamination. We are indeed kept by the power of God through faith unto salvation (1 Pet. 1:5), but this is not automatic. Faith must be maintained."[63] When God put his seal on Jesus, it was not to protect him but to designate him as his Son who gives eternal life (John 6:27). In the Old Testament the seal indicated the price was paid and the transaction completed (Jer. 32:9–10).

"The seal in the New Testament also has the idea of designation of ownership, a trademark indicating we are His workmanship (Eph. 2:10). Since an ancient seal often impressed a picture, the seal may be related to the fact that the Spirit brings the impress of Christ 'until Christ be formed in [us]' (Gal. 4:19). The seal is also a mark of recognition that we are indeed sons, and an evidence that God has indeed accepted our faith."[64]

The significance of the seal as an experience after conversion can be seen in Ephesians 1:13: "And you also were included in Christ when you heard the word of truth, the gospel of your salvation. Having believed, you were marked in him with a seal, the promised Holy Spirit." Because the context emphasizes spiritual life rather than power for service, many commentaries deny that the sealing here refers to Spirit baptism. However, 2 Corinthians 1:21–22 (see above) mentions anointing with the sealing and that can indicate service or ministry. "Others say we belong to the Lord the moment we are saved and we cannot make God's ownership dependent on a later experience. But that argument is not well taken either. The seal did not cause ownership, it only recognized ownership. Thus, the blood of Jesus is the purchase price. By faith we believe and are made His. Then the baptism in the Holy Spirit comes as the seal, the assurance by Jesus that God has accepted our faith."[65]

The seal was always a visible demonstration those around could recognize (as in the case of those Spirit-filled in the house of Cornelius). Thus, it means more than believing. Some believe even the sealing of the 144,000 (Rev. 7:3) included Spirit baptism. "It is true that they are sealed with a mark in their foreheads. But even in the Old Testament God did not command an outward sign without the inward reality to go with it. David was anointed with oil, but the Holy Spirit came upon him from that day forward."[66]

Another important passage is 1 Corinthians 12:12–13: "The body is a unit, though it is made up of many parts; and though all its parts are many, they form one body. So it is with Christ. For we were all baptized by the one Spirit into one body—whether Jews or Greeks, slave or free—and we were all given the one Spirit to drink." Comparing the local assembly to a human body shows "the unity that the Spirit brings is the unity of a living organism. It retains its variety. It is able to adjust to new situations and meet new opportunities and challenges."[67]

Then we see a distinction between the Spirit baptizing believers into the one body and being "given the one Spirit to drink." The latter phrase could be translated "made to drink with the same Spirit," which "can mean we are watered, imbued, or saturated with the one Spirit like that on the Day of Pentecost (cf. Isa. 29:10 where the Septuagint translates the Hebrew *nasakh*, 'pour out,' with *pepotiken*, 'made to drink'; see also Isa. 32:15; 44:3). This implies not only the initial baptism in the Spirit but a continuing experience with the Spirit. . . . As Ephesians 5:18 commands us, we need to 'ever be filled with the Spirit' (Williams translation)."[68]

Romans 6:3 and Galatians 3:27 similarly mention baptism into Christ, meaning into the body of Christ. But this is different from John the Baptist's promise that Jesus would baptize in the Holy Spirit. "If this distinction is not maintained, we have the strange idea that Christ baptizes into Christ!"[69]

In a class I took at Gordon Divinity School, a Baptist student said, "Since the Holy Spirit is a person, you can't split him up. You get all of him when you are born again. You can't get any more of him. The only thing you can do is give more of yourself to him." I responded, "Aren't you a person? If you can give more of yourself to him, he can give more of himself to you." The professor then spoke up and said, "Yes, there are always different degrees and levels of personal relationships."

Since the Father gives the Spirit to Jesus to distribute, we can have this experience if we ask. Jesus said, "How much more will your Father in heaven give the Holy Spirit to those who ask him?" (Luke 11:13). This promise is still available to those who are believers looking to their heavenly Father. As Pentecostals, we believe that the "one baptism" of Ephesians 4:5 is the baptism by the Spirit into the body of Christ. It is the one that is essential for our salvation. But baptism in water is essential for the expression of our faith, and Spirit baptism is essential for our witness and contributes to our spiritual life, worship, and ministry.

By receiving the baptism in the Spirit, we become more open to the gifts of the Spirit (1 Cor. 12:7–11). It helps us to live victorious lives that glorify Christ, as Paul brings out in Romans 8:5, 13: "Those who live according to the sinful nature have their minds set on what that nature desires; but those who live in accordance with the Spirit have their minds set on what the Spirit desires. . . . For if you live according to the sinful nature, you will die; but if by the Spirit you put to death the misdeeds of the body, you will live."

And as we read in Galatians 5:25, "Since we live by the Spirit, let us keep in step with the Spirit." That is, we continue to be open to the Spirit's prompting and guidance. It may also mean we are responsive to the Spirit and receive special fillings to meet special needs. For example, when Peter and John were brought to trial before Annas, Caiaphas, and other rulers and elders in Jerusalem, the same group that had condemned Jesus, Peter was no longer afraid. He was "filled with the Holy Spirit" as he began to speak (Acts 4:8). The Greek verb (in the aorist) indicates a new, fresh filling. "This does not mean he had lost any of the power and presence of the Spirit he received on the Day of Pentecost. In view of the pressures of this critical situation, the Lord simply enlarged his capacity and gave him the fresh filling to meet this new need for power to witness."[70]

Paul also had new, fresh fillings. On Paul's first missionary journey, he faced Elymas the sorcerer who was trying to turn the proconsul Sergius Paulus from the faith, that is, from the gospel of Christ that Paul preached. Paul, like Peter was "filled with the Holy Spirit" as he looked at Elymas and pronounced God's judgment on him (Acts 13:7–10). This was not his own idea but was directly prompted by the Spirit. From this point on the Holy Spirit also gave Paul the leadership in the missionary endeavor.[71]

Speaking in Tongues as the Initial Outward Evidence

The Day of Pentecost

When the 120 were filled on the Day of Pentecost, they "began to speak in other tongues as the Spirit enabled them" (Acts 2:4). Hardy Steinberg points out that this was unprecedented so that "no one can say they were psychologically conditioned for such an experience. It happened without their expecting it. It was a sovereign and supernatural manifestation of the Holy Spirit."[72] Nowhere in ancient Judaism was there any speaking in tongues (["languages," often called] glossolalia, from the Greek, *glossais lalein*).[73]

In this passage we can see a double use of the word *tongues* (Greek, *glossais*). It is used of the single tongue like a flame that rested on each of the 120 (2:3). Then it is used of the languages the Spirit enabled them to speak (2:4). "This was the first perceptible expression *from within* the disciples that they had been filled with the Spirit. They who were mostly Galileans began to speak in what observers from Rome to Mesopotamia and Arabia individually recognized as their 'own language'" (*idia dialekto*) (2:6, 8). Reference to this fact is made a third time in 2:11 using *"hemeterais glossais* 'our languages' in which *glossai* is manifestly used synonymously with *dialektoi.*"[74]

Notice that the filling preceded the speaking in tongues. The Holy Spirit took full possession of their spirit, heart, and mind. Then they spoke. "These were not 'ecstatic sayings' that were unintelligible, but were clearly discernible languages . . . that were recognized. (If anyone was 'ecstatic' in the *disorganized* sense of the word, it was the *observers* as seen in one of the words descriptive of their reaction—*existanto*—lit. 'they stood outside themselves,' i.e., 'were amazed.')"[75] Certainly, babbling could not be considered a gift or work of the Holy Spirit. Nor does the verb *lalein* used of "speaking" in tongues imply unintelligible speech. See 1 Corinthians 14:29 where it is used of the gift of prophecy. See also 14:26 where speaking in tongues is used with the word *legein,* a very common word for *speak.*

Because of the mention of "hearing" in Acts 2:6, 8, 11, some suppose the 120 did not speak in languages other than their native Galilean dialect. Instead they propose that by a miracle the Spirit enabled them to hear a translation of what was said. Dr. Anthony Palma refers to Max Turner who points out, however, that the Holy Spirit had filled the believers. He was working in them and through them. Turner also notes that even John Calvin recognized that such a miracle of hearing would mean that the Spirit was given to the unbelievers rather than the believers.[76]

I have been asked the question: Does 1 Corinthians 13:1 support the idea that when we speak in tongues we may be speaking in languages of angels? I answered:

Some Jews did believe angels had their own heavenly languages. Some in Corinth "may have thought they were speaking 'tongues of angels.'" However, it is more likely that "tongues of angels" was a figure of speech (a hyperbole) indicating the high regard the Corinthians had for speaking in tongues. (See my commentary on *I and II Corinthians* [Springfield, Mo.: Logion Press, Gospel Publishing House, 1999], p. 125). Later, Paul, to encourage the gift of interpretation, says, "Undoubtedly there are all sorts of languages in the world, yet none of them is without meaning. If then I do not grasp the meaning of what someone is saying, I am a foreigner to the speaker, and he is a foreigner to me. So it is with you. Since you are eager to have spiritual gifts, try to excel in gifts that build up the church. For this reason anyone who speaks in a tongue should pray that he may interpret what he says" (1 Corinthians 14:10–13, NIV). Here Paul seems to recognize tongues as human languages ("in the world"). He does not seem to leave room for any of them being languages of angels. No other passage indicates that when we speak in tongues they are anything but human languages. There are more than 4,000 languages and dialects in the world today and probably another 4,000 or 5,000 ancient languages, so the Holy Spirit has plenty to choose from.[77]

One of my students, Randy Hurst, told the class that when he was a boy in China his missionary father, Wesley Hurst, was ministering in an interior village where white men had not been before. After a number accepted the gospel, missionary Hurst prayed for them to be baptized in the Holy Spirit. Randy said he heard one young woman speak in tongues in perfect English.

My friend, Mrs. Kofsmann from Jerusalem, was visiting in Central Assembly of God in Springfield, Missouri, when someone spoke out in tongues and a woman who knew no Hebrew gave the interpretation. Mrs. Kofsmann told me the tongues speech was modern Hebrew, and the interpretation was correct.

Another friend of mine, a medical doctor who grew up in a German-speaking home in Florida, had one of his patients persuade him to attend an Assembly of God service. During the service a man spoke in German, and another man stood and gave the interpretation in English. My friend supposed the first man was a German newcomer and that a friend was helping him out. So he went up to the first man and began speaking to him in German. The man turned out to be a farmer who didn't understand a word of German. That medical doctor joined the Assemblies of God and, while still carrying on his medical practice, has been instrumental in starting about a dozen new Assemblies of God.

See C. Peter Wagner, *Spreading the Fire* [(Ventura, Calif.: Regal Books, Gospel Light, 1994), 95], for an account of a multilingual Arab Muslim who was converted when a British pastor prayed for him in tongues that he knew was fluent Iranian, and later prayed in fluent Ugaritic.

Some say that the tongues speaking they have heard has no known language structure. The Greek, however, definitely means languages, not nonsense syllables.

If it seems like nonsense syllables, so did the language of the Assyrians seem to the Hebrews (Isaiah 28:11, 13). To those who do not know Hebrew, it would sound like nonsense syllables as well. "Our Father" in Hebrew is pronounced "ah-vee-noo." "I will fear not evil" is "lo-ee-rah ra." Since tongues is often a matter of worship and praise, ejaculations and repetitions should be expected, as in many Psalms. Psalm 150:2, "Praise him for his mighty acts," is pronounced, "hah-le-loo-hoo bih-g'voo-roh-taw." Then "ha-le-loo-hoo" is repeated again and again in the next few verses.

No matter how it sounds . . . tongues means languages both in Acts and in Corinthians. When we pray in tongues our spirit prays, since our spirit is the medium through which the gift operates, and thus involves yielding spirits and our wills to God as well as our tongues and vocal organs for the operation of the gift (1 Corinthians 14:14). The result is language, as the Spirit gives utterance.[78]

That they "began" to speak implies that they continued to do so (see the use of "began" in Acts 1:1). It also implies that tongues speaking continued to accompany other instances of Spirit baptism. The speaking was as the Spirit "enabled" them. *Enabled* (Greek, *apophtheggesthai*) is a word used in the Septuagint of divinely inspired, bold speech (1 Chron. 25:1). It is used also in Acts 2:14 when Peter, filled with the Spirit, "raised his voice and *addressed* the crowd." What Peter said is often called his first sermon, but it was not a sermon. He did not sit down and figure out three points. He spoke as the Spirit gave him the words. It was an expression of the Spirit's gift of prophecy. Then when Festus shouted to Paul, "Your great learning is driving you insane," Paul replied, "What I am saying is true and reasonable" (Acts 26:24–25). "Saying" (Gk. *apophtheggomai*) also indicates that what Paul was saying was spoken as the Spirit enabled him—just as Spirit-inspired speaking in tongues is not the result of our own thinking or reasoning.

From Peter's experience and from his reference to Joel's prophecy (2:16–18) where he indicates that those speaking in tongues "will prophesy," some might ask how speaking in tongues is related to prophecy. "Both oral prophesying and speaking in tongues involve the Holy Spirit coming upon a person and prompting the person to speak out."[79] Those who prophesy speak in their own language. Those who speak in tongues speak in a language they have never learned. But the same Holy Spirit prompts them both in the same way. Tongues, however, are not for evangelism.[80] Those who heard on the Day of Pentecost heard praise. It was not until Peter spoke out in the gifts of prophecy and exhortation that the three thousand were converted.

Other evidences of Spirit baptism will also follow, as noted in the Assemblies of God *Statement of Fundamental Truths* above. "The Spirit is the source of the love, zeal, and state of heart that enables us to serve the Lord acceptably with 'spiritual fervor' (Rom. 12:11)."[81]

The Samaritan Believers

When Simon saw that the Spirit was given at the laying on of the apostles' hands, he offered them money and said, "Give me also this ability so that everyone on whom I lay my hands may receive the Holy Spirit" (Acts 8:18–19). Luke does not describe what caught Simon's attention. But there is only one thing it could have been. Simon had already observed the miracles in Philip's ministry. He would not have recognized a prophetic utterance in his own language as something unusual or supernatural. MacDonald notes also that "some new sign" is unlikely, for Luke probably would have mentioned it.[82] Simon must have heard them speak in tongues as the Spirit enabled them, as on the Day of Pentecost. This would be easily recognized.

It should be noted that Luke does not mention every detail when other passages make his point. For example, he does not mention water baptism every time people are converted, even though the book of Acts as a whole makes obvious that believers were always baptized in water. Furthermore, Luke was especially concerned to point out Simon's wrong attitude, so he quickly goes on to deal with that and does not take up space to mention tongues. Tongues speaking also did not have the same effect as in Acts 2, for there were no others who spoke foreign languages.

Some say this passage is irrelevant to our discussion here due to Luke's primary intent. But, as Robert Menzies points out, "A passage must be understood in terms of its original setting and intention, but the theological freight it carries may transcend its 'primary intent.' . . . An exclusive focus on an author's 'primary intent' or 'intention to teach' too often leads to a form of tunnel vision which ignores the implications of an individual text for the theological perspective of the author."[83]

The Apostle Paul

When Ananias placed his hands on Saul, he said, "Brother Saul, the Lord—Jesus, who appeared to you on the road as you were coming here—has sent me so that you may see again and be filled with the Holy Spirit" (Acts 9:17). We should note here that Jesus did not send apostles as he did to Samaria, but Ananias was an ordinary believer who was native to Damascus. There is nothing to indicate any apostle laid hands on him either. He was just obeying the command of Jesus to him.

Again Luke is more concerned about recording Paul's outstanding healing and the call to ministry Jesus gave Paul. So he does not mention speaking in tongues. But it should be obvious Luke was referring to the same experience the 120 had on the Day of Pentecost. We can see parallels between God's sending Peter to Cornelius and sending Ananias to Saul. Undoubtedly, Saul was filled with the Spirit immediately, before he was baptized in water, as in the case of those in the house of Cornelius.[84] He must also have spoken in tongues, for he says later to the Corinthians, "I thank God that I speak in tongues more than all of you" (1 Cor. 14:18). "Titus 3:5–7 confirms this by showing that the Holy Spirit was poured out on both Saul and Titus abundantly. Each had his own personal Pentecost."[85]

What then does Paul mean when he asks the question, "Do all speak in tongues?" (1 Cor. 12:30). The way the question is phrased calls for the answer, "No, all do not speak in tongues." Paul, however, is not talking about tongues as the initial evidence of the baptism in the Holy Spirit. The Corinthian believers all had that experience. Paul, in this context, is talking about the gifts of the Spirit and makes clear that not everyone will be used by the Spirit for every spiritual gift in the local assembly. The Greek continuous present tense could be translated, "Do all continue to speak in tongues?" "implying that not everyone will have a continuing ministry in the local assembly of speaking tongues,"[86] that is, in the exercise of that gift when prompted by the Spirit.

The Gentile Believers

For the second time Luke specifically mentions the fact that those filled with the Spirit spoke in tongues. "The circumcised believers who had come with Peter were astonished that the gift of the Holy Spirit had been poured out even on the Gentiles. For they heard them speaking in tongues and praising God" (Acts 10:45–46).

It took a vision from heaven and a command of the Spirit for Peter to be willing to go to the home of a Gentile (Acts 10:9–20). This was not ordinary prejudice. The Jews over the years had to take a stand against Gentiles (such as Antiochus Epiphanes) who tried to wipe out the worship of the one true God the Jews served. Furthermore, the Roman conquerors were considered enemies, even though some did come under the influence of Jewish teachings about God. Because Peter knew he would be called on the carpet and perhaps condemned for entering into a nonkosher home and fellowshipping, even eating with Gentiles, he brought six good Jewish believers with him as witnesses. (Note that Peter was not acting on his own authority but on the Spirit's.)

The Lord knew, too, that there would have to be a convincing evidence that God had accepted these Gentiles as true believers and as part of the church. The evidence given was that they spoke in tongues and praised God. The speaking in tongues was the primary evidence, the initial evidence. That it was the work of the Holy Spirit was further evidenced by the outflow of praise to the true God. Spirit baptism had satisfied their hearts and filled them with joy. Now they knew God and Christ in a new and personal way that no one could deny.

As Peter expected, when he went back to Jerusalem "the circumcised believers criticized him and said, 'You went into the house of uncircumcised men and ate with them'" (Acts 11:2–3). Peter then explained his vision and the Spirit's prompting him to go. He drew attention to the fact that "the Holy Spirit came on them as he had come on us at the beginning. Then I remembered what the Lord had said: 'John baptized with water, but you will be baptized with the Holy Spirit.' So if God gave them the same gift as he gave us, who believed in the Lord Jesus Christ, who was I to think that I could oppose God?"

Though at this point Peter does not specifically mention speaking in tongues, the fact that he calls this baptism in the Spirit the same (identical) gift assured them that nothing was lacking in their Pentecostal experience. They spoke in tongues just as the 120 did on the Day of Pentecost. Just as the six witnesses could not deny that God had accepted them, so the Jerusalem believers could not deny it either (Acts 11:18). The question for us is: "Do we need this convincing evidence today, or should we simply hope or suppose we have been Spirit-baptized?"

The fact, too, that the evidence of speaking in other tongues is found in Acts chapter 2 and in chapter 10, thus bracketing chapters 8 and 9, should be taken as a help to understand what happened at Samaria and at Saul's filling with the Spirit.[87]

The Ephesian Disciples

After Paul baptized the Ephesian disciples in water, he "placed his hands on them, the Holy Spirit came on them, and they spoke in tongues and prophesied" (Acts 19:6). Again, speaking in tongues was the initial outward evidence of Spirit baptism. That they not only spoke in tongues but also prophesied ("spoke for God") was further evidence that the speaking in tongues was genuine and that the Holy Spirit had enabled them to do so as Acts 2:4 tells us. That this occurred during Paul's third missionary journey at a long distance from Jerusalem shows speaking in tongues continued to be "a recurring evidence of the Spirit baptism."[88]

Pentecostals believe that these passages show that speaking in tongues is the normative evidence for being baptized in the Spirit. Though no Scripture passage says specifically that tongues is the normative evidence, yet when Acts 2:4 says "all of them" and 10:45 says, "For they heard them speaking tongues," this makes it clear. Speaking in tongues is indeed normative.[89]

The Purpose of Spirit Baptism

As Pentecostal believers we recognize that Spirit baptism is primarily "a point of entrance into a life of Spirit-empowered witness for Christ."[90] We see this on the Day of Pentecost when the 120 believers received what Jesus called "the gift my Father promised . . . in a few days you will be baptized with the Holy Spirit" (Acts 1:4–5). Jesus said further, "You will receive power when the Holy Spirit comes on you; and you will be my witnesses in Jerusalem, and in all Judea and Samaria, and to the ends of the earth" (1:8).

Then the rest of the book of Acts shows how this witness was carried out first by Peter through the gift of prophecy. Peter did not sit down and think of three points for a sermon. He stood up, "raised his voice," and "addressed the crowd" (2:14). The term *addressed* (Greek, *apephthenxato*) is literally "spoke forth" and is a form of the same verb *apophthengesthai* "to speak out" used in 2:4 of speaking in tongues. Thus, Peter, inspired by the Spirit, was speaking with the gift of prophecy. As Peter concludes, "with many other words he warned them; and he pleaded with them, 'Save yourselves from this corrupt generation'" (2:40). The phrase "he pleaded with them" (Greek, *parekalei autous*) could be translated "he exhorted them." First Corinthians 14:3 includes exhortation as part of the gift of prophecy, though Romans 12:8 lists it as a distinct gift of the Spirit. (We do not find hard-and-fast lines between the gifts of the Spirit in the Bible.) Thus, Peter became an agent of the Holy Spirit to carry out the work Jesus spoke of in John 16:8: "When he [the Counselor, the Holy Spirit] comes, he will convict the world of guilt in regard to sin and righteousness and judgment." The result was that three thousand were saved, baptized in water, and baptized in the Holy Spirit (Acts 2:38–39, 41).

Peter also assured us that "the promise [the promise of the Father, Spirit baptism] is for you and your children and for all who are far off—for all whom the Lord our God will call" (Acts 2:39). We know that God is still calling people to salvation, calling people to himself, calling people to accept Christ and live for him. Thus, the promised Spirit baptism is for us today.

The Pentecostal results continue today. When the Assemblies of God was formed, the Holy Spirit impressed two visions upon those Pentecostal pioneers. One was to send missionaries throughout the world. The other was to establish Bible schools to train national workers to continue the spread of the gospel. At that time many missionaries were establishing mission compounds and, in a paternalistic way, acting as pastor for a few nationals gathered around them. Few were giving any opportunity for the Spirit to give nationals gifts of administration or leadership. But our Pentecostal leaders saw the need for indigenous churches that would themselves become spreaders of the gospel. Within the Assemblies of God, missionary Melvin L. Hodges has been a great exponent of indigenous principles.[91]

The result has been development of great Pentecostal mission agencies as well as strong missions emphasis in our Pentecostal colleges and seminaries. Missionaries have carried the same vision overseas with Bible schools established in every field that is open to the gospel. Recent statistics of the Assemblies of God show that in Europe we have 322 missionaries and 112 missionary associates in 35 countries with 16,014 national ministers, 10,760 churches and preaching points, and 2,076,872 adherents. In Africa we have 297 missionaries and 85 missionary associates in 47 countries with 31,972 national ministers, 36,896 churches and preaching points, and 10,843,625 adherents. In Latin America and the Caribbean we have 437 missionaries and 132 associates in 35 countries with 143,925 national ministers, 159,423 churches and preaching points and 23,654,543 adherents. In Eurasia (including India) we have 291 missionaries and 87 associates in 41 countries with 22,571 national ministers, 10,449 churches and preaching points, and 1,340,211 adherents. In Asia-Pacific (including the Philippines) we have 274 missionaries and 90 associates in 32 countries, with 16,808 national ministers, 18,672 churches and preaching points, and 3,322,925 adherents.[92] All these churches are reaching out to needy people, feeding and teaching needy children, and discipling believers.

Global University in Springfield, Missouri, now distributes correspondence courses to the United States and the world. They include courses to bring people Christ, courses for new believers, courses of Bible study, college courses and seminary courses that lead to a master's degree. Spirit-filled instructors in countries where little education is available use many of these. Others are used in many Bible colleges overseas. They have been effective in spreading the gospel and bringing people to the Pentecostal experience. "An Assemblies of God national church is listed as the largest or the second largest Protestant denomination in almost a quarter of the countries of the world, making it clearly one of the most effective vehicles for extending the historical Christian faith in our time."[93]

Another example of what can be done is "Top Chrétien Francophone, a Christian Web site supported by French believers, . . . currently the most visited French Christian Web site. In 2002 . . . [it] received more than 1.5 million visits . . . and today is assisted by a 200-member team. . . . Last year, more than 2,000 people wrote . . . indicating they had made a decision to accept Jesus as Savior while visiting the Web site."[94]

The growing Pentecostal movement has also affected the renewal or Charismatic movement in major denominations. As I have written elsewhere, this

caught the attention of Evangelical leaders, including those involved in the Evangelical Theological Society. I joined that Society not long after it was formed. Many of the members were gracious and friendly. A high point for me came when Dr. Burton Goddard had charge of the program and asked me to help arrange a dialogue between Pentecostals and Evangelicals at the annual meeting which was in Grand Rapids, Michigan, December 28, 1963. Two papers were presented on glossolalia (speaking in tongues). One was by Dr. Bastian Van Elderen of Calvin Seminary, and the other by Dr. William MacDonald, then teaching at Central Bible College. A panel that included Dr. Russell Spittler, who was also teaching at Central Bible College, and myself, followed this.

Dr. Van Elderen emphasized two points. First, he said extraordinary gifts ceased at the end of the first century, and only ordinary gifts such as teaching and preaching remain. Second, he said tongues can be misused and therefore should be avoided. Before any of the Pentecostals could say anything, professors from Wheaton College and Trinity Evangelical Divinity School asked where in the Bible there was any distinction between ordinary and extraordinary gifts. All the gifts are extraordinary. They also said water can be misused, but that does not mean we should not drink water.

Then MacDonald presented his paper, which gave an excellent scriptural defense for speaking in tongues. [It was later published by the Gospel Publishing House, Springfield, Mo.] After the presentation I heard Dr. Kenneth Kantzer, then editor of the magazine *Christianity Today,* say MacDonald's paper was definitely better than Dr. Van Elderen's.

Dr. Spittler told me later that he expected to be almost crucified when the panel presented its papers and the meeting was open for question and answers. The reverse was true. Everyone was sympathetic and really wanted to know what we believed. It was after ten o'clock when they finally dismissed the meeting. Several then followed us up to our rooms and we continued to talk about the Lord and the Holy Spirit until after midnight. The next morning, at breakfast, a Baptist pastor sat beside me and said, "How do you receive the baptism in the Holy Spirit?"[95]

Even the Roman Catholics have been stirred. When I visited Belgium, Cardinal Suenens gave me a signed copy of his book, *A New Pentecost*, in which he wrote, "As we await the Parousia which will reveal to us the majesty of God, the Spirit is secretly at work. His presence can be felt on every page of the book of Acts more real and more active than the men whose names and deeds are recorded there. Even when Luke does not mention him explicitly we can discern traces of his presence, a 'water-mark' on each page of the sacred text. The Spirit guides the thread of apostolic activity, weaves its secret course."[96]

Some, especially some extreme dispensationalists, argue that "tongues . . . will be stilled . . . when perfection comes" (1 Cor. 12:8, 10), taking perfection to mean the completion of the New Testament canon. But the context in verses 9–13 indicates that the perfection is when "we shall see face to face" and know fully as we are fully known. That kind of perfection will not come until we are resurrected, "changed—in a flash, in the twinkling of an eye, at the last trumpet . . . and death is swallowed up in victory" (1 Cor. 15:51, 52, 54).[97] Until then prophecy, tongues, and other gifts of the Spirit will still function through those who, in faith and obedience, are open to the Spirit's enabling.

On the Day of Pentecost, Peter, speaking by the enabling of the Spirit, told the people to repent and be baptized. Then after receiving forgiveness of their sins, they would receive the gift of the Holy Spirit. This promise, he added, "is for you and your children and for all who are far off—for all whom the Lord our God will call" (Acts 2:38–39). Clearly Spirit baptism is available to all today, since the call to salvation is still going forth wherever the gospel is preached.[98]

"To argue that Charismatic gifts were necessary only for the first century Church and that they are not needed today in our individual and corporate worship is contrary to the teachings of the Scriptures as well as the experience of millions of Pentecostal/ Charismatic believers who are living in all continents of the world."[99] The Pentecostal revival and its Charismatic counterpart have continued to spread. In the year 2000 there were, worldwide, nearly 66 million denominational Pentecostals, 176 million Charismatics, more than 295 million independent neo-Charismatics. They are active in 80 percent of the 3,300 large metropolises in the world. About 29 percent of the members are white, 71 percent are nonwhite. They include the majority of the megachurches that have more than 50,000 members each. They show powerful dynamic in penetrating the media, publishing and distributing literature and in evangelistic campaigns. In addition, Spirit-inspired social programs have sprung up for the youth, the poor, the aged, disaster relief, and prisoners. They include Teen Challenge, Convoy of Hope, orphanages, hospitals and clinics, schools and feeding programs for children in many countries. "Over one-third of the world's full-time Christian workers (38%) are Pentecostals/ Charismatics/Neo-Charismatics."[100] Pentecostals in many countries around the world are sending out missionaries. Everywhere, they are depending on the power of the Holy Spirit to help them fulfill the Great Commission. The Spirit inspires them to obey Christ's command to witness.

Del Tarr tells of an example in Burkina Faso, West Africa, where national pastors prayed and fasted for weeks asking God for the Holy Spirit to be outpoured. Less than one-third of the 15,000 Assemblies of God believers there had been Spirit baptized. When God answered their prayers, meetings continued day and night for three months. Even Muslims were converted and were baptized in the Holy Spirit, speaking in tongues. The church soon grew to over 400,000 members.[101] This fits in with Luke's clear "assumption about tongues as the most significant sign of the bringing together of Jew and Gentile in the one mission of God."[102]

The Command to Witness

In Acts, "filled with the Holy Spirit" most often occurs "in places where inspired speaking is the dominant theme."[103] However, too often the command to witness is taken to be simply what we say. "But effectiveness in reaching the spiritually lost requires a witness beyond words."[104]

Paul gives us important guidance in our witness. In 1 Corinthians 2:1–5 Paul wrote: "When I came to you, brothers, I did not come with eloquence or superior wisdom as I proclaimed to you the testimony about God. For I resolved to know nothing while I was with you except Jesus Christ and him crucified. I came to you in weakness and fear, and with much trembling. My message and my preaching were not with wise and persuasive words, but with a demonstration of the Spirit's power, so that your faith might not rest on men's wisdom, but on God's power."

I had a public speaking professor in the University of California, Berkeley, who said, "Anyone who uses elocution ought to be electrocuted." He said also that if you can use two little words instead of one big word and reach more people, do it. Paul, by refusing to use eloquence in the style of Greek orators, would agree. He kept his message simple so ordinary people could understand it. The Holy Spirit inspires communication, not language that simply impresses people by the extent of your vocabulary. Neither did Paul attempt to display the breadth of his earthly knowledge or human wisdom. Nor was he like so-called "liberal" theologians whose wisdom is more human philosophy than Bible. He focused on "Jesus Christ and him crucified" so that people would know "the testimony about God." People must receive redemption through Christ before seeking the promise of the Father, Spirit baptism.

As Christ's witnesses we must not depend on our own strength and wisdom. "God chose the weak things of the world to shame the strong . . . so that no one may boast before him" (1 Cor. 1:27, 29). Paul includes himself among the "weak things." He shamed the wise, not by persuasive words, "but with a demonstration of the Spirit's power." The world cannot grasp the truth of the gospel, but the Holy Spirit gives power to witness, "not just with words but miracles, signs, and wonders that demonstrate the Spirit's power (Acts 2:32–33; 4:28–31; 5:12; 8:5–6; 14:3; Rom. 15:19;

1 Thess. 1:5; 2:13; Heb. 2:4). These demonstrations, including the baptism in the Holy Spirit with the initial evidence of speaking in tongues, give undeniable, visible proof of God's desire to save, heal, restore, and give new direction to our lives."[105]

Paul continues in 1 Corinthians 2:6–10:

> We do, however, speak a message of wisdom among the mature, but not the wisdom of this age or of the rulers of this age, who are coming to nothing. No, we speak of God's secret wisdom, a wisdom that has been hidden and that God destined for our glory before time began. None of the rulers of this age understood it, for if they had, they would not have crucified the Lord of glory. However, as it is written: "No eye has seen, no ear has heard, no mind has conceived what God has prepared for those who love him"—But God has revealed it to us by his Spirit.

Using the first person plural, Paul most probably indicates that what he says is inspired by the Spirit. In his witness Paul did not use words of human wisdom. He had a higher wisdom from God. Paul calls it a secret wisdom because it goes beyond any of the wisdom of Proverbs and was not revealed in any part of the Old Testament. God destined this wisdom for our glory. Before time began, God planned a salvation through Christ that would make it possible for us to share in his eternal glory. Paul brings this out in Romans, where he shows the gospel means justification by faith (chap. 4), assurance (chap. 5), victory over sin (chaps. 6–7), and our sharing in the glory of God and Christ (chap. 8). All this is included in the full, free salvation God prepared for us and made available through the cross. We have a first installment of the glory now through the gift of the Holy Spirit (2 Cor. 1:22; 5:5; Eph. 1:14; 3:8, 10). This assures us of what will be ours in the final state of the redeemed.[106]

Paul goes on to emphasize the importance and function of the Holy Spirit in 1 Corinthians 2:11–16:

> The Spirit searches all things, even the deep things of God. For who among men knows the thoughts of a man except the man's spirit within him? In the same way no one knows the thoughts of God except the Spirit of God. We have not received the spirit of the world but the Spirit who is from God, that we may understand what God has

freely given us. This is what we speak, not in words taught us by human wisdom but in words taught by the Spirit, expressing spiritual truths in spiritual words. The man without the Spirit does not accept the things that come from the Spirit of God, for they are foolishness to him, and he cannot understand them, because they are spiritually discerned. The spiritual man makes judgments about all things, but he himself is not subject to any man's judgment: "For who has known the mind of the Lord that he may instruct him?" But we have the mind of Christ.

We can trust the Holy Spirit because he is God and he knows "the deep things of God." This goes beyond anything the most brilliant minds of men can know, but the Holy Spirit reveals them as he chooses to the simplest of believers. As the Spirit of truth, he brings glory to Christ by taking what is Christ's—which is also the Father's—and making it known (John 16:12–15). This has been central in the Pentecostal movement because its "orientation is primarily Christological. Pentecostals believe the power of the Holy Spirit is given to preach Christ . . . in such a way that conviction of sin takes place, lives are changed, and the Church grows."[107]

We can also trust the Holy Spirit that we have received because he is from God and is so different from the spirit of the sinful world. (That we have received him "in a specific, definite experience" is indicated by the Greek aorist tense.) Because he is from God, we see another purpose of the gift of the Spirit. Through receiving Spirit baptism, we are further assured that the Holy Spirit is indeed the true author of all the written Word of God. ("Not in a mechanical way, of course, but by preparing the writers so that He could use their vocabulary and style to bring out the truth the way God wanted us to have it."[108])

What the NIV translates as "the man without the Spirit" is the Greek *psuchikos anthropos,* "a natural or sensual human being." Such a person cannot make proper judgment of spiritual things any more than a blind man can make judgments of a great artist's beautiful painting. (See also James 3:15–17, which adds that natural wisdom may be full of envy and selfish ambition.) "Such 'wisdom' does not come down from heaven but is earthly, unspiritual, of the devil [Gk. *daimoniodes,* 'of demonic nature or origin']. . . .

But the wisdom that comes from heaven is, first of all, pure; then peace-loving, considerate, submissive, full of mercy and good fruit, impartial and sincere." This indicates that the natural or sensual human being has no way to grasp or evaluate the truths of God's Word, for they are "spiritually discerned." A person who is Spirit filled has extra help to examine and evaluate spiritual truths "in a manner consistent with the Holy Spirit."[109] To Paul this also means having "the mind of Christ." Here we see "another reason why the unbeliever cannot understand biblical truths or Spirit-filled people. Only when minds are joined with the mind of Christ through the activity of the Holy Spirit are such knowledge and understanding possible."[110] This indicates that our manner must show the fruit of the Spirit as well.[111] The apostle Paul declared the same thing in one of his first letters: "Our gospel did not come to you in word only, but also in power and in the Holy Spirit and with full conviction, just as you know what kind of men we proved to be among you for your sake" (1 Thess. 1:5 NASB).

Randy Hurst, commissioner of evangelism for the Assemblies of God, agrees. "Paul's witness was not merely *what* he said ('*not . . . in word only*'), but also *how* he said it ('*in power and in the Holy Spirit with full conviction*') and *who* he was (you know what *kind of men we proved to be* among you for your sake'). Our witness is comprised of *what we say* (vocal), *how we say it* (vital) and *who we are* (valid)."[112] Hurst goes on to point out that what we say must focus on Jesus, "the sinless Son of God who gave His life to pay the penalty for our sins." How we say it must always be with grace, gentleness, and respect (Col. 4:5–6; 1 Pet. 3:15–16). Who we are means our manner; our actions must be consistent with and affirm our message.[113] In all of this the Holy Spirit, who reveals Jesus to us through his Word, makes Jesus the pattern for us to follow (John 15:26). The Holy Spirit is our counselor (Greek, *parakletos,* basically meaning one who comes alongside to help). He is the Spirit of truth who guides us into all truth and brings glory to Jesus (John 16:13–14).

Other Benefits of Spirit Baptism

Pentecostals recognize a distinction between the "gift" of the Spirit which Jesus gives us and the "gifts" of the Spirit that the Spirit gives "as he determines" (1 Cor. 12:11). In addition to power for witnessing, the Holy Spirit often uses Spirit-filled people for spiritual gifts and for signs and wonders as means for service and for spreading the gospel, just as he did in the book of Acts. The Spirit also gives "encouragement, wisdom, and direction to the church (6:3, 4; 9:31; 11:24, 28; 13:52; 15:28; 20:28)" as well as "personal guidance (20:23; 21:4, 11)."[114] Sometimes the Spirit's message to the local assembly is through interpreted tongues:

> Lest the Corinthians jump to the conclusion that there was no place for speaking in tongues in the public worship, Paul quickly draws their attention to Isaiah 28:11–12. In the context of Isaiah's prophecy, proud Israelites were saying that Isaiah was treating them like spiritual babies and they resented it. Isaiah then made it clear that because of their unbelief, the message meant for blessing [and refreshing] would bring judgment. God would send foreign conquerors whose language they would not understand, but whose actions would make it clear that these Israelites were separated from God, cut off from His blessing and under His judgment. Paul applies this to speaking in tongues (languages) they did not understand. So speaking tongues is necessary as a judgment sign to unbelievers, making them realize that they are separated from God and cannot understand His message.[115]

On the Day of Pentecost tongues first of all drew the crowd together. When they heard them declare the wonders of God, it got their attention, amazed them, and brought questions to their minds—questions Peter answered through the enabling of the Spirit.

Palma lists three reasons God ordained glossolalia for the Day of Pentecost. First, it was a new thing signaling a new era. Second, it drew attention to the Great Commission to spread the gospel to all nations. Third, "He who speaks in a tongue edifies himself" (1 Cor. 14:4).[116]

To desire to edify yourself, that is, to build yourself up spiritually, is not wrong. Paul goes on to say that he "would like everyone of you to speak [keep on speaking] in tongues" (1 Cor. 14:5). He also said, "I thank God that I speak in tongues more than all of you" (1 Cor. 14:18).[117] Since he called for limits on speaking in tongues in the public worship (1 Cor. 14:27), he must have meant that he spoke in tongues in his private devotions, receiving that edification. In fact, he makes clear that he both prayed and sang in tongues: "For if I pray in a tongue, my spirit prays, but my mind is unfruitful. So what shall I do? I will pray with my spirit, but I will also pray with my mind; I will sing with my spirit, but I will also sing with my mind" (1 Cor. 14:14–15). He goes on to imply that the Corinthians were "praising God with their spirit" and "giving thanks" (14:1, 17).

His concern in mentioning these things was to show that since this praying, singing, praising, and giving thanks were not understood by the people in the local congregation, they were not edified. Personal edification was not enough in the public meeting. The believers needed to be concerned with one another. But Paul is careful to be sure they were not to think that he was against speaking in tongues. He says, "Do not forbid speaking in tongues" (1 Cor. 14:39). With this command we should keep in mind verse 20: "Brothers, stop thinking like children. In regard to evil be infants, but in your thinking be adults." We should use our intelligence with regard to speaking in tongues. "The baptism in the Spirit should make us better thinkers. It should help us conform in our thinking to the will of God."[118] Paul definitely shows that speaking in tongues in private devotions is not only edifying but also "desirable and universally available. In short, all should speak in tongues."[119]

The edification that speaking in tongues brings can help in any situation. For example, when I was working on my dissertation for the doctor of theology degree, I had gathered a great deal of material that showed the Babylon passages in Isaiah fitted Isaiah's own day, not the later time of Cyrus.[120] I had even spent two weeks going through German journals in the basement of the Harvard Divinity School library, for Germans had been prominent in the excavation of Babylon's ruins. But when I came to the task of putting it all together in a logical fashion, I was having great difficulty. Finally, I knelt down alone in my study and began to pray, then to pray in tongues. Soon I felt the Spirit's edification in an unusual way. I went back to my desk, and everything fell right into place.[121] On many other occasions, when I didn't know what to pray or was too weary even to think, as I prayed in tongues, I was refreshed and encouraged in a marvelous way—and soon I would be interceding in English, still prompted by the Holy Spirit.

As the apostle Paul said, "I will pray with my spirit, but I will also pray with my mind" (1 Cor. 14:15). Jude 20 says, "But you, dear friends, build yourselves up in your most holy faith and pray in the Holy Spirit." Many take this to confirm that speaking in tongues is often "a prayer language."[122] It is a way of praising God. Harold Horton of England put it this way: "There is a deep in the spirit of the redeemed that is never plumbed by the mind or thought. That deep finds expression at last in the Baptism of the Spirit, as unaccustomed words of heavenly coherence sweep up to the Beloved from the newly opened well of the human spirit—flooded as it is with the torrential stream of the divine Spirit."[123]

When we understand the nature of spiritual gifts and exercise them, moved by the love God pours out in our hearts by the Spirit (Rom. 5:5), we will not degrade any gift as inferior.[124] They, including tongues, are wonderful, supernatural gifts that we can exercise as the Spirit determines. As Jack Hayford points out, "Today's interest in spiritual language isn't prompted by a shallow search for novelty. You'll find it borne of a desire for God's fullest resources, borne of a passion for anything biblical that will draw me nearer His heart in prayer, which will assist my exalting Him more grandly in private praise."[125]

Edification or building up spiritually must also mean the encouragement of righteous living and the fruit of the Spirit. Paul wrote, "Therefore, I urge you, brothers, in view of God's mercy, to offer your bodies as living sacrifices, holy and pleasing to God—this is your spiritual act of worship. Do not conform any longer to the pattern of this world, but be transformed by the renewing of your mind. Then you will be able to test and approve what God's will is—his good, pleasing and perfect will" (Rom. 12:1–2).

Receiving Spirit Baptism

Pentecostals encourage believers to look to Jesus to receive the baptism in the Holy Spirit. Sometimes the Lord surprises them without their seeking the experience—as in the case of the Romans in the house of Cornelius and in the case of my grandmother (related earlier in this chapter)—and I have seen new converts come up out of the waters of baptism speaking in tongues. But we recognize that all the gifts of God are by grace through faith, and that faith includes obedience, must be based on God's written Word, and must be faith in God. As the apostle Paul said to the Galatians, "Did you receive the Spirit by observing the law or by believing what you heard?" (Gal. 3:2). The believing would be shown by obedience to the gospel they heard—which Paul said he received "by revelation from Jesus Christ" (Gal. 1:12). So what did Jesus say?

Jesus encouraged us first of all to ask: "So I say to you, Ask and it will be given to you; seek and you will find; knock and the door will be opened to you. For everyone who asks receives, he who seeks finds, and to him who knocks, the door will be opened. Which of you fathers, if your son asks for a fish will give him a snake instead? Or if he asks for an egg, will give him a scorpion? If you then, though you are evil, know how to give good gifts to your children, how much more will your Father in heaven give the Holy Spirit to those who ask him" (Luke 11:9–13). Since all believers have the Spirit at the new birth without asking for it, since the Spirit accomplishes the new birth, Jesus must be talking about Spirit baptism here. Thus Jesus promises that you will not be turned away when you ask, nor will you receive something hurtful, such as being deceived by a demon.

"Jesus is saying that Father God is going to see that you receive all that is holy and glorifying to Him."[126] Before he went to the cross, he told his disciples "If you love me, you will obey what I command. And I will ask the Father, and he will give you another Counselor to be with you forever" (John 14:15–16). Before he ascended to heaven, Jesus promised, "I am going to send you what my Father has promised; but stay in the city until you have been clothed with power from on high" (Luke 24:49). After Jesus ascended, they had returned to Jerusalem with great joy and were "continually in the temple praising God" (Luke 24:53). On the Day of Pentecost, all the 120 were together in one place (Acts 2:1). Jesus had reaffirmed his promise, commanding them, "Do not leave Jerusalem, but wait for the gift my Father promised which you have heard me speak about. For John baptized with [in] water, but in a few days you will be baptized with [in] the Holy Spirit" (Acts 1:4–5). Therefore, they were waiting and asking with expectation and faith.

From this, Pentecostals encourage believers who desire Spirit baptism to come together with other believers and, in an atmosphere of believing prayer and real praise, expecting Jesus to fulfill the same promise of the Father to them. Because Jesus is the baptizer, we encourage them to seek Jesus, not tongues—though we show them from Scripture that tongues will be "part of the package."[127] We encourage them to continue seeking. "They all joined together constantly in prayer" (Acts 1:14). "Ideally, one should receive the enduement of power immediately after conversion, but actually there may be circumstances of one kind or another" that make it necessary to continue seeking in faith. "Faith is the most essential element."[128] But an extended time of prayer, focused on Jesus the mighty baptizer, "creates a hunger for the presence of God, generates a right attitude, and subdues the stubborn human spirit,"[129] thus making us more receptive to receiving the promise of the Father, the gift of the Spirit.[130]

This was my own personal experience. I was nineteen years old, a student at the University of California, Berkeley. In my science courses I heard and read statements that were contrary to what I had been taught about the Bible. I remember kneeling by my bed in the attic room where I lived and crying out to the Lord, "I know I'm saved, but I don't know how to answer the questions that are being raised." Then the Lord reminded me of how my grandfather was operated on for prostate cancer.

Somehow the surgeons cut something that caused poison to come out through the wound. They sent him home to die. I remember the black ambulance coming and how they carried him upstairs on a stretcher. Our relatives all came, some to see him die. But my uncle, Joseph Clark from England, was then pastor of the Assembly of God in North Hollywood. I don't remember the words of his prayer, but I'll never forget the way the power of God came on him. The next morning my aunt went up to change the bandages that were collecting the poison. The wound had healed up except for half an inch and that was perfectly clean. Grandpa Horton was seventy-five then and lived to be eighty-seven. I don't believe he would have died then except that my grandmother died, and all he wanted to do was to go to be with Jesus and her.

Then the Lord reminded me of my cousin Charles Fisher, who at seven years of age came down with polio. The doctors didn't recognize it at first and thought he had stomach trouble. When the paralysis set in, they said, "Sorry, we can't help you." His parents took him to Angelus Temple where Aimee Semple MacPherson prayed for him. He walked out of there, played football in high school, and never had any further signs of polio.

Next, the Lord reminded me of what he had done for my younger brother, Donald. While Don was in high school, he became bitter against his father and against God. He still went to church because that is what our family did. When the teacher of his high school Sunday school called the roll, each student was asked to respond with a Scripture verse personally selected and learned during the week. Don would respond with something from one of the imprecatory psalms, not to be funny but because he was bitter. The previous Christmas when I was home, he was a changed person. He was born again and filled with the Holy Spirit and now had a wonderful, intimate relationship with Christ.

These memories did not answer the questions I had at the time, though later studies did. But they created a hunger in my heart to be baptized in the Spirit. In an all-night prayer meeting, I felt that Jesus was so near I could touch him. Without any effort I spoke in tongues briefly. The next night at another prayer meeting I prayed, "Lord, if there is a freedom in this experience, I want it." Immediately, it was like a dam broke. Tongues poured out of my mouth. For weeks after that I could hardly pray in English— though I did. The mother of one of our missionaries said to me, "Stanley, don't let a day go by without letting the Spirit recreate this in you and guide your life." Though God had often blessed me as I prayed, there is an intimacy with the Savior in my experience since then that I had not known before. He has guided me in many situations, usually in a different way each time. He has been with me in forty-six years of teaching in Assemblies of God colleges and seminaries and has made possible for me to do archaeological digging in the Holy Land and to teach and minister in twenty-five countries—especially since I have retired. God is so good! Over the years I have proved in my own experience that the baptism in the Holy Spirit is not "an end within itself, but only an opening to a life in the Spirit."[131]

Each person who receives Spirit baptism will have his own personal experience, of course. Two books that many have found helpful are: *How to Pray for the Release of the Holy Spirit: What the Baptism or Release of the Holy Spirit Is and How to Pray for It,* by Dennis Bennett[132] and *A Handbook on Holy Spirit Baptism,* by Don Basham.[133] As Dennis Bennett states, "To lead a person to Christ and not see to it that he is baptized in the Holy Spirit is like giving someone a car, filling it with gasoline, but not showing him how to start it or drive it."[134]

Responses to Stanley M. Horton's Pentecostal Perspective

Response by Larry Hart

Dr. Horton exemplifies the primary contribution that the worldwide Pentecostal movement has made to the church of the twentieth and twenty-first centuries: that the work of the Holy Spirit is more than merely a doctrinal tenet; it is the primal *experience* of the Christian faith. Before the Pentecostals arrived as a global mission force, the Holy Spirit was all but ignored in many quarters of the church. He was too often spoken of in tones of embarrassment. Especially where Enlightenment rationalism reigned supreme, the Pentecostal experience was most often met with disdain. Undaunted, the Pentecostals proceeded to bring a spiritual sea change to the church. Theirs was truly a revival movement which spread the gospel across the earth.

At first, unsurprisingly, their theological rationale was rather unsophisticated. Today, as Dr. Horton's presentation exemplifies, they are making a substantial theological contribution. Almost inadvertently, the Pentecostals of the last century forced Evangelicals to look afresh at their New Testament hermeneutic, allowing Luke, for example, a theological voice alongside Paul's. Further, even theological critics, such as James D. G. Dunn, evinced an unexpected warmth toward "the Pentecostal contribution" in terms of "the place they give to the Holy Spirit in doctrine and experience and in their various theologies of conversion, initiation and baptism."[135]

Dr. Horton's case rests squarely on the book of Acts. He asks the reader to look honestly at the five key narratives (Acts 2, 8, 9, 10, 19) related to Spirit baptism along with other relevant New Testament texts, noting the salient characteristics of these pneumatic events as well as the powerful and successful mission they generated. Then, when one reflects on the contemporary Pentecostal mission thrust and connects it with the Acts narratives, a powerful rationale for the Pentecostal experience emerges! As an apologetic, this approach is virtually unassailable. As a theological argument, however, it may be found lacking by other ecclesial traditions.

For example, though they are not alone, the Pentecostals have never seemingly worked out a theology of the Christian life that would provide interpretation for the wide diversity of Christian experience. Are we simply to conclude that those saints never having experienced a distinctive second blessing empowerment are spiritually defective in some sense? Does the Holy Spirit always work in such a punctiliar fashion? This is certainly not true when it comes to conversion. Contrast, for example, the testimonies of Ruth and Billy Graham. Ruth Graham is unable to pinpoint a precise moment of conversion, whereas Billy's sawdust trail testimony is well-known. Both are obviously exemplary Christians. Might not the same be true in terms of experiences of spiritual empowerment?

The sign of speaking in tongues must also come up for reexamination. Does the New Testament warrant making a "law" of tongues, as it were, as *the* sign of spiritual empowerment. If so, then how does one explain the seemingly powerless and unfruitful tongues-speaking saints, which almost any Pentecostal pastor would have to acknowledge exist? One response on the part of the Pentecostal theologian would be to hold forth the differentiation between spiritual empowerment for service and spiritual progress in sanctification. But I am referring specifically to spiritual empowerment here and want to hold the Pentecostals' feet to the fire. Another possible response would be in relation to the "many fillings" subsequent to Spirit baptism. But would this not lend itself just as readily to a more nuanced approach which allows for more diversity of experience?

Having said all this, however, I would be eager to affirm the bulk of the Pentecostal argument. The book of Acts does portray a "high voltage" Christianity, a vital faith that is definitely needed in our day. Worldwide Pentecostalism is a revival movement. At the same time it has generated in the latter part of the twentieth century a significant body of scholarship, much of which is skillfully displayed by Dr. Horton. No other tradition has explored the Pentecostal reality with greater depth and understanding. Further, Pentecostals have consistently kept the *purpose* of Pentecost—world evangelism—before their people. And no other body of believers has lived out that Great Commission vision with greater effectiveness than the Pentecostals. Dr. Horton stands at the forefront theologically of a now firmly established ecclesial tradition—a tradition whose voice needs to be heard. And Dr. Horton is one of its most esteemed spokespersons.

Response by Walter C. Kaiser Jr.

It is difficult to respond to such a good friend as Dr. Stanley Horton, indeed, even one who is a graduate of the seminary of which I am its president. We both have too much respect and good will for each other as fellow servants in the body of Christ to respond too quickly or harshly to each other. Nevertheless, I will attempt to point out just a few matters that struck me as being major differences between us as I read his essay on the Pentecostal perspective of baptism in the Holy Spirit.

The experiences Dr. Horton relates are most interesting and supportive, in a way, of his thesis. One cannot gainsay the fact that God has used his Holy Spirit in a wonderful way in the lives of those believers to whom he has pointed. That is not an issue in this discussion.

But what is an issue is this: should we give such experiential evidence the pride of place over the Scriptures in places where Scripture does not give us a direct statement? Dr. Horton quoted approvingly Roger Stronstad, who affirmed that "spiritual experience . . . gives the interpreter of relevant Biblical texts an experiential presupposition *which transcends* the rational or cognitive presuppositions of scientific exegesis, and, furthermore, results in an understanding, empathy, and sensitivity to the text."[136] Even more unsettling in this same direction is Robert Menzies' claim that "a passage must be understood in terms of its original setting and intention, but the theological freight it carries *may transcend* its primary intent. . . . An exclusive focus on an author's 'primary intent' or 'intention to teach' too often leads to a form of tunnel vision which ignores the implications of an individual text for the theological perspective of the author."[137]

It must be conceded, as we really do, that the Holy Spirit is a person. But can we argue from that given to a position that an experience and a relationship can, on occasion, take front and center over Scripture? The experience still may be very real, but can its grounds rest on itself and be its own authority in the absence of specific scriptural teaching? Rather, must we not as Evangelicals declare that experience cannot be its own authority but must rest on the clear teaching of the Word of God if we are to build a doctrinal case for a particular teaching?

However, that is precisely the point at which the case for baptism in the Holy Spirit with the speaking in tongues as its primary physical evidence breaks down. As Dr. Horton concedes, "No Scripture passage says specifically that tongues is the *normative evidence* [of being baptized in the Holy Spirit]" (emphasis mine). That concession is one of the most important statements in Dr. Horton's whole essay. But that is precisely the sort of authority we need to ground our case.

If Scripture is not available to determine what is normative for us as the initial physical evidence for being baptized in the Holy Spirit, what then makes tongues in this situation normative? Dr. Horton replies, it is the simple notation in Scripture that "all of them" (Acts 2:4; cf. 10:45) experienced the gift of speaking in tongues. But are these secure enough grounds for such an important distinctive, especially since no single Scripture can be cited as teaching that tongues are the normative evidence for a genuine baptism in the Holy Spirit? This is an important issue, for it does not simply pit Luke-Acts versus the apostle Paul, but it raises the stakes for all of Scripture now.

Even so, despite the importance of the question we have just raised, the debate as to whether speaking in tongues is the initial physical evidence of being baptized in the Holy Spirit *must take a backseat* and a *secondary position* to the question of whether the baptism in the Holy Spirit is what happens at conversion or subsequent to conversion. Dr. Horton would teach that there are at least two distinct baptisms here: one that is essential for our salvation and the other that is essential for power in witnessing. Can this distinction, made popular by Pentecostalism, be sustained?

This separation is key to the whole debate. Surely there are a continual number of fresh *infillings* of the Holy Spirit for the believer, just as Ephesians 5:15–21 teaches us. We are continually to keep on being filled with the Holy Spirit, as I argue in my chapter. And there is just as strong a teaching that we all have been incorporated into one body and made to drink one drink by the baptizing work of the Holy Spirit (1 Cor. 12:12–13). I have argued in my chapter that this later baptism is the same one John the Baptist promised and the one Jesus warned was not many days in coming, prior to the Day of Pentecost.

I enjoyed the tone and the frequent use of illustration that Dr. Horton used in his chapter. Moreover, his constant appeal to Scripture, despite his emphasis on experience, made our conversation all the more profitable, since that is our common base of authority which neither one of us can surrender. But our differences lay in the handling of the disputed passages in the book of Acts, as I have already argued in my essay. To be sure, we are not in dispute about the centrality or the importance of the person, presence, or the necessity of the power of the Holy Spirit. What we are in gentle disagreement over is the separation of the Spirit's work at the time of our conversion into a subsequent coming of the Holy Spirit for power in the work of the gospel. We have tried to argue that the subsequent "infillings" flow from the earlier baptism in the Holy Spirit when we allowed that the grace of God that brought salvation to be the same grace of God that we responded to in faith and obedience for the mighty working of God's Holy Spirit in our lives.

May our Lord grant to us his good wisdom and grace as we continue to speak in love to one another because we care deeply about what our Lord wishes for each of us and we desire to see the fullness of that grace worked out in each of our lives. May the discussion continue to the blessing of all God's men and women for his honor and glory.

Response by H. Ray Dunning

Two statements in the early pages of Dr. Horton's essay are interesting. The first I mention is found on page 10 as a concluding statement of an argument for the validity of a "spiritual hermeneutic," which, in the words of Peter Wagner, "gives the interpreter of relevant biblical texts an experiential presupposition which transcends the rational or cognitive presuppositions of scientific exegesis, and, furthermore, results in an understanding, empathy, and sensitivity to the text." Horton's conclusion from this is that "we need both traditional Protestant hermeneutics and Pentecostal presuppositions." This approach to biblical interpretation is significantly different from the Wesleyan approach where the *ideal* is a presuppositionless approach to the text. In full awareness of the impossibility of reading any text free of presuppositions, the *ideal* still remains to use every possible safeguard to seek to determine what the original writer intended to communicate and not read one's own assumptions into the text. Furthermore, this is, in fact, the ideal of "traditional Protestant hermeneutics." Experience functions in the Wesleyan methodology as a confirming source of exegetical conclusions. The interpretation of Scripture that impinges on Christian experience is tested by experience either to confirm or to deny the validity of the interpretation. In his *Plain Account of Christian Perfection,* John Wesley reflects this method in relation to his teaching about Christian Perfection: "If I were convinced that none in England had attained what has been so clearly and strongly preached by such a number of preachers, in so many places, and for so long a time, I should be clearly convinced that we had all mistaken the meaning of those Scriptures; and therefore for the time to come, I too must teach that 'sin will remain till death.'"[138]

The other statement found in the first sentence of the essay states that Pentecostals have always understood Spirit baptism "as the coming of God's Spirit into the believer's life in a very focused way." I seriously doubt that any Christian in any theological tradition would say otherwise. The question is the shape and character of this experience.

Dr. Horton affirms the Pentecostal view to be twofold: (1) Spirit baptism "is an experience that follows conversion, and (2) is evidenced by speaking in tongues."

His arguments from Scripture pertinent to the first point resulted in a *deja vu* experience for me since all the popular literature of the Holiness movement used the same arguments to "prove" the "secondness" of entire sanctification. Horton affirms what others have discovered, that this was at least one reason for the emergence of Pentecostalism out of this movement. My own chapter suggests an alternate exegesis of the same passages.

Furthermore, "scientific exegesis" must allow that the presence of tongues speaking was an aspect of the early experiences in Acts in some cases. Since Luke is recording a transitional period in *Heilsgeschichte*, it was important, if not necessary, for there to be a special type of evidence that the new age of the Spirit was dawning. And since his narrative records an ever-widening circle of inclusion into the benefits of this new age, this evidence appeared at the point where the new age moved to a more inclusive level. In a word, the Age of the Spirit dawned in stages. Wesleyan interpreters have always, in this light, referred to these physical phenomena as "inaugural manifestations."[139] But even with this qualification, biblical scholar F. F. Bruce is doubtless on the mark in his comments regarding the physical phenomena that accompanied the first Pentecost: "the mere fact of *glossolalia* (gift of languages) or any other ecstatic utterance is no evidence of the presence of the Holy Spirit. In apostolic times it was necessary to provide criteria for deciding whether such utterances were of God or not, just as it had been necessary in Old Testament times."[140]

Because of this qualification, Wesleyans have always, like St. Paul, focused more on the fruit of the Spirit than the gifts of the Spirit. The gifts may be counterfeited and used for carnal purposes, as was the case in Corinth. Consistent with the total thrust of the New Testament concerning the experience of the Holy Spirit, Wesleyans fully concur with the classic words of Friederich Schleiermacher that "the fruits of the Spirit are . . . nothing but the virtues of Christ."[141] The necessary moral qualifications at least bring the position that the essential mark of Spirit baptism is speaking in tongues into question.

I was tremendously startled to note that Horton insists that the gift of tongues is always an intelligible language understandable by some language group. While I have had almost no direct exposure to the practice, I cannot make any informed judgment, but everything to which I have been exposed suggests differently. If his claim is valid, it invalidates all so-called glossolalia I have heard about, including what may have been practiced at Corinth.

When I returned to graduate school after several years in the pastorate, I was assigned to a rural church composed of a wonderful congregation of people who were happy for me to spend the week-days at the university. One regular attendant was a delightful gen-tleman who could neither speak nor hear. We soon developed the ability to communicate, even though neither one of us knew sign language. One Sunday evening during my tenure there, Orville came to the altar along with several other people when the invita-tion was given. I was at a loss, at first, to know how to help him, but it occurred to me that he could read. So I took my Bible, and moving from verse to verse, we worked our way through his seek-ing. I shall never forget the broad smile, radiance of countenance, and beautiful expression that came to his face as we reached the cli-max of this pilgrimage to his experience of faith unto salvation. From that time on, he maintained the spiritual glow. But never did he hear a word of the sermons I preached, although he seldom missed a service. Never did he speak a word, intelligible or other-wise, because by an accident of birth, he did not have the physical capability. How would Orville know he had been filled with the Spirit?

Response by Ralph Del Colle

One truth must be acknowledged in this volume. There would be no discussion (or debate!) on Spirit baptism except for the clas-sical Pentecostal witness to it. Granted, the term was employed prior to Charles Parham's initial-evidence teaching in 1900–1901 and its spread by William Seymour in the Azusa Street Revival of 1906–1909. Stanley Horton is quick to note proto-Pentecostal usages of the term in Wesleyan Holiness, Keswick, and revivalist circles. However, even considering the doctrinal status of Spirit baptism as a subsequent work of entire sanctification in the Wesleyan and Nazarene churches, it was the Pentecostal move-ment that elevated its usage with its consequent controversy in the recent history of Christianity.

Two aspects of the classical Pentecostal doctrine have provoked the most controversy: subsequence and tongues (*glossolalia*) as initial evidence. Horton is not shy in his articulation and defense of each of these doctrines. His approach is to combine various and complementary approaches in Pentecostal witness and teaching. He combines testimony—including personal testimony and auto-biography—an emphasis on experience, and the integrity of the

Word. At the same time he dispels any illusions that Pentecostals are not thoroughly Christological—even Christocentric—in their strong pneumatological emphases.

Horton's use of Scripture in the pursuit of Bible evidence for the Spirit baptism typically employs the narrative portions of the Acts of the Apostles to make his case. This continues to be an old and continuing debate, especially between Pentecostals and Evangelicals, and needs no further comment on my part except to note my explanation of the Catholic approach to Scripture, tradition, and dogma in my response to Walter Kaiser's essay. One should note, however, that biblical exegesis is not the only tool in Horton's arsenal. I have mentioned his use of testimony. This extends not only to personal testimony but also to the overwhelming corporate testimony of the Pentecostal and Charismatic movements. At the very least their evangelistic and missionary zeal is certainly evidence of the power of the Spirit attending Pentecostal witness and preaching. Without the biblical evidence the Pentecostal witness would not be convincing for Horton, but without the experiential testimony there would be something missing from that witness that he and every full-blooded Pentecostal expects. The reason is clear. Through one's experience the Pentecostal is aware that the Spirit has descended with power and that its most distinctive feature, *glossolalia,* is a source of personal edification and an ecclesial sign.

Stating all this in the positive vein that I intend it, one is still obliged to respond to the distinctly Pentecostal doctrine of Spirit baptism including initial evidence. In my essay I demonstrate that it was the classical Pentecostal doctrine of Spirit baptism that was received and revised in the Catholic Charismatic renewal. The issue was not so much subsequence itself, as contested by many Evangelicals, but how subsequence as a new experience of the Spirit could be integrated into the church's sacramental economy. In other words, because Catholics already distinguish the work of the Spirit in the sacraments of baptism and confirmation, it is not too problematic to conceive of a new, even gateway, experience of the Spirit subsequent to Christian initiation/conversion. The debate among Catholic Charismatics, as we have seen, has been whether Spirit baptism is a release of sacramental grace or a new experience apart from the sacraments.

Even if one were was to respond from a strictly sacramentalist position—held at the very least by all Catholics in the sense that all Catholics acknowledge the work of the Spirit in the sacraments—a distinction should be made between the washing of water in baptism and the laying on of hands and anointing in confirmation. In a normative sense the latter is still a sacrament of initiation and thus will be administered to adults at conversion, but the work is still distinct from, even if related to, baptism. The disagreement with Horton is that classical Pentecostals do not associate Spirit baptism with initiation, although it may take place then, and that it lacks an ecclesial interpretation. (Note Horton's statement that Pentecost is not the birthday of the church but simply the promised enduement with power.)

Perhaps the best way to compare the Catholic doctrine with the Pentecostal one is to follow the New Testament lead that baptism and the laying of hands are distinct but inseparable dimensions of Christian initiation (Heb. 6:1–5; Titus 3:5–7). Both entail the work of the Holy Spirit; indeed, each imparts an indelible sacramental character to the recipient (meaning the sacrament cannot be repeated). The relationship between the two can be summed up in the phrase that confirmation imparts "to the newly baptized by the laying of hands the gift of the Spirit that completes the grace of Baptism."[142] The term "Spirit baptism" is not used; nevertheless, the "gift of the Spirit" is, and it connotes something distinct from what is received in baptism. Hence, the formula used in confirmation: "Be sealed with the gift of the Holy Spirit."

The analogy between the two traditions seems to hold. Horton distinguishes between new birth and Spirit baptism as an enduement with power. Catholics also distinguish between the effects of each of these sacraments. "Thus, the two principal effects [of baptism] are purification from sins and new birth in the Holy Spirit."[143] The "effect of the sacrament of Confirmation is the special outpouring of the Holy Spirit as once granted to the apostles on the Day of Pentecost."[144] Of course, the difference between sacramental and nonsacramental communication of grace is significant. Nevertheless, an initiatory outpouring of the Holy Spirit in the life of the believer holds true and is to be distinguished from both baptism/conversion and subsequent infillings and anointings with the Spirit. In this regard perhaps the conciliatory approach to

Evangelicals is that the initial filling of the Holy Spirit, either at conversion or more likely subsequent to it, is foundational for all subsequent fillings, whether the original one be termed Spirit baptism or not. It will also be the basis for operation of the gifts of the Holy Spirit (for the Catholic already present in baptism[145]) and the *charismata* as acknowledged by Horton.

Finally, I cannot affirm the classical Pentecostal doctrine of initial evidence, although *glossolalia* is considered normative by many Catholic Charismatics. My own view is that *glossolalia* has been a signifier in Pentecostalism, one that has pointed to the outpouring of the Holy Spirit and, therefore, has enabled that movement to be at the service of the church catholic. While this is not a hard and fast doctrine that *glossolalia* is the initial evidence or normal sign of Spirit baptism, it does hark back to its recognizable function in the Acts of the Apostles where the various outpourings of the Holy Spirit are clearly seen and heard (Acts 2:33; 8:18; 10:44–46). In this respect we all owe a depth of gratitude to the Pentecostal movement.

CHAPTER 3

Spirit Baptism: A Dimensional Charismatic Perspective

LARRY HART

What Does It Mean to Be "Baptized in the Holy Spirit"?

A half century ago the news first hit the national media that a "Charismatic movement" was underway within the mainline churches of America. Virtually every segment of American Christianity has been affected by the renewal, and many individual lives have been forever changed—including my own. In terms of statistics alone, with some half billion self-professed Pentecostal and Charismatic Christians in the world, this widely variegated spiritual phenomenon can be seen as perhaps the greatest revival movement in the history of the church.

At the core of the movement's ideology is an experience and teaching most often referred to as "the baptism in the Holy Spirit." Most Pentecostals and Charismatics view Spirit baptism as the crux of their movement. Further, speaking in tongues has been both the sign and the scandal of the movement—especially in relation to other Evangelical and mainline churches. How does one evaluate this doctrine and, more importantly, this experience? The phenomenon of Pentecostal religion may be relatively new on the scene in terms of the totality of the church's history, but its salient characteristics can be found at key junctures throughout that history. Certainly Puritanism, Pietism, Wesleyanism, and revivalism all played formative roles in the emergence of twentieth-century Pentecostalism.[1] And as one shifts the focus to specifically American religious history, clear preparations, both experiential and doctrinal, can be found.

Nineteenth-century Holiness preaching increasingly reverberated Pentecostal themes as the focus began to shift from purity to power.[2] In addition, many of the key leaders of the nineteenth- and twentieth-century Evangelical revival claimed some sort of empowering experience subsequent to their conversion that transformed their ministries. And many called this anointing "the baptism in the Holy Spirit." Unfortunately, modern Evangelicals have forgotten—or worse, suppressed—this fact.

Some of the finest existing Evangelical institutions were founded by stalwart preachers who claimed such a Spirit baptism. Dwight L. Moody insisted until the day he died that the two greatest blessings of his life were his conversion and his infilling with the Holy Spirit. He loved for his colleague, R. A. Torrey, to preach on the baptism in the Holy Spirit. Torrey's writings themselves were crystal-clear on the subject. In fact, they served as textbooks for the first Pentecostals in America. Torrey stated simply that he studied the subject, determined that he lacked this empowerment, and set about to receive it. Subsequently, he averred, his ministry was never the same. The fact that he later turned against the Pentecostals does not lessen the significance of his testimony. Charles Finney, of an earlier generation—and a man who left an indelible mark on American revivalism—also claimed this same experience.

A. J. Gordon, likewise, clearly differentiated between the work of the Holy Spirit in conversion and the empowering dimension which he termed variously as "baptized," "filled," or "anointed." John Pollock relates the story of one of the many turning points in Billy Graham's ministry when the fledgling evangelist met, studied, and prayed with Stephen Olford concerning the fullness of the Holy Spirit. Graham said, "This is a turning point in my life, this will revolutionize my ministry."[3] The list could go on.

David Yonggi Cho, pastor of the world's largest church, in Seoul, Korea, once said: "Write that we are the largest in the world because of the Baptism of the Holy Ghost that empowers our people to win the lost." In fact, it is true that the majority of the largest churches worldwide are Pentecostal or Charismatic in nature. These folk have also led the way in the use of television to spread their "full gospel" message. Many Christians echo the perplexity of the Jewish leaders before whom Peter and John stood: "What shall we do with these men? For that a notable sign has been performed through them is evident to all the inhabitants of Jerusalem, and we cannot deny it" (Acts 4:16 ESV). Is the baptism in the Holy Spirit precisely what the Pentecostals and Charismatics say it is? Should we conclude instead that they are deluded and their doctrine false in this respect? Or do they simply have a "right experience by a wrong name"? A handful of characteristic responses to these questions has emerged in our day, rendering emblematic positions on the nature of Spirit baptism.

Billy Graham and the Evangelicals remain faithful to the view that Spirit baptism belongs to the reality of becoming a Christian; that is, it refers to the indwelling of the Holy Spirit at the new birth. Scholars such as James D. G. Dunn and John R. W. Stott ably defend this position. A modified form of this understanding can even be found among Charismatics who either term themselves "Third Wave" (Evangelical in theology, Charismatic in experience) or who develop an "organic/sacramental" view which guards the unity of Christian initiation.

Pentecostals generally defend the insights of their forebears that the baptism in the Holy Spirit is an experience distinct from and subsequent to conversion for the purpose of power for ministry and with the "initial physical evidence" of speaking in tongues. They would build this doctrinal understanding primarily on the book of Acts, chapters 2, 8, 9, 10, and 19, whereas Evangelicals would shy away from using such narrative portions of Scripture as a basis for formulating doctrine (preferring "didactic" passages, generally Pauline).

Is another tack possible in these chaotic doctrinal waters? I believe so. I perceive a developing consensus among some Charismatic scholars which combines the best of the above characterized traditions and builds bridges among them. My own version of this newer approach I term "dimensional."

In simplest terms I am suggesting that we broaden the metaphor, Spirit baptism, to its proper biblical parameters and recover a renewed appreciation for the various *dimensions* of this profound biblical teaching. It is this dimensional view which I will attempt to develop and defend, with the help of a number of other Evangelical and Charismatic scholars, in the paragraphs that follow.

Scientists are now telling us that there must have been at least seventeen dimensions present at the Big Bang for a four-dimensional universe to have emerged and persisted to the present. To say the least, this assertion is mind-expanding! But does not a similar dimensionality come into play in our conceptualities of such profound Christian realities as our Triune God and his immanent/transcendent relation to both space and time? I believe the same is true in relation to the work of the Holy Spirit. Postmodern experientialists are much more comfortable with these mysteries than rationalistic modernists of both liberal and Evangelical/Fundamentalist stripes. The theological continuum, being a curved rather than a straight-line reality, brings extreme liberals and extreme Funda-mentalists together as uncomfortable bedfellows with tidy theological notions but often truncated religious experience. Surely we owe a debt to our Pentecostal brothers and sisters for raising the issues and keeping the question ever before us: Just what does it mean to be baptized in the Holy Spirit? It just may be that one day we will all come to appreciate the holistic, eschatological nature of Spirit baptism. And it is this broader perspective that will, in my view, do more to promote Great Commission energies and godly living than any of our previous, somewhat parochial positions. At the very least, we will rediscover the value of learning from one another and working alongside one another.

What is Spirit baptism then? Strictly speaking, Spirit baptism is a metaphor, not a doctrine. Further, it is a metaphor whose usage is clearly not univocal within the New Testament. I will be arguing that in the New Testament Spirit baptism refers to the following: (1) Jesus' eschatological redemptive work; (2) Christian initiation; (3) the Christian life; and (4) empowerment for Christian mission and ministry. In addition, it is essential that this understanding be fully integrated within a larger pneumatology. Therefore, I will offer a brief analysis of the work of the Holy Spirit, comparing Johannine, Pauline, and Lukan perspectives. Finally, it is important to acknowledge that this approach is merely one among a plethora of positions one may encounter in the study of Charismatic theology.[4] There is no one "Charismatic position" on Spirit baptism. It is true, however, that the term *Spirit baptism* has taken on a life of its own theologically, and this is so largely because of the massive spread and pervasive influence of Pentecostal/ Charismatic religion. That influence raises at least as many practical and spiritual issues as it does theological.

It was only in the later decades of the twentieth century that the Pentecostal/Charismatic tradition began to take theology seriously. At least at the grass roots level there was a veritable disdain for theology.[5] Now, of course, Pentecostals and Charismatics have earned their rightful place at the theological table. One need only consult the promising biblical, historical, and theological scholarship issuing from such fertile sources as the Society for Pentecostal Studies, the *Journal of Pentecostal Theology,* Sheffield Academic Press, and Hendrickson Publishers to corroborate this fact. But various intractable spiritual and practical issues have also accompanied this pneumatic revival.

What do we do with speaking in tongues today? What about the various claims to divine healing, prophetic utterances, words of knowledge, and the like? Is this "signs and wonders" movement as a whole authentic or spurious? Is it really a revival? Do we even want such a revival? Obviously, a responsible reply to such concerns would go far beyond the boundaries of this chapter. But one's understanding of Spirit baptism would be foundational to a responsible answer to such concerns. Therefore, a consideration of spiritual and practical matters must be included in any treatment of this crucial theological issue.

Our journey should begin, I suppose, with the poignant pronouncements of Jesus' forerunner, John the Baptist. His prediction of a Spirit-and-fire baptism to be administered by the Messiah drew everyone's attention, and it is germane to both Jew and Gentile down to the present. The debate over what such a Spirit baptism entails is surely one of the most significant of contemporary Christianity.

"The Word of God Came to John"

No Spirit! No prophecy! For nearly four hundred years this had been the experience of God's people when John the Baptist burst onto the scene.[6] This eschatological/apocalyptic prophet from the Perean desert (east of the Jordan and the Dead Sea) stepped forth into the spiritual wilderness of his day with a message of both peril and promise. The peril was the impending judgment of the people of Israel. The promise was the soon-coming Messiah! Thus, John's ministry truly was the "beginning of the gospel of Jesus the Messiah, the Son of God" (Mark 1:1, author's translation).

John's uncompromising message of repentance, accompanied by a baptismal rite that would surely alienate the priestly establishment with their temple sacrifices, also addressed the Roman political order. His rebuke of Herod Antipas's illicit marriage to Herodias would eventually cost him his head. John, prophet of Yahweh, from the wilderness (symbol of Israel's purity), had thrown down the gauntlet. "John's fierce loyalty to his faith pitted him against a temporizing high priest and a Hellenizing tetrarch."[7] Thus, after centuries, the Spirit of prophecy was again on the move among God's people.

Indeed, John presented himself "like one of the prophets of old, in particular one of the northern prophets, especially Elijah (cf. the leather belt in 2 Kings 1:8)."[8] Unlike Elijah, however, John would not be a wonder-worker (John 10:41). Jesus himself would display this Charismatic dimension of prophetic ministry with great signs and wonders—a ministry which would continue, as Luke would argue, through the church. But Jesus praised John as one of the greatest persons ever born and as "more than a prophet" (Luke 7:24–28/Matt. 11:7–11). Perhaps in a not so subtle swipe at the shaky, showy leadership of Herod Antipas (who had minted a coin with a reed on it and who dressed in royal robes), Jesus averred that John was no "reed shaken by the wind" and wore no "soft robes" like those of the palace (Luke 7:24–25/Matt. 11:7–8).[9] Again, the prophets were back and were heralding an end-time message of the kingdom of God!

As the "messenger" of Malachi 3:1 and the "voice" of Isaiah 40:3, John came to clear a path for the Messiah (Matt. 3:1–6; Luke 3:1–6; John 1:23). His impact was immediate and enduring:

As the people were filled with expectation, and all were questioning in their hearts concerning John, whether he might be the Messiah, John answered all of them by saying, "I baptize you with water; but one who is more powerful than I is coming; I am not worthy to untie the thong of his sandals. He will baptize you with the Holy Spirit and with fire. His winnowing fork is in his hand, to clear his threshing floor and to gather the wheat into his granary, but the chaff he will burn with unquenchable fire" (Luke 3:15–17 NRSV).

Mark omits the mention of fire, but the older Q version of Matthew and Luke includes it. Is John referring to two baptisms, a Spirit baptism of the righteous and a fire baptism for the wicked? Probably not. Syntactically, the preposition *en* would likely govern both elements (a hendiadys), and John is referring to a "Spirit-and-fire baptism." Any attempt to ascertain the New Testament understanding of Spirit baptism surely begins here. What did John mean by such a baptism?

This is eschatological, even apocalyptic, language. John's words resonate with the Old Testament promises of an end-time outpouring of divine judgment and blessing. Isaiah had long ago predicted that the Messiah would one day revive Israel by his Spirit (*ruach*)—"by a spirit of judgment and by a spirit of burning" (Isa. 4:4 ESV). Numerous Old Testament prophecies pointed to an eschatological outpouring of God's Spirit, bringing both purification and punishment, depending on the human response (Joel 2:28–32; Ezek. 36:25–27; 39:29; Mal. 3:2–3; cf. Isa. 11:15; 29:10; 30:28; 32:15–17; 44:3).[10] Thus, in comprehensive language, John summarizes the total impact of Jesus' saving mission, which continues to this very day!

Max Turner ably summarizes the vision here: "The imagery of washing/cleansing with Spirit and fire was clearly capable of being applied by the Evangelists (i) to the Spirit *in* Jesus' ministry, (ii) to the continuation of his ministry through the church in Jesus' Lordship over the Spirit, and (iii) to the final act of judgement and re-creation, without requiring it to be applied *exclusively* to any one."[11]

In other words, John is speaking in the broadest terms of how Jesus both inaugurates and consummates the kingdom. Spirit baptism is thus introduced at the outset as an eschatological reality descriptive of all of Jesus' saving activity. The entire sphere of the Spirit's work is in purview. In relation to the Christian life, which is most often the concern of dialogue across ecclesial traditions, Spirit baptism encompasses all the saving, sanctifying, and empowering dimensions of the Spirit's activity. Craig Keener has, in my opinion, provided the most satisfying treatment of this approach in his *Gift and Giver: The Holy Spirit for Today.*[12]

To be sure, different New Testament writers will focus on, or emphasize more, a given dimension, which we shall see, but the *unity* of the Spirit's work should not be lost: This unity will aid in our efforts "to maintain the unity of the Spirit in the bond of peace" (Eph. 4:3 NRSV)!

What happens next is surprising, when one reflects on it: Jesus himself comes to be baptized by John! This is certainly not a story the New Testament church would have invented, for John's was a baptism of *repentance*. The various New Testament perspectives on Jesus' baptism are crucial to our full appreciation of Spirit baptism.

"Then Jesus Came from Galilee to John at the Jordan"[13]

Matthew addresses the issue head on: "Then Jesus came from Galilee to John at the Jordan, to be baptized by him. John would have prevented him, saying, 'I need to be baptized by you, and do you come to me?' But Jesus answered him, 'Let it be so now; for it is proper for us in this way to fulfill all righteousness.' Then he consented" (Matt. 3:13–15 NRSV).

Why would Jesus need John's repentance baptism? Matthew's account makes clear that John himself would agree with our first blush response: Jesus, the sinless one, should be baptizing John! And yet Jesus was intent on being baptized. He was there by divine necessity "to fulfill all righteousness" (v. 15). Jesus' "repentance" was in terms of his prophetic identification with the people and their sins, his submission to God's will, and his commitment to his divine calling.[14] In actuality, all four Gospel writers deemphasize the water rite itself and focus more on Jesus' messianic anointing. This was an epoch-making event. Jesus was leaving obscurity now and launching out in his world-changing ministry in the power of the Spirit.

Mark's account adds another important insight. He alone tells us that Jesus *saw* "the heavens torn apart and the Spirit descending like a dove on him" (Mark 1:10 NRSV). Jesus was having an apocalyptic visionary experience. The heavens were rent (*schizo*), just as the curtain of the temple was at Jesus' crucifixion (Mark 15:38). In typical apocalyptic language, Mark emphasizes Jesus' *vision* of heaven (cf. Rev. 1:10; 4:1–2; 10:1; 19:11, 17, 19; 20:1, 4, 11; 21:1–3). This was Jesus' messianic empowerment and an essential key in interpreting his earthly mission.[15]

Luke, however, wants to keep us rooted in history by adding that "the Holy Spirit descended upon [Jesus] *in bodily form* [*somatikos*] like a dove" (Luke 3:22 NRSV). This was more than a visionary event; it was an observable *historical* event. It was "an objective, externalized, and physical manifestation of the Spirit."[16] Further, as we shall see later, Jesus was empowered for his ministry, which as Luke will illustrate, was at least partially paradigmatic for the early church's ministry.[17]

John's Gospel reports another revelation associated with this event—that of the Baptizer himself: "And John testified, 'I saw the Spirit descending from heaven like a dove, and it remained on him. I myself did not know him, but the one who sent me to baptize with water said to me, "He on whom you see the Spirit descend and remain is the one who baptizes with the Holy Spirit." And I myself have seen and have testified that this is the Son of God'" (John 1:32–34 NRSV).

John the Baptist's role in the fourth Gospel is solely that of *witness*. Nothing else is said about him. And his witness is a profound one: (1) "Here is the Lamb of God who takes away the sin of the world!" (2) "[This] is the one who baptizes with the Holy Spirit." (3) "This is the Son of God" (John 1:29–34). Add to these the Father's voice from heaven (Matt. 3:17; Mark 1:11; Luke 3:22) declaring that Jesus is God's beloved Son (Ps. 2:7) with whom he is well pleased (Isa. 42:1), and we have the full testimony of this event as to who Jesus really is. Jesus is the Davidic Messiah. He is Isaiah's Suffering Servant. He is God's Lamb, slain for our sins. He is the Baptizer in the Holy Spirit. He is the Son of God.[18]

In other words, Jesus' baptism was a profoundly Trinitarian event, but the focus that day was on Jesus himself. This fact is instructive for present-day debates on the Holy Spirit, Spirit baptism, spiritual gifts in general, and speaking in tongues in particular. If, as here at the Jordan, we could keep our focus on Jesus and the crucial need to bear witness of him to a world in chaos, surely we ourselves could better experience *together* the Spirit's unifying and empowering work. And in this the Father would be pleased. In fact, my observation is that the present generation has grown weary of our internecine warfare and simply wants to get on with knowing and following Jesus. When we get off this track, we become spiritually dysfunctional whatever our label—Evangelical, Pentecostal, Charismatic, traditional. And there are encouraging signs—not the least of which a respectful dialogue such as this one—that the Holy Spirit is definitely moving us in that direction!

The question remains, however: was Jesus "baptized with the Holy Spirit" at the Jordan? In other words, in what way, if any, was his experience of the Spirit paradigmatic for us? This is clearly a sticking point in the present dialogue. Howard M. Ervin, my highly esteemed colleague here at ORU, would answer unequivocally, "Yes, it was paradigmatic." Chapter 2 of his *Conversion-Initiation and the Baptism in the Holy Spirit,* a critique of Dunn's classic, *Baptism in the Holy Spirit,* is entitled "Jesus' Baptism in the Spirit."[19] Even Dunn himself admits that "we may legitimately speak of the descent of the Spirit on Jesus at Jordan as a baptism in the Spirit; and we certainly cannot deny that it was this anointing with the Spirit which equipped Jesus with power and authority for his mission to follow (Acts 10:38)."[20]

But Dunn's classic, appreciative as it is of the Pentecostal contribution (see his preface), is, nonetheless, a theological *tour de force,* attempting to *refute* any sort of second blessing account of Spirit baptism. Unfortunately, in the eyes of some, he may be guilty of foisting Paul's theology (of which he is a master) on Luke, for example, in this way: Clearly Luke's focus is on *salvation* and on history as the arena of God's saving events. But Dunn seems to want to impose a rigid salvation-history scheme on these baptismal narratives in general so that any empowering dimension as paradigmatic for the church is diminished. There is evidence, however, that Dunn—and his disciples—are listening with greater appreciation to the newer theological perspectives of the Pentecostal/Charismatic tradition. Who knows! Perhaps one day a consensus can be reached!

My argument here is simply that Jesus' empowerment at the Jordan *is* paradigmatic for us. This does not mean that one must therefore adopt a kind of "haves and have-nots" theology and mentality, which is spiritually deadly and divisive. I am simply asking for a fuller acknowledgement of this *dimension* of the Spirit's work, which is vital to fulfilling our mission. The next logical step for our consideration of Spirit baptism would therefore be to examine Luke's narrative in Acts of the early church on mission, giving special attention to the key debated chapters, 2, 8, 9, 10, and 19. What do we make of Pentecost and of the subsequent outpourings of the Spirit which Luke narrates?

"When the Day of Pentecost Had Come"

Without a doubt Acts has been the storm center in the debate over Spirit baptism.[21] In all honesty, Luke's description of first-century Christianity has often seemed foreign to our present experiences. How many of us, for example, would feel comfortable giving an evangelistic invitation in precisely the same words Peter used in his Pentecost sermon? "Repent, and be baptized every one of you in the name of Jesus Christ so that your sins may be forgiven; and you will receive the gift of the Holy Spirit" (Acts 2:38 NRSV). For some of us, even the word *repent* has been neglected. Then the mention of water baptism makes others of us uncomfortable as we tend to diminish the importance of baptism or the church. But the last straw is Peter's mention of the gift of the Holy Spirit, especially as it is portrayed on the Day of Pentecost! We would rather stay with the safer words "receive Christ." Those words, as we shall see, are not without biblical warrant, but why have we shied away from Pentecostal language?[22] More importantly, why have we been afraid of the power of Pentecost itself?

Ken Hemphill, former president of Southwestern Baptist Theological Seminary in Fort Worth, Texas, addresses the issues head-on: "Pentecost marks the beginning and the empowering of the New Testament church. It marks a unique transformation in the lives of the members of the early church. After Pentecost we see high-voltage Christianity. If we ourselves and our churches do not have a Pentecost experience, we will never be bold witnesses and never know supernatural church growth."[23]

Hemphill has the testimonies of both Scripture and Christian history to back him up. But how do we experience Pentecostal power today? And what is the significance of Pentecost biblically, historically, theologically, and practically?[24]

When I was writing my own systematic theology, I was appalled to discover how little has been said by the theologians about the significance of Pentecost. Here we have one of the most significant events in redemptive history, and we are virtually silent on the subject. What follows in the next few paragraphs is a brief accounting of *one* theological perspective (my own), since an exhaustive survey of options would extend far beyond assigned parameters.

The Pentecostal/Charismatic tradition has correctly argued, in my opinion, that Pentecost is *both* a key event in salvation history *and* a dimension of empowerment essential to the church's completing her mission. Luke is the New Testament Gospel writer (and historian, theologian, and medical missionary!) to whom we must turn for the most relevant scriptural materials. Pentecostal and Charismatic theologians are fast convincing those of other traditions that there is much to be gained doctrinally from the narrative portions of Scripture. If not, then we are certainly impoverished theologically, since a major portion of the Bible is narrative! Luke has a distinctive pneumatology, about which more will be presented later. But he definitely provides plenty of grist for our theological mills in his narrative depiction of Pentecost.

It was Easter Sunday evening. Jesus had made a dramatic resurrection appearance to his disciples in which he had interpreted his saving mission in the total, tripartite Hebrew canon of Scripture ("the Law of Moses, the prophets, and the psalms [the writings]," Luke 24:44). But then he told them to wait. They were not yet ready to proclaim "his name to all nations" (v. 47). I suppose, as a Southern Baptist, I might have been tempted to challenge Jesus that day. More than three years of personal training and discipleship, a conclusive resurrection appearance, a comprehensive Bible study interpreting Jesus' saving work, led by the Master himself—what more do we need! Let's just get organized, derive our programs, write up our literature, and exhort each other to *go*! But Jesus said *wait*: "And see, I am sending upon you what my Father promised [lit. the promise of my Father]; so stay here in the city until you have been clothed with power from on high" (Luke 24:49 NRSV). Jesus said they needed empowerment first.

(margin handwriting: broad Christian theology concerned with the Holy Spirit)

The first chapter of Acts further elaborates Jesus' teaching: "While staying with them, he ordered them not to leave Jerusalem, but to wait there for the promise of the Father. 'This,' he said, 'is what you have heard from me; for John baptized with water, but you will be baptized with the Holy Spirit not many days from now'" (Acts 1:4–5 NRSV).

Clearly Jesus is referring to Spirit baptism, evoking the words of John himself. When the disciples queried Jesus as to the timing of the restoration of the kingdom to Israel, Jesus replied, in effect, that it was none of their business. They were missing his point: "But you will receive power when the Holy Spirit has come upon you; and you will be my witnesses in Jerusalem, in all Judea and Samaria, and to the ends of the earth" (vv. 6–8).

For what was Jesus preparing his disciples? Was he preparing them for the new birth? The traditional answer is yes. Pentecostals and Charismatics have argued the opposite: *Jesus was preparing them for their empowerment for mission.* Who is right? There may be a kernel of truth in each of these competing perspectives.

James D. G. Dunn, in his highly influential *Baptism in the Holy Spirit,* speaks for many with these kinds of programmatic statements: "Pentecost is a new beginning—the inauguration of the new age, the age of the Spirit—that which had not been before" (p. 44). "For Luke Pentecost is also the beginning of the new covenant for the disciples" (p. 47). "Pentecost inaugurates the age of the Church" (p. 49). "[As a new epoch in salvation history], Pentecost can never be repeated" (p. 53). "But in another sense [becoming a Christian], Pentecost, or rather the experience of Pentecost, can and must be repeated" (p. 53). "The Baptism in the Spirit, as always, is primarily initiatory, and only secondarily an empowering" (p. 54). ⭘

In common parlance, Spirit baptism, then, is being born again, regenerated by the Spirit, indwelled by the Spirit, and baptized into Christ's body; it is the quintessence of "becoming a Christian." One could certainly use Paul's pneumatology to back this position, for Paul clearly uses the Spirit baptism metaphor in this initiatory sense in 1 Corinthians 12:13. The question to be raised, however, is whether this reality is the primary focus of Luke's use of the Spirit baptism metaphor.

Howard Ervin would ask in rebuttal, if Jordan (Jesus' baptism) and Jerusalem (Pentecost) are parallel, in terms of Dunn's conversion-initiation model, then where are the baptismal waters for the 120? Further, what would be the significance of Jesus' Last Supper words of institution ("the new covenant in my blood": Matt. 26:28; Mark 14:24; Luke 22:20; 1 Cor. 11:25), if the new covenant only began for the disciples at Pentecost?[25] Ervin speaks for most Pentecostals and Charismatics when he defines the purpose of Spirit baptism as being "power-in-mission."[26] "The purpose of Pentecost is unmistakably world evangelism," he would strongly argue.[27]

So who is right? On the one side are the Evangelicals safely entrenched behind Paul's 1 Corinthians 12:13. And on the other, the Pentecostals and Charismatics fortify themselves with Luke's Acts 2:4. Who is right? Both are right. In the Pauline sense of the metaphor, all believers have experienced Spirit baptism. In the Lukan emphasis on the empowering dimension of Spirit baptism, we may not all be "filled with the Spirit"! The traditional view that Spirit baptism in its regenerational dimension is what all true believers have in common is correct. But the Pentecostal/Charismatic tradition is also on target in arguing that Luke uses the metaphor (along with at least six others) in an empowering sense.

In broadest theological terms, both the regenerational/indwelling and empowering dimensions of the Spirit's work are included in Spirit baptism as far as the believer's experience is concerned. As we have already seen, however, from our study of the preaching of John the Baptist, there is an eschatological perspective to this scriptural teaching which should never be lost: The last days started with Jesus' arrival and will be consummated at his second coming. All that Jesus has done as the Messiah (Jewish language), the Christ (Greek language), the Anointed (English language)—both in his earthly ministry and since his ascension—is subsumed under the Spirit baptism rubric. All that we ourselves personally experience in his saving work—new birth, sanctification, empowerment for witness, and giftedness for mutual upbuilding within his body—should also be included in this concept.

Thus, when a believer avers, "I was baptized in the Holy Spirit at the new birth, according to 1 Corinthians 12:13," they would be scripturally and theologically correct. And when a believer experiences an empowerment for witness and ministry and exults, "I was baptized in the Holy Spirit just like in the book of Acts!" they would also be correct biblically and doctrinally. (As a halfway house for the present, perhaps we could *all* refer to being "filled with the Spirit" or "empowered" when communicating with one another— but more on that later!)

But Spirit baptism is only one major issue raised by the Pentecost narrative. Luke states explicitly that "they were all filled with the Holy Spirit and began to speak in other tongues as the Spirit gave them utterance" (Acts 2:4 ESV). Does speaking in tongues alone signify Spirit baptism and entrance into the Spirit-filled, Charismatic dimension of the Christian life, as many Pentecostals and Charismatics would argue? We would need to probe further into the Acts narratives to answer that question.

"They Received the Holy Spirit"

When did the first disciples "receive" the Holy Spirit?[28] Again, unless we allow for a diversity of uses of a given metaphor (in this case, the gift metaphor), our differing answers can only confuse the issues. *Receive* can mean different things in different contexts in the Bible. Clearly every true Christian has "received" the Holy Spirit (Gal. 3:2; Rom. 8:9). But again Luke chooses to use this language in a broader empowering sense as well, which often confuses our (sometimes less-than-flexible) attempts to conceptualize the Spirit's work.

Peter promised in part on the Day of Pentecost, "you will receive the gift of the Holy Spirit" (adding "for the promise is for you," Acts 2:38–39). What is the gift of the Holy Spirit, the promise of the Father? And how do we evaluate Luke's variegated language in terms of the coming of the Holy Spirit?

First, we will look at Luke's pneumatological language. He uses seven different phrases to describe the coming of the Spirit: First, the believers are "baptized in the Holy Spirit" (Acts 1:5; 11:16). Second, the Holy Spirit "comes upon" (Acts 1:8; 19:6). Third, the believers are "filled with the Holy Spirit" (Acts 2:4). Fourth, the Holy Spirit is "poured out" (Acts 2:17, 18, 33; 10:45). Fifth, the believers "receive the Holy Spirit" (Acts 2:38; 8:15, 17, 19; 10:47; 19:2). Sixth, the Holy Spirit is "given" (Acts 8:18; 11:17). Finally, the Holy Spirit "falls upon" them (Acts 8:16; 10:44; 11:15). The term *dorea* (gift) itself is also central to Luke's thought in these passages (Acts 2:38; 8:20; 10:45; 11:17; cf. 5:32; 15:8).

When one correlates this terminology with Luke's narrative of the worldwide spread of the gospel by the Spirit-empowered church, the results are fascinating:

Pentecost (Acts 2)

Acts 1:5 NRSV: "You will be baptized with the Holy Spirit." Acts 1:8: "But you will receive power when the Holy Spirit comes on you." Acts 2:4 NRSV: "All of them were filled with the Holy Spirit." Acts 2:17–18, 33 NRSV: "I will pour out my Spirit . . . he has poured out." Acts 10:47 NRSV: "Who have received the Holy Spirit just as we have." Acts 11:17 NRSV: "God gave them the same gift that he gave us when we believed." Acts 11:15 ESV: "The Holy Spirit fell on them just as on us at the beginning."

Samaria (Acts 8)

Acts 8:15, 17, 19: "Receive(d) the Holy Spirit." Acts 8:18 NASB: "The Spirit was given." Acts 8:16 NASB: "[The Holy Spirit] had not yet fallen upon any of them."

Caesarea (Acts 10)

Acts 11:16 NRSV: "Baptized with the Holy Spirit." Acts 10:45 NRSV: "The gift of the Holy Spirit had been poured out even on the Gentiles." Acts 10:47 NRSV: "Who have received the Holy Spirit just as we have." Acts 11:17 NRSV: "God gave them the same gift that he gave us when we believed." Acts 10:44; 11:15 NRSV: "The Holy Spirit fell upon."

Ephesus (Acts 19)

Acts 19:6 NRSV: "The Holy Spirit came upon them." Acts 19:2: "Did you receive the Holy Spirit when you believed?" (ESV).

Add to these Luke's references to being "filled with the Holy Spirit" (*pimplemi*: Luke 1:15, 41, 67; Acts 2:4; 4:8, 31; 9:17; 13:9; *pleroo*: Acts 13:52) and the picture becomes even more intriguing. John the Baptist and his parents are filled with the Holy Spirit before Pentecost in the infancy narratives of Luke's Gospel! Peter, Paul, and other disciples apparently experienced numerous infillings of the Spirit. How do we interpret all this?

The Jewish context of Luke's thought world is our first clue. For Luke, the Holy Spirit is the "Spirit of prophecy." Notice how

Peter interprets Pentecost in terms of Joel's prophecy (Acts 2:16–21/Joel 2:28–32). In effect Luke is announcing "the *prophethood* of all believers," to use Roger Stronstad's ingenious and insightful phrase.[29] Further, this new prophetic activity, absent for centuries, even predated John the Baptist's ministry. John was filled with the Holy Spirit in his mother's womb, and both of his parents prophesied (Luke 1:15, 41, 67). Luke's is a *prophetic* pneumatology in large measure.[30]

Roger Stronstad's groundbreaking study, *The Charismatic Theology of St. Luke*,[31] shows how Luke ransacks the vocabulary of the Septuagint (the Bible of the early church) in its description of the Charismatic and prophetic activity of the Holy Spirit in Old Testament times to depict the same kinds of activity in the New Testament era. Without question, Luke draws special attention to these phenomena both in Jesus' ministry and in that of the early church.

Thus, when Peter referred, in his Pentecost sermon, to receiving the "promise of the Father" and the "gift of the Holy Spirit" (Acts 2:33, 38–39; cf. Luke 24:49; Acts 1:4; and Paul's words: Gal. 3:1–5, 14; Eph. 1:13), he was referring to both conversion and charisma! Whenever people "received the Holy Spirit" or "received the gift of the Holy Spirit" or were "baptized in the Holy Spirit" in Acts—that is, whenever they became Christians—the Charismatic dimension was already present within their lives! It might find immediate expression with speaking in tongues or prophecy, for example, or eventual expression in future ministry. But it was already present and ready to be released. Further, they could expect future empowerments to complete their task in the enterprise of discipling the nations. In fact, Jesus himself taught that we can continually ask the Father to give us the Holy Spirit (Luke 11:13). And we all should! We need his power—continually! Surely we should aspire to be like those table servants of Acts 6 (v. 3), like Stephen (Acts 7:55), like Barnabas (Acts 11:24), and even like Jesus himself (Luke 4:1)—to be "*full* [*pleres*] of the Holy Spirit," "*continually* filled (*pleroo*) with Spirit," as Paul would put it (Eph. 5:18).

"All of Them Were Filled with the Holy Spirit"

Luke specifically states that they were all "filled with the Holy Spirit" on the Day of Pentecost.[32] It is interesting that he does not use that specific phrase to describe what happened at Samaria (Acts 8), Caesarea (Acts 10), or Ephesus (Acts 19). He does, however, indicate that three days after Saul's dramatic conversion and commissioning on the road to Damascus he was "filled with the Holy Spirit," when Ananias laid his hands on him (Acts 9:17 NRSV). Earlier, *after* Pentecost, Peter found himself before the Jewish council where, "filled with the Holy Spirit," he gave bold witness to the Christ (Acts 4:8 NRSV). And later we see the "Little Pentecost," where Peter, John, and friends are "filled with the Holy Spirit and spoke the word of God with boldness" (v. 31 NRSV). Luke reports another infilling of the Spirit for Paul on Cyprus at the start of his first missionary journey (Acts 13:9). Finally, Luke summarizes the disciples' response to persecution with these words: "And the disciples were filled with joy and with the Holy Spirit" (v. 52).

Because of these narratives, most can agree that there is a Spirit-filled life available to all believers and that this is something to be pursued. In fact, it is even commanded in the New Testament (Eph. 5:18). But what the Pentecostals have alerted us to is that this is precisely how Luke describes the event of Pentecost itself. In fact, Luke uses all seven of his descriptive phrases with reference to Pentecost (see the above list), including "baptized in the Holy Spirit" (Acts 1:5). *Thus, it is not a mistaken notion to associate empowerment with Spirit baptism.* Jesus said, "You will receive power" (Acts 1:8), and they did. They proceeded to turn the Roman Empire upside down!

However, the Pentecostals are also quick to point out that something else happened that day as well as subsequently in Acts: They spoke in tongues (Acts 2:4). Here is where the debate really heats up. Should we expect speaking in tongues to signify Spirit-filled living today? Going back through the Acts narratives, most Pentecostals and Charismatics would want to draw our attention to how often Luke either explicitly states that speaking in tongues occurred at the coming of the Spirit or strongly implies that it did.

"[They] Began to Speak in Other Tongues"[33]

The "second blessing" concept of Spirit baptism, with the normal accompanying sign of speaking in tongues, rests squarely on Luke's Acts narratives: *Pentecost* (Acts 2): They were baptized-in/filled-with the Holy Spirit and spoke in tongues. *Samaria*

(Acts 8): Tongues are strongly implied, since Simon offered money to be able to bestow the Spirit. *Paul* (Acts 9): Again, tongues are strongly implied, since later the apostle thanked God that he spoke in tongues more than all the Corinthian believers (1 Cor. 14:18). *Caesarea* (Acts 10): They spoke in tongues. *Ephesus* (Acts 19): They spoke in tongues and prophesied.

Most Pentecostals would endorse a virtual "law of tongues," viewing speaking in tongues as the "initial physical evidence" of Spirit baptism. Charismatics, on the other hand, are somewhat "softer" on tongues: One may or may not speak in tongues when baptized in the Holy Spirit, but speaking in tongues is still seen as a normal part of Spirit-filled living available to all. Then, of course, opponents of Charismatic renewal may view present-day tongues speaking as marginal at best, if not delusional. Among these folk would also be dispensationalists who see such sign gifts as disappearing with the apostles. It is those "exceptions" to a given pattern in Luke's narratives which cause problems on all sides.

The traditional Pentecostal/Charismatic view finds a strong argument in the "Samaritan Pentecost" of Acts 8, where the gift of the Spirit is delayed. However, their tongues-as-evidence argument is weakened by no explicit mention of tongues in the narrative. Paul's encounter with disciples of John, some thirty-five years after Pentecost (Acts 19), meets the tongues criterion but raises the troublesome question of the "rebaptism." Their response would be, of course, that this was Christian baptism. But, ironically, the most problematic passage of all is Pentecost itself.

If the 120 of Pentecost were already "born again" believers and thus now candidates for Spirit baptism, when did this new birth take place? Some would appeal to John 20:22. Actually, a rather strong case can be made here.[34] However, that does not account for the total number at Pentecost. Again, an argument from silence must be used. But the coin can be turned.

For opponents of the view that Luke uses Spirit baptism as an empowerment metaphor and that Charismatic activity such as tongues speaking and prophecy may be associated with it, Acts is rife with problems. Pentecost (Acts 2), Caesarea (Acts 10), and Ephesus (Acts 19) are explicit in this regard, and Samaria (Acts 8) strongly implies it: Charismatic phenomena accompanied the gift of the Spirit. Only a dispensational model—convenient, but contrived—can adequately deal with this issue. Also, the delay of the gift of the Spirit in Acts 8, though an obvious exception to the normal pattern of Acts, still leaves open the possibility of a time lapse between conversion and the gift of the Spirit.[35]

Without a dimensional approach we are left at an impasse here, a dilemma. In fine Hegelian fashion the thesis (traditional views) and antithesis (Pentecostal/Charismatic views) must find a synthesis (a dimensional view).[36] Spirit baptism in the New Testament refers to conversion-initiation, initial sanctification, and spiritual empowerment as well as the outworking of these realities in the total Christian life.

There is an already-not yet eschatological tension that pervades the New Testament teaching on the Christian life. Our salvation is a process, a pilgrimage. We are already dead to sin (Rom. 6), but this also has to be worked out in our lives (Rom. 7–8). We have already been sanctified (1 Cor. 6:11) but are also being sanctified daily. We have already been saved (Eph. 2:8–9), but we are also being saved (1 Cor. 1:18). And we shall be saved: "For salvation is nearer to us now than when we first believed" (Rom. 13:11 ESV). There are many breakthroughs in the Christian pilgrimage—the conquering of besetting sins, deeper levels of consecration, sovereign empowerments for ministry, and the like. There is no arrival point. Theologies that are plagued with an "arrival syndrome"—"I got it all when I was saved, Brother!" or "I've been saved, sanctified, and baptized in the Holy Ghost!"—end up promoting spiritual stagnation.[37]

There *is* a second blessing in the Christian life—and a third and a fourth and a fifth and so on.[38] I know from almost four decades of participation in the Charismatic movement that Charismatics themselves often get stuck here. That is why the Toronto and Pensacola revivals were so encouraging to many of them: There *is* always something more! We do not need simply to pine for the past (or seek to recreate it). Being filled with the Spirit and speaking in tongues twenty years ago is not enough. What about the *present* dimensions of that Spirit baptism? J. I. Packer phrased it well when he affirmed the fact that we need to *broaden* "the categories of Spirit baptism, ongoing charismata, and current manifestations of the Spirit" if we want to remain faithful to the New Testament witness and move toward peace, unity, and mutual edification in the church.[39] God obviously never intended Spirit baptism to be a divisive issue. That is why it behooves us to return to Paul's initiatory use of the metaphor as the startingpoint for all our discussions.

"For in One Spirit We Were All Baptized into One Body"[40]

First Corinthians 12:13 is a problematic passage for those of the Pentecostal/Charismatic persuasion who hold rigidly to the concept that Spirit baptism refers solely to a subsequent empowerment after the new birth. One way of getting around the difficulty, of course, is to adopt the rendering, "*by* one Spirit," which many English translations do. This approach is grammatically possible but exegetically and theologically fraught with problems. Thus, a Charismatic might argue that at conversion we are baptized by the Holy Spirit into the body of Christ, and at our empowerment for service we are baptized by Jesus in the Holy Spirit. But where else in the New Testament is there a reference to the Spirit's being the baptizer? Thomas R. Schreiner provides an apt summary: "The word *en* in 1 Corinthians 12:13 should not be translated as 'by,' but 'in,' for elsewhere in the New Testament the agent of baptism is regularly designated by *hypo* (e.g., Matt. 3:6, 13–14; Mark 1:5; Luke 3:7; 7:30) and the element with which they are baptized by *en* (Matt. 3:6, 11; Mark 1:8; Luke 3:16; John 1:26, 31, 33; Acts 1:5; 11:16)."[41]

Without doubt Paul is referring to Spirit baptism here. And he is doing so for the purpose of promoting unity in the body of Christ.

What an irony that we have let debate over Spirit baptism divide us. Just as Paul penned 1 Corinthians 12–14 in part to correct the Corinthians' overemphasis on speaking in tongues, so Charismatics often turn to these passages to overemphasize speaking in tongues! (I suppose that is no more culpable than those who use these same chapters to *exterminate* tongues.) It is difficult for us Protestants consistently to submit our traditions to biblical authority. What are the implications of 1 Corinthians 12:13 for our present situation?

Without exception in the New Testament, when instruction is given on spiritual gifts and ministries, the themes of unity within diversity, love, and humility are emphasized (Rom. 12; 1 Cor. 12–14; Eph. 4:1–16; 1 Pet. 4:7–11). This is precisely Paul's burden in 1 Corinthians 12:13: "For in one Spirit we were all baptized into one body—Jews or Greeks, slaves or free—and all were made to drink of one Spirit" (ESV). Gordon Fee quickly adds this clarifying comment: "What needs to be pointed out, however, is that, . . . Paul's present concern is *not* to delineate *how an individual becomes a believer,* but to explain *how the many of them, diverse as they are, are in fact one body.* The answer: The Spirit, whom all alike have received."[42]

Our diverse gifts and ministries will always tend to divide us if we fail to acknowledge and celebrate God's lavish gift of his Spirit to all.

Howard Ervin accepts Paul's initiatory use of the Spirit baptism metaphor in the first part of this verse but argues that the second part, "all were made to drink of one Spirit," refers to Pentecostal empowerment, which all in our day simply do not have.[43] Fee, however, seems to have the upper hand exegetically, seeing in this passage "a Semitic parallelism, where both clauses argue essentially the same point."[44] However, Paul *is* making an experiential appeal here. The gift of the Spirit, as in Galatians 3:2–5, is portrayed as a vivid, manifest reality, too often missing in the contemporary church.[45] And this is precisely the Pentecostal contribution. The gift of the Spirit is not "a deduction to be drawn from a correct confession or properly administered sacrament" but rather something the apostle "could refer them to directly," says Dunn correctly and in consonance with Pentecostal/Charismatic spirituality.[46]

"The Gift of the Holy Spirit"

The gift of the Holy Spirit is the culmination of Christian initiation, however experienced. Our pilgrimages are about as diverse as our personalities.[47] The Pentecostal/Charismatic tradition has alerted us to the empowerment dimension of this gift, and the contemporary church is surely its debtor for this. But the "unwrapping" of this gift, as it were, is a lifelong discovery. The gift of the Holy Spirit is something the whole church should continually celebrate together.

Luke's terminology here is intriguing. The word for gift used in this phrase is *dorea.* It is a term that is used eleven times in the New Testament by four authors and in six different books: John (John 4:10: "the gift of God"); Acts (Acts 2:38: "the gift of the Holy Spirit"; Acts 8:20: "the gift of God" [ESV]; Acts 10:45: "the gift of the Holy Spirit"; Acts 11:17: "the same gift that he gave us"); Paul

(Rom. 5:15: "the gift"; Rom. 5:17: "the gift of righteousness" [NASB]; 2 Cor. 9:15: "[God's] indescribable gift"; Eph. 3:7: "the gift of God's grace"; Eph. 4:7: "Christ's gift"); Hebrews (Heb. 6:4: "the heavenly gift"[48]). It could be that this was a technical term of the New Testament era used with reference to the Holy Spirit's coming into a person's life in all the above mentioned dimensions. If so, then we have further biblical warrant for viewing Spirit baptism as a supremely unifying concept in the New Testament.

The highly revered Charismatic scholar, J. Rodman Williams, has provided a rich and virtually exhaustive treatment of the gift of the Spirit from the Charismatic perspective of empowerment.[49] Although some would be put off by the second blessing schema, his edifying analysis can be beneficial to all. Do we really know what we have in this gift? The Pentecostal/Charismatic tradition has prompted a new appreciation for God's "indescribable gift" (2 Cor. 9:15).

David du Plessis, known as "Mr. Pentecost" and as a worldwide ambassador for Pentecostalism, had a colorful and engaging way of communicating God's truth in a bridge-building fashion. I vividly remember interviewing him while doing my Ph.D. dissertation critiquing Pentecostal theology. He was known for using a cooking analogy to get his message across. I will adapt it to my own upbringing.

In West Texas we love to barbeque. There is nothing like a juicy, thick barbequed sirloin steak! It is one thing to have possession of that steak in the freezer. It is quite another to have it sizzling on an open grill (and then, of course, enjoying it!). The church has always had possession of the truth of Spirit baptism. The Pentecostals have simply helped us get it out of the freezer and onto the grill![50]

The One Work of the Holy Spirit

Any analysis of a given subject tends to compromise the *unity* of the subject, and this is especially true in relation to the work of the Holy Spirit.[51] Because God is one God, his revelation is a unified revelation. And because there is one Spirit (Eph. 4:4), his work will be a unified work. Especially in the West we tend to derive tidy categories and rigid schemes. This tendency, of course, works against our conceptualizing the Spirit's work; for "the wind blows where it chooses" (John 3:8), and there always remains a mystery to the Spirit's ways. Nonetheless, a careful observation of the

New Testament's portrait of the Spirit's work reveals three fundamental dimensions, which I have termed Paschal, Purifying, and
Pentecostal and charted as follows:

Paschal	Purifying	Pentecostal
Salvation	Sanctification	Service
Conversion	Consecration	Charisma
How to Get *Started*	How to Get *Straight*	How to Get *Strong*
John	Paul	Luke

Paul refers to Jesus as our Paschal Lamb (1 Cor. 5:7), and the
paschal dimension refers, therefore, to the Holy Spirit's work in
applying Christ's saving work to us through regeneration. It is his
initiating work, bringing about a new birth and imparting to us
eternal life. And it is John, perhaps more than any other New
Testament writer, who focuses on this essential dimension of the
Spirit's work.

In present-day discussions of Spirit baptism, prompted by the
Pentecostal and Charismatic movements, attention often turns to
Paul's letters, particularly 1 Corinthians 12–14. Paul does have much
to say about the charisms and the Charismatic life of the church. But
I believe a thorough reading of the Pauline materials reveals that
Paul is the proponent *par excellence* of the purifying dimension of
the Spirit's work. Finally, we have already seen that Luke champions
the Pentecostal dimension, the Spirit's empowering work.

To be sure, it would be artificial to keep these categories rigid,
for each writer touches on all the dimensions of the Spirit's work,
as we shall see. However, I am amazed at the manner in which
seemingly the Spirit, in his inspiration of the Scriptures, sover-
eignly chose to use a given writer to accent a particular dimension
of his work. What follows, then, is a brief overview of these dimensions in the Johannine, Pauline, and Lukan pneumatologies.

The Paschal Dimension

The apostle John has a special interest in the Spirit, the water,
and the blood (1 John 5:6–8). In fact, he weaves these together in
his theological tapestry to provide one of the most profound and
moving portrayals of our salvation to be found in all the Scriptures.
John's is a cross-centered pneumatology. It may be at the rooftop
of the New Testament in terms of its development and integration.

Years ago, in *Christianity Today,* Timothy L. Smith wrote of the "dialects" which have developed in the Christian community.[52] Some speak a "Calvary dialect," emphasizing the cross and the call to discipleship, while others evince more of a "Pentecost dialect," which highlights the power of the Holy Spirit and the necessity of the spiritual gifts. Smith called for an *integration* of these languages in a more holistic perspective on the Christian faith and life. One thinks of the Calvary orientation of contemporary Evangelicalism and the Pentecost orientation of the present-day Charismatic movement. What Smith called for, John masterfully delivers in his Gospel, letters, and Apocalypse.

Calvary and Pentecost are inseparable. To emphasize one to the neglect of the other is to distort and enervate the faith. In John's pneumatology the cross and the Spirit are bonded together. John brackets his Gospel with this message. At the beginning, John the Baptist steps forth to announce the Messiah as the (1) "Lamb of God who takes away the sin of the world" and (2) "the one who baptizes with the Holy Spirit," culminating with the declaration, "this is the Son of God" (John 1:29–34 ESV). At the end, Jesus' side is pierced by one of the soldiers "and at once blood and water came out" (19:34 NRSV). Blood: "Behold, the Lamb of God, who takes away the sin of the world!" (1:29, ESV). Water: "This is the one who baptizes with the Holy Spirit" (v. 33, author's translation).

The parallel to these passages in John's epistles is found in 1 John 5:6–8 NRSV: "This is the one who came by water and blood, . . . There are three that testify: the Spirit and the water and the blood." John is emphatic about the truth of his own testimony to the blood and water, in his Gospel account of the crucifixion (John 19:35), and even more so about the Spirit's testimony to the water and the blood in his epistle (1 John 5:6). Water and Spirit are so closely aligned in the Gospel (cf. John 3:5) that the parallels between these two passages become striking. Gary M. Burge has concluded that "the parallels between John 19:34 and 1 John 5:6–8 indicate that they are conceptually in the same school: blood, water, testimony, and the Spirit all converge."[53] The concern of the Gospel passage is atonement, and the epistle addresses Christological concerns. And John's "living water/Spirit metaphor" serves both.[54]

Only through Jesus' atoning death do we receive the living water of the Spirit. And only because he was the one who went *both* to the Jordan (baptism) and to Jerusalem (the cross)—Gnostic heresy would deny this, believing that "the Christ" descended upon Jesus at the Jordan and left him at the cross (i.e., no incarnation)—could he be the atoning sacrifice for our sins and the source of eternal life? Thus, allusion is ultimately made to our own baptism in the water of the Spirit (John 3:5), that is, to Spirit baptism.[55]

So the testimonies coincide, those of John the Baptist, John the apostle, the Spirit, the water, and the blood. Jesus alone is the Lamb and the Baptizer—the Son of God. He alone can give us eternal life. The Holy Spirit wants to bring us to Jesus' side so that we can be cleansed by his blood and baptized in the Spirit. The Contemporary English Version's rendering of 1 John 5:6–8 vividly communicates these truths: "Water and blood came out from the side of Jesus Christ. It was not just water, but water and blood. The Spirit tells about this, because the Spirit is truthful. In fact, there are three who tell about it. They are the Spirit, the water, and the blood, and they all agree."[56]

This paschal orientation in John's pneumatology sets him apart. He is most interested in alerting us to the Spirit's work in bringing us to Christ and to eternal life. This is his consistent emphasis throughout his Gospel. A brief survey of relevant passages will forcefully corroborate this conclusion.

"Born of the Spirit"

Nicodemus could never have anticipated what Jesus was going to say to him that night![57] It was rather remarkable that such a Pharisee and leader of the Jews would approach Jesus at all. And when he did, he immediately acknowledged to Jesus that his miraculous signs surely indicated that he was from God (John 3:1–2). But that was far from enough for Jesus. He abruptly announced to Nicodemus that he needed a new birth from heaven by the Spirit, a birth as mysterious as the wind (vv. 3–8).

Nicodemus needed to be "born from above" or "born again" (vv. 3, 7). The term *anothen* can signify "from above," as in verse 31, where Jesus is described as the "one who comes from above [*anothen*]," or it can mean "again" or "anew." To be born from above is to be born "of God" (John 1:13). The second birth that brings one into the kingdom is a spiritual birth. As the saying goes: Born once, die twice; born twice, die once! Jesus authoritatively announced to Nicodemus: "Very truly, I tell you, no one can enter the kingdom of God without being born of water and Spirit" (John 3:5 NRSV). To what is Jesus referring here?

In all probability, we have another hendiadys, one preposition governing the two nouns, water and Spirit. Thus, a probable and helpful rendering would be "born of the water of the Spirit." *This is another important reference then to Spirit baptism.* Nicodemus was familiar with the idea of a Gentile experiencing proselyte baptism as a cleansing and "new birth" into Judaism. It must have been at least a little offensive to hear Jesus say, in effect, he needed a similar initiation through repentance and rebirth into the kingdom of God. Nicodemus had difficulty making the transition from physical birth and being "born of the Spirit" (John 3:4–9).

This new birth is mysterious like the wind, Jesus explained: "The wind blows where it chooses, and you hear the sound of it, but you do not know where it comes from or where it goes. So it is with everyone who is born of the Spirit" (v. 8 NRSV). The play on words is clear to those who know biblical Greek, for the term *pneuma* found here is translated either "wind" or "Spirit," according to the context. Jesus is telling Nicodemus that the ways of the Spirit are mysterious and unpredictable. We need to review that lesson in our own day, when it comes to the new birth and the Spirit-filled life. The things of the kingdom do not come through some formula but through the sovereign action of the Holy Spirit. Here again we note John's paschal emphasis on the regenerating/initiatory work of the Spirit. There is no entrance into the kingdom of God without this baptism in the water of the Spirit (v. 5).

Water, Water, Everywhere!

John has a special interest in water! Whether it is the waters of the Jordan, where John was baptizing (1:31–33), the ceremonial water pots in Cana of Galilee (2:6), the Jewish proselyte baptismal waters we just mentioned (3:5), the water of Jacob's well in Sychar (John 4), or the pools of Bethesda (John 5) or Siloam (John 7 [spring of Gihon] and 9) in Jerusalem—John portrays Jesus himself and the living water of salvation, which he alone can give, as *superior* in every way. The Spirit baptism he offers transcends any Jewish religious rites and any ancient healing shrines.[58] Take, for example, the woman of Samaria at Jacob's well.

The drama in John's narratives tempts one to expound far beyond the focus of this study: Jesus' encounter with the Samaritan woman is filled with meaningful detail. But John's quintessential pneumatology is given vivid expression in Jesus' words: "If you knew the gift [*dorea*] of God, and who it is that is saying to you, 'Give me a drink,' you would have asked him, and he would have given you living water. . . . Everyone who drinks of this water [Jacob's well] will be thirsty again, but those who drink of the water that I will give them will never be thirsty. The water that I will give will become in them a spring of water gushing up to eternal life" (John 4:10, 13–14 NRSV).

Again we encounter John's (and Jesus') water analogy: living water, an artesian well of the Spirit, springing up to eternal life! Perhaps an even more dramatic example of this sort occurs later in Jerusalem during the Feast of Tabernacles (John 7).

King Solomon, centuries earlier, had probably dedicated his temple during this feast (1 Kings 8:2), and Ezekiel had seen a vision during the time of the exile of a restored temple with water flowing from beneath the threshold (Ezek. 47:1). It was the fall of the year, and Jesus had quietly observed the ongoing activities of the festival. But then came "the last day of the festival, the great day" (John 7:37). For centuries there was strong Jewish expectation that the Messiah, now hidden, would make himself known at this feast. The priest took water in a golden pitcher from the spring of Gihon, which fed the pool of Siloam, as the choir sang, "With joy you will draw water from the wells of salvation" (Isa. 12:3). Various psalms were sung as the crowds followed in joyous procession through the Water Gate and up to the altar, where the water was poured out. Zechariah had prophesied the Messiah's coming (chs. 9–14) at such a time: "On that day a fountain shall be opened for the house of David and the inhabitants of Jerusalem, to cleanse from sin and impurity" (Zech. 13:1 NRSV).

At this most dramatic moment of the festival, Jesus stood forth and cried out (John 7:37–38 NRSV): "Let anyone who is thirsty come to me, And let the one who believes in me drink." Jesus was announcing himself as the source of the "rivers of living water" (v. 38). And John adds editorially that Jesus was speaking of the Spirit who would be given after Jesus was glorified, that is, crucified, resurrected, and ascended (v. 39).[59] Note again the bond between the cross and the Spirit in John. As with Nicodemus and the woman of Samaria, Jesus was offering salvation in the gift of the Holy Spirit. The Spirit himself is the living water. He indwells every believer and brings eternal life. The culmination of these pneumatic passages in the Gospel is the great insufflation of John 20.

"He Breathed on Them"

John 20:19–23 is often called the "Johannine Pentecost."[60] If the intention of this terminology is to indicate John's ignorance of Pentecost or to suggest that no impartation of the Spirit actually transpired that Easter evening, then it is indeed an unfortunate descriptive term. John demonstrates historical precision here with the intention of communicating a momentous event in those disciples' lives.

Jesus suddenly appears to the disciples, who were cowering behind locked doors. He greets them with the traditional Jewish *Shalom!* He shows them his hands and side, and the disciples rejoice. Then Jesus says again to them, "Peace be with you" (vv. 19–21). His next words and actions are truly significant: "'As the Father has sent me, so I send you.' When he had said this, he breathed on them and said to them, 'Receive the Holy Spirit. If you forgive the sins of any, they are forgiven them; if you retain the sins of any they are retained'" (vv. 21–23 NRSV).

Jesus *could* be preparing them for the future Pentecost event, but the nature of Jesus' words and actions as reported by John suggests much more. Jesus' breathing on the disciples evokes Genesis 2:7. The new humanity has begun! Then comes the command to receive the Holy Spirit, whom Jesus is imparting through the insufflation. The gift of the Spirit is preceded by the display of the marks of the cross.

But more is found here. The sending of the disciples with the gospel of forgiveness echoes the Great Commission event of Matthew 28:16–20. The Spirit is given not just as a private possession but to empower for mission. These same disciples, along with others, would be filled with the Holy Spirit on the Day of Pentecost and launched on their worldwide mission (Acts 2). The rubric of Spirit baptism would then encompass both events. But our survey of Johannine pneumatology would not be complete without a careful look at Jesus' upper room teachings prior to his passion.

or on, on, being baptized

The Paraclete

I personally encountered Jesus Christ as Lord and Savior when I was a seven-year-old boy, sitting with my parents and pastor in the pastor's study at the First Baptist Church in Fort Stockton, Texas. Years later, as a teenager, I began to hunger for a greater intimacy with Christ and for boldness in bearing witness to him. During those days, it was as if God gave me personally as a gift chapters 14–16 of John's Gospel, in which Jesus taught his disciples about the ongoing ministry of the Holy Spirit about to take place in their lives.

What originally caught my attention was this statement of Jesus: "Nevertheless I tell you the truth: it is to your advantage that I go away, for if I do not go away, the Advocate [Paraclete] will not come to you; but if I go, I will send him to you" (John 16:7 NRSV). What could be better than having Jesus physically by one's side? Indeed, the disciples often seemed to be dismal failures when he was not there. But Jesus was preparing them for the gift of the indwelling Spirit, whereby both he and the Father could be *in* them twenty-four hours a day!

I also noticed Jesus' words, "He will take what is mine and declare it to you" (v. 14 NRSV). The ministry of the Holy Spirit is to make Jesus more real to us, to reveal him to us and to glorify him through us. That was what I was hungering for! It was the witness and example of my Pentecostal aunt and uncle that gave these words concrete reality in terms of present-day experience. Traditionally, the scholars note five "Paraclete sayings" in John 14–16.

The term *paraclete* signifies "one called alongside to help us" and is often rendered Counselor or Helper. Jesus used this term to describe the ministry of the Holy Spirit in the believer's life as follows: *Helper* (14:15–24): Through the Father's giving us the Spirit the Trinity takes up residence within us. *Teacher* (14:25–26): The Father will send us the Spirit to continue Jesus' teaching ministry among us. *Witness* (15:26–27): Jesus sends the Spirit from the Father to empower our witness. *Judge* (16:4–11): Jesus leaves the earth bodily in order to send the Spirit, who will convict the world of sin, righteousness, and judgment. *Guide* (16:12–15): The Holy Spirit guides us into all truth—the things of Jesus and the Father.[61] Thus, even though John's primary pneumatological focus is ontological, that is, in relation to regeneration, he also includes the functional dimension in terms of an empowered witness.[62]

John's pneumatology then is cross-centered and Christ-centered. It is a needed corrective in some Charismatic circles which have moved toward triumphalism and materialism. Gary M. Burge, a specialist in Johannine pneumatology, expresses it well:

Finally, this dual message of John—that the Spirit is released through the cross and that Christ and Spirit must never be separated—has an important contemporary relevance. Any theology which separates salvation from the life-creating Spirit is inadequate (contra many "second-blessing" theologies). Any theology which separates the acceptance of Jesus from the gift of the Spirit is incorrect. Our experience of the Spirit is wrapped up in our experience of Christ's sacrifice on the cross.

Similarly, the anchor for unbounded enthusiasm must be the glorification of the historical person of Jesus.[63]

But if John is the theologian of the paschal dimension of the Spirit's work, surely Paul is the champion of the purifying dimension.

The Purifying Dimension

Paschal and Pentecostal themes abound in Paul's theology, but the hallmark of his pneumatology is his emphasis on the Spirit's empowerment *for holy living*. As with John, Paul's approach is cross-centered and Christ-centered. He highlights how the Holy Spirit *applies* Christ's saving death and resurrection in our lives—not just at conversion but on a daily basis.

Paul reminded the carnal Corinthians, "But you were washed, you were sanctified, you were justified in the name of the Lord Jesus Christ and in the Spirit of our God" (1 Cor. 6:11 NRSV). His reminder of their past cleansing is also an implicit imperative for holy living in the present. He ties together regeneration, sanctification, and justification and points to the Spirit's work in effecting spiritual transformation through Christ's death and resurrection.[64] In one of Paul's oldest epistles (1 Thess.), the apostle rings a clarion call to holiness by appeal to the Holy Spirit and his work.

He reminds his readers, "For this is the will of God, your sanctification [or holiness, *hagiasmos*]" (1 Thess. 4:3 NRSV). His specific ethical instruction is culminated with these words: "For God did not call us to impurity but in holiness. Therefore whoever rejects this rejects not human authority but God, who also gives his Holy Spirit to you" (vv. 7–8 NRSV). In this perhaps first mention of the gift of the Holy Spirit in Paul's letters, the accent falls on the sanctifying dimension of the Spirit's work. His argument is poignant and penetrating: God calls us to holiness, and the infallible proof of this is that he has given us his *Holy* Spirit. The emphasis on "Holy" in the original is also a reminder that both the Spirit's name and his reality are at stake here. To live sinful lives is to sully his name and deny his reality. Further, God continually "gives" us his Spirit, which is the only means by which we are enabled, or empowered, to live holy lives.[65] Spirit baptism effects not only new birth and empowered witness; it also enables a continually transformed lifestyle. The gospel of Christ is at issue here. And nowhere does the apostle make this clearer than when he presents the gospel (Rom.) and defends it (Gal.).

Romans could easily be named "The Gospel According to Paul." It is his systematic presentation of the gospel and its effects. In reality, it could be called Paul's systematic theology. He joins inseparably in these chapters justification, sanctification, and the gift of the Holy Spirit. But what he has joined we have too often separated. We have preached justification without sanctification and offered, in effect, a "cheap grace" which produces an insipid Christianity. Or we have preached sanctification without justification, which results in crushing legalism or pharisaical pride and deception.[66] But even beyond these errors, we have too often neglected the Holy Spirit's role in these matters. Again, it is "in the Spirit of our God" that we are washed, sanctified, and justified, as well as "in the name of the Lord Jesus Christ" (1 Cor. 6:11 NRSV).

In presenting the human problem of sin and the divine answer of the gospel in the first five chapters of Romans, Paul elevates God's justifying grace above the pervasive problem of sin. Thus, the fifth chapter begins with the triumphant announcement of justification by faith, peace with God, grace, and the hope of glory (Rom. 5:1–2). He concludes that "where sin increased, grace abounded all the more, so that, just as sin exercised dominion in death, so grace might also exercise dominion through justification leading to eternal life through Jesus Christ our Lord" (vv. 20–21). The obvious objection by the opponents to Paul's gospel would be, "Should we continue in sin in order that grace may abound?" (6:1 NRSV). And with these words the apostle launches into the doctrine of sanctification (chs. 6–8). It is a seamless transition.

Romans 6 shows how our identification with Christ's death and resurrection liberates us from sin. We die to sin with Christ to walk in newness of life as slaves of righteousness, which is true freedom. C. E. B. Cranfield has mastered the apostle's concept here.[67] Our death with Christ takes place in four ways, according to the apostle, and this fourfold sense of our identity with Christ's death is being applied in this chapter. Paul's programmatic statement in this regard is: "one has died for all; therefore all have died" (2 Cor. 5:14 NRSV). Here are the four senses: *The Juridical Sense*: By God's gracious decision, when Christ died we all died; God was beginning a whole new humanity in the person of his resurrected Son (2 Cor. 5:14; Col. 3:1–4). *The Baptismal Sense*: We died with Christ and were raised with him at our conversion (Rom. 6:1–4; Col. 2:12). *The Moral Sense*: We experience Christ's death daily as we, by the Spirit, mortify sin in our lives (the major argument of Rom. 6; 8:13; cf. 1 Cor. 15:31; 2 Cor. 1:9; 4:11, referring to Paul's suffering for the gospel). *The Eschatological Sense*: The battle with sin comes to an end with our physical death, and the resurrection completes our redemption from sin and death (Rom. 8:23).

Thus, Christ's death is central to our sanctification. Spirit baptism ultimately applies Christ's death and resurrection to bring about a transformed life. This is the purifying dimension of the Spirit's work. The next two chapters of Romans explain how this takes place.

Romans 7 transports us back to the garden where the first couple fell. Sin, like Satan, seizes the opportunity of God's commandment to deceive us and kill us (Rom. 7:7–12/Gen. 3:1–13). Consequently, we are all "sold into slavery under sin" (v. 14). We suffer from a sort of spiritual schizophrenia (vv. 14–21). Sin now has its camp in our physical bodies, preventing us from fulfilling God's law (vv. 22–25). What is the answer to this moral and spiritual dilemma? It is the cross. It is Christ. It is the Holy Spirit. God does for us what we could never do for ourselves. *Our sanctification is just as much a work of God's grace as our justification!* This is the culmination of Paul's teaching on the Spirit's sanctifying work (Rom. 8).

What the law of Moses could not do because of human depravity *God did*; sending his own Son "in the likeness of sinful flesh" and as an offering for sin, God "condemned sin (cf. the noun form of this verb in v. 1) in the flesh" so that we might fulfill the law by walking "according to the Spirit" (vv. 3–4). "For the law of the Spirit of life in Christ Jesus has set you free from the law of sin and of death," Paul begins (v. 2 NRSV). Three laws are in purview here: (1) the Law of Moses, (2) the law of sin and death, and (3) the law of the Spirit of life in Christ Jesus. Moses' law is powerless to liberate us from the downward pull of sin. The law of sin and death, like gravity, continually pulls us downward. But the law of the Spirit of life in Christ Jesus, like the law of aerodynamics, lifts us to a new level of living! We can now live in the Spirit (v. 4) and have the mind-set (*phronema*) of the Spirit (vv. 5–8). "By the Spirit" we can put to death the evil deeds of the body (v. 13).

We were given the gift of the Holy Spirit to empower us for holy living, not just to do signs and wonders. In fact, as Paul would say elsewhere, without Christlike character, our miraculous gifts are hollow and meaningless (1 Cor. 13). The Spirit wants to liberate us from selfish, sensual, and stingy living into the freedom of a life of loving service to God and others. It is this freedom in the gospel that the apostle defends in his Galatian epistle.

The Galatian believers were being enticed by false teachers to go back under the law by requiring circumcision for salvation. But Paul would have none of it; he had already been down that road:

> You foolish Galatians! Who put a spell on you? Before your very eyes you had a clear description of the death of Jesus Christ on the cross! Tell me this one thing: did you receive God's Spirit by doing what the Law requires or by hearing the gospel and believing it? How can you be so foolish! You began by God's Spirit; do you now want to finish by your own power? Did all your experience mean nothing at all? Surely it meant something! Does God give you the Spirit and work miracles among you because you do what the Law requires or because you hear the gospel and believe it? (Gal. 3:1–5 GNB).

Notice here how all three dimensions of the Spirit's work—paschal, purifying, and Pentecostal—are made available through the gospel. *The gift of the Spirit, Spirit baptism, brings with it new birth, new life, and miraculous ministry.* Only the Spirit himself can regenerate, sanctify, and empower us. And all of this has its source in the gospel of Christ, publicly portrayed as crucified.

The apostle was exhorting his readers to refuse to lose their freedom in Christ: "For freedom Christ has set us free. Stand firm, therefore, and do not submit again to a yoke of slavery" (Gal. 5:1 NRSV). To receive circumcision after receiving the gospel was to cut oneself off from Christ, to fall from grace (vv. 2–4). "For through the Spirit, by faith, we eagerly wait for the hope of righteousness" (v. 5 NRSV). Living in the Spirit liberates us from the bondage of sin and the destructive works of our fallen nature (vv. 16–21). Now we are free to harvest the Spirit's fruit in our lives (5:22–23; 6:7–8). "And those who belong to Christ Jesus have crucified the flesh with its passions and desires" (5:24 NRSV). Again, the Spirit applies Christ's cross in our lives.

And here is Paul's bottom line: "Since we live by the Spirit, let us keep in step with the Spirit" (v. 25). The words "keep in step" translate the Greek term *stoikeñ,* which is a military term: Since we have our very lives by the Spirit, we are under obligation to let him direct our lives. When we do so, we are enabled to love one another and thus fulfill the whole law (v. 14).

This was the gospel Paul defended. The "full gospel," to use a popular Charismatic phrase, entails justification *and* sanctification as well as Charismatic empowerment. And it is only by the power of the Spirit that we can "rightly proclaim, savingly appropriate, and effectively live out the gospel."[68] But the Pentecostals and Charismatics still have a point: The Spirit *has* come "to empower us to do the same kingdom work our Lord did in his earthly ministry. And that work was in major part a *Charismatic* work!"[69]

The Pentecostal Dimension

Luke's two-volume work is centered on salvation. As the song of Simeon says in part: "for my eyes have seen your salvation, which you have prepared in the presence of all peoples, a light for revelation to the Gentiles and for glory to your people Israel" (Luke 2:30–32 NRSV).

Jesus said to Zacchaeus, "Today salvation has come to this house" and then announces of himself, "For the Son of Man came to seek out and to save the lost" (19:9–10 NRSV). Thus, Luke depicts the spread of the gospel of the kingdom from Galilee to Jerusalem (Jesus) and from Jerusalem to Rome (the early church), a saving gospel for both Jew and Gentile and for every strata of society.[70] And without doubt, Luke highlights the role of the Holy Spirit in the spread of this gospel. From the infancy narratives onward the Spirit is explicitly mentioned as the enabler of the mission. "The Holy Spirit, then, is the means, the person who empowers the disciples as well as Jesus for preaching, teaching, and healing."[71]

Further, the ministry in which we see Jesus and the disciples engaged is in large measure *Charismatic* in nature. Using the terminology of the Old Testament (LXX), narratives of the Spirit's Charismatic activity (e.g., the judges, Samuel, Elijah, and Elisha), Luke pens an account of Jesus and the early church rife with pneumatic activity—signs and wonders of every sort, both in Luke and Acts. His is truly a Pentecostal/Charismatic pneumatology.[72]

But how should we relate to Luke-Acts in our own day? To be sure, Charismatic activity is found only sporadically in Israel's history and in the history of the church. The Pentecostal phenomenon of the twentieth century is virtually nonpareil in this regard. How should we interpret this? Are these the last days? Every time, in every century, when such increased spiritual activity emerges, eschatological expectations run high. Only God knows the day and the hour. But one thing is certain: Pentecostalism reminds us, as does the book of Acts, that the secret to our success in mission is the power of the Spirit.

Present-day Pentecostals have led the way in world missions, and we have tried every way possible to explain their success in pragmatic terms alone. Could their success be tied to their name? Could it be that these sacrificial saints have simply tapped into the power of Pentecost, the empowering dimension of Spirit baptism, and many others of us simply have not?

I have learned much about the Holy Spirit—as a student, as chaplain of the university, and as a faculty member—from the dear saints of Oral Roberts University. When Oral Roberts addressed the first class of the university on September 7, 1965, he laid down a vision in terms of a "quest for the whole person." He said in part: "Your spiritual development includes a new birth through repentance and faith in the Lord Jesus Christ, a constant cleansing of your inner self from sin, the baptism in the Holy Spirit in the

Charismatic dimension for empowerment and personal edification, a manifestation of the gifts of the Holy Spirit through you for meeting the needs of others, a personal witness of your Master to your fellow man, and a daily application of Christian principles to the demands of daily life."[73]

It is that "baptism in the Holy Spirit in the Charismatic dimension" which I am presenting and defending in this chapter. It is what Luke poignantly depicted in Luke-Acts, and it is what Pentecostals and Charismatics in general have been recommending to the church at large for a century now.

In short, the Pentecostal dimension of Spirit baptism reminds us of our need perennially for *revival*. But revivals are not neat. They are chaotic, disruptive. There are excesses and counterfeits. But they also get us off dead center and help us overcome spiritual inertia. They are sovereign outpourings of the Holy Spirit, like Pentecost, and they move us along in mission.

Martyn Lloyd-Jones, great Evangelical expositor and theologian, unsettled many in his call for this dimension of the Spirit's work. Consider these prophetic words:

Examine your doctrine of the Holy Spirit, and in the name of God, be careful lest, in your neat and trimmed doctrine, you are excluding and putting out this most remarkable thing which God does periodically through the Holy Spirit, in sending him upon us, in visiting, in baptizing us, in reviving the whole Church in a miraculous and astonishing manner.[74]

Do you believe in revival, my friend? Are you praying for revival? What are you trusting? Are you trusting the organizing power of the church? Or are you trusting in the power of God to pour out his Spirit upon us again, to revive us, to baptize us anew and afresh with his most blessed Holy Spirit? The church needs another Pentecost. Every revival is a repetition of Pentecost, and it is the greatest need of the Christian church at this present hour.[75]

In these passages and throughout these works, Lloyd-Jones, careful exegete that he is, uses the Spirit baptism metaphor in the empowering sense, as does Luke. Perhaps we should examine again our rigid rubrics. There is always more. We can anticipate and welcome future outpourings of the Spirit.

The Holy Spirit is the executive of the church on mission. John V. Taylor expresses it well: "The chief actor in the historic mission of the Christian church is the Holy Spirit. He is the director of the whole enterprise. The mission consists of the things that he is doing in the world. In a special way it consists of the light he is focusing upon Jesus."[76]

Therefore, the church of the twenty-first century must seek anew the Pentecostal empowerment in order to fulfill her mission. The world needs Jesus Christ, and God has given us his Spirit to bring him in all his fullness to all the peoples of the world.

Jesus went about teaching, preaching, and healing (Matt. 4:23; 9:35). And he is "the same yesterday and today and forever" (Heb. 13:8). Why should there not be a Charismatic/healing dimension to our own ministry today, if we truly are his body? Luke's pneumatology serves as a constant reminder that there *is* an empowering/Charismatic/revival dimension to Spirit baptism. There is more after conversion than merely "gutting it out 'til glory." But the church has known this all along. A brief perusal of past revitalization movements corroborates this fact.

Puritanism

There would have been no twentieth-century Pentecostal/Charismatic tradition without the Puritans. At first blush, such a statement seems ludicrous. What two traditions could be further apart in religious ethos? We have the rational versus the experiential, Calvinism versus Arminianism. But the Puritans are like the Pentecostals in a number of striking ways. Furthermore, American religious soil, enriched by the Puritan vision well into the twentieth century, produced a kind of Charismatic Christianity which evinced a continuation of Puritan values.

The Puritans were biblical restorationists, seeking to return to the simplicity of worship and witness of the New Testament church. They inherited the mysticism and intense personal quest for holiness of St. Augustine, and St. Bernard, and the whole medieval tradition from which Puritanism emerged. Assurance of faith became increasingly associated with a crisis experience, a mentality that would dominate the Great Awakening. Jonathan Edwards exemplified this spiritual set, and today even some theological leaders in the Pentecostal/Charismatic tradition would reflect Edwards's appreciation for the life of the mind in service to God.[77] Perhaps the greatest influence of Puritanism was doctrinal.

Puritan pneumatology was linked primarily to assurance of faith. The Puritans prepared themselves for the grace of conversion in much the same way as the early Pentecostals prepared themselves for a personal Pentecost, with great emphasis on the work of the Holy Spirit.[78] In America the quest for knowledge of one's being elect led to the belief in an experience of assurance subsequent to one's conversion. Martin E. Marty describes this phenomenon thus: "In seventeenth-century America, New England Puritans, already members of the covenant, had to have an experience of 'owning the covenant' in order to become spiritually elite. This act compares to the pentecostal quest for a second blessing."[79]

Perhaps the Puritan's greatest influence would be exerted through John Wesley. More will be said about this later.

In our own day Charismatic Southern Baptist broadcaster Pat Robertson could be called a contemporary Puritan. Believing that the faith should be applied to all of culture and possessing a strong experiential faith, while at the same time valuing the life of the mind, Robertson often grates on modern and postmodern viewers who long ago capitulated to rationalism and relativism. J. I. Packer, though not known as a Charismatic, still promotes the Puritan vision while at the same time evincing an appreciation for and affirmation of the Pentecostals and Charismatics. And John Piper, popular writer and pastor, also combines the best of Puritan and Charismatic spirituality. As the Evangelical and Charismatic streams continue to merge, lines of demarcation increasingly blur. Each movement is learning from the other, and local churches now often bring both together in Christian fellowship and service.

The Puritans were pietistic in their approach to spirituality. Today, unfortunately, piety is most often viewed as a pejorative term. Nevertheless, present-day Evangelicalism in general and Pentecostalism and Charismatic renewal in particular, are simply incomprehensible apart from their roots in European Pietism.

Pietism

F. Ernest Stoeffler, in his specialty studies of Pietism, has helped alert us all to the pervasive influence of this tradition.[80] There was a Lutheran Pietism, an English Puritan Pietism, and a

Reformed Pietism, according to Stoeffler. And there were four major characteristics of this widely influential movement. The first was an emphasis on religious experience, which certainly has its parallels in the twentieth- and twenty-first centuries. There was a clarion call to holiness in this movement. And strong appeal was also made to the Bible as the norm for faith and practical living. Finally, there was the prophetic call to the church, lacking in these areas, to reform and renewal.[81] We see these same dynamics today.

Philipp Jakob Spener (1635–1705) exemplifies Pietism at its best. His *Pia Desideria* remains a classic to this day, and much of his advice has been heeded. Spener argued cogently for the priesthood of the believer and the role and function of laity in ministry. He established small Bible study groups—what would be called cell groups today—for the purpose of greater interaction and more direct discipleship. This method, too, has been implemented today with great effectiveness. David Yonggi Cho pastors the world's largest church in Seoul, Korea, on this model. Spener wanted to reform the training of ministers on a more practical model and stressed personal piety and simplicity of doctrine. All of these ideas have become important in our own day.[82]

Count Nikolaus Ludwig von Zinzendorf (1700–1760) would be a leader in the Charismatic movement were he alive today! He was a product of the Pietism advocated by Spener and perpetuated at the University of Halle. Both leaders had an ecumenical spirit, much as is witnessed in the Charismatic movement today. But it was the missionary zeal of Zinzendorf and the Moravians that etched them on the memories of Christians since their day. Again, contemporary Pentecostalism leads the way in this regard as well. It was just that missionary zeal and confident assurance of faith that influenced John Wesley toward the vital life and ministry that would profoundly impact the church down to the present.

Wesleyanism

John Wesley is the father of the contemporary Pentecostal/Charismatic tradition. His experience during that perilous storm on the Atlantic, which ultimately led him to Aldersgate, would launch a movement whose impact is felt even to this day. In John Wesley, Puritanism and Pietism converge and coincide. Stoeffler states it well: "What we are dealing with, then, when we are talking of Methodist origins in America is a confluence of Puritan and Pietist impulses, the resulting Evangelicalism being as closely patterned on its Pietist as on its Puritan model."[83] Thus, we are all children of Wesley. It was particularly Wesley's perfectionism that would be bequeathed to the Pentecostals.

Wesley taught a doctrine and experience of Christian perfection or entire sanctification: a punctiliar experience of purification that freed the believer from the power of sin. The influence and importance of this teaching can hardly be overemphasized. James D. G. Dunn aptly summarizes these developments as follows: "Within more radical and pietistic Protestantism there has grown up a tradition which holds that salvation, so far as it may be known in this life, is experienced in two stages: first, the experience of becoming a Christian; then, as a later and distinct event, a second experience of the Holy Spirit. For many Puritans the second experience was one of assurance. For Wesley the first stage was justification and partial sanctification, the second the divine gift of entire sanctification or Christian perfection."[84]

Without doubt, this concept of the Christian life strongly impacted Pentecostalism and the Charismatic movement. The early Pentecostals either added a third blessing of Spirit baptism or stayed with two blessings, conceiving sanctification more in terms of a lifetime process. This concept of *subsequence* is all-important in Pentecostal theology to this day.

How does one evaluate this doctrine and experience? Wisdom teaches us never to belittle or write off anyone's experience, but to discern it according to the Scriptures. Could it be that a dimensional approach provides insight in this regard? Surely Craig Keener is correct when he concludes that "the whole sphere of the Spirit's work becomes available at conversion, but believers may experience some aspects of the Spirit's work only subsequent to conversion."[85] Therefore, one *could* have an authentic experience of purification or empowerment subsequent to the new birth. The error creeps in with the "punctiliar fallacy" that this one experience constitutes a person as permanently "perfected" or "Spirit-filled."

Wesley was a revivalist at heart. His Arminian approach combined with George Whitefield's Calvinistic approach to form the revival ethos of American Christianity. And, if anything can be asserted incontrovertibly about the Pentecostal/Charismatic tradition, it is that this tradition teaches, embraces, and promotes revivalism.

Revivalism

American Christianity, rooted in the spread of the church across the "frontier," has always been enamored with and fascinated by revivalism. Revivalism has been profoundly formative of our religious ethos. And the "Pentecostals claim a direct lineage from the religious revivals."[86] It is difficult to overestimate the significance of the handful of revival outbreaks which have molded American Christianity. The last is the greatest: worldwide Pentecostalism.[87] But in America, clear experiential and doctrinal preparation came in the form of the Holiness revivals of the nineteenth century which called the Evangelicals (a major portion of whom were Methodists) back to the revival fires of Wesley.

The leaders of the twentieth- and twenty-first-century Pentecostal/Charismatic revivals have not been as impressive theologically as those of previous eras: Edwards, Whitefield, Wesley, Luther, and Calvin, for example. But their influence nonetheless has been widespread. The Pentecostals are the present-day harbingers of hope in a chaotic and violent world. William J. Seymour led the way at the turn of the twentieth century in the great Azusa Street revival in Los Angeles, which launched the worldwide movement. Harvey Cox states it well:

> Pentecostalism has become a global vehicle for the restoration of primal hope. The movement started from the bottom. A partially blind, poor, black man with little or no book learning outside of the Bible heard a call. Seymour was anything but a Paul of Tarsus, trained by the leading religious scholars, or an Augustine of Hippo, schooled by the most polished Roman rhetoricians, or a Calvin or Luther educated in the original languages of scripture. He was a son of former slaves who had to listen to sermons through a window and who undoubtedly traveled to Los Angeles in the segregated section of the train. Yet under Seymour's guidance, a movement arose whose impact on Christianity, less than a century after his arrival in Los Angeles, has been compared to the Protestant Reformation.[88]

Seymour's leadership is needed today. He evinced a humility too often missing among Charismatic preachers who strut and huff and puff across our television screens today. He also demonstrated a wisdom and honesty so desperately missing in some quarters. Seymour did not care how many tongues a person had spoken in: if their hearts were still filled with racism, there was no way they could claim to be baptized in the Holy Spirit.[89] Seymour was, in effect, the father of a great tradition of Christianity, a possible fourth branch of Christendom, and much gratitude is owed this humble servant who died in obscurity.

Thus, the massive spiritual forces which reached our shores from Europe did much to form who we are today. And we have much more in common than we think, as we trace our common religious lineages. This perspective enables us to respect and receive from one another more readily. Scratch deeply enough and you will find a Puritan and Pietist in us all. Some of us, particularly the Pentecostals and Charismatics of this study, will identify more readily with John Wesley than with others. And our responses to revival outbreaks will continue to be diverse. Nevertheless, we are spiritual siblings who are inextricably bound to one another, like it or not. And maturity demands that we learn to like it.

Historical Mileposts

Historical perspectives, as we have already seen, can often clarify theological debates. In addition to the broader movements noted above, one could also trace Charismatic outbreaks down through church history and note that the Charismatic dimension did not simply die out with the apostles. But more helpful still for our theological purposes in this study would be an overview of Pentecostalism and the Charismatic movement as specifically American phenomena. A perusal of historical mileposts is instructive on a number of fronts. As the movement developed, diversified, and spread into the mainline churches, all sorts of new theological issues and challenges emerged, and more will be said about this later. But a brief list of key dates and events provides perspective in sifting through present issues:

1901   "Outpouring" at Charles F. Parham's Bethel Bible College, Topeka, Kansas

1906   The beginning of the Azusa Street Revival in Los Angeles, California
1932   End of the primary formation of classical Pentecostal denominations
1948   The appearance of the healing revivalists such as William Branham and Oral Roberts
1951   Founding of the Full Gospel Business Men's Fellowship International
1960   Dennis Bennett, rector of St. Mark's Episcopal Church, Van Nuys, California, announces his Charismatic experience to his congregation: beginning of public awareness of a Neo-Pentecostal movement and more rapid spread of the movement
1966   First stirrings of Catholic Charismatic renewal (well under way in 1967)
1971   The Jesus Movement comes to public attention (stirrings began around 1967)
1975   Emergence of the shepherding-discipleship controversy
1981   The "Third Wave" Evangelical/Charismatic movement emerges
1993   The Toronto Revival begins
1995   The Pensacola Revival begins

As the above events unfolded, Christians of all stripes were increasingly being confronted with searching questions in relation to the work of the Holy Spirit.

What is the nature of the Spirit-filled life? What does Spirit baptism signify according to the Scriptures? What is the place of speaking in tongues in the Christian life and the life of the church? What about healing and other Charismatic gifts? As the renewal spread into the traditional churches, adherents were faced with the challenge of providing a theological basis compatible with their given tradition. But revival does not lend itself easily to theological analysis. How does one gauge present realities?

Flux and ferment are the norm at present. Old forms of revival and renewal have lessened in vitality in many quarters, and new forms are only beginning to emerge. A blending of ecclesial cultures is now taking place, the future parameters of which are impossible to predict. Speaking in tongues is more widely accepted, and yet it is less emphasized than it was during the apex of the original renewal. Christians think decreasingly in terms of a discreet sequence of experiences and more in terms of a pilgrimage of discipleship. The Great Commandment and Great Commission are becoming increasingly formative of the churches' overall vision. These are truly exciting and intriguing times!

Effective strategies for the future require sound theological foundations. Thus, the explorations and dialogue of the present volume seem all the more crucial. The theological and practical suggestions which follow are meant to further this overall process.

Theological Issues

The doctrinal lineage which lies behind the traditional understanding of Spirit baptism in the Pentecostal/Charismatic tradition explains in large measure the dynamics of the present debates. A direct line can be drawn from Pentecostalism back to the nineteenth-century Holiness movement to John Wesley himself and on to Anglicanism and finally Roman Catholicism. All these traditions are comfortable with the concept of subsequent works of grace. Thus, the Reformed heritage, on largely a separate track, will balk at Spirit baptism as taught by the Pentecostals and Charismatics. Yet even among those of this shared heritage of subsequence, a wide doctrinal diversity persists. Profound differences continue on issues of sacramentalism, perfectionism, and Pentecostalism. Perhaps the dimensional approach to the work of the Holy Spirit can shed further light on a number of theological issues.

The Pentecostal/Charismatic tradition has placed eschatology on the front burner. Not only do expectations run high for the return of Christ. The view of the nature of the Christian life has also been clarified. There is an "already-not yet" dimension to Christian life and experience which too often was ignored in the past. Salvation is seen as a *process* of past, present, and future dimensions. At present, "we know only in part, and we prophesy only in part" (1 Cor. 13:9 NRSV). The Spirit's work is a *continuing* work. There is no one experience which constitutes us as sanctified or empowered. A dimensional approach to Spirit baptism sees Christ's eschatological ministry continuing on into the new millennium. And our walk in the Spirit anticipates innumerable spiritual breakthroughs. There is no arrival until the King himself arrives!

Water baptism and the Lord's Supper can also take on new significance. One can anticipate manifestations of the Spirit's presence in the waters of baptism, much as in the book of Acts. The Lord's Supper becomes an occasion for a vivid communion with the risen Savior and all the saints. The ordinances (or sacraments) become the means of faith, and the Spirit himself is the means of grace. Grace is seen as God's Spirit in saving action on our behalf—rescuing, transforming, comforting, consolidating.

Spiritual gifts have already taken on renewed significance in our day. Twentieth-century Pentecostalism and Charismatic renewal have influenced large segments of the church to learn afresh what God's Word teaches in this area. The twenty-first-century church shows the greatest promise ever in terms of a people mobilized in worldwide ministry. We have learned that the total ministry of the church is Charismatic in nature. The *charismata* listed in the New Testament are both real and representative, and all are vital. We are learning that we *can* do the works that Jesus did (John 14:12)! We truly are his body.

We are being increasingly confronted, in the face of the pressing needs all around us, with the crucial question of precisely what it means to be empowered by the Holy Spirit. Necessity has become the mother of discovery! We are becoming more appreciative of our interdependence and the need for cooperation. And awareness of the supernatural has increased.

Perhaps a brief look back at how Charismatics in their various ecclesial contexts have attempted to theologize the work of the Spirit will be instructive for us as we attempt to tie loose theological threads together and explore the practical implications of our findings.

The Theology of Charismatic Renewal

The one constant in life is change, and this maxim is especially applicable to the Pentecostal/Charismatic tradition. Between 1901 and 1932 some two hundred Pentecostal denominations were formed in America. Two to three decades later, Pentecostalism had begun to spread into the mainline churches. By the sixties and early seventies, the shift upward socially had created a widely variegated movement. One notices across the board a broad diversity of doctrine, polities, styles of worship, and cultural orientations.

At the same time there is a demonstrable unity in terms of a basic conception of Spirit baptism. Scratch the average Charismatic, and underneath one finds a classical Pentecostal. The virtually monolithic perspective on Spirit baptism among both classical Pentecostals and Charismatics is that of (1) subsequence and (2) speaking in tongues. Spirit baptism is viewed as a definite experience subsequent to conversion, and the generally anticipated sign of this experience is speaking in tongues. As has already been mentioned, Charismatics are "softer" on the tongues issue. Nevertheless, it is usually held that even though one may not initially speak in tongues when baptized in the Spirit, that experience is available and will most likely manifest itself shortly thereafter.

Pentecostals generally view tongues as the "initial physical evidence" of Spirit baptism; this is a doctrinal distinctive. This "law of tongues," as their critics have often described it, sets them apart from even the Charismatics themselves. And yet the Pentecostals and Charismatics are not dramatically different in their broader conception of the nature of Spirit baptism and the Spirit-filled life. Certainly in the early days of the spread of Charismatic renewal in the mainline churches, the Charismatic message was couched almost verbatim in classical Pentecostal language: "Have you received 'the baptism,' brother?" followed with the further clarifying question, "Have you spoken in tongues?" It is easy to understand why there was resistance to this approach. One does not easily foist one tradition upon another! I have vivid personal memories in this regard.

I served for five years, during my seminary training, as an associate pastor in a Southern Baptist church that was promoting Charismatic renewal. The doctrinal dissertation upon which I was laboring was a critique of American Pentecostal/Charismatic theology. During our regional conferences I kept exhorting the pastors to begin laboring on a theology of renewal which flowed out of Baptist tradition. But in the main they seemed to be content to "foist Assemblies of God doctrine on Southern Baptists," as I phrased it. Because of personal friendships and even family relations with Assemblies of God folk, I had tremendous respect for this denomination, which continues to be a leading denomination both here and abroad. Nevertheless, I had already seen how Charismatic renewal was being more favorably received by Presbyterians, Episcopalians,

Methodists, Roman Catholics, and others who had sought to provide a theological undergirding for the renewal compatible with their respective traditions. What follows is a broad-stroke depiction of some of these efforts along with a brief analysis of present progress.

Larry Christenson was an early pioneer in the field of neo-Pentecostal, or Charismatic, theology. A Lutheran pastor, theologian, and author, Christenson was perhaps the first to forge new trails in Charismatic theology. His *Speaking in Tongues and Its Significance for the Church* was possibly the first major attempt to interpret Charismatic renewal in non-Pentecostal terms.[90] Christenson provided balanced guidelines for the renewal in an effort to promote congregational unity. Nevertheless, some of his counsel must have been as shocking to Pentecostals and Charismatics as to traditionalists: "When a person feels that this experience [speaking in tongues] is not for him, that the Holy Spirit is working in his life in other ways, that is his decision, and there should be no implication that he is 'less of a Christian' than someone else who speaks in tongues. In fact, it misses the whole spirit of 1 Corinthians 12 to compare one Christian to another in such a way. We are members of His body—each one unique, each one dealt with by the Lord in individual ways."[91]

Later Christenson related how Catholic Charismatic leaders had impressed upon him the need to develop renewal theologies in consonance with one's tradition rather than simply borrowing from classical Pentecostal categories. He also observed that in the early days of the renewal among Lutherans, too often a rather uncritical and unreflective theology with a less-than-adequate hermeneutic was evident.[92]

In his matured Charismatic theology Christenson argued for an "organic" approach which sees renewal experiences as simply a release, flowering, or actualization of the power of the Spirit received at Christian initiation. He rejected the idea of Spirit baptism as a "second baptism" distinct from Christian baptism.[93] Curiously, however, Christenson differentiated between a doctrinal and an experiential significance to Spirit baptism. Every true Christian has been baptized in the Holy Spirit according to the Bible's *doctrinal* teaching, but not necessarily so in an *experiential* sense.[94] But what biblical basis could he offer for such a distinction? His counsel on speaking in tongues was similarly ambivalent.

He states that "it may well be that [speaking in tongues] does have a special relationship to the baptism with the Holy Spirit," but he never expounds this statement. Instead, he affirms that all do not speak in tongues, even in Pentecostal churches, and that this fact should not be alarming:

> As a pastor, it does not disturb me that some of my members do not speak in tongues. I feel no urgency to highlight this particular gift, except as a member might inquire about it, or as it would come up in a sermon text or Bible study. Yet, if *nobody* in the congregation had this gift, then I would be concerned—just as I would be concerned if I discovered that nobody was praying, nobody was studying Scripture, nobody was being healed, nobody was giving, nobody was growing in holiness. These are the kinds of things which *should* be happening in a normal congregation.[95]

If speaking in tongues has a special relationship to Spirit baptism, then it *should* concern him as a pastor if all do not speak in tongues. However, he ironically states a pastoral position that many on every side of the Spirit baptism issue would find attractive. There seems to be a disjunction here between the theological and the pastoral.

More recently Christenson has explicated the Christian life in general and life in the Spirit in particular by use of a parable (or allegory): the Lewis and Clark expedition. The explicit Trinitarian perspective and sage advice throughout strongly recommend his presentation. His views on Spirit baptism and speaking in tongues remain the same, with one significant exception: he has moved from speaking about the "release" of the Spirit to asserting the preferability of using the term *receive*.[96] Thus, both theological and pastoral questions remain.

Christenson provides a helpful case study in the development of Charismatic theology. There seems always to have been a hesitancy among Charismatic scholars to break cleanly from classical Pentecostal categories. J. Rodman Williams, renowned Presbyterian Charismatic scholar, evinces similar tendencies. Williams's earlier works argued for an "organic" approach similar to that of Christenson, viewing renewal experiences as a *release* of that which had already been received in Christian initiation.[97] However, his later thinking seems to move back toward traditional classical Pentecostal categories.[98]

Both scholars give exemplary counsel against artificial and divisive "haves and have-nots" categories, and both have a sincere and legitimate desire to communicate the significance and beauty of renewal experiences. The doctrinal tack adopted, however, still works against some of their shared goals. British Charismatic Tom Smail would take the discussion a step further.

Smail states straightforwardly that second blessing teaching— Holiness, Pentecostal, and Charismatic—tends to divide the Christian life into artificial categories divorced from the centrality of the gospel of grace. It tends further to divide Christians into superior and inferior categories, a sort of spiritual elitism: "The Charismatics dare not claim to be exclusively Charismatic, but simply to remind the Church of the neglected Charismatic element that is at the basis of its life."[99] Yet even Smail gets caught in the second blessing thicket, asserting that, biblically, Spirit baptism refers to an experience of Charismatic empowerment subsequent to regeneration.[100]

As a Protestant theologian, I can fully appreciate the concerns of these sterling scholars. How is it possible to interpret the "new-ness" of Charismatic life in traditional categories? The burden lies in how to interpret biblically and theologically the *new* things the Holy Spirit is doing in our midst. But alas we finally discover that the new is as old as the Bible itself and that traditional categories have plenty of room for the Charismatic dimension. Perhaps the scholars of the Catholic Charismatic renewal have led the way in this regard.

Catholic Charismatic renewal was unique in its origins in that leading scholars and clerics were involved from the outset. Historically, Roman Catholicism has often had an easier time of assimilating renewal movements of all kinds by simply "baptizing" them into the church—forming new orders and/or immediately placing the movements under ecclesial and pastoral supervision. After the initial Pentecostal explosion in the Catholic church,[101] scholars immediately went to work interpreting and correcting the movement. And, more often than not, these scholars were *partici-pants* in the movement, or at least sympathetic observers.

Ultimately, Léon Joseph Cardinal Suenens, one of the four moderators of the Vatican II Council, internationally renowned and respected scholar, and a participant in Charismatic renewal himself, was appointed by the pope to oversee Catholic Charismatic renewal worldwide. Suenens was careful to guard the church's teaching on Spirit baptism as integral to Christian initiation, yet was also able engagingly to interpret and even recommend the renewal to one and all. His *A New Pentecost?* was a landmark in the theology of Charismatic renewal. In effect, Suenens announced that the message of the Charismatic renewal to the church was twofold: (1) "Be converted!" and (2) "Be filled!"[102] He viewed the Pentecostal outpouring of the Spirit as a hopeful sign to be welcomed, in the main, by the church. At the same time, he warned against elitism: "Every Christian is Charismatic by definition; the difference lies in our degree of faith, our awareness of this fundamental and necessarily common reality."[103]

A more recent publication coming out of this vast field of scholarship is the magisterial *Christian Initiation and Baptism in the Holy Spirit,* by two leading Catholic Charismatic scholars, Kilian McDonnell and George T. Montague.[104] Providing a thorough overview of biblical teaching on Spirit baptism as well as the teaching and practices of the church in the first eight centuries, McDonnell and Montague demonstrate the soundness biblically, theologically, and pastorally of refusing to violate the unity of the Scriptures' teaching on Spirit baptism as a shared, common reality of the entire church.

A summary comment by Montague expresses well the wisdom of this perspective. Montague concludes that, biblically, the initial gift of the Spirit, Spirit baptism, *"is not static but is meant to grow"* (Titus 3:5; 2 Cor. 3:18). He continues:

> The Pentecostal experience is a reality in the modern church, and the fact that as a means of evangelization it is far outdistancing the efforts of the mainline churches should make the more sacramentally oriented pay attention. The element which the Pentecostals have touched on is the one largely neglected in the mainline sacramental churches—that the Spirit received is manifested Charismatically and will indeed do so, if one has such an expectation and has not *a priori* excluded it. God, of

course, is not limited by our subjective disposition. But ordinarily God takes us where we are.[105]

The insights of this sacramental approach to the theology of Charismatic renewal can be easily translated into a nonsacramental perspective.

A dimensional approach to Spirit baptism gleans the benefits of all the above insights from both Protestant and Catholic Charismatic scholars.[106] The biblical and theological unity of Spirit baptism is maintained. Spiritual elitism is avoided. A static punctiliar and "arrival" mentality is averted. And hope is given for further renewal and empowerment.

First, a dimensional approach takes us back to the original announcement of John the Baptist of Jesus' eschatological redemptive work. This is a Christ-centered and cross-centered approach. Spirit baptism points to the totality of Christ's saving work—past, present, and future. This is a Trinitarian approach which refuses to allow the violation of the *unity* of the redemptive work of our Triune God.

Second, Spirit baptism is seen biblically as referring unambiguously to Christian initiation. "For in one Spirit we were all baptized into one body—Jews or Greeks, slaves or free—and all were made to drink of one Spirit" (1 Cor. 12:13 ESV). A contemporary paraphrase and doctrinal application of this programmatic verse might be: We have all received Spirit baptism—whether Catholic or Orthodox, Pentecostal or Baptist, Methodist or Presbyterian, and so forth—we have all been made to drink of one Spirit. There truly is one body, one Spirit, one hope, one Lord, one faith, one baptism, one God and Father of us all, "who is above all and through all and in all" (Eph. 4:4–6 NRSV).

Third, Spirit baptism encompasses the entirety of our Christian lives (Titus 3:5; 2 Cor. 3:18). It entails not only regeneration, but also the ongoing sanctification of life. Christian living is an eschatological reality, an already-not yet pilgrimage of faith enabled by the Holy Spirit.

Fourth, Spirit baptism provides empowerment for Christian mission and ministry. Thanks to the Pentecostals, we are recovering this Charismatic dimension of the baptism in the Holy Spirit. And despite all its foibles and fallacies, the Charismatic movement—comprised of *people,* not angels—has done a great service for the church as well. Prophetic movements in general keep the church from "playing church." We have to be prodded perennially to be honest and humble in our quest for divine direction and empowerment.

Finally, there are a number of practical benefits in taking a dimensional approach to conceptualizing and appropriating the Spirit's work in our lives. The practical issues I will address below derive primarily from my own pilgrimage of faith and personal observations of the contemporary church scene. Thus, the scope will be necessarily limited and patently incomplete. Nonetheless, these issues have already proven their importance to the spiritual health and effectiveness of the church, and they are worthy of exploration.

The Empowered Church

Whatever our views of Spirit baptism, we all share the common goals of an empowered church fulfilling her God-given mission. *Marturia* is the source of all that the church does as she reaches out to a lost and dying world. *Koinonia,* that supernatural participation we share in the Holy Spirit, brings us together in worship, fellowship, and discipleship. And *diakonia* mobilizes us in loving service to one another and to the world. The Holy Spirit is the executive director of this entire mission—a mission which is inspired and guided by the vision of the Great Commandment (Mark 12:29–31) and the Great Commission (Matt. 28:18–20).

Anyone at all familiar with the church growth scene would know that I am echoing here the teachings of Rick Warren, senior pastor of the highly influential Saddleback Church in Lake Forest, California.[107] The Saddleback model for doing church has influenced churches of every stripe, including the Assemblies of God, which have adopted and adapted this model (from a Southern Baptist church!) for their own uses. Warren has addressed their national conferences and in general has been a generous, unselfish friend, as he is to all churches and church leaders asking for help.

Another increasingly influential megachurch is Southeast Christian Church in Louisville, Kentucky, with some seventeen thousand in weekend attendance.[108] Having lived in Louisville for nine years and having kept in touch with the miraculous growth of this vital congregation, I have observed that large numbers of Charismatics have been attracted to this church, while many of their former churches have struggled in church growth. If Charismatics corner the market on the Spirit's power, then why are many nonCharismatic congregations outstripping them in growth? Could it be that there is more to being empowered by the Spirit than is traditionally understood in Charismatic circles? The fact of the matter is that there are many dysfunctional Pentecostal and Charismatic churches (just as there are the same in other traditions). They have the name of being alive but are, in all honesty, dead (cf. Rev. 3:1).

In another writing I have characterized a number models for doing church—traditional models (mainline, Evangelical, Charismatic), the Saddleback model (purpose-driven), the Willow Creek model (seeker-targeted), the Apostolic model (apostolic leaders), the Toronto model (revival orientation), the Metachurch model (cell-based), and even Leonard Sweet's AquaChurch model, reaching out to postmoderns![109] I have noted that there are examples of vital, growing churches using each of these models (or hybrids thereof). What is the secret of their empowerment? My opinion is that they have all, in their own way, tapped into the power of Spirit baptism.

Sooner or later, Charismatics are going to have to admit that there is more to being empowered by the Spirit than a crisis infilling and speaking in tongues. I know too many carnal, powerless, fruitless, even mean-spirited tongues speakers who claim to be "Spirit filled." James D. G. Dunn is precisely correct when he states: "The powerless non-Pentecostal Christian has a need no different from that of the powerless Pentecostal Christian."[110] When Randy Clark, at the time a Vineyard pastor, shared his testimony in Toronto of simply getting honest with God and admitting that he, a tongues-speaking Charismatic pastor who believed in miracles and all of the gifts of the Spirit, was spiritually barren and powerless, the Toronto revival burst forth and is still having repercussions! The way up is always down! When we humbly admit our need and ask for help in dependent prayer, God shows up!

Prayer and the Power of the Spirit

What are the signs of a truly Spirit-empowered church? What is the secret to vital Christianity? Everyone has an answer, as Rick Warren often relates. Some say the secret is mobilizing the saints in personal evangelism. Others argue that it is a strong discipleship emphasis, as people come to church with Bibles and notebooks, eager to learn God's Word. Still others say vitality lies in Spirit-led worship. Then some say the answer lies in the service ministries of the church. Who is right? They are all right. It takes *all* of these dimensions to have a vital church.

The debate over Spirit baptism is integrally related to these questions. A church is only as spiritually healthy as its individual members. Their spiritual health is related, in turn, to their vital connection to Christ (and one another) in the Holy Spirit. Which brings us back to Spirit baptism. Pentecostals and Charismatics affirm that the reality of being baptized in the Holy Spirit with the accompanying prayer language of the Spirit (tongues) is the key to vital Christianity. And they can easily point to the massive spread of the Pentecostal/Charismatic movement worldwide in corroboration.

Jesus said, "By this all people will know that you are my disciples, if you have love for one another" (John 13:35 ESV). Love is the one indispensable mark of the church.[111] Paul, of course, reminds us that charismatic gifts as such can be hollow without love. Thus, our ultimate goal will be love (1 Cor. 13:1–14:1). Nevertheless, there remains the question of the source of power to fulfill our Great Commandment-Great Commission mission; and Luke, "the Charismatic theologian of the New Testament," takes us to the heart of the issue.

An amazingly consistent pattern in Luke-Acts enables us to conclude that Luke is also "the theologian of prayer" in the New Testament. Luke makes crystal clear that the secret to the spiritual power of Jesus' ministry as well as that of the early church was prayer. Virtually all spiritual empowerment, all spiritual breakthroughs in Luke-Acts are linked in some way to prayer, beginning with the infancy narratives. The power of the Spirit is inseparably linked with prayer.[112]

People were praying outside when Zechariah, inside the sanctuary, received Gabriel's announcement concerning the birth of John (Luke 1:10). The prophetess Anna spent her time in continual fasting and prayer in the temple, and to her came the revelation concerning the Christ child (2:36–38). Then as the narrative turns to Jesus' earthly ministry, Luke's prayer emphasis really becomes striking. Luke alone among the Gospel writers tells us that it was while Jesus was *praying* that the heaven was opened, the Holy Spirit descended upon Jesus in bodily form like a dove, and the Father's voice spoke from heaven (3:21–22). The crowds were clamoring after Jesus, "but he would withdraw to deserted places and pray" (5:16 NRSV).

Luke alone tells us that Jesus spent the entire night in *prayer* before he chose the Twelve. In fact, Luke mentions prayer twice in that narrative: "Now during those days he went out to the mountain to pray; and he spent the night in prayer to God" (6:12 NRSV). Again, only Luke tells us that Jesus was *praying* when Peter made the great confession that Jesus was the Messiah (9:18–20). Luke alone relates that Jesus went up on the mountain with Peter, John, and James specifically to *pray* and that "while he was praying" he was transfigured (9:28–29 NRSV).

Jesus "was praying in a certain place, and after he had finished, one of his disciples said to him, 'Lord, teach us to pray, as John taught his disciples'" (11:1 NRSV), and Jesus gave them the model prayer (vv. 2–4). This also is a unique Lukan redaction. We might have been tempted that day to ask Jesus to instruct us to preach and teach as he did, to lead as he did, or to heal as he did. But the disciples had already learned through observation what Jesus' secret was: prayer. A song I heard in chapel during seminary days has never left me; it asks: If Jesus needed to pray, how about you?

Only Luke relates Jesus' parable about the importunate friend at midnight, a story encouraging persistent prayer (5–8). And Luke's redaction of the "ask, seek, and knock" saying (Q) is exceptionally enlightening. In Matthew's Sermon on the Mount, Jesus says, "How much more will your Father in heaven give *good things* to those who ask him!" (Matt. 7:11 NRSV, italics added). In Jesus' prayer discourse in Luke, Jesus says, "How much more will the heavenly Father give *the Holy Spirit* to those who ask him!" (Luke 11:13, italics added). In Luke's narrative the saying is in the context of the Lord's Prayer and our daily *bread* needs (vv. 1–13). Jesus is teaching a daily appropriation of the Holy Spirit.[113] *He is saying that we should ask the Father for the Holy Spirit every day!* We are to be *continually* filled with the Holy Spirit (cf. Eph. 5:18).

Luke alone gives us the parables of the persistent widow and the unjust judge (18:1–8) and the Pharisee and the tax collector (vv. 9–14), both centered on prayer. Jesus, of course, went to Gethsemane as the other Gospels indicate. But Luke alone mentions that Jesus *twice* told his disciples to pray that they might not enter into temptation (22:40, 46). In addition, only Luke mentions the appearance of the angel from heaven to give Jesus strength and that Jesus in "his anguish . . . prayed more earnestly, and his sweat became like great drops of blood falling down on the ground" (vv. 43–44). All the Gospels relate the crucifixion event, but only Luke reports Jesus' prayer: "Father, forgive them; for they do not know what they are doing" (23:34). And Luke alone records Jesus' final prayer: "Father, into your hands I commit my spirit!" (v. 46 ESV).

The pattern continues in Acts. Immediately, we see the disciples devoting themselves to united prayer in preparation for their empowerment for mission (Acts 1:14). After the first ingathering on the Day of Pentecost, the disciples, we are told, "devoted themselves to the apostle's teaching and fellowship, to the breaking of bread and the prayers" (2:42 NRSV). Churches today who do these same things—preaching and teaching God's Word, worship and fellowship in the Holy Spirit, and *prayer*—will also be healthy, world-changing churches.

Shortly after Pentecost another outpouring of the Spirit took place at a prayer meeting: "When they had prayed, the place in which they were gathered together was shaken; and they were all filled with the Holy Spirit and spoke the word of God with boldness" (4:31). Later the apostles explain: "But we will devote ourselves to prayer and to the ministry of the word" (6:4 ESV). Then Peter and John "went down [to Samaria] and prayed for them that they might receive the Holy Spirit" (8:15 NRSV). Ananias was told by the Lord in a vision that Saul "at this moment is praying" (9:11). Luke makes special note of Cornelius's prayer life (10:2, 4, 30–31) and Peter's noontime prayer (v. 9) as the context for spiritual revelation and breakthrough. Chapter 12 highlights the church's prayer life (vv. 5, 12).

Luke's pattern and point are unmistakable: Prayer and the power of the Spirit are inseparable. We do not have one without the other. People are amazed at David Yonggi Cho's response when he is asked the secret to building the world's largest church. He says simply, "We pray and we obey!" And then he chuckles. We may debate Spirit baptism and speaking in tongues until Jesus comes. But this pattern is undebatable. The question is, Will we *do* it? This pattern clearly suggests that the fullness of spiritual power is a continual reality, not a once-for-all appropriation.

Continual Fullness

In summarizing Luke's pneumatology, Catholic Charismatic Bible scholar George Montague observes: "Even for the primitive community (and by implication for the later church), the fact that the Holy Spirit filled them once does not exclude later 'fillings.' And for such experiences there is no need to repeat baptism: prayer suffices. This is abundantly clear in Luke's catechism of prayer [Luke 11:1–13]."[114] Montague adds that the context of Luke's catechism clearly indicates spiritual empowerment: "Charismatic ministry" and "prayer for the outpouring of the Holy Spirit."[115] It is those future fillings which I would like to highlight in this section.

All direct references to being "filled with the Holy Spirit" in the New Testament are found in Luke-Acts—except for one. And even this one exception may have Luke's signature on it: Ephesians 5:18. I often like to shock my seminary students by asserting in class that the apostle Paul did not write Romans. (The Pauline authorship of Romans is virtually unquestioned.) Then I have them turn to and read Romans 16:22: "I Tertius, the writer of this letter, greet you in the Lord." So, Paul really was the author, but Tertius was his amanuensis or secretary.

The Pauline authorship of Ephesians, in contrast to Romans, is often challenged because of differences in style, vocabulary, and the like. The style of the Greek in Ephesians is similar to that of Luke-Acts. What if Luke, Paul's missionary companion, was Paul's secretary in the writing of Ephesians? This could in large measure explain how the one other reference, outside of Luke-Acts, to being filled with the Spirit got into the text of Ephesians! It is at least an interesting theory. What is not theoretical is what Paul is commanding here.

The command is in the present imperative passive, second person plural: (1) a command, not a suggestion; (2) passive voice: "allow the Spirit to fill you," not "psyche yourself"; (3) plural: this applies to *everyone*. A continual appropriation of the Spirit is in purview here. As many Pentecostals say, "One baptism, many fillings." Evangelicals would usually agree, *except* to say that the one baptism is initiatory. They are both right. Spirit baptism according to the dimensional model I am suggesting here encompasses both. But there may be an ecumenical strategy to be gleaned at this point. If all could agree that spiritual empowerment is an ongoing reality and can be legitimately referred to as being "filled with the

Holy Spirit," then we have come a long way toward a rapprochement! But there is more to be gleaned from this passage. The command is followed by a string of imperatival participles: "speaking to one another in psalms and hymns and spiritual songs, singing and making melody in your heart to the Lord, always giving thanks for all things in the name of our Lord Jesus Christ to God the Father, and submitting yourselves to one another in the fear of Christ" (Eph. 5:19–21, author's rendering). Paul describes here a Spirit-filled congregation. This is how a Spirit-filled congregation is characterized, *and* this is how to become a Spirit-filled congregation! Notice that the context is corporate. It is a worshipping congregation of mutually submitted believers. I have noticed a further pattern when this passage is placed alongside the Acts narratives.

Persons are filled with the Spirit when they come together in unified prayer (Acts 1:14/2:4; 4:23–31) and praise (Eph. 5:18–21). They are also filled with the Spirit when as individuals they are out on mission in obedience to the Lord's command (Acts 4:8; 13:9). And we can be *continuously* filled with the Spirit (Acts 13:52; Eph. 5:18).

Perhaps to some degree because of the witness and example of the Pentecostal/Charismatic tradition, the church is rediscovering worship in our day. There is a real hunger for it. It may be that this is so because believers are discovering afresh the experience of being filled with the Spirit in this context. In addition, we have begun to take our God-given mission seriously in obedient lives of service and are discovering the fullness of the Spirit in this context as well. But what do we make of spiritual gifts in general and speaking in tongues in particular in relation to Spirit baptism and the Spirit-filled life? A few additional comments are in order.

Spiritual Gifts

Again, it could be argued that Pentecostalism and Charismatic renewal have strongly influenced the church to reexamine what it teaches and practices in the area of spiritual gifts. The Pentecostal/Charismatic tradition itself most often sees Spirit baptism as an experience of empowerment subsequent to conversion (signified by tongues, in the opinion of most) which also initiates one into the manifestation of spiritual gifts. Too often the implication is that those not claiming such an experience are not fully available for use by the Spirit in spiritual gifts. Put most crassly, those who do not speak in tongues cannot be substantially of use to the body in spiritual gifts. Fortunately, this fallacy is dying out in the tradition because of interaction with the larger body of Christ and a general maturing of the tradition.

A dimensional approach to Spirit baptism views 1 Corinthians 12–14, for example, as applicable to the whole body of Christ, not just to a select pneumatic few. *Every* Christian is gifted for a functioning place of ministry. Spiritual gifts inventories may be of some value in discovering our place, but the more natural process of personal prayer, study of the Scriptures, and interaction with others will most often reveal what God has in mind. In addition, Pentecostals and Charismatics are quick to remind us that at any given moment any of us can be used in any particular spiritual gift according to the need being addressed.

Also, there is some truth in the experience of many that tongues can help usher one into the flow of spiritual gifts and ministry. In effect, one is learning to cooperate with the Holy Spirit by faith in carrying out his desires. Everything we receive from God is by grace through faith. And sometimes learning to cooperate with the Spirit in a personal prayer language, as it is often called, is a beginning step in the pilgrimage of Spirit-empowered ministry.

One myth that needs to be exploded in Charismatic circles, however, is the teaching that Christians do not *have* gifts but are only conduits of any particular gift at any particular time. The New Testament clearly teaches the opposite; we do *have* gifts. For example, Paul wished that the Corinthians had his gift of celibacy. "But each has his own gift [*charisma*] from God, one of one kind and one of another" (1 Cor. 7:7 ESV). Paul wrote to the Romans: "Having gifts that differ according to the grace given to us, let us use them" (Rom. 12:6 ESV). Peter wrote: "As each has received a gift, use it to serve one another, as good stewards of God's varied grace" (1 Pet. 4:10 ESV). It could not be expressed any more plainly.

As mentioned earlier, the major passages dealing with spiritual gifts and ministries, without exception, stress unity within diversity, love, and humility (Rom. 12; 1 Cor. 12–14; Eph. 4:1–16; 1 Pet. 4:7–11). These themes are too often overlooked when spiritual gifts are taught. Every believer is absolutely essential to the body of Christ. Repeatedly and pointedly these key passages ring this bell, but when will we hear it? Space does not permit a detailed discussion in this area, but the following observations seem appropriate.

Increasingly, Christians of all stripes are discovering the naturalness of moving in the supernatural. Wayne Grudem, for example, masterfully explains how the gift of prophecy can be used in a natural and edifying way in any given congregation.[116] Charles Hummel's *Fire in the Fireplace,* Jack Deere's *Surprised by the Power of the Spirit,* and Doug Banister's *The Word and Power Church* are only a few examples of how this discovery of the Spirit's gifts is spreading throughout Christ's body.[117]

James Simmons, a Southern Baptist pastor of a traditional congregation in Murray, Kentucky, felt strongly led to reestablish an ongoing discipleship program in his church as a part of his doctor of ministry work. One aspect of the training program was an exploration of the spiritual gifts mentioned in the New Testament, with a view toward enabling his parishioners to discover what areas of service God might have in mind for them. No charism mentioned was left out, including the more controversial ones such as healing and tongues. What surprised both the pastor and his people was the amazing discovery of how many spiritual gifts were already in operation in their midst, including faith and authority over the demonic. Very often all that is needed in a given congregation is simply enabling the members to become aware of what the Holy Spirit is already doing in their midst![118]

Charismatic worship, often referred to as the "praise and worship" model, has also had a profound influence on the church at large. But sometimes "worship wars" have ensued during times of transition or debate about the choice of worship style. Paul Basden's *The Worship Maze: Finding a Style to Fit Your Church* is a helpful guide in this arena as is Sally Morgenthaler's *Worship Evangelism.*[119] But without doubt, speaking in tongues remains a troublesome issue in many quarters and deserves further practical comment.

Speaking in Tongues

Making a "law of tongues" as the sole signifier of spiritual empowerment is, as has already been argued, a mistake. But what should be the place of speaking in tongues in the church today? Pentecostals, for decades now, have been keeping the church honest as to why certain of the more "unusual" gifts have dropped off in the church. If Jesus went about preaching, teaching, *and* healing, why do we, his body, not do so? If speaking in tongues was evidently widespread and common in early Christianity, why not today?

Even a cursory perusal of Acts would indicate that *many* times speaking in tongues accompanied spiritual empowerment in the first-century church. Why until the twentieth century was it so sporadic? Since the days of Charles Parham and William J. Seymour, Pentecostals have honestly faced these facts and simply begun to *expect* such things to happen when praying for spiritual empowerment. And when it does, why are we so alarmed? Some might say, "It may be Bible, brother, but it's not Baptist!" But when we do so, are we not in danger of "making void the word of God through [our] tradition" (Mark 7:13 NRSV)?

Pastoral wisdom would lay down at least the following basic guidelines on this issue. First, making a "law of tongues" can only create problems. It can easily produce a sense of superiority in those who do speak in tongues ("I've got the baptism, brother; why don't you?") or it can frustrate those who do not ("God can't use me in spiritual gifts, since I haven't spoken in tongues"). I have observed the latter problem firsthand many times over the last three decades.

Second, speaking in tongues should never be viewed as the *sine qua non* of spirituality. Tongues are simply not the panacea of the church's ills. Any Charismatic pastor can document this observation! But the obverse is also true. Tongues speakers are not spiritual lepers either, mentally unstable and frothing at the mouth. Some traditionalists relate to tongues speakers in this manner. The Great Commandment does not allow us the luxury of such superficial attitudes of superiority in either direction. But what should be the place of speaking in tongues today?

Paul evidently valued the experience highly: (1) "Now I would like all of you to speak in tongues, but even more to prophesy" (1 Cor. 14:5); (2) "I thank God that I speak in tongues more than all of you" (14:18). The apostle sought to *regulate,* not *exterminate,* the rampant tongues at Corinth. At the same time he clearly taught the private, personal value of this sort of prayer. He uses the subjunctive mood in 1 Corinthians 14:5: "I *wish* you all did." But all do not—not in any Pentecostal or Charismatic church I have ever known and, of course, not in traditional churches. And Paul saw only a limited use for tongues in corporate worship (14:13–38).

But speaking in tongues as a private language of prayer to aid devotion and intercession is valued by millions today. Are they all deluded or demonized? Some cessationists would say yes. But fairer-minded folk would be kinder.

Is speaking in tongues available to all believers? Paul's words above would imply the affirmative. Is a person's spirituality defective if he or she does not desire to do so?—absolutely not. God deals with us in many ways and on many matters. We have to let our Savior and Shepherd determine what is most needed at a given time in a believer's pilgrimage.

Concluding Comments

We see in the Pentecostal/Charismatic tradition a megachurch, metachurch, parachurch, revival, and renewal phenomenon of unparalleled proportions in church history. The tradition has raised the issue of the importance of *religious experience* to a new level.

Years ago world religion expert Ninian Smart pointed out that every living religion has a cognitive dimension (system of beliefs), a cultic dimension (manner of worship), an ethical dimension (teachings on right and wrong), and the like. But what keeps it a *living* religion is the *experiential dimension.*[120] Pentecostals and Charismatics often view James D. G. Dunn as their nemesis, when in reality he is one of their greatest advocates. For decades, in almost every work he has published, Dunn has asserted "the primacy of experience in shaping the course and character of first-generation Christianity."[121] And Dunn sees Pentecostals and Charismatics as major forces in restoring this balance to the rationalism of our own day. Our *experience* of Spirit baptism is at the heart of who we are as twenty-first-century followers of Christ.

Craig Keener may have provided the body of Christ with the surest guide through the current maze of opinions concerning the Spirit and his gifts in his *Gift and Giver: The Holy Spirit for Today.* And one of his concluding comments in his Spirit baptism discussion bears repeating:

> Second-work Pentecostals and their theological
> cousins in the Wesleyan and Holiness traditions have
> brought a gift to the rest of Christ's body by reminding us
> that we all need an experiential empowerment of the

Spirit, just as other traditions have rightly emphasized the need to depend on the finished work of Christ. Whether we think of that empowerment as implicit in our conversion, in our water baptism, or in a second or third special work, we recognize that in practice we must yield more fully to God's grace and power in our lives.[122]

Especially, in the current chaotic shift toward postmodernism, with its experiential, communal, and unfortunately relativistic ethos, a strong integration of heart religion and head religion is essential.

Millard Erickson points us to this same truth in his cogent analysis of postmodernism: "Postmodernism has reminded us, correctly, that we are not purely cognitive or rational creatures. Experience plays a major part in our understanding and our beliefs."[123] And Leonard Sweet, in his inimitable style, exhorts us: "God is birthing the greatest spiritual awakening in the history of the church. God is calling you to midwife that birth. Are you going to show up?"[124]

Southern Baptists by the thousands have been helped by Henry Blackaby and others to *experience God*. And that is the cry of the human heart in every generation: "Really knowing God only comes through experience as He reveals Himself to you."[125] This is why in-depth discussion of the reality of the baptism in the Holy Spirit is so crucial in our day.

To be sure, the troublesome fallacy of a punctiform conception of Spirit baptism, or for that matter sanctification or salvation itself, must be honestly addressed. But at the same time, our experience of God sometimes far outstrips our conceptions of him. The lack in the latter should not be seen to invalidate the authenticity of the former. Thus, some may object strongly to much of the pneumatology of the Pentecostal/Charismatic tradition, but the validity of its vital spirituality should not be lost sight of in the process. The best is yet to be for God's people as we continue to listen to and learn from God and each other.

In the final analysis, Spirit baptism can become the rallying cry for a new generation of Spirit-filled believers going into all the world with the saving gospel of Jesus Christ. Two Charismatic utterances will be found on our lips: (1) "Abba! Father!" (Rom. 8:15) and (2) "Jesus is Lord!" (Rom. 10:9). Our consuming passion will be to glorify God by our obedience to his Great Commandment and his Great Commission. We will have learned afresh to celebrate the unity within our vast diversity. And God's Spirit will transform us, empower us, and guide us. "For in one Spirit we were all baptized into one body" (1 Cor. 12:13 ESV).

Responses to Larry Hart's Dimensional Charismatic Perspective

Response by Ralph Del Colle

If it is the case that many Charismatics have adopted in some form (often with slight revision) the classical Pentecostal doctrine of Spirit baptism, this is not true with regard to Larry Hart. His reception of it is critical and revisionary and one that attempts to integrate various elements that arise in any discussion of Spirit baptism. I characterize his position as revisionary, for although a Southern Baptist, he basically affirms the Pentecostal/Charismatic experience while denying any notion of subsequence in the matter. Methodologically he prefers to identify his approach as postmodern, dimensional, and holistic. Theologically, the dominant and overarching theme is the eschatological nature of Spirit baptism.

Since part of Hart's intent is to move beyond the Pentecostal/ Evangelical impasse, one should consider how successfully he accomplishes this. In this respect his efforts are similar to some "third-wave" understandings that deny subsequence but maintain a focus on the power of the Spirit for life and ministry. However, Hart's analysis and the specifics of his proposal in my judgment are not best categorized by this moniker. I am not so sure that his postmodern, holistic approach is the best way to characterize the new methodology as compared to previous positions. At least as he phrases it— "postmodern experientalists" versus "rationalistic modernists of both liberal and Evangelical/Fundamentalist stripes"—it is not helpful. Many are invoking the play of the postmodern these days to say a number of things including subsequence, or the denial thereof. The main point, however, and one that I think is well taken, is that the meaning of being "baptized in the Holy Spirit" is somewhat fluid in the New Testament and may best be captured by his strategy to characterize it as a "metaphor, not a doctrine," one that underscores the eschatological nature of salvation. In this respect his usage of "dimensional" best encapsulates his intent, namely, to uncover and not ignore (or reduce) the several aspects of Spirit baptism he finds in the Scriptures and as experienced throughout the history of the church (an important point not to be dismissed in his essay).

There is one aspect of this approach and of his subsequent definition of Spirit baptism that I will consider. I shall then conclude with some reflections on the reception by the faithful of their inheritance in the Holy Spirit.

Gleaning from the prophetic and apocalyptic tendencies of the Old Testament and the preaching of John the Baptist, it is clear that the promised coming of the Holy Spirit inaugurates an eschatological fulfillment that encompasses both the already and the not yet. I agree with Hart in this theological evaluation of the outpouring of the Holy Spirit. Only in the light of the divine promise can we appreciate the biblical scope of the coming of the Spirit. Certainly in Paul's estimation the reception of the Holy Spirit marked the fulfillment of God's promise to the nations through Abraham (Gal. 3:14). However, I prefer to add another dimension to this aspect of Spirit baptism.

As I argue in my chapter, the outpouring of the Holy Spirit also helps constitute the church. The church exists in the outpouring of the Holy Spirit. The ecclesiological dimension is not incidental to the eschatological one. *Lumen Gentium,* the Second Vatican Council's Dogmatic Constitution on the Church, states that the kingdom of Christ is present in mystery in the church and now "grows visibly through the power of God in the world."[126] It is in and through the church that the nations are brought into the outpouring or baptism in the Holy Spirit. This is true for those converted to Christ and also for believers who enter into its experiential reality subsequent to their conversion or Christian initiation. Nor is this intended to restrict the sovereignty or freedom of the Spirit who blows where he wills (John 3:8). It is to say that the work of the Spirit is always related to and proceeds from the gospel entrusted to the church proclaimed through the Holy Spirit sent from heaven (1 Pet. 1:12).

Hart's definition of Spirit baptism is comprehensive. It embraces Jesus' eschatological redemptive work, Christian initiation, the ongoing Christian life, and empowerment for Christian mission and ministry. He also parses it in terms of its saving, sanctifying, and empowering dimensions, or as he nicely puts it, the paschal, purifying, and Pentecostal dimensions of Spirit baptism. He uses other variations on the same theme. For example, regeneration, the indwelling of the Spirit and being baptized into the body of Christ—the typical Evangelical themes—are included. He also mentions conversion, initial sanctification, and spiritual empowerment; or in another place, new birth, new life, and miraculous ministry.

Suffice it to say that the eschatological outpouring of the Holy Spirit imparts the entire work of salvation and the entire spectrum of the *ordo salutis* with no temporal disjunction among its various elements. In an irenic move at the end of his essay, Hart affirms the popular Pentecostal phrase, "one baptism, many fillings," by arguing that they and Evangelicals are both right; the former in a necessary initiatory reception of the Spirit, and the latter in locating that event at conversion. No matter the difference, the important point is to affirm the ongoing and continuous work of the Spirit, the only adequate perspective in which to situate the Christian life.

Hart's definition of Spirit baptism is attractive for a number of reasons. From the point of view of God's work, surely the Pentecostal outpouring is the culmination of the work of redemption. In the Catholic liturgical year, the Solemnity of Pentecost is the end of the Easter season, not the beginning of a new season. In other words, Christ's saving death and resurrection in the paschal mystery requires Pentecost for its communication and impartation in and through the church in witness and mission to the nations. In this regard (in agreement with Hart) one cannot restrict the effects of the outpouring to empowerment alone. It also includes the paschal and purifying dimensions that he identifies. Indeed cross and Spirit, Calvary and Pentecost, are the inseparable foundations for the fullness of saving grace.

Viewed from the perspective of the human reception of grace, however, some distinctions can be made. In fact, the traditional Reformed *ordo salutis* makes such distinctions, even temporal distinctions at the ontological level of cause and effects, without imposing a temporal order of subsequence that characterized the Wesleyan and Pentecostal doctrines of entire sanctification and Spirit baptism. I do not doubt that Hart would allow for such theological distinctions in the work of grace as long as one does not yield to subsequence. From a Catholic perspective I am sympathetic to his position, but I must also give an account of such distinctions in the works of grace in light of the sacraments.

The difficulty that the doctrine of subsequence entails concerns the identification of the reception of particular works of grace in the subjective experience of the believer. Therefore, entire sanctification in the Wesleyan-Holiness tradition and Spirit baptism in Pentecostalism both beg for some verification, hence the initial physical evidence of *glossolalia* for the latter. Also, as Hart argues, can one really restrict the operation of spiritual gifts or the power of the Spirit only to so-called Spirit-baptized believers? Evidences of spiritual gifts such as miracles and anointed preaching, to name just two, are not absent from church history, and his account of various ecclesial movements, from Puritanism to revivalism, confirms this.

Therefore, I am in agreement with much of what Hart proposes, especially the notion that new life, sanctification, and power ought not to be separated in the life of the believer, even though they may be distinguished. Viewed from a sacramental perspective, Catholics affirm that the gift of the Spirit in the sacrament of confirmation increases the gifts of the Holy Spirit for sanctity (the sevenfold gifts) and the *charismata* for service. Undue separation disrupts the integrity of the Christian life. Nevertheless, the distinction between the graces received in baptism and those received in the sacrament of confirmation is still valid.

I realize the difficulty of persuading a nonsacramentalist of a sacramentalist position. That is not so much my intent as it is simply to highlight the New Testament witness that water baptism and the laying on of hands were a part of Christian initiation. The washing of water and anointing may be administered at the same time (as in adult Christian initiation in the Catholic Church today), but they are still distinct. The latter is certainly related to the former. The Spirit is present and active in baptism as well as in confirmation. He is received in both sacraments. Yet there is a distinct giving of the Spirit in the anointing with the laying of hands that increases and strengthens all of the elements of grace—new life, sanctification, empowerment—that Hart is concerned to integrate.

The advantage of the sacramentalist position resides in the priority of God's grace in the matter. God always offers and imparts new life and the Holy Spirit in the sacrament. The fruitfulness of sacramental reception depends on the faith and cooperation of the recipient. This may indeed lead to further anointings, infillings, and manifestations of the Spirit in holiness, witness, and ministry, something that all the contributors to this volume want to affirm.

Response by Stanley M. Horton

I am happy for the spread of Spirit baptism and the gifts of the Spirit among Charismatics. Dennis Bennett sent me autographed copies of his books, and when I was vice president of the Society for Pentecostal studies, I invited him to speak at our annual banquet. He was not as soft on tongues as Larry Hart and many other Charismatics. At least he said there, "Tongues is part of the package." Dennis and Rita Bennett's *The Holy Spirit and You* has helped Assemblies of God young people to receive the Pentecostal experience.

I appreciate Larry Hart's emphases on the eschatological perspective of the Spirit's work, on the fact that all born-again believers have the Spirit, on the need for the present dimension of being filled with the Spirit, and on the fact that the secret of our success in mission is the power of the Spirit. I agree that we perennially need revival and that the power of the Spirit is inseparably linked with prayer in the Bible and in our Pentecostal experience. It was in prayer that my parents and my children and I were baptized in the Spirit. In prayer God called me to a teaching ministry. Prayer has been central in the Bible colleges and seminary where I have taught. Pentecostal preachers and teachers constantly urge daily prayer and prayer for revival. In their preaching I hear constant teaching centered on Christ and the cross. In fact, I hear far more about Jesus and a call to holy living than sermons specifically about the Holy Spirit.

I am sorry Larry Hart finds too many carnal, powerless, fruitless, even mean-spirited speakers who claim to be Spirit filled. God does not wait for believers to be mature and free from problems or even sins before the Spirit gives them gifts—as Paul in First Corinthians clearly shows. However, in my experience in every part of the United States and in twenty-five other countries, I have found the vast majority of Pentecostals to be godly, kind, and helpful—many of them having suffered for their witness to Christ. Everywhere, I find young people who are on fire for God, studying his Word, and ready to follow Christ wherever he leads.

As Pentecostals today, we do not view tongues as the *sine qua non* of spirituality. We are more concerned about living the Spirit-filled life. However, as I look at what happened in the early days of the Pentecostal revival, it is evident that it would not have happened if it were not for seeing that Acts 2:4 is for today; they were all filled and all spoke in tongues as the Spirit enabled them. It is evident also that in some places, such as Nyack, New York, where the revival broke out and where leaders later decided that speaking in tongues was not necessarily the initial physical or outward evidence, soon no one was seeking to be baptized in the Spirit. I hope that will not happen in America as a whole in the present century. If it does, missionaries from other parts of the world will be coming here to spread the truth and call for a new Pentecostal revival.

Response by H. Ray Dunning

As a Wesleyan I resonate with many of the emphases advocated in this wide-ranging essay, especially the repeated stress on the importance of the ongoing character of the Spirit-filled life. Too many in my own tradition have relied on a momentary experience as the *ne plus ultra* of the Christian life, and the earlier apologetics of the Holiness movement tended to formulate the doctrine of sanctification largely in these terms. This raises for me the question of theological formulation, which is always articulated (whether self-consciously or not) in philosophical terms.[127] Most of the popular theology of Christian experience to which I have been exposed was informed by the traditional concept of "substance," and the doctrine of sanctification was formulated in these terms. This way of thinking inevitably fostered a static view of the Christian life.

In writing a systematic theology under assignment for the denomination to which I belong, using a relational paradigm, I was amazed to discover the opposition I encountered from older (and some younger) theologians in the church who thought in Aristotelian terms. When Christian experience is viewed in relational terms, it provides a conceptuality that removes it from a static domain to a dynamic one and opens the door to a developing spirituality resulting from increased understanding of the Christian faith, obedience to new light, and the fostering of a more intimate relationship with God through spiritual disciplines. This pattern seems to be clearly implied by 2 Peter 3:18, the key verse that encapsulates a major emphasis of the epistle.

The matter of theological conceptuality raises another issue that has been of interest to me in the process of participating in this project. How do we conceptualize the "Holy Spirit"? Professor Hart concurs with my own essay on the corporate nature of spirituality. There is doubtless great significance in the promise of Jesus that where two or three were gathered in his name, he would be in the midst (Matt. 18:20). This is not essentially a word of comfort when only a few show up for church but an affirmation that Christ is present when and where his people are gathered. And the Holy Spirit vouchsafes that presence. In such a gathering we often say there was a good spirit present. The question is, was it the *Holy* Spirit or merely a spirit of congeniality or enthusiasm, or what? And since the whole thrust of the New Testament confirms that the Holy Spirit is the Spirit of Jesus, it seems safe to say that the Spirit of Christlikeness is the one assurance that the spirit of our communal life is the *Holy Spirit.*

This suggestion, which requires further thought and clarification, seems to be perfectly consistent with the Trinitarian theology of St. Augustine that has profoundly influenced Western thought about the Triune nature of God. St. Augustine interpreted the Trinity in relational terms. The Son is Son in relation to the Father; the Father is Father in relation to the Son, and the Spirit is the bond of love uniting the two. In a word, the Spirit *is* the relation and, like love, is personal in nature.[128] Such a view validates the corporate nature of the Spirit's presence and work since a relation is of necessity between or among persons.[129]

In the light of this Christological understanding of the Spirit, I have some serious questions about the whole concept of "power" which, according to Professor Hart's analysis, is a (if not the) central thrust of the Charismatic understanding of Spirit baptism. The aphorism validated by centuries of experience that "power corrupts and absolute power corrupts absolutely" raises perplexing issues about Jesus' offer of the bestowment of power upon his followers. If it is some mysterious force that turns us into "seven day wonders," as E. Stanley Jones put it, or overwhelms others so that their will is broken, or even the capacity to manipulate God, what is to guarantee that it would not corrupt the one who possesses this power? Or how would it differ from the Old Testament experience of the Spirit of Yahweh. My own sense is that the entire development of the ministry of Jesus in the "power" of the Spirit results in a radical reorientation of the concept of power so that as Christlike in nature, the power Jesus promises is the power of suffering love.

It is certainly true that there are Charismatic persons who are mightily used by the Spirit in ministry. Persons who are radically open to God are channels through which the Spirit's influences may be manifested. But this cannot be manipulated, it can only occur at the sovereign initiative of the Lord, and the character of that initiative has been decisively defined by Jesus Christ.

The distinction between the Charismatics and the Pentecostals appears from these essays to be primarily the way tongues speaking is viewed. The former, as Hart says, is "softer on tongues," and tends to see it as a prayer language, rather than as an evidential phenomenon. A highly respected Wesleyan theologian, before his untimely death, was Timothy L. Smith, professor of American church history at Johns Hopkins University and an ordained minister in the Church of the Nazarene. Dr. Smith was invited to present the keynote address to the annual meeting of the Society for Pentecostal Studies in 1975. His address was presented and published under the title of *Speaking the Truth in Love*. This address contains what I believe would be the studied Wesleyan response to the whole idea of a "prayer language." Smith says:

> Now, the biblical view of prayer is that God talks with us and we talk with Him. . . . Yet, quite clearly, prayer in both Old and New Testaments is more than intelligible communication; it is communion. . . . [Our Lord's prayer] at Gethsemane represented much more than could be conveyed by the words in which, profoundly enough, He affirmed His dedication at the cost of a cross. Prayer, then, however verbalized, takes Christians at their deeper moments of spiritual crisis to the limits of their comprehension. Paul knew well the loneliness of unphraseable prayers. . . . Charismatic Christians are not illogical to wish to break though these limitations to prayer in an utterance of syllables which stand for things which no earthly language can say.
>
> But I believe Paul was showing the Romans, and us, a better way. When our prayers have reached the limit of our understanding, we are to wait in faith and listen

before the Lord. For the Holy Spirit makes intercession for us in such moments with a clarity that need not be confused by our moving lips and singing voices, and with a love from which nothing is able to separate us—neither life nor death, principalities nor powers. Praying in an unknown tongue at that point, I think, may sometimes divert our attention from the awesome communion we ought to have with a suffering Saviour, disconnecting our minds at the very moment when we ought to be listening most intently for what God has to say to us.[130]

Response by Walter C. Kaiser Jr.

Dr. Hart has forged a new tact for our discussion by defining Spirit baptism as a metaphor rather than insisting on the fact that it is a doctrine! Moreover, it is a metaphor that is "not clearly univocal within the New Testament." This metaphor, Larry teaches, may refer to: (1) Jesus' eschatological redemptive work, (2) Christian initiation, (3) the Christian life, or (4) empowerment for Christian ministry. Since there are a plethora of positions, Larry concedes that, "There is no one 'Charismatic position' on Spirit baptism." Instead, it has taken on a life of its own theologically.

It would appear that this is just another way of acknowledging the fact that no single text in Scripture distinctively teaches that the baptism John and Jesus predicted is distinct from the baptism that occurs when one is initiated into the Christian faith, or that no single text exists that would authoritatively back up the claim that speaking in tongues is the initial physical evidence that this baptism in the Holy Spirit is a subsequent and distinct event occurring once some time after our initiation-conversion.

What does Dr. Hart mean by his metaphorical language? His use of this term is seen most clearly in his extended discussion of Jesus' baptism at the Jordan River by John the Baptist. Hart says Jesus was equipped with power and authority for his mission when Jesus was anointed by the Spirit at the Jordan River. In that sense, "Jesus' empowerment at the Jordan is *paradigmatic* for us" in the sense that there is a "fuller acknowledgment of this *dimension* of the Spirit's work."

This makes me nervous, however. Must we think that our Lord was any less divine, less powerful, and less authoritative at any point from his birth up to his resurrection while he walked this earth in his human flesh? Could such ways of describing what happened at the Jordan lead to another form of the *kenosis* theory where Jesus is incorrectly described as bereft of all his divine attributes except love (with apologies to Wesley's great hymn, "And Can It Be," which claims just that). It is difficult to set forth "any sort of *second blessing* account" of Jesus' baptism. To do so runs the risk of diminishing the full deity and known mission of our Lord. And if that caution is of any value, then how can what happened to our Lord be "paradigmatic for us" in the sense of our being equipped with power and authority for our mission?

In an effort to make peace between Evangelicals who are "safely entrenched behind Paul's 1 Corinthians 12:13" and the Pentecostals who "fortify themselves with Luke's Acts 2:4," Hart declares neither is wrong, but "both are right." Hart decides that in the Pauline sense of the baptism metaphor, "all believers have experienced Spirit baptism," while in the Lukan sense "we may not all be 'filled with the Spirit.'" Hence, what we all need is both the regenerational sense of baptism and the empowerment sense of baptism!

This certainly is a magnanimous suggestion that leaves room for both parties to shake hands and go on their way rejoicing in the separate works of God in each of their lives. But it begs the main question: Is the baptism forecasted by John the Baptist and Jesus the same one that Paul referred to in 1 Corinthians 12:13? One side claims it is and the other side claims it is not. Scripture cannot mean two opposite things at the same time! What is the truth intention of the writers of Scripture? That is the question. It will not go away until we wrestle with the intention of the writers of these texts.

Of course, I agree with Hart that after the conversion-initiation work of the Holy Spirit, all believers can also enjoy the special infilling and empowerment of the Holy Spirit over and over again, as each experiences the grace of God in their lives. But my only biblical reservation is that such infilling and empowerment does not seem necessarily to be linked with the baptism in the Holy Spirit that was promised by John or Jesus.

Hart turns to the second major issue: "Does speaking in tongues alone signify Spirit baptism and entrance into the Spirit-filled, Charismatic dimension of the Christian life?" After surveying the "seven different phrases to describe the coming of the Spirit" in the New Testament, Hart concludes that when Peter referred in his Pentecost sermon to the "promise of the Father" and the "gift of the Holy Spirit," he was "referring to both conversion and charisma!" For Hart, this means that when persons became Christians, "the Charismatic dimension was already present in their lives." We agree with these results, of course, but how will this satisfy both parties who are attributing two separate meanings to the same expressions? We agree that believers are commanded by our Lord to be filled continually with the Holy Spirit as an ordinary outcome of their conversion to Christ. Hart, therefore, concludes that there is a "second blessing," which is ordinarily accompanied with speaking in tongues. In so saying, he depicts Charismatics, compared to Pentecostals, as being "somewhat 'softer' on tongues": one may or may not speak in tongues when he or she is baptized in the Holy Spirit.

But why must the answer be yes and no at the same time for the same biblical expressions? Is a second blessing taught or not? Why may some speak in tongues when they are baptized in the Spirit and others may not? Is this a spiritual luxury? Is it distributed randomly? Does one need to prequalify for this work of God? Why may tongues be regarded by Charismatics as "marginal at best," but "normative" for Pentecostals? What is required for Evangelicals?

I am not sure a Hegelian dialectical model explains anything except the form in which this argument is being cast: i.e., the thesis is the traditional view, the antithesis is the Pentecostal (Charismatic?) view, and the synthesis is a so-called Hart "dimensional view." Is the impasse avoided altogether by this dialectical solution?

Should the "time lapse" advocated by Hart between one's conversion and infilling of the Holy Spirit be answered by his "dimensional" scheme? Hart points more realistically to an inaugurated eschatological model in which there is always the "now" and the "not yet." Given the fact that our salvation is a pilgrimage in which we were saved, are now being saved, and ultimately will be saved (all three tenses of the verb used in Scripture), we too agree with Hart that there are second, third, fourth, and more blessings in the Christian life. If that is what Hart finally ends up with, then we too agree. But we do not attribute this fact to an exegesis of the "baptism in the Holy Spirit," but to an understanding of all the teaching on the Holy Spirit in the Bible.

In what sense, then, did 1 Corinthians 12:13 help or hinder Hart's discussion? Hart adopts Criag Keener's conclusion. Said Keener, "The whole sphere of the Spirit's work becomes available at conversion, but believers may experience some aspects of the Spirit's work only subsequent to conversion." For Hart, that summarizes the paschal emphasis of John, the purifying emphasis of Paul, and the Pentecostal emphasis of Luke. All three dimensions of the Spirit's work are made available through the gospel.

If I understand what Hart is developing here, I believe he has grasped the majority of what I think is at stake in this discussion, with faithfulness to Scripture. I would want to reserve a few caveats for his use of some of the upper room discourse statements that are directed to the apostles who would later author Scripture, rather than directing these texts specifically to us as believers [Note: we did not walk with Jesus since the beginning of his ministry, and the like].

Where then is all the fuss and ferment? Hart concludes that it lies in the "punctiliar fallacy": i.e., that "one experience constitutes a person as permanently 'perfected' or 'Spirit filled.'" That seems to be the final way of stating the key point in tension. How do we interpret the biblical statements about the "promise of the Father" and the works of the Holy Spirit? To be avoided at all costs are all concepts of an "arrival mentality" in which there is little or no need for any further work of the Holy Spirit in your life and mine. Moreover, whatever else we may say about the Spirit, he has been given for the "unity" of the body and not for dividing it up.

This essay was a joy to read. It is filled with great pastoral counsel and compassionate appeals for the various positions to see the biblical strengths in each others' arsenal of verses. Therefore, its spirit is right, and it follows the commands for love that are incumbent on all of us as believers. In that sense, my caveats were minor in comparison to the major tasks to which we are jointly called by our Lord.

CHAPTER 4

A Wesleyan Perspective on Spirit Baptism[1]

H. RAY DUNNING

Attempting to describe the Wesleyan view of any aspect of the Christian life presents the interpreter with a difficult task since there is considerable ambiguity in how the tradition is interpreted.[2] John Wesley himself gave careful attention to examining the Scripture and applying his interpretation of it to the Christian life but never addressed a number of issues that have preoccupied more recent scholars. Doubtless one reason for this was his perspective, which predated the Enlightenment influence that began the process of elevating private religious experience to the level of an axiom. Wesley shared the biblical perspective of the corporate nature of religion. This is clearly seen in his oft-quoted statements that "there is no holiness but social holiness," and "Christianity is essentially a social religion; and to turn it into a solitary one is indeed to destroy it."[3] Recognizing this perspective would obviously influence one's interpretation of the book of Acts, which is pivotal to this study (see below).

Furthermore, even in Wesley's lifetime, some of his followers began developing an interpretation of the Christian life that led to a significant reorientation of his own perspective,[4] resulting in a bifurcation in the Wesleyan tradition that continues to the present day. The most relevant change, for our purposes, concerns the relation of the Holy Spirit to sanctification.

It would thus seem appropriate to first explore Wesley's own teaching and then examine the transformation of his views that primarily occurred in the nineteenth and early twentieth centuries during the spiritual awakenings, commonly referred to as the "Holiness revivals." A number of self-proclaimed "Wesleyan" denominations emerged out of these revivals.[5] Finally, I would attempt to state what, from my understanding, would be a normative, or authentic, Wesleyan view of the Christian life. The reader should recognize that this might not represent every form of theology that identifies itself as Wesleyan.[6]

The reader may be asking how this approach impinges on the issue of "Spirit baptism," which is the focus of this collection of essays, and which on the surface may appear to be simply an exegetical issue. The answer is that the doctrine of the Holy Spirit in traditional Christian theology is directly related to the doctrine of sanctification; and in its broader meaning in the New Testament, sanctification basically refers to the Christian life, particularly in its ethical aspects. Hence one's doctrine of sanctification is virtually synonymous with the understanding of the "Spirit-filled life."

One of the most important considerations in an investigation such as this is to recognize the importance of distinguishing between a particular term and the reality to which it refers. One can become so preoccupied with defending a particular use of a term that he misses the larger truth to which it points, particularly if that truth is made to stand or fall on the acceptance of a specific linguistic reference to it. As Ludwig Wittgenstein reminded us, language can be bewitching. This is nowhere truer than in theological language.

Succinctly put at the outset, John Wesley's understanding of the Christian life was Christological in focus and emphasis, whereas the nineteenth-century developments in the Wesleyan tradition became primarily pneumatological in emphasis.[7] In my opinion, John Deschner correctly argues that Christology is the presupposition of Wesley's theology and comments: "[My] conviction is that an explicit examination of Wesley's great presupposition can lead to a clarification and even correction of preaching in the present-day Wesleyan tradition."[8] This statement reflects the contrast between Wesley's own views and the developments among his successors in the American Holiness movement.

A further significant contrast between Wesley and the majority of his successors in the American Holiness Movement should be noted initially. As befitted an Oxford scholar, Wesley developed his theological views in dialogue with the larger, mainstream Christian theological tradition. With minor exceptions his successors generally were myopic in this regard, virtually becoming exclusively preoccupied with one issue; and most of their views on this issue were derived from experience. Their strength was clearly not in the area of hermeneutics.

The Role of the Spirit in Wesley's Theology

Wesley came to understand his central mission to be to restore the biblical balance between justification and sanctification, a balance that had been skewed toward sanctification by the Catholic tradition and toward justification by the Protestant. He identifies the distinctiveness of his emphasis in his sermon "On God's Vineyard": "It is, then a great blessing given to this people, that as they do not think or speak of justification so as to supersede sanctification. They take care to keep each in its own place, laying equal stress on one and the other. They know God has joined these together, and it is not for man to put them asunder: Therefore they maintain, with equal zeal and diligence, the doctrine of free, full, present justification, on the one hand, and of entire sanctification both of heart and life, on the other; being as tenacious of inward holiness as any Mystic, and of outward, as any Pharisee."[9]

George Croft Cell, in a pioneering work on Wesley, described his position as a synthesis of the Protestant ethic of grace and the Catholic ethic of holiness.[10] Albert Outler, one of the leading Wesley scholars in the twentieth century, advocated the same analysis in his affirmation that the genius of Wesley was his persistent holding together of "faith alone" and "holy living."[11]

The Catholic emphasis on holiness, Wesley saw, was based on a faulty understanding of justification. While he struggled to formulate an adequate interpretation of this salvation metaphor himself, he rejected the confusion between justification and sanctification in the Catholic tradition that stemmed from St. Augustine, who defined justification as "making holy." For Augustine this holiness, which was the basis for acceptance with God, was a divine gift. In time it came to be seen as the result of good works.

Like Martin Luther before him, Wesley came to recognize the bankruptcy of this form of piety out of his own experience. Throughout his early life, he had sought to be justified by "being good." He provides a quaint description of this whole process. Reflecting on his years at school, he recalled that "restraints being removed, I was much more negligent than before, even of outward duties, and almost continually guilty of outward sins, which I knew to be such, though they were not scandalous in the eye of the world." But he goes on to explain his religious attitude at that time: "However, I still read the Scriptures, and said my prayers, morning and evening. And what I now hoped to be saved by was, 1. Not being so bad as other people. 2. Having still a kindness for religion. And, 3. Reading the Bible, going to church, and saying my prayers."[12]

But he became much more serious later in life, still to no avail, even going to Georgia as a missionary. He sadly lamented at the conclusion of this ill-fated experiment, "I went to America to convert the heathen, but O who shall convert me." Looking back on these events, he later described them:

I diligently strove against all sin. I omitted no sort of self-denial which I thought lawful: I carefully used, both in public and in private, all the means of grace at all opportunities. I omitted no occasion of doing good: I for that reason suffered evil. And all this I knew to be nothing, unless as it was directed toward an inward holiness. Accordingly this, the image of God, was what I aimed at in all, by doing his will, not my own. Yet, then after continuing some years in this course, I apprehended myself to be near death, I could not find that all this gave me any comfort, or any assurance of acceptance with God. At this I was then not a little surprised; not imagining I had been all this time building on the sand, nor considering that "other foundation can no man lay, than that which is laid" by God, "even Christ Jesus."[13]

His journal records his preaching of justification by faith during this period, even before his own experience at Aldersgate. His descriptions are almost humorous as he reports where he preached followed by wry comments such as, "I was not to preach any more in either of those churches," "I was afterwards told, 'Sir, you must preach here no more,'" "I was quickly apprized that at St. Ann's, likewise, I am to preach no more." From these experiences he felt he learned "how intolerable the doctrine of faith is to the mind of man; and how peculiarly intolerable to *religious* men."[14]

But Wesley also found Luther's interpretation of justification to be faulty since he continued to hold that acceptance with God was based on ethical righteousness but interpreted this to mean that we are accepted on the basis of an "alien righteousness." The implication of this view was minimizing the significance of the holy life, or sanctification. In Luther's famous phrase, the believer was *simul justus et peccator.* Wesley vigorously objected that in no sense does the biblical view of justification "imply that God is deceived in those whom he justifies; that he thinks them to be what, in fact, they are not; that he accounts them to be otherwise than they are." On the so-called problem of "imputed righteousness," he declared that God "can no more . . . confound me with Christ, than with David or Abraham."[15]

It was on this particular point that Wesley saw himself as supplementing the Protestant Reformers, especially Martin Luther, going beyond their understanding to complete the work that they had only begun.

After having read Luther's Commentary on Galatians, Wesley reacted with strong feeling: "He is quite shallow in his remarks on many passages, and muddy and confused almost, on all; . . . he is deeply tinctured with mysticism throughout, and hence often dangerously (1st ed., "fundamentally") wrong . . . how blasphemously does he speak of good works and of the law of God—coupling the law with sin, death, hell, or the devil; and teaching that Christ delivers us from them all alike. . . . Here (I apprehend) is the real spring of the grand error of the Moravians. They follow Luther, for better, for worse."[16]

It was Luther's lack of stress upon sanctification that caused Wesley's great distress, even though it was Luther whose writings had been influential in bringing Wesley to justification by faith, both in doctrine and experience.

Wesley's sustained interest in and emphasis on sanctification meant that he was deeply committed to the work of the Holy Spirit.

But as with certain other significant doctrinal issues (such as the Atonement), Wesley did not develop any extensive expositions of the doctrine of the Holy Spirit. Two sermons are included in the Jackson edition of his *Works*,[17] but Randy Maddox points out that these were actually abridgements that Wesley made of others' sermons for his use, the first by John Cambold and the second by William Tilly. Maddox does concede that one can assume that these sermons are at least amenable to Wesley but suggests that they should not be used as primary sources for his pneumatology. The fullest discussion in the primary sources is a letter written in response to a tract on "The Office and Operations of the Holy Spirit" by Bishop William Warburton that was intended to attack Methodist "enthusiasm" [fanaticism], *A Letter to the Right Reverend the Lord Bishop of Gloucester* (26 Nov. 1762), found in *Works* 9:117ff.[18]

The most appropriate way to understand Wesley's view of the work of the Spirit arises out of its close correlation with sanctification. The significance of this relationship can best be seen through his balanced emphasis on grace, which is twofold in its meaning. The first aspect may simply be defined as "God's unmerited favor," his mercy that is the basis of pardon for the repentant sinner. The second aspect refers to grace as transforming power, the dynamic. That Wesley self-consciously held these two meanings in balance may be seen in his sermon "On the Witness of Our Spirit":

> By "the grace of God" is sometimes to be understood that
> free love, that unmerited mercy, by which I, a sinner,
> through the merits of Christ am now reconciled to God.
> But in this place it rather means that power of God the
> Holy Ghost which "worketh in us both to will and to do
> of his good pleasure." As soon as ever the grace of God
> (in the former sense, his pardoning love) is manifested to
> our soul, the grace of God (in the latter sense, the power
> of his Spirit) takes place therein. And now we can per-
> form through God, what to [ourselves] was impossible
> . . . a recovery of the image of God, a renewal of soul after
> His likeness.[19]

Maddox says, "It seems fair to say that the aspect of grace as the power of the Holy Spirit was most definitive for him."[20]

It is important here to take further account of Wesley's distinction between justification and sanctification. Justification, he said, is a relative change whereas sanctification is a real change. This radically broadens the concept of sanctification from a narrow spectrum of the Christian life (as in much popular teaching in the Holiness movement) and likewise broadens the realm of operation of the Spirit. Clearly included in this comprehensive definition is the "new birth," "entire sanctification," and "growth in grace" or progressive sanctification.

Although pneumatological language is not prominent in the discussions of these subjects, implicit in Wesley's extensive expositions of them is the conviction that the Holy Spirit is the dynamic agency here, including in his pervasive understanding of prevenient grace.

Sanctification is the only salvation metaphor derived from a distinctly religious context, and its original context was cultic. Hence, the primary meaning is "to set apart." By a ritual of consecration, something or someone is "set apart" to belong to God or to be used in his service, that is, sanctified. Based on the nature of Yahweh, the Old Testament understanding came to denote ethical implications, especially in the prophetic understanding. This prophetic understanding became the normative view of sanctification in the New Testament where most uses of the term have reference to the holy life (e.g., 1 Thess. 4:3).

Consistent with this New Testament emphasis, the language Wesley consistently used to talk about sanctification was primarily ethical in nature. He regularly referred to it in terms of "perfect love" and "Christian perfection," but dominantly with the biblical language of being "renewed in the image of God" and "having the mind that was in Christ." He never referred to it as the "baptism with the Holy Spirit" or "the fullness of the Spirit."

While in no sense did he downplay the work of the Spirit or avoid altogether ceremonial language such as "cleansing from sin," he doubtless understood that pneumatological language was always in need of definition, whereas the ethical, especially when informed by Christological concepts, was self-defining. Daniel Steele, professor of theology at Boston University and perhaps the leading Holiness scholar in the nineteenth century, in answer to a questioner, stated that he had counted twenty-six terms used by

Wesley to refer to the experience of sanctification, and added: "But 'the baptism of (or with) the Spirit,' 'fullness of the Spirit,' are not phrases used by him, probably because there is an emotional fullness of a temporary nature, not going down to the very roots of the moral nature."[21]

This insightful observation highlights the unvarying emphasis of Wesley on sanctification as ethical in nature. In fact, all his doctrinal work was primarily practical. Consequently, many of his interpreters argue that his greatest contribution was in the area of practical religion. They insist, as Frank John McNulty says, that "moral reformation was the essence of the Wesleyan crusade."[22] However, recent studies have shown great appreciation for his contribution to theology; but even in discussing his theology, it is nevertheless widely acknowledged that "his single, sufficient motive in theologizing was to reinforce the spiritual and ethical concerns of his societies in particular and the Church in general."[23]

Wesley himself bears witness to this passion when, in a response to accusations by the bishop of London, he appeals in defense to the ethical results of his labors, which no man should disparage:

What have been the consequences . . . of the doctrines
I have preached for nine years last past? By the fruits shall
ye know those of whom I speak; even the cloud of witnesses, who at this hour experience the gospel which
I preach to be the power of God unto salvation. The habitual drunkard that was, is now temperate in all things; the
whoremonger now flees fornication; he that stole, steals
no more, but works with his hands; he that curses or
swore perhaps at every sentence, has now learned to serve
the Lord with fear, and rejoice unto him with reverence;
these formerly enslaved to various habits of sin are now
brought to uniform habits of holiness.[24]

Allen Lamar Cooper's statement that "the Wesleyan system of Christian ethics rests securely on the foundation of the theology of John Wesley" not only calls attention to the essentially practical concern of Wesley, but also points out the necessity to examine the theological basis of his ethical understanding.[25]

As the distinctively Wesleyan doctrine of Christian perfection was being formed in Wesley's mind, his consistent concern was to maintain ethical integrity. It was this concern that led him in the early years to his break with the Moravians, whose quietism repelled him.[26] Later on, this same aversion to antinomianism caused him to separate from the Calvinistic Methodists. In John Peters' words, "For Wesley, Christian Perfection had been from the very first a concept intensely ethical in its stress."[27] Cooper is correct in seeing that for Wesley, "Christian perfection . . . was conceived as an inherent ethical change in man and the Christian life represented as a progressive development towards it."[28]

In his "Remarks on the Life and Character of John Wesley" appended to the 1847 edition of Southey's *Life of Wesley,* Alexander Knox, one of Wesley's contemporaries, bears clear testimony to the ethical aims of all that the first Methodist did. Although there may be some anomalies in Wesley's mind, "the ultimate object is uniformly pure and excellent; be the prescribed means of advancement what they may, the point aimed at is consummate virtue, in every temper and in every action." It is this character that sets his doctrines above those of Whitefield. "In fact," says Knox, "Mr. Wesley's practical principles had ever been such as to insure perfect moral consistency. From his first years of serious reflections, his standard of Christian virtue was pure and exalted." Knox further reinforces the view here proposed about Wesley's relation to the Protestant Reformers by pointing out that in adopting the doctrine of justification by faith from the Reformed tradition through Peter Bohler, Wesley cast it in his own mold, the formative concept being moral. "It will, in fact, be seen in all Mr. Wesley's statements on the subject, that it was the moral liberation on which he relied as the true criterion of the justified state."[29]

Certain formulae may be used to illustrate the development from Catholicism through Luther to Wesley as adjustment is made between faith and love. For Roman Catholic theology, following Thomas Aquinas, the order of the Christian life may be characterized as "faith formed by love." Luther rejected this because it made sanctification (love) precede justification and replaced it with the formula "faith formed by Christ." Wesley, however, with his ethical concerns took for his motto a phrase from Paul found in Galatians 5:6, "faith working by love."

This formula held together, he thought, his stress upon faith as the foundation of the Christian life and his strong insistence that love is the result of that life. Thus, as Albert Outler says: "It was of set purpose that he held the Revival to his own compounded premise of 'salvation, faith and good works.' This put him into tension with other viewpoints in which, as it seemed to him, the essential integrity between Evangelical faith and Christian ethics was split, one way or the other. Against all such disjunctions, he asserted the reciprocal unity of belief and behavior."[30]

Wesley used the term *sanctification* in at least two clearly distinguishable senses, although it is not always completely clear in which sense it is employed in some particular contexts. His broadest definition would be "to be renewed in the image of God, 'in righteousness and true holiness.'"[31] This same definition can be employed in a limited way in defining other terms. For instance, regeneration is interpreted as "restoring man to the image of God,"[32] and entire sanctification in the same way.[33] These apparent contradictions may be explained by allowing that these limited uses of the broad definition refer to stages in the total process and not to the culmination of the process. The ultimate *telos* is the complete image of God perfectly reflected in man's character, but this is not within man's grasp in this life; it always eludes him. Rather it becomes the dynamic force that makes the Christian life a constantly enlarging enterprise.

True religion, says Wesley in expounding the Sermon on the Mount, is characterized by "hungering and thirsting after righteousness." Righteousness is the image of God. (The meaning of the "image of God" is not exhausted by this term.) Therefore, the hunger and thirst in the soul is "after the image of God" and is "the strongest of all our spiritual appetites, when it is once awakened in the heart; yea, it swallows up all the rest in that one great desire— to be renewed after the likeness of Him that created us."[34]

The more comprehensive definition of the image of God, as Wesley defined it, is love. From this perspective one can clearly see his understanding of the Christian life as a process of developing love that moves along, in part, by way of crisis stages. Love is instilled in the heart in regeneration. From then on, there is a gradual development that knows no *finis,* not even death. Wesley insisted that there is no "perfection of degrees, as it is termed, none which does not admit of continual increase."[35] Nevertheless there is a stage in the process that may be called perfect love or entire sanctification, but perfect only in the sense of being unmixed.

In the light of this consistent emphasis, one can determine Wesley's view of the role of the Holy Spirit in Christian experience. His definitive sermon on *Scriptural Christianity* was preached from the words of Acts 4:31: "And they were all filled with the Holy Ghost" (KJV). After dispensing with the suggestion that the *extraordinary gifts* of the Spirit were central to this experience he declares, "It was, therefore, for a more excellent purpose than this, that 'they were all filled with the Holy Ghost.'" Its central purpose was to "give them (what none can deny to be essential to all Christians in all ages) the mind which was in Christ, those holy fruits of the Spirit which whosoever hath not, is none of his; to fill them with 'love, joy, peace, longsuffering, gentleness, goodness.'"[36]

The preceding quotation, along with numerous others that could be cited, makes it unequivocal that Wesley would identify the *fruit* of the Spirit as the essential marks of true religion rather than the *gifts* of the Spirit. The latter can be counterfeited and manifested in a carnal fashion, which is precisely the phenomenon Paul encountered at Corinth.

His sermon on *The New Birth* makes essentially the same point. The rationale for the birth by the Spirit is based on the assumption that humanity was created in the image of God. This image was lost (or badly distorted) in the fall, so God's redemptive intention is to restore human beings to their lost estate. In the accomplishment of this goal, the new birth is "that great change which God works in the soul when he brings it into life; when he raises it from the death of sin to the life of righteousness. It is the change wrought in the whole soul by the almighty Spirit of God when it is 'created anew in Christ Jesus'; when it is 'renewed after the image of God, in righteousness and true holiness'; . . . In a word, it is that change whereby the earthly, sensual, devilish mind is turned into the 'mind which was in Christ Jesus.'"[37]

Here we see Wesley's application of his generic definition of sanctification to one phase of God's therapeutic work in human life. Unlike many of his successors in the Holiness movement, he sees a continuum in the work of the Spirit since each stage of the believer's pilgrimage partakes of the same character. What then is the distinction between the new birth and entire sanctification?

The most pointed answer to this question is found in his sermon *On Patience* (1788). Entire sanctification, he says:

Does not imply any new *kind* of holiness: Let no man imagine this. From the moment we are justified, till we give up our spirits to God, love is the fulfilling of the law. . . . Love is the sum of Christian sanctification; it is the one *kind* of holiness, which is found, only in various *degrees,* in the believers who are distinguished by St. John into "little children, young men, and fathers." The difference between one and the other properly lies in the degree of love.[38]

In the second crisis of entire sanctification, all sin is taken away and the heart is purified: Til this universal change was wrought in his soul, all his holiness was mixed. . . . His whole soul is now consistent with itself. . . . There is no mixture of any contrary affections: All is peace and harmony after.[39]

But after this instantaneous change, "he still grows in grace, in the knowledge of Christ, in the love and *image of God*: and will do so, not only till death, but to all eternity."[40]

So it may be concluded, in Lindström's words, that in "the process of salvation this idea of gradual development is combined with an instantaneous element." It is an order of salvation that is aimed at the perfection of human persons. "With this teleological aim his conception of salvation must obviously be determined principally by the idea of sanctification."[41]

Wesley's use of sanctification in the wide sense to refer to the whole process of restoring humanity to the image of God is its most proper use, says Lindström, and is explicitly recognized in this way by Wesley in his sermon on the *New Birth* (1760). He distinguishes between the new birth and sanctification, denying that the former is a *progressive* work.

This is undeniably true of sanctification; but of regeneration, the new birth, it is not true. This is a part of sanctification, not the whole; it is the gate to it, the entrance into it. When we are born again, then our sanctification, our inward and outward holiness begins; and thenceforth we are gradually to "grow up in Him who is our head." . . . A child is born of God in a short time, if not in a moment. But it is by slow degrees that he afterward grows up to the measure of the full stature of Christ. The same relation, therefore, which there is between our natural birth and our growth, there is also between our new birth and our sanctification.[42]

This understanding of "sanctification" is in perfect accord with the definition given by E. C. Blackman in the *Interpreter's Dictionary of the Bible* that sanctification is "the realization or progressive attainment of likeness to God or God's intention for men."[43]

John Peters insists that Wesley, also, at times, implies a distinction between entire sanctification as an event and Christian perfection as a continuing process of which that event is a part, "a distinction which he generally fails to maintain."[44] If this be the case, Christian perfection in its wider connotation partakes of the same teleological character as does sanctification is its wider usage.[45]

We may summarize the role of the Spirit in Christian experience as follows: the Holy Spirit is the life-giving agent in the new birth by which the process of being transformed into the image of God is begun; and the Spirit continues to function as the Agent of growth and transformation with this same goal until it is finally achieved in its fullness at the consummation.

These insights enable us to discern how Wesley would interpret the effulgence of the Spirit at Pentecost as recorded in Acts. First, it seems significant to note that his corporate understanding of the Christian religion would inform his understanding of Luke's account of the early church. In his brief note explaining the significance of Acts in relation to the Gospels he says: "The Gospels treat of Christ the Head: the Acts show that the same things befall His body, which is animated by His Spirit, persecuted by the world, defended and exalted by God."[46] This implies that the primary thrust of Acts relates most centrally to the theological doctrine of ecclesiology. While Wesley does not explicitly take account of it, it is significant that there are no accounts of an individual *qua* individual receiving the Spirit. The one apparent exception to this is the case of Saul of Tarsus, but his reception of the Spirit awaited the coming of the church in the person of Ananias.[47]

The logical implication of this fact suggests forcibly that questions about the order of individual Christian experience are questions that Luke had no interest in addressing and can be extrapolated only by indirect implication. It is further apparent that the identification of Pentecost as the "birthday of the church" is an exegetically valid observation.

More important than the foregoing is the way Wesley understood what it meant to be a New Testament Christian. In the context of an argument that the Eucharist can function as a "converting ordinance," he basically defines those who are "converted," those who are "believers in the full sense," as those "who have received the Holy Ghost."[48] This and numerous other quotations solidly support the conclusion of Maddox that for Wesley, "the 'baptism' of the Spirit's renewed Presence comes at the beginning of our Christian life, and provides the indispensable empowerment for our growth in holiness all along the Way of Salvation—including the potential attainment of Christian Perfection."[49]

Succinctly stated then, Wesley's understanding of the nature of *Christian* experience would interpret the bestowal of the Holy Spirit upon the disciples as that event that ushered them into the New Age of the Spirit, and was the foretaste of what all subsequent authentic conversions would entail. Does this mean that the disciples were first saved at Pentecost? Absolutely not! To raise that possibility is a red herring that directs attention away from the real issue Luke was emphasizing.

Rob Staples, in an unpublished paper addressing the issue of using "baptism with the Holy Spirit" to refer to entire sanctification, summarized his findings:

> At times [Wesley] does use the expression "fullness of the Spirit," but he is not consistent in his application of the term and perhaps never used it with doctrinal precision, even when the important matter of chronology is taken into consideration. In his sermon "The First Fruits of the Spirit," preached in 1745, the expression "filled with the Holy Ghost" is used to describe the justified believer who has not yet been cleansed from inward sin. And in 1758, Wesley says that Paul's experience of being "filled with the Holy Ghost" was a part of the apostle's *conversion*. On the other hand, in 1771 he can use the term "fullness of the Spirit" as an equivalent of Christian perfection. But even in cases such as the latter he does not relate this "fullness

of the Spirit" to what happened at Pentecost. Usually
Pentecost is described as the "receiving" of the Holy Spirit
by the disciples, and such "receiving" of the Spirit is what,
in Wesley's mind, constituted the "conversion" or the justification and regeneration of the disciples. The evidence
for this is abundant and unequivocal.[50]

One of the clearest statements is found in his work on
A Farther Appeal to Men of Reason and Religion where he says
concerning several Scriptures about the Holy Spirit, including Acts
2: "From this passage I learn, First that every true Christian now
'receives the Holy Ghost,' as the Paraclete or Comforter promised
by our Lord, John XIV.16: Secondly, that every Christian receives
him as 'the Spirit of truth,' (promised John XVI,) to 'teach him all
things:' and, Thirdly, that 'the anointing,' mentioned in the first
Epistle of St. John, 'abides in every Christian.'" A couple of pages
later he adds, "I assert that till a man 'receives the Holy Ghost,' he
is without God in the world."[51]

Staple's findings suggest that Wesley doubtless used such
pneumatological terminology in the same wide-ranging fashion as
he did the concept of the *imago dei,* applying it to virtually every
phase of one's redemptive relation to God.

But as we noted in our introductory summary, some of
Wesley's followers began speaking about sanctification more specifically in terms of being "baptized with the Holy Spirit" and related
it to Pentecost. The most notable of these was John Fletcher, whom
Wesley had appointed to succeed him as leader of the Methodist
movement. However, Fletcher preceded Wesley in death. Joseph
Benson, another of Wesley's associates, became prominent in using
this language.

Wesley's response to these terminological developments was
irenic in tone. He wrote to Benson on December 28, 1770:

Is there no deliverance, no salvation from this inbred
enemy? Surely there is; else many great and precious
promises must fall to the ground. "I will sprinkle clean
water upon you, and ye shall be clean; from all your filthiness and from all your idols will I cleanse you." "I will
circumcise thy heart" (from all sin), "to love the Lord thy
God with all thy heart and with all thy soul." This I term
sanctification (which is both an instantaneous and a

gradual work), or perfection, the being perfected in love, filled with love, which still admits of a thousand degrees. But I have no time to throw away in contending for words, especially where the thing is allowed. And you allow the whole thing which I contend for—an entire deliverance from sin, a recovery of the whole image of God, the loving God with all our heart, soul, and strength.[52]

Later in the same letter, Wesley reveals the issue that is apparently at stake and encourages Benson to confirm the brethren "(2) in expecting a second change, whereby they shall be saved from all sin and perfected in love." This is clearly a reference to Wesley's emphasis on entire sanctification. To make the issue clear, he cautions Benson, "If they like to call this 'second change' 'receiving the Holy Ghost,' they may; only the phrase in that sense is not scriptural and not quite proper; for they all 'received the Holy Ghost' when they were justified."[53]

Apparently Benson resisted conforming to Wesley's advice as well as developing other teachings contrary to sound doctrine since in a letter on March 9, 1771, Wesley urges him to "abstain from speaking of Universal Salvation and Mr. Fletcher's late discovery."[54] While it is not an unequivocal inference, it seems quite certain that Fletcher's "late discovery" was the doctrine of "receiving the Holy Ghost" as another way of referring to entire sanctification. Wesley thought this was unscriptural.

To Fletcher himself, Wesley wrote on March 22, 1775: "It seems our views of Christian Perfection are a little different, though not opposite. It is certain every babe in Christ has received the Holy Ghost, and the Spirit witnesses with his spirit that he is a child of God. But he has not obtained Christian perfection. Perhaps you have not considered St. John's threefold distinction of Christian believers: Little children, young men, and fathers. All of these had received the Holy Ghost; but only the fathers were perfected in love."[55]

This discussion leads to the conclusion that John Wesley would no doubt fully concur with the statement of James D. G. Dunn that "whatever their [the 120] old covenant experience of the Spirit, it was only at Pentecost that they entered into what Paul might have called the abba-relationship with the Father, in which the filial relation of Jesus to God is repeated in the experience of the Christian through his reception of the Spirit of the Son. And since it is this relationship which alone may be called 'Christian,' it was only at Pentecost that the 120 became Christians."[56]

Since the teaching of John Fletcher seems so pivotal in initiating the bifurcation in the Wesleyan tradition regarding the "baptism with the Holy Spirit," or being "filled with the Holy Spirit," it appears appropriate to explore more carefully what he actually taught. Virtually everyone who recognizes the influence of Fletcher appears to assume that he equated entire sanctification with the baptism with the Holy Spirit. Randy Maddox is typical as he notes, "The Holiness branch of the Methodist family tended to follow Fletcher in equating entire sanctification with the baptism of the Holy Spirit."[57] But David Cubie and Rob Staples have demonstrated that Fletcher did not actually equate the two experiences.[58]

In his classic work, *Checks to Antinomianism,* Fletcher is giving direction to those seeking Christian perfection and presents an apologetic in the process that is identical to John Wesley's. He first cites a number of Scriptures that define the *precept* of perfection and exhorts his reader, "Let then your faith deliberately rest her right foot upon these precepts and then let faith place her left foot upon the following *promises.*" In reference to a number of biblical promises, he declares: "Always rest the doctrine of Christian perfection on this Scriptural foundation, and it will stand as firm as revelation itself."[59]

He then turns to the subject of the baptism with the Holy Spirit promised by Joel in the Old Testament, John the Baptist in Matthew 3:11, and Jesus in Acts 1:4–5. He refers to the fulfillment of these promises in the Pentecostal outpouring of the Spirit as "a *specimen* of the power which introduces believers into the state of Christian perfection."[60] On the Day of Pentecost "the kingdom of God . . . began to come with a new power; then were thousands wonderfully converted, and clearly justified; then . . . the love of Christ and of the brethren began to burn the chaff of selfishness and sin with a force which the world had never seen before."[61] Note the significance of the words, "specimen" and "began."

Regarding the language of Acts 4:31–33, identical to that used of the Pentecostal outpouring, he says: "Some time after, another glorious baptism, or capital outpouring of the Spirit, carried the disciples of Christ farther into the kingdom of grace which perfects believers in one. And therefore we find that the account which St. Luke gives us of them after this second, capital manifestation of the Holy Spirit, in a great degree answers to our Lord's prayer for their perfection. He had asked 'that they all might be one' . . . and that they might be perfected in one, John 17:23. And now a fuller answer is given to his deep request."

Staples calls attention to the fact that Fletcher does not use the popular explanation of the difference between these two "fillings" by speaking of "one baptism, many fillings." Instead, he noted, "these were two steps, two baptisms with the Spirit, which carried Christ's disciples farther along the path to perfection."

Once again using the imagery of John Wesley, Fletcher addresses the matter of whether those who received the Spirit as recorded in Acts 4:31 were all made perfect in love. He admits the possibility that some were, but uses the example of Ananias and Sapphira to suggest that this was not the case with all. It may be, he says, that some were "strong in the grace of their dispensation" and thus "arose then into sinless fathers." But "this does not necessarily mean that they were all equally strong in grace; for unity and happiness may rest upon a whole family where the difference between a father, a young man, and a child continues to subsist."[62] However, he did allow the possibility that all entered this high stage of grace by God's permission.

Perhaps the most crucial statement for Fletcher's view is the following:

> Should you ask, how many baptisms, or effusions of the sanctifying Spirit are necessary to cleanse a believer from all sin, and to kindle his soul into perfect love. . . . I should betray a want of modesty if I brought the operations of the Holy Ghost, and the energy of faith, under a rule which is not expressly laid down in the Scriptures. If you ask your physician how many doses of physic you must take before all the crudities of your stomach can be carried off, and your appetite perfectly restored; he would probably answer you, that this depends upon the nature of those crudities, the strength of the medicine, and the manner in which your constitution will allow it to operate; and that in general you must repeat the dose, as you

can bear, till the remedy has fully answered the desired end. I return a similar answer; if one powerful baptism of the Spirit "seal you unto the day of redemption, and cleanse you from all [moral] filthiness," so much better. If two or more be necessary, the Lord can repeat them. . . . Before we can rank among perfect Christians, we must receive so much of the truth and Spirit of Christ by faith, as to have the pure love of God and man shed abroad in our hearts by the Holy Ghost.[63]

Thus as David Cubie says, "Fletcher teaches that the baptism with the Holy Spirit is repeated in a succession of events beginning with the new birth and concluding with glory."[64] Based on these passages from Fletcher a few things are clear: (1) he did not merely equate entire sanctification with the baptism with the Holy Spirit; (2) his primary concern was the same as Wesley in holding tenaciously to the ethical aspect of the Christian life as definitive; (3) one could legitimately use the terminology of "baptism" of a number of spiritually renewing experiences including the new birth and also entire sanctification. Nevertheless, a reading of the nineteenth-century Holiness literature reveals that virtually without exception, it describes its theology as Wesleyan but at the same time speaks with rare exceptions, so far as my reading can discover, of entire sanctification as the "baptism with the Holy Spirit," and uses Pentecost as the paradigm for the "second work of grace."

Fletcher's most influential contribution to the Wesleyan revival occurred in the controversies with the Calvinists and was expressed in his major work entitled *Checks to Antinomianism*. For purposes of our inquiry (and proposals in the last section of this essay), the most relevant of his ideas are found in an essay on "A Portrait of St. Paul, the Ideal Pastor," which has to do with his doctrine of dispensations. It should be stated in the strongest possible terms that Fletcher's use of this language has nothing in common with the currently popular teaching known as dispensationalism, which arose in the nineteenth century with the Plymouth Brethren movement.

While one cannot be dogmatic, Fletcher apparently made two moves in the development of this teaching that led to his use of pneumatological language as related to sanctification. The first was fairly traditional and was historical in nature. He viewed history as divided into three dispensations corresponding to the three persons of the Trinity. The crucial element here is the degree of knowledge of God given through revelation. He refers to the dispensation of the Father variously as "the natural law," "the remains of the Creator's image in the human heart," "the secret grace of the Redeemer which is more or less operative in every man," "Gentilism," or "Judaism." The dispensation of the Son reflects a more perfect divine disclosure while that of the Spirit is the highest.

The second move was to transfer this "theology of history"[65] to individual experience. It was this latter move that eventually resulted in relating the Pentecostal event with the entire sanctification of the 120 (though not as a one-to-one correlation by Fletcher himself), and describing it in pneumatological language and thus moved him away (at least linguistically) from Wesley's way of formulation sanctification references. Fletcher's way of elaborating the divine-human relation was the outcome of his wide-ranging application of the distinctive Wesleyan doctrine of prevenient grace. Possibly it was this doctrine that was the point of contact that resulted in the later Wesley making some comments that appeared to reflect the influence of Fletcher's dispensational theology. In his sermon "On Faith," Wesley refers to "a small degree of light [that] is given to those that are under the heathen dispensation."[66] The concept and language is clearly Fletcherian.

In the opinion of this writer, the way Fletcher explained the nature of the three dispensations ultimately provides a *rapprochement* between his views and those of his mentor. He understood each dispensation as having two aspects, a cognitive and an existential or experiential. The former formatively influenced the latter. Fletcher understood the relationship between these two aspects as having practical significance to the pastor, and this was his primary concern. Like St. Paul the ideal pastor should seek to discern the spiritual state of his parishioners in order to determine in which dispensation they were in their experience. His task was then to lead them cognitively to the recognition of a higher level of relationship with the goal that they should enter that relation existentially.

This analysis of the various dispensations was based on a synergistic understanding of the divine-human relation and thus was of a piece with Fletcher's opposition to Calvinism with its logically implied practical (ethical) implications. A contrast can be seen in the following monergistic interpretation by Ned Stonehouse. In discussing the activity of the Spirit in the book of Acts, he says: "The baptism with the Spirit on that day [Pentecost] constituted a unilateral, eschatological action on the part of Christ, as immediate and miraculous as the resurrection of Jesus. If human cooperation or a human response had been indicated as being of the essence of what took place, the foundational significance of Pentecost would have been obliterated or obscured."[67]

The case of the twelve disciples at Ephesus (Acts 19:1–7) is a near-perfect example of the application of Fletcher's view that experience is directly related to the cognitive aspect. This insight will be a significant factor when we come to the last part of our discussion.

The Nineteenth-Century Holiness Movement

As already noted, the preachers and teachers of the Holiness revivals in the United States came to speak with one voice about entire sanctification as the "baptism with the Holy Spirit," and underscored its significance as being both instantaneous and subsequent to conversion, thus a "second work of grace."

In 1974, Charles W. Carter published a book entitled *The Person and Ministry of the Holy Spirit: A Wesleyan Perspective,* which included a major section on "The Baptism with the Spirit in the Pentecostal Experience."[68] Carter recognized that Wesley was "reticent" to use "baptism with the Holy Spirit" language but argued that more recent Holiness writers have "improved upon the structure and expression" of Wesley. He further insisted that "Wesley meant theologically and experientially essentially the same Biblical truth as they believe and teach."[69] Earlier in his book, Carter explicitly rejects the widely held view among Wesleyans that Pentecost was the birthday of the church.[70] This rejection reflects the individualizing of religious experience that seems to have marked the shift from a biblically based corporate understanding to a privatistic interpretation of religion. But its intent is to avoid the inherent contradiction involved in affirming both that Pentecost was the birthday of the church and equating it with entire sanctification, thus implying that only the entirely sanctified constitute the "church."

The most significant thing about Carter's work, for our purposes, was that a statement was printed in the front as a virtual *imprimatur* from the Christian Holiness Association, which represented the majority of Holiness groups in the United States. It stated: "The Christian Holiness Association has defined and proclaimed the Wesleyan interpretation of Scripture since 1867. Dr. Charles W. Carter's book . . . is considered by us to be a scholarly and exhaustive exposition within the Wesleyan interpretation of the Holy Spirit as presented in the Scriptures. It is for this reason that we give our full endorsement."

Without intending to sound pejorative, it should be noted here that few scholars were involved in the nineteenth-century Holiness awakenings. The one obvious exception was Daniel Steele, Boston University theology professor, whose teachings were consistent with that of the popular writers but more theologically and exegetically informed. Wesley Tracy's description of these "Holiness fathers" is quite illuminating:

They had, predictably, a natural built-in resistance to intellectuals. After all, it was the intellectuals—the scientists, theologians, philosophers, and scholars who could read Greek and Hebrew Bibles—who had destroyed the world they had inherited from their parents.

In an almost instinctive survival move they, more or less, cut themselves off from the biblical scholarship, the theological reflection, and the philosophical hypothesizing then taking place. Avoiding such things it is not surprising that the good people of this movement came early to rely heavily on testimony and religious experience. They developed a way of being that was long on personal experience and short on in-depth understanding of the Scriptures and open-minded theological reflection.[71]

Perhaps more influential as informing the "theology" of Holiness during the revivals of the post-Civil War period is the situation lamented by Mildred Bangs Wynkoop in a presentation to the Wesleyan Theological Society in 1979:

There was a vigorous Wesleyanism composed of theological interpretations from other [than Methodist] traditions. Many of the so-called "Holiness classics" were produced by this non-Wesleyan side. An examination of

the long lists of books and pamphlets printed and recom-
mended for the holiness people shows that as the nineteenth century progressed there were fewer and fewer of
Wesley's own writings made available. Today, Wesley's
works are so limited and expensive that most of the
Holiness preachers and students have never read Wesley
and often stoutly maintain that they are not really
Wesleyan. A precious heritage is going by the board.[72]

As young people in the movement began to seek advanced
degrees in academic institutions, resulting in better historical, theological, and exegetical consciousness, they began to explore their
"Wesleyan roots," with interesting results.[73] Coming to terms with
the disparity between Wesley and his nineteenth-century successors, however, was not easy to do. In 1964, Leo George Cox published his doctoral dissertation (University of Iowa) entitled *John
Wesley's Concept of Perfection*.[74] Cox recognized the discrepancy
between Wesley himself and his successors but, like Charles Carter,
attempted to argue that "the idea is implicit in Wesley" that the
instantaneous experience of entire sanctification is the equivalent
of the Pentecostal experience in Acts.[75] In the light of the overwhelming evidence to the contrary, this can only be evaluated as a
case of special pleading.

Others among my own peers, including myself, in doing
advanced research came to discover a "different" Wesley than the
one we had learned about in the popular preaching and teaching of
the Holiness movement. Among the several contrasts we discovered had to do with the understanding of the equivalence between
the Pentecostal "baptism with the Holy Spirit" and entire sanctification. But we generally said little about it and certainly did not
intend to make an issue out of it.

However, the issue exploded in Wesleyan academic circles in
1972 at the annual meeting of the Wesleyan Theological Society
with a paper listened to on tape recorded by Herbert McGonigle of
England. McGonigle's paper was entitled "Pneumatological
Nomenclature in Early Methodism." McGonigle, a dedicated John
Wesley scholar, argued that the Wesleys said little about the baptism with the Holy Spirit but that this emphasis "arose in America,
rather than, British Methodism." While McGonigle's paper did not
adequately take account of British Wesleyans like John Fletcher

and argued that Wesley was remiss in his failure to make the pneumatological emphasis, it did serve as a catalyst for a vigorous debate that stretched over several years and that at times became quite high-pitched.[76]

One wonders why this issue created such near pandemonium among many Holiness people. Perhaps one reason is that the use of Pentecost as the paradigm for entire sanctification provided a clear-cut illustration of the two issues that had been at the forefront of the dissention between the mainline Methodist followers of Wesley and the Holiness people, namely the secondness or subsequence and instantaneousness of entire sanctification. Other New Testament evidence from the Gospels and Epistles entailed considerable ambiguity.[77] John Wesley himself said of the question about whether sanctification was gradual or instantaneous, "the scriptures are silent on the subject." This partially explains his flexibility regarding the structure of Christian experience.

No doubt, one of the cultural factors that precipitated the issue becoming public was the emergence of the Charismatic revival. Donald Dayton, in his doctoral dissertation (University of Chicago), had demonstrated that the shift to pneumatological language by the Holiness movement was one of the major factors that occasioned the rise of modern Pentecostalism. He concludes his chapter on this development: "It is thus no accident that Pentecostalism emerged when it did. All that was needed was the spark that would ignite this volatile tinder."[78]

Rob Staples perceptively notes that the transition from Christological to pneumatological categories "unwittingly opened the door to the question of 'evidence,' to which the Pentecostals had a 'neat' answer." By contrast, if holiness is described as "Christlikeness," that is a self-defining term. Scholarship in the Holiness movement began to recognize that there was no difference in the theology that had become standard in the "right-wing" Wesleyan tradition and Pentecostal theology, and with the outbreak of "tongues speaking" in Wesleyan churches, a phenomenon that had always been viewed as unacceptable,[79] they disconcertingly found that there was no exegetical or theological basis in the prevailing theological formulations about sanctification for rejecting the practice. The only recourse was to ecclesiastical pronouncement on the basis of denominational commitment.

Timothy Smith, professor of American church history at Johns Hopkins University and devoted participant in the Holiness movement, offered a thesis that credited Charles G. Finney with being the decisive influence in the shift to "baptism with the Holy Spirit" language. Unlike Wesley, said Smith, Finney drew upon Moses and the prophets and the Old Testament promises, interpreting them according to the tradition of Puritan or covenant theology. Finney's study of the promises led him to turn to the language of Pentecost to expound the covenant of grace. Smith said in his paper to the Wesleyan Theological Society: "The transfer of Finney's Pentecostal language into American Methodism was direct and immediate. George O. Peck, editor of the influential Methodist weekly, The New York *Christian Advocate,* paid close attention to Finney's lectures as they appeared in *The Oberlin Evangelist* in 1839 and 1840. In the fall of the latter year, he became the first Methodist since John Fletcher to equate the experience of entire sanctification with the baptism with the Holy Ghost."[80]

If Smith is correct, it illustrates Mildred Bangs Wynkoop's contention that influential factors that formed the theology of the Holiness movement came from outside authentic Wesleyan perspectives. This influence resulted in what Rob Staples called a "hybrid theology" resulting from crossbreeding Wesleyan perfectionism with covenant theology. We will explore some of the implications of this later.

In a condensed version of his WTS paper published in *Christianity Today,* Smith observed that "one of the fascinating questions surrounding the history of the Holiness movement in America and Britain is how the heirs of John Wesley moved from his almost exclusive use of Calvary language to declare the promise and describe the experience of sanctification" in terms of the "baptism with the Holy Spirit." In the light of this implicit interpretation of Wesley, Smith makes the judgment that "to discover and combine in one rhetoric of redemption the idioms of Pentecost and Calvary [was] an improvement upon John Wesley."[81]

In Herbert McGonigle's paper, referred to earlier, he also says that the emphasis of Wesley's characteristic language was upon Calvary and the atonement, rather than upon Pentecost, as the ground of our sanctification. Rob Staples is certainly correct in pointing out that it is not accurate to claim that Wesley almost exclusively used "Calvary language" to "declare the promise and describe the experience of sanctification," and supports his critique by the fact that Wesley was careful to distinguish between *justification* as "what God does for us through his Son," and *sanctification* as "what God works in us by his Spirit."[82]

While recognizing that Wesley unequivocally related sanctification to the work of the Spirit, I would suggest that a much more appropriate linguistic reference is to characterize his perfectionist language as "incarnational." Since the debate over the equation of entire sanctification with the baptism with the Holy Spirit in the seventies has apparently subsided, Wesley scholars have become increasingly aware of the influence of the Eastern church fathers upon Wesley's understanding of sanctification.[83] This tradition has stressed the redemptive significance of the work of Christ in terms of transformation (deification) and attributes this result to the incarnation. In the famous formula of Irenaeus and Athanasius, "He became what we are, that we may become what He is." This insight will inform our discussion in the final part of this essay.

Another consequence of the shift from the pristine Wesleyan understanding of the work of the Spirit under the influence of the Oberlin theology was a gradual transition from emphasizing purity to emphasizing power as a concomitant of the "baptism with the Holy Spirit." Donald Dayton has demonstrated in his dissertation research that this shift brought about an increased emphasis on spiritual gifts and the gift of prophecy and "by the turn of the century attention had expanded to include the more 'supernatural' gifts of healing and miracles. . . . Those who stayed closest to the Wesleyan tradition emphasized the *ethical* consequences and the 'graces' rather than the gifts of the Spirit, but the push was increasingly toward the 'spiritual gifts *and* graces'—especially where the fascination with Pentecost was most intense."[84]

Dayton's thesis is that this is one aspect of the developments that resulted, theologically, in the rise of Pentecostalism. The tension between purity and power resulted in the rise of the idea among some that the baptism with the Holy Spirit was a third blessing, adding power to the cleansing of sanctification. Theologians like A. M. Hills, whose systematic theology was the text for the minister's course of study in the Church of the Nazarene for some time, profoundly influenced by the Oberlin theology, wrote extensively arguing for the coalescence of "holiness and power."[85]

Mildred Bangs Wynkoop states the authentic Wesleyan response to this development in her observation in an early book: "Among the very many terms he [Wesley] used for entire sanctification, never did he call it the baptism of the Holy Spirit or any like term because of the danger of seeking the Holy Spirit for some accompanying gift or emotion instead of seeking Christ and His will. Wesley's ethical insights are seen in the fact that he does not point us to the gifts of the Spirit but to the fruits of the Spirit."[86]

A Proposed Wesleyan Interpretation

One who presents a theological interpretation of any aspect of the Christian faith should make clear at the outset the methodology to be employed in arriving at the conclusions. Wesleyan theology uses an approach that has been popularized by Albert Outler as the "Wesleyan Quadrilateral." Actually, there is little that is unique in this method, which builds its theological commitments on a complex of four "sources."

These four—Scripture, reason, tradition, and experience—have been generally employed within the Christian tradition.[87] It is the way in which these are incorporated into theological reflection that is distinctive. Properly understood, reason, tradition, and experience function in subordination to the authority of Scripture and should never have independent authority, although each has assumed that prerogative at various times in Christian history. The theologian who claims to derive his beliefs from the Bible alone, without any formative influences from one or more of these subsidiary sources, is only engaged in self-deception.

Having committed to the final authority of Scripture, it then needs to be affirmed unequivocally that it must be the Bible rightly interpreted. As John Bright puts it, "The Bible can seem to mean, and can be made to mean, many things; to acknowledge it as authoritative settles nothing so long as the principles by which it is to be interpreted are not agreed upon."[88]

My own hermeneutical method, which is widely employed by other students, includes two major exegetical steps. The first is commonly referred to as grammatico-historical exegesis. This means that "the text is to be taken as meaning what its words most plainly mean in the light of the situation (historical situation or life-situation) to which they were originally addressed: the 'grammar' is to be interpreted against the background of 'history.'"[89] This is indispensable to avoid as fully as possible the skewing of the meaning of the text by subjective factors. This classical approach implicitly rejects the approach to the text that denies the possibility of discovering the original "intention" of the Scripture, characteristic of an aspect of so-called post-modernism.[90]

The second step is to do a "theological exegesis" of the text(s) under consideration. This step is intended to exegete the text in its theological depth, to identify the theology that informs the text. Doing this exercise requires that one must recognize that the Bible is not an encyclopedia or dictionary in the sense that a word or term or concept means the same throughout, but various writers (e.g., Luke and Paul) have their own theological formulations within the larger context of a consistent vision of the gospel. This is a particularly important insight in relation to the issue under investigation in this volume.

Before exploring the specific New Testament data about the Holy Spirit, it is important to survey briefly the Old Testament's eschatological hope concerning the Age of the Spirit, which must be understood against the background of the Old Testament experience of the Spirit (*Ruach*).

Here, the mysterious, invisible, and unpredictable power or energy of the wind provided a paradigm to identify the activity of the *Ruach* (breath, wind, spirit) of Yahweh. Hence, when men (or women) were seized with a power from beyond themselves and behaved in commensurate ways, they were identified as men (or women) of the Spirit. In the earliest sources this was often depicted as an unexpected, intermittent experience that energized otherwise obscure and less-than-competent persons to do mighty exploits in the interest of national freedom. It was a temporary endowment given in times of crisis and for the purpose of dealing with that crisis. In a word, it produced Charismatic (Spirit-gifted) leaders (cf. Judg. 3:10; 6:34; 11:29).

Early prophecy in Israel also shared in this "Spirit seizure," which elevated the prophet's natural capacities to an intensity that caused him (or her) to behave in unusual ways. This Spirit possession was often, if not universally, precipitated by music and dancing (see 1 Sam. 10:6ff; 19:20ff).[91]

Saul of Kish, in the time of his preparation for kingship, is a classic example of this early picture of the experience of the Spirit of Yahweh (1 Sam. 10:6, 9–10). Some have suggested that the outcome of the seizure, brought on by stimulation within the group accompanied by music, was a type of glossolalia. However, one Old Testament scholar has demonstrated the uncertainty of this opinion and argued that instead of "strange utterances," the distinguishing characteristic of ecstasy was "strange actions."[92] It was this strange behavior that called forth the words of ridicule: "What has come over the son of Kish? Is Saul also among the prophets?" (v. 11).

Aside from the striking aspects of these few experiences that we may classify as abnormal behavior, there is a distinctive feature of the Old Testament experiences of the Spirit that has great significance. Such Charismatic (Spirit-gifted) experiences are chiefly limited to those who function as leaders in Israel. Walther Eichrodt argues that the validation of leadership by Charismatic endowment stems from Moses himself. Pointing to the difficulty of classifying Moses under any traditional category such as prophet, king, or other title, he insists that Moses' unusual combination of gifts, enhanced by the initiating energy of the Spirit, is the key to his uniqueness. In this, Moses places his stamp upon all subsequent claims to leadership. Eichrodt concludes: "At the very beginning of Israelite religion we find the charisma, the special individual endowment of a person; and to such an extent is the whole structure based upon it, that without it, it would be inconceivable."[93]

This explains the central importance of judges and prophets having the power of the Spirit to demonstrate that they are sent of God. William Barclay's more popular treatment also suggests the same thing when he says: "The great leaders of the Old Testament are men who possess the Spirit, who have been possessed by the Spirit, and in whom the Spirit dwells."[94]

Later prophets did not generally manifest the same ecstatic traits or claims as the earlier prophets, but their authenticity was still verified by the fact that God put his Spirit within them and gave their message (cf. Num. 11:25ff.; Mic. 3:8; Ezek. 2:2; 3:24; etc.).[95]

No doubt it was the principle of Charismatic leadership that was the basis for much opposition to the institution of kingship in early Israel. The transition was bridged, thinks John Bright, by the first kings being Charismatic leaders. David was the exemplar in this regard (cf. 1 Sam. 16:13–14; 2 Sam. 23:2).[96] There may be a similar significance attached to the anointing of kings at their induction into office: the hope that they would be Charismatic rulers.

In addition to these more obvious endowments of the Spirit in the Old Testament understanding, there was also a less explosive and spasmodic endowment that inspired and equipped to more mundane tasks such as craftsmanship (Exod. 28:3; 31:3; 35:31). More permanent gifts of the Spirit's power are also suggested in a few exceptional cases, such as Moses and Joshua (Num. 11:17; 27:18; Deut. 34.9).

It is to be noted that these experiences we have surveyed are task oriented. Furthermore, there does not seem to be any necessary ethical accompaniment to the special endowments. Not all reflected the low moral tone of a Samson, but ethical stipulations are generally absent from the description of Spirit possession. One might argue that an exception to this is the classic prophets who, under the inspiration of the Spirit, decried unethical behavior among God's people and enjoined conformity to the covenant law.

With this background we may now note the eschatological dimension of the Old Testament understanding, which builds solidly upon these views. First, there is a chord of hope that longed for, and then predicted, a democratization of the Spirit. The distribution of the Spirit of leadership upon the seventy elders, enabling them to share Moses' burdens, was a fore-gleam. But its broader realization was longed for in Moses' magnanimous words in the face of jealousy over his own position as a Spirit-endowed leader: "Would that all the Lord's people were prophets, that the Lord would put his spirit up them!" (Num. 11:29 ESV).

The prophecy of Joel explicitly envisions the sequel to the Day of the Lord being the universal outpouring upon all flesh (by which he obviously meant "Jewish" flesh, as did Peter, in quoting this passage in his Pentecost sermon) in 2:28–29.[97] It is important to note here that this vision relates directly to prophecy and thus stands in direct continuity with the central Old Testament understanding of the work of the Spirit as task oriented.

In addition to these expectations is a theme of hope that the coming of the Spirit in the eschatological age will bring moral renewal. In this regard, these passages move beyond the orbit of the usual Old Testament perception and doubtless grow out of a profound sense of need for such inner transformation for both the individual and the community.

In the Psalms, notably 51, there are prayers for inner renewal to provide strength to do God's will. In this psalm (v. 11), along with Isaiah 63:10–11, we have the only instances of the phrase "Holy Spirit." The usual Old Testament designation is "Spirit of Yahweh," but here we have not so much an anticipation of New Testament terminology as recognition that God's Spirit is the Enabler to holiness. The phrase may literally be translated "Spirit of holiness." In Isaiah 63:10, "'the grieving of the holy spirit' means the rejecting of the prophetic instruction by which God sought to guide his people towards holiness and righteousness."[98]

In Ezekiel 36:26ff., the priest-prophet implicitly recognizes the inadequacy of a restored ritual and, along with Jeremiah (31:31ff.), anticipates an eschatological time of heart transformation. He explicitly attributes this to the operation of the Spirit: "I will put my spirit within you, and cause you to walk in my statutes" (Ezek. 36:27 ESV). The vision of the valley of dry bones (37:1–14) may also convey the same motif.[99]

Furthermore, there is a strand of eschatological hope that relates the Spirit to two ideal figures: the Messianic King and the Servant of the Lord.[100] In both cases, a permanent endowment with the Spirit is a prominent feature (see Isa. 11:2; 42:1–4).

While there is a solid core of evidence in the canonical Old Testament itself regarding the Spirit-anointed character of the Messianic King (which is in accord with the validation of rulership referred to above), this theme is much more fully developed in intertestamental Judaism. Such a development is doubtless intensified by the rabbinic belief that the Spirit of prophecy had been withdrawn from Israel, which explains the need for apocalyptic writers to attribute their visions to an ancient writer who lived during the prophetic age. Hence there is, in rabbinic literature, a frequent reference to the Spirit of prophecy.[101]

Building solidly upon Isaiah 11:2, the rabbis depicted the coming Messiah as endowed with the Spirit of prophecy. Through him the Golden Age of the Spirit would return. Since the Spirit was withdrawn because of Israel's sin, his return would be accompanied by sanctification: "The evil impulse would be taken out of Israel's heart in the age to come, and the Spirit, as a power for moral renewal, would rest upon her."[102] The same motif is found in the "Manual of Discipline" among the Dead Sea Scrolls: "United through the holy spirit of God's truth, man shall be cleansed of all his iniquities: because of an upright and humble spirit his sin shall be atoned" (1QS 3:6–7). Hill comments: "Here we are in touch once more with the thought expressed in Psalm 51 that the powerful influence on man's life of God's truth and righteousness creates the desire for and will to achieve holiness through obedience and righteous conduct."[103]

Thus, the themes of a universal outpouring of God's Spirit, the Spirit-anointed ministry of the ideal King, and the anticipated moral regeneration of the human heart are intertwined in Jewish expectation on the threshold of the New Testament.

Our next step, on moving to the New Testament, is to engage in a brief grammatico-historical analysis of the texts relevant to "Spirit baptism." The phrase "baptism with the Holy Spirit" (which incidentally is not found in the New Testament) is primarily derived from two biblical sources, the announcement of John the Baptist (Matt. 3:11; Mark 1:8; Luke 3:16; John 1:33) and the words of Jesus in Acts 1:5, repeated in 11:16. Even though Luke's description of Pentecost uses the language of "filling," it seems reasonable and exegetically sound to relate the baptism of which they spoke to that event, even though its meaning and implication may not have been exhausted on that day. In light of the methodological statement above, we must observe that because being baptized in the Spirit and being filled with the Spirit are equivalent expressions for Luke does not mean that they are for any other writer.[104]

All of these uses are in the form of a promise that those who respond to the messianic word will be baptized in the Holy Spirit, and it is the Messiah who will baptize them with the Spirit. In a careful study of the various experiences recorded in Acts that would be considered the fulfillment of this promise, Robert Lyon has demonstrated that each one is an initial experience whereby each group (or person in the case of Saul of Tarsus [but see above]) is initiated into the promised Age of the Spirit or, what is the same thing, incorporated into the body of Christ. This entails the conclusion that one cannot draw a one-to-one parallel between the experiences recorded by Luke of those who are involved in this transitional age and subsequent Christian experience. By the very nature of historical existence, it is impossible for a later person to live prior to the initial giving of the Spirit, which, in Luke's understanding, clearly occurred in stages corresponding in large part to the expanding inclusiveness of the New Age. Lyon concludes his exegetical study in the following summary statement: "From Pentecost on, all believers receive at conversion the Holy Spirit as promised—in his fullness. No biblical basis exists for a distinction between receiving the Spirit and being baptized in, or filled with, the Spirit. The Acts of the Apostles shows *au contraire* that they are interchangeable expressions. All references involving the language of baptism reinforce that conclusion, for they are all inclusive as a descriptive of every believer."[105] This grammatico-historical exegesis substantiates the understanding of John Wesley himself.

Thus, in the light of Luke's understanding, it seems clear that he understood the effulgence of the Spirit at Pentecost as the inaugural event that ushered in the Age of the Spirit. Hence, if one views this pivotal moment as a transitional stage in salvation history, it is a nonrepeatable event. But if one would go further, as many are wont to do, and see it as paradigmatic for subsequent Christian experience, a number of questions are raised. Is what occurred in the experience of the 120 the same as that which should occur in every Christian's experience of the Holy Spirit? How does this differ from the three thousand who were "converted" in response to Peter's sermon to whom he offered the "gift of the Holy Spirit"? If Pentecost is paradigmatic, should we anticipate the same, or similar, outward signs to accompany every such experience? If the answer to this question is affirmative, what are the criteria for selecting only one of the several that were present at the initial outpouring, or should one insist on all including the sound of wind and visible tongues of fire? These and others are questions that have preoccupied much New Testament scholarship.[106] Dogmatism is therefore ill-advised. Hence, I present the following with some diffidence.

However we may address these and numerous other questions that arise, I would argue that the most important matter to be explored is theological, with every effort being made to avoid allowing dogmatic considerations to skew this task.

What clues should we look for in trying to identify the distinctive and unique features of these early experiences of the Holy Spirit as recorded by Luke? Two primary factors may be suggested. First, Luke's purpose in writing these accounts. The question of purpose suggests that his theological perspective will influence the meaning that will be overtly stressed, but that does not necessarily exclude other meanings that may be covertly or implicitly present. Raising the question of purpose at the outset is an attempt to guarantee that we ask the right questions when we approach the text of Acts.[107]

Within certain limits, there is an amazing degree of unanimity among scholars regarding the purpose of the writer of Acts. A summary of statements might read like this: Luke's broadest and primary intent was to demonstrate how, in the power and under the direction of the Holy Spirit, the church, which originated as a Jerusalem-based, Judaism-oriented sect of Jewish believers, became a chiefly Gentile, worldwide phenomenon reflecting a belief in universal salvation based on grace alone.[108] "William M. Greathouse substantially restates this purpose in his commentary on Acts: Luke has one master purpose in mind as he writes Acts: to sketch the Spirit-empowered witness of the Church as it begins in Jerusalem, spreads into surrounding regions, and extends to the wide world. His particular concern is with the preaching of the gospel and the planting of the Church in radiating centers throughout a large part of the Roman Empire."[109]

Alex Deasley, professor of New Testament at Nazarene Theological Seminary, in a paper presented to the Wesleyan Theological Society, affirms that Luke's primary concern in Acts is "with the Spirit as the agent of mission; hence the emphatic insistence at each of the nodal points in the advance of the gospel that the Spirit is poured out. His basic intent is to show that the Christian era is the era of the Spirit; that there is no Church without the Spirit; no Christian without the Spirit; and wherever the gospel goes in power, it goes in the power of the Spirit."[110]

However, as we hinted earlier, there may also be secondary purposes that can be identified. There is an apologetic purpose to demonstrate that Christianity is not politically dangerous and that Jews and not Christians instigated the violence that accompanied its spread. Luke may also intend to help heal the conflict between Jewish and Gentile believers by his treatments of Peter and Paul, but the primary purpose is clear and unequivocal.

With this hermeneutical insight as a benchmark, we may exclude a number of proposed interpretations of Acts. It is not Luke's primary intention to provide a normative or normal pattern of individual experience. Obviously, there are implications to be drawn here, but to attempt to make this an exegetical principle will lead to mass confusion since there is such a diversity of patterns present. Fee and Stuart point this out clearly: "When he [Luke] records individual conversions there are usually two elements included: water baptism and the gift of the Spirit. But these can be in reverse order, with or without the laying on of hands, with or without the mention of tongues, and scarcely ever with a specific mention of repentance, even after what Peter says in 2:38–39."[111]

Daniel Steele, nineteenth-century Holiness scholar, recognized the significance of this insight in answering a question concerning Wesley's reticence (refusal) to use baptism with the Holy Spirit as equivalent to entire sanctification. He said:

We learn from books and from the lectures of some theological professors that both regeneration and entire sanctification are states of grace sharply defined, entered upon instantaneously after certain very definite steps, and followed by certain very marked results. But the young preacher soon learns that there are eminently spiritual members of his church whose experiences have not been in accordance with this regulation manner. They have passed through no marked and memorable crises. Hence they have no spiritual anniversaries. The young pastor is puzzled by these anomalies. At last, if he is wise he will conclude that the books describe normal experiences to which the Holy Spirit does not limit itself, and that an abnormal method of gaining a spiritual change or elevation is by no means to be discounted.[112]

Understanding Luke's purpose in the way suggested here would immediately suggest the idea of *mission*. That is precisely the theme that confronts us at the outset and overwhelms us with its pervasiveness. It is the motif that dominates Luke's thinking from the beginning to the end of his "history of early Christianity."

This means that he would tend to stress the gift of the Spirit as endowment, one of the major strands of the Old Testament eschatological hope.

The opening words of Acts provide a clear clue as to his intention: "In the first book, O Theophilus, I have dealt with all that Jesus began to do and teach" (1:1 ESV). The implication is that the present writing intends to speak of what Jesus continued to do through the Spirit operative in his disciples. Jesus' last command to his disciples explicitly emphasizes this theme: "But you shall receive power when the Holy Spirit has come upon you; and you shall be my witnesses in Jerusalem, and in all Judea and Samaria, and to the end of the earth" (1:8 NKJV).

The events of the Day of Pentecost focus on factors that highlight the universality of the message about the risen Christ (the resurrection is what is to be witnessed to) and the power to proclaim it. The signs, especially the gift of languages, are unmistakably intended to focus on this truth. Finally, when Peter provides the explanation to the questioning crowd concerning the meaning of the disciples' behavior, he does so by quoting the Joel passage that deals with endowment for prophecy. Other passages could have been quoted (or reported as quoted) if Luke (or Peter) intended to stress other meanings (e.g., Jer. 31:31ff or Ezek. 36:26ff).

This dominant theme makes it possible for some interpreters to evaluate the early accounts of the experiences of the Spirit in Acts as little more than Old Testament phenomena. On the surface this might be a valid interpretation. However, given the situation, it is impossible to settle for this explanation as completely adequate. This moves us to a second consideration.

Even the concept of mission had been transformed in light of the fact that it was the continuation of the work of Christ. And this new understanding involved moral renewal (sanctification) because only by a radical reorientation of one's inner being, as well as his understanding of the nature of power, can the servant role be adopted. Thus we are quickly introduced to the second strand of the Old Testament eschatological hope.

As a result of this transformation, we must now acknowledge a different meaning in Luke's use of being "filled with the Holy Spirit" in connection with the birth narratives and his use of it here in describing the disciples' experience. Hull puts it poignantly: "We may say for the moment that it was the same Spirit, the Holy Spirit Himself, who filled Elizabeth and Zechariah and the disciples also. But while Elizabeth and Zechariah were only able to feel that they were filled with the Spirit of One whom they had not seen, namely God, the disciples were aware that they were filled with the Spirit who had been in One they had seen, namely, in Christ Himself."[113]

This diversity of meanings may partially account for the ambiguity earlier noted as being present in the Wesleyan movement from the beginning, first emerging in a discussion between John Wesley and John Fletcher. Alex R. G. Deasley, in exploring this ambiguity, calls attention to the qualifications that Daniel Steele made in his expositions of Holiness theology. Steele explicitly recognized that the phrase "baptism or fullness of the Spirit" has multiple meanings: There is an "ecstatic fullness," involving a flood of peace, joy, and power that "may prostrate the body without cleansing the soul"; there is a "Charismatic fullness," in which one may be endowed with some extraordinary gift of the Spirit; and then there is an "ethical fullness," which implies entire sanctification.[114]

W. F. Lofthouse has argued that the novelty of the conception of the Spirit as it appears in Acts is not often noted because of familiarity. It is so new, he argued, that it is quite different from the Old Testament conception, nor could the Old Testament have suggested it. He proposes that this new element is the understanding of the Spirit that comes to expression in the Fourth Gospel, especially chapters 14–16, which provides the background for the understanding in Acts.[115]

Although there is more to be said for the contributions of the Synoptic Gospels to the understanding of the Spirit in Acts than Lofthouse and other New Testament scholars allow, it is more implicit in these documents than explicit. Hence, it is important to note the input of Jesus' last sayings, which significantly come on the threshold of his passion.

In particular we are here enabled to see the relation between Jesus' high priestly prayer and the experiences(s) of the Spirit in Acts. In John 17, the theme of mission is likewise inescapably present and can be avoided only by prior dogmatic presuppositions. The burden of Jesus' prayer for his disciples was that "the world may believe that thou hast sent me" (v. 21). In the course of the prayer, he dedicated (sanctified) himself to the completion of his mission and prayed that God would dedicate (sanctify) his disciples to the continuance of that mission. The carrying out of this mission involves far more than persuasive speech; it entails a unity ("that they may be one" [v. 22, cf. 21]) that can occur only through a metamorphosis of their nature. Thus, the Pentecostal outpouring as well as subsequent ones have as their aim the moral renewal (sanctification) of the disciples so they may carry out this mission. The descriptions of the corporate life of the early church validate that Pentecost was clearly effective in accomplishing this result.

The premise that informs our discussion here is the insight of John Fletcher regarding the three "dispensations" as applied to personal (or corporate) religious experience. Each "dispensation" or level or stage of experience has both a cognitive and an existential element with the former giving shape to the latter. In applying this analysis to the experiences of the Spirit in Acts, we are proposing that how we interpret those experiences is directly related to the understanding of the recipients.

One of the crucial factors in attempting to identify the disciples' understanding of what the outpouring of the Spirit upon them meant is the charge of Jesus in Acts 1:4–5 ESV: "And while staying with them he ordered them not to depart from Jerusalem, but to wait for the promise of the Father, which, he said, 'you heard from me, for John baptized with water, but you will be baptized with the Holy Spirit not many days from now.'" What is the "promise of the Father"? Lofthouse has argued that since Luke asserts that Jesus spoke it, it can only refer to the Johannine passages dealing with the promise of the Paraclete. However, expanding our analysis to include the entire fourth Gospel will enhance our understanding of the crucially significant nature of this insight.

What is presented in John is more or less making explicit what is taught in a more inferential way in the Synoptic Gospels. It presents us with an illuminating structure with regard to its teachings about the Holy Spirit.[116] There are twelve references, divided equally into two groups of six each. In the first six, the reference is to the Spirit in relation to the ministry of Jesus, climaxing with the sixth (John 7:38–39), which emphasizes the Spirit not being bestowed until Jesus' glorification (John's shorthand term for his death, resurrection, and ascension). The second group refers to the

Spirit's relation to the followers of Jesus, climaxing with 20:22, where Jesus "breathed" the Holy Spirit into his disciples following the resurrection. In the first part Jesus is presented as the Bearer of the Spirit and in the second part as the One who bestows the Spirit. While these emphases are not hermetically separated, the distinction is generally valid.

John 1:32–33

This is the account of Jesus' baptism by John (although that fact is not explicitly made) and records some unique features. John is to recognize the fulfillment of his own work by the descent of the Holy Spirit in the form of a dove. That is, Jesus is authenticated thereby to be the Messiah. The distinctive emphasis is upon the Spirit's remaining, in contrast to the temporary visitation on the Old Testament Charismatic persons. Thus, there is a much stronger emphasis than the Synoptics on Jesus' possession of the Spirit. This fact identifies Jesus as the One who will baptize with the Spirit. Jesus receives the Spirit in order that others may share his indwelling.

John 3:1–8

This passage is perhaps the most difficult to fit into the pattern suggested for the Johannine teaching about the Spirit. It can best be done by noting the "vertical dualism" that is characteristic of John and that is in contrast (not contradiction) to the Synoptic "horizontal dualism."[117] Hence the birth of the Spirit is "from above" (margin), which is to be preferred to "again" (KJV) in 3:3. Since Jesus himself is from above (8:23), it may be inferred that the Spirit "from above" effecting regeneration is from him.

In Matthew and Luke the activity of the Spirit in relation to the conception and birth of the Messiah emphasized the creating power and activity of God bringing into being the new creation. There appears to be a parallel here to the Spirit, who is the life-giving Power making humanity anew.

John 4:14–24

In this passage Jesus is pictured as the Source of the Spirit and the Teacher of true worship in the Spirit. Jesus' description of "true worship" as being in "spirit and truth" is reflexive. Truth came through Jesus Christ (1:17), and it is in the light of this truth that spiritual worship occurs. "This union of 'spirit and truth' is the most distinctive teaching about the Spirit in Johannine thought (see 1 John 5:7)."[118] One of the most characteristic Johannine titles for the Holy Spirit is "the Spirit of truth" (used three times). David Hill argues that the language suggests that "'spirit and truth' are to be considered as one entity." He goes on to insist that the clue to understanding the passage is Jesus' affirmation that "God is Spirit," and that this is to be understood Hebraically rather than as a Stoic concept of spirit as a semi-materialistic substance permeating all things. He concludes: "When John says that God is 'Spirit' he is asserting his nature as creative life-giving power in relation to his people. To worship 'in spirit' is therefore to worship in the sphere of this divine activity, which was supremely manifested in Christ who is 'truth.'"[119]

If "truth" here is also to be understood Hebraically, as it is throughout the fourth Gospel, it is equivalent to *emeth,*[120] which refers to the faithfulness of God. In this case it would then doubtless refer to the faithfulness of God to his promises to transform the worshipper through the Spirit as implied by certain Old Testament promises (e.g., Jer. 31:31f.)

John 6:35–65

The life-giving power of the Spirit is stressed again in the discourse on the Bread of Life, as the explanatory section makes clear (6:63). "Life" is the Johannine way of speaking of the content of salvation. The church has traditionally understood this passage to have a Eucharistic significance, thus the flesh (Eucharistic elements) is but the vehicle of the Spirit. But by parallel, since the elements symbolize the body and blood of Christ, it is ultimately through him that the Spirit is mediated to the believer. In this case it is his words that specifically are the source of life, thus of the Spirit.

There is no disparagement of the historical Jesus here (flesh) but the recognition that it is the earthly, physical, incarnate Christ who is the occasion for the knowledge of God in the Spirit. As G. Eldon Ladd says, "It is basic to Johannine theology that flesh becomes a vehicle of the Spirit."[121] The incarnational principle in relation to the Christian experience of the Spirit is thus explicitly affirmed while recognizing that flesh alone apart from the Spirit's activity is ineffectual.

John 7:38–39

We now come to the pivotal passage in the Johannine structure, and it must occupy more attention since it really defines the perspective not only of the fourth Gospel but of the entire New Testament. We are explicitly told that the bestowing of the Spirit upon Jesus' followers awaits the completion of his work.

One major textual problem concerning this passage needs addressing since it bears on the theological issue at stake. There is a disputed question concerning the punctuation in verse 38. One form (the Eastern text) refers "out of his inmost being shall flow rivers of living water" to the believer in Christ. This is the form followed by the King James Version. The other (the Western text) relates it to Christ. The latter finds massive support among contemporary scholarship, and to interpret it this way makes the saying internally consistent with regard to the source of the outflowing Spirit. Raymond E. Brown calls attention to the difficulty of identifying the Old Testament Scripture referred to in the text if the Eastern form is adopted, and he points out further that there is a dogmatic prejudice involved in the Eastern hesitancy to accept the view that the Spirit "flows from" Christ. This reference is to their rejection of the *filioque* teaching of the Western church.[122] Brown suggests, on the other hand, that it is plausible to refer the Old Testament Scripture referred to in this passage to the event in which Moses struck the rock and water flowed from it (Exod. 17:6). "This rock," he points out, "was seen in the early Church as a type of Christ (1 Cor. 10:4), and therefore this background would favor the Christological interpretation of the source in John's citation."[123]

If this is a proper interpretation, we have the crowning moment in the Johannine teaching that as the Bearer of the Spirit, Jesus puts the stamp of his own person upon the content of the Spirit that is bestowed upon his followers. The remainder of the Gospel's teaching about the Spirit is developed in this light.

What is of profound and revolutionary significance is the affirmation that the bestowal of the Spirit awaits Jesus' glorification. Why is this the case? It must be said first that it is not because there is here an ontological beginning. Literally, verse 39 reads, "The Spirit was not yet." But to interpret this ontologically is to deny the biblical teaching about the Trinity. William Barclay has expressed the true implication clearly in these words: "It often happens that at some given point in time, and because of some action and event, men enter into a completely new experience of something which has already for long existed."[124]

E. Stanley Jones provides the most satisfactory explanation of the issue this writer has yet found.[125] Jones suggests two reasons the Spirit could not be given until Jesus was glorified. First, if the power of the Spirit was to be Christlike power, it was necessary to see that power manifested throughout the whole of his life from the carpenter's bench to the throne of the universe. It has to be seen in humiliation and triumph, on the cross and in the resurrection. Second, the disciples had to see that this power manifested in Jesus was the ultimate power. Such an insight would come to them in a shocking manner, challenging all their preconceived notions about the messianic mission. They had "been nurtured in the idea that messianic power would be manifested in overwhelming display that would compel acceptance." But how different was Jesus' actual expression of power!

In a word, there had to be involved a total reorientation of the concept of the power of the Spirit of God. If they had been endowed with the gift of the Spirit before that gift had manifested its full range of meaning in Jesus, they would have doubtless become raging nationalists, swinging weapons like Samson of old. But they would never have recognized the power of love. "It would have been the Spirit of the Lord, but not the Holy Spirit."

Paraclete Texts and the Bestowal of the Spirit

The words of H. B. Swete provide an excellent transition from the first section of John to the second and thus to our discussion of the latter: "The Fourth Gospel in its earlier chapters reveals the Holy Spirit as the author of the Spiritual life in men, and our Lord as the giver of the Spirit to those who will come to Him for the gift. In the latter part of the book, which contains the private instructions given to the disciples on the night before the Passion and after the Resurrection, the Holy Spirit is regarded in another light; the relation in which the Spirit will stand to the Christian brotherhood, the offices which it is to fulfil towards the future Church represented by the company assembled in the upper room, come here into view."[126]

The second section of the Gospel, as we have noted, contains six sayings about the Spirit. There are five Paraclete passages (14:15–17; 14:25–26; 15:26–27; 16:5–11; 16:12–15) and the climactic one (20:22) referring to the bestowal of the Spirit by Jesus upon the assembled disciples after his resurrection by "breathing on them."

I would propose a thesis that captures the thrust of the Paraclete sayings taken collectively: *The Holy Spirit must be understood as inseparably related to the person of Jesus Christ.* There are five truths that support this thesis.

The Spirit's coming is dependent on Jesus' going. This truth is initially proposed by the proclamation of Jesus at the Feast of Tabernacles (7:37–39) but is explicitly stated in 16:7 NRSV: "Nevertheless I tell you the truth: it is to your advantage that I go away, for if I do not go away, the [Paraclete] will not come to you; but if I go, I will send him to you." We have already noted that the primary reason for this is so that the completed work of Christ, including the Ascension, can give character to the work of the Spirit.

The meaning of the Spirit's name implies a continuation of the work of Christ. Much discussion has occurred as to the origin and meaning of the term chosen by Jesus to name the Spirit. Various translations include "Advocate," "Counselor," and "Helper." All are agreed that in today's linguistic context, "Comforter" is less than satisfactory. I would suggest that "Helper" is probably the broadest and best rendering.

The best way to see the significance of this term is to think of the situation to which Jesus spoke. The despair of the disciples over Jesus' announcement that he was leaving them was doubtless due to the dependency they felt toward him. In their stumbling understanding and efforts to follow him, he had always been present with words of encouragement and moral support, to say nothing of divine promises. For this support to be taken away could only produce frustration. Now Jesus is promising to provide for them *another Helper,* One who would continue this work that he had been providing and in a more internal, consistent, and uninterrupted fashion. It seems safe to say that the thought involves a continuation of Jesus' ministry to his disciples.

The reception of the Spirit is dependent on a prior knowledge of Jesus. The world, Jesus said, cannot receive the promised Helper because it does not see or know him. But "you know him, for he dwells with you and will be in you" (14:17 ESV). It is noteworthy that this saying is introduced by identifying the Spirit as the "Spirit of truth." When this is related to verse 6 of the same chapter where Jesus says, "I am the truth," we have an interesting correlation. In light of Jesus' self-identification with "truth," "know" may carry the connotation of "recognize." The disciples will recognize the Helper when he comes because they have already become acquainted with him by way of the Master, who models the nature of the promised Spirit—the Helper will be a Christlike boon.[127]

Jesus identifies the Spirit's coming with his own personal, abiding presence. There is an illuminating interplay of pronouns in these sayings: "I," "him," and "we." They seem to be used interchangeably, so that, as A. M. Hunter says, "The Spirit comes not so much to supply Jesus' absence as to accomplish His presence."[128] The Spirit is not taking Jesus' place; his presence is tantamount to the presence of the risen Lord. Alan Richardson argues that this is true of the entire New Testament understanding, so that "the Risen Christ and the Holy Spirit are not differentiated, so far at least as their operations are concerned."[129]

Finally, and more generally, *the Spirit's work is decisively Christ centered.* In 14:26 (ESV), the Helper is sent by the Father in Jesus' name, and his function will be to "bring to your remembrance all that I have said to you." In 15:26 (ESV), Jesus sends the Spirit and declares, "He will bear witness about me." And in 16:13–14 (ESV) it is declared that the Spirit's teaching ministry is not of his own authority, but it will come from the person of Jesus: "He will glorify me, for he will take what is mine and declare it to you."

This brings us finally to the "bestowment" passage: "And when he had said this, he breathed on them, and said to them, 'Receive the Holy Spirit'" (20:22 ESV). The context is pervaded with the sense of mission. Jesus finds his disciples behind closed doors for fear of the Jews, having nothing of the boldness that he had promised them and that they would need to carry out his continuing ministry in the world. Greeting them with a Jewish *shalom,* he immediately utters a commission: "As the Father has sent me, even so I send you." Following the insufflation, he speaks again of the continuation of his own mission through them: "If you forgive the sins of any, they are forgiven; if you retain the sins of any, they are retained" (v. 23). In this setting, "the gift of the Spirit signifies power and authority to declare the gospel of redemption."[130] Ladd's words are pointed: "However this verse be interpreted, it means at the least that Jesus was bestowing on his disciples the same Spirit that had descended on him at his baptism and had filled him during his ministry."[131]

It is obvious that the language used here has in mind the original creation of humanity when God breathed into Adam the breath of life. This further parallels the initiating activity of the Spirit in Jesus' ministry as noted above. While this passage may not directly impact the point of this study, it does present the interpreter with a difficult problem. How does this event relate to the Pentecostal outpouring? Many have identified this as the "Johannine Pentecost," suggesting that it is an alternate account of the same happening. Ladd offers some potent arguments against this view: (1) it is difficult to believe that any Christian writing at the end of the first century did not know about Pentecost; (2) it is difficult to believe there were two impartations of the Spirit; (3) the fourth Gospel itself teaches that the Spirit could not be given until Jesus' ascension, and so if this is the actual bestowment, there would need to be two ascensions; (4) there is no evidence that the disciples began to carry out their mission until after Pentecost.

Ladd's own proposal seems to accord best with the evidence. He suggests that this "inbreathing" was "an acted parable promissory and anticipatory to the actual coming of the Spirit at Pentecost." While there are numerous parallels between the passages suggesting two reports of the same event, there is no overpowering reason one cannot be promissory of the other.[132]

With this background, we have rather solid evidence to support the position that the understanding of the first participants in the Pentecostal outpouring of the Spirit was informed by the teaching of Jesus and that, in addition to the empowerment for witnessing, there occurred the transformation of their natures that qualified them to "continue the work of Jesus." For these who had lived through the three years of Jesus' Spirit-empowered ministry, listened to his teachings that we have just surveyed, and experienced the forty-day training session about what had happened and what was about to happen, it doubtless led them to the full dispensation of the Spirit (Fletcher), and their baptism with the Spirit resulted in full or entire sanctification. There may have been those, notably the three thousand, whose initial experience of the gift of the Spirit led them only so far as regeneration.[133] What we are seeking to support is that both the measure and character of the Spirit's work were the result of the understanding faith of those who appropriated him at any point in their experience. Like Fletcher, and reflecting this thesis, John Wesley, following "Macarius the Egyptian," taught that one of the prerequisites for the reality of the Spirit's sanctifying fullness was understanding of both need and provision.[134]

Substantially, Alex R. G. Deasley articulated the same position from much the same evidence. He concludes: "I would suggest with great diffidence that what Luke is doing is using the phrase 'baptism in the Holy Spirit' with the same breadth that the root *hagios—hagiazo* is used in the New Testament epistles. . . . Luke's understanding of salvation, expressed in terms of the Holy Spirit, is in harmony with this [use]. However, that is not his prime concern in Acts. His concern is rather with the Spirit as the agent of mission. . . . In keeping with this his language is correspondingly wide, and terms such as 'salvation' and 'fullness' can bear whatever degree of meaning is appropriate to their context."[135]

The bottom line of all this is that early Christian experiences of the Spirit are interpreted Christologically, whether in terms of endowment or in terms of moral renewal (sanctification); and that furthermore the result of the Spirit's filling is correlative to the recipient's understanding and appropriating faith. This means that the phrase "baptism with the Holy Spirit" may legitimately be applied to the new birth, subsequent infillings, and the transformation Wesleyans have referred to as entire sanctification or Christian perfection, and that each of them has for its divinely intended purpose the renewing of human persons in the image of God which is perfectly embodied under the conditions of existence by Jesus Christ. Furthermore, this use of the phrase cannot be legitimately restricted exclusively to any one of the above mentioned "experiences."

In the light of this conclusion, an apparent anomaly is present in H. Orton Wiley's *Christian Theology,* which has served for most of the twentieth century as the authoritative theological voice for much of the Holiness movement. In his chapter on "The Person and Work of the Holy Spirit," Wiley defines the baptism with the Spirit as "the induction of newborn individuals into the full privileges of the New Covenant," but in the same section affirms that "entire sanctification is effected by the baptism with the Spirit."[136] Unless Wiley can be charged with a gross contradiction within the space of a few sentences, his identification of the "baptism with the Spirit" with both the new birth and entire sanctification obviously reflects the same flexibility in use of the term as is proposed here.

John Gresham's study of Charles G. Finney concludes that Finney's understanding of Spirit baptism is quite similar. He states in his concluding remarks: "Finney believed in repeated Baptisms in the Spirit as a normal part of the Christian life, and he experienced several such Baptisms."[137]

What is implicit in the Acts about the Holy Spirit is made explicit in the teaching of St. Paul. W. T. Conner expresses a generally held understanding when he says:

> The teaching of the Apostle Paul on the subject of the Spirit is the richest section of the biblical material on this subject. It might not be true to say that Paul goes any deeper into this subject than do the Johannine writings (the Gospel & 1st Epistle), but it is certainly true that Paul goes into the question more extensively and sets out the subject in a more comprehensive and ample manner. No writer in the New Testament sets out the function of the Spirit in the Christian life in such an illuminating and stimulating way, as does the great apostle to the Gentiles. Paul more definitely than any other New Testament writer discusses the work of the Spirit as something to be experienced on the part of the recipient.[138]

This is true because the genius of Paul was in his development of the implications of the application of the work of Christ to personal experience. It is the Holy Spirit who is the active agent in this application. He does not develop a doctrine of the Spirit so much as he develops the implication of life "in the Spirit" or the activity of the Spirit.

James S. Stewart's evaluation of Paul's contribution to the understanding of the Spirit resonates with the emphasis of John Wesley:

> In the primitive Christian community there was a tendency at the first—perhaps quite natural under the circumstances—to revert to the cruder conceptions of the Spirit, and to trace His working mainly in such phenomena as speaking in tongues. It was Paul who saved the nascent faith from that dangerous retrogression. Not in any accidental and extraneous phenomena, he insisted, not in any spasmodic emotions or intermittent ecstasies were the real tokens of God's Spirit to be found; but in the quiet, steady, normal life of faith, in power that worked on moral levels, in the soul's secret inward assurance of its sonship of God, in love and joy and peace and patience and a character like Jesus.[139]

One of the most discussed, as well as illuminating features of Paul's thought is his close correlation of Christ and the Spirit.[140] Some have even raised the possibility that the two are identical in the apostle's mind. Passages such as 2 Corinthians 3:17 seem clear: "Now the Lord is that Spirit: and where the Spirit of the Lord is, there is liberty" (KJV, "the Lord" usually refers to Jesus in the Corinthian correspondence). But this identification is ontologically impossible in the light of the total Pauline teaching. "It would never have occurred to Paul that this personal Being, this historic Christ, and the Spirit of God were simply to be identified."[141] But this phenomenon nonetheless points to the close connection between Jesus and the Spirit in Paul's theology.

The words of C. H. Dodd capture the crucial significance of Paul's virtual identification of the experience of the Spirit with the experience of the indwelling Christ: "It saved Christian thought from falling into a non-moral, half-magical conception of the supernatural in human experience, and it brought all 'spiritual' experience to the test of the historical revelation of God in Christ."[142]

In conclusion, this survey of the biblical accounts and teachings concerning the experience of the Spirit has solidly supported the thesis propounded at the outset. The sweep of biblical revelation reflects a clear pattern of a developing understanding of experience with a pronounced emphasis emerging in the New Testament on the necessity for a distinctive revelation as prerequisite for the eschatological bestowment of the Spirit. Following this clue, all theologizing about the Holy Spirit that is informed by biblical revelation will take seriously this Christological character and insist that all facets of Christian experience be evaluated by this Christological criterion. Since the unique work of the Holy Spirit envisioned in the New Testament is *sanctification* seen in its broadest and deepest meaning, a Christian theology of sanctification will be Christological in character. Or to say the same thing differently, New Testament pneumatology is through and through Christological.

Responses to H. Ray Dunning's Wesleyan Perspective on Spirit Baptism

Response by Walter C. Kaiser Jr.

Wesley "did not develop any extensive expositions of the doctrine of the Holy Spirit." Rather, in his exposition of the doctrine of sanctification we get some of Wesley's best teaching on the Holy Spirit. In fact, as noted in Dunning's essay, of the twenty-six terms used by Wesley to refer to sanctification, the expressions "baptism in the Holy Spirit" and "fullness of the Spirit" are not found at all or occur only rarely.

Wesley's followers, Dr. Dunning observed, began speaking about sanctification in terms of being "baptized with the Holy Spirit." Most notable among them was John Fletcher, the one Wesley had appointed to succeed him in the Methodist movement. Wesley, in fact, warned against Mr. Fletcher's "late discovery," which apparently was his doctrine of "receiving the Holy Ghost." It was thought to be an alternate way of referring to entire sanctification. Wesley wanted Fletcher and others to abstain from referring to this "late discovery." Fletcher ended up saying that baptism could be used of a number of spiritually renewing experiences, including one's new birth and one's entire sanctification.

Through Fletcher a division came in the Wesleyan tradition, noted Dunning. The Holiness branch of the Wesleyan family usually followed Fletcher in equating entire sanctification with the baptism of the Holy Spirit. Thus it was that preachers and teachers of Holiness revivals in the United States came to view entire sanctification as the baptism with the Holy Spirit. It was both an instantaneous act and one that was subsequent to conversion, a "second work of grace."

But when the issue exploded in 1972 at the annual meeting of the Wesley Theological Society about whether entire sanctification was instantaneous or secondary and subsequent to salvation, the issue was not easily resolved. Wesley himself had said Scripture was silent on the issue and left it at that. But now the Charismatic movement was forcing the issue anew. Wesley at this point is more biblically anchored than many of those who later were to follow him.

Some pointed to Charles G. Finney as the reason for the shift in the Wesleyan movement to "baptism with the Holy Spirit" language. This shift, to what some called the "Oberlin Theology" (after the school of Charles Finney), moved Wesleyan pneumatology from emphasizing purity, ethical living, and Christlikeness to one of emphasizing power as a result of the baptism in the Holy Spirit. In place of ethical concerns of earlier Weslyanism, now the gifts of the Spirit became dominant. Such a tension gave rise to a "third blessing," adding *power* to the *redeeming* and the *cleansing* work of Christ and the Spirit.

Dr. Dunning calls for reason, tradition, and experience to be subordinate to Scripture in the so-called "Wesleyan Quadrilateral." But more is needed, as we all know, than merely the statement that the Bible is the final authority for faith and practice: the Bible has to be interpreted properly as well. Such interpretation would begin with the grammatico-historical exegesis of the text. The plain, natural meaning of the text understood in light of its historical situation is basic to this endeavor. But one has to do "theological exegesis" as well.

In this second step of exegesis Dr. Dunning makes a move that is hard to understand. He argues that the fulfillment of a text like Joel 2:28–29 transcends its literal or intended meaning, for it is impossible to make a correlation between the prophecy of Joel and its fulfillment! But Dunning has understood Joel to mean that God would pour out his Spirit only on all "Jewish" flesh, when instead Joel had referred to men servants and maid servants in the Jewish homes, who were always Gentile!

Then Dunning notes that Luke's use of being baptized in the Spirit and being filled with the Spirit came in a transitional age as one moved toward the initial giving of the Holy Spirit. Therefore, argues Dunning, one could not draw a one-to-one parallel from the experiences recorded by Luke of those in this transitional age to subsequent Christian experience. Accordingly, the events noted in Luke were nonrepeatable.

This is a curious line of reasoning. Naturally one must be wary of automatically assuming that similar expressions in other parts of the Bible mean exactly what they meant in the places where they appeared first. That is not in debate here: what is at risk is the labeling of the Spirit's work in the book of Luke as transitional. It would seem to demand that one was not regenerated up to this point in history by the Holy Spirit, infilled by the Holy Spirit, or empowered by the Holy Spirit in the days prior to Pentecost. This, we have argued elsewhere (and referenced in our chapter) is a mistake, and it fails to take the statements of Scripture at their face value. It is a sort of dispensational logical argument that needs to be fortified, at the very minimum, with scriptural evidence.

One of the most interesting aspects of Dunning's article is his study of what is meant by the "promise of the Father." He suggests that the twelve references in John tell us what the promise of the Paraclete was, with the first six dealing with the Spirit in relation to the ministry of Jesus (climaxing in the sixth, John 7:38–39), and the final six dealing with the Spirit's relation to Jesus' followers (climaxing in John 20:22).

The bestowment or insufflation passage of John 20:22 is a difficult problem for all, where Jesus says to the 120 gathered, "Receive the Holy Spirit." How, then, does this text relate to the outpouring of the Holy Spirit at Pentecost? Surely John, writing well toward the end of the first century, knew about Pentecost. It is doubtful, argued George Ladd, that there were two impartations of the Spirit (here and later at Pentecost), and that the 120 began to carry out their mission even before Pentecost. Dunning correctly accepts Ladd's explanation: This inbreathing was "an acted parable promissory and anticipatory to the actual coming of the Spirit at Pentecost."

Dunning concludes, therefore, that the phrase "baptism with the Holy Spirit" can legitimately be applied to conversion, subsequent infillings, and entire sanctification. But if it means all these things, will it not end up meaning nothing at all? We are afraid that is true. How can we show the exegetical intention of the author simultaneously to mean all these things at once? I do not believe we can.

I enjoyed the strong historical studies in this essay. There was also a strong desire to stay close to the text, but in the end ecclesiastical harmony was given pride of place of Scripture, I'm afraid. Everyone was declared to have a piece of the correct answer, and the term "baptism in the Holy Spirit" must be shared in meaning with all, even if it cannot be shown from an exegetical standpoint of the biblical author's intention and definitions of his own terms and usages.

Response by Ralph Del Colle

The roots of the Pentecostal doctrine of Spirit baptism in Wesleyan theology are well known. H. Ray Dunning's essay provides further nuances to that story, especially in regard to how the term "Spirit baptism" has been employed. Its initial use by John Fletcher, not simply identical with its later usage in the nineteenth-century Holiness movement, points to distinctly Wesleyan constructive possibilities for the interrelationship of the pneumatological dimensions of sanctification, Christian perfection, and the power of the Spirit. Combined with Wesley's foundational influence, the historical account enables Dunning to offer a Wesleyan perspective that is not bound by the later Holiness developments. More than that, his proposal remains thoroughly Wesleyan and not surprisingly can also engage some specifically Catholic concerns.

Two main emphases emerge in Dunning's essay—the inseparability of the Christological and pneumatological aspects of Spirit baptism and an application of the term in broader perspective than either the Holiness or Pentecostal usages. Throughout he argues that moral perfection is the dominant theme of the Spirit's work. Whether this leads to a neglect of the gifts of the Spirit in favor of grace and purity requires further evaluation, a point to which I shall return.

First, let me note some natural points of contact between Wesleyan and Catholic sensibilities. Both traditions are concerned with sanctification and the call to Christian perfection, the latter understood as the fullness of divine love or charity. Dunning notes this commonality in his essay although he is quick to point out Wesley's differences from Catholic doctrine, the former being faithful to the Reformers in his insistence that justification (and later sanctification) are by faith alone with good works following, e.g., faith working through love rather than faith being formed by love.

Much could be said on this matter. It is sufficient to note from a Catholic perspective that since love is the form of all virtues, faith without love may still entail belief in God, a posture still distinct from its contrary, unbelief ("Even the demons believe—and shudder" James 2:19 ESV). Unbelief is the sin against faith and may still exist even after grievous sin, although it is no longer a living faith. Therefore, Thomas Aquinas can argue "the movement of faith is not perfect unless it is quickened by charity."[143]

I mention this confessional difference in order to emphasize how Dunning's typically Wesleyan concern that purity and ethical change is the primary work of the Holy Spirit in the believer possesses a slightly different configuration in Catholic theology. Whereas Wesley distinguished between grace as God's unmerited favor and grace as transforming power (in this regard he remains true to the Reformation), Catholic teaching understands grace to be the supernatural gifts given whereby the believer participates in the divine nature. Grace is infused and by its presence in the soul it heals and elevates it to become holy. Hence, the Council of Trent affirms that the "single formal cause [of justification] is the justice of God, not that by which He himself is just, but that by which He makes us just."[144] Ontologically speaking, this is sanctifying grace, a created supernatural gift that is infused by God and inheres in the soul.[145] The comity of sanctifying grace, that which is infused concurrently with sanctifying grace, includes the theological virtues of faith, hope, and love, together with moral virtues, the gifts of the Holy Spirit and various *charismata* as the Spirit wills.[146]

I repeat this (since I dealt with it in part in the essay) to empha-size that the nature of grace is to transform the believer in an inte-gral and fully orbed modality. Thus sanctifying grace makes the person actually righteous (the rectitude of divine love, as the *Catechism of the Catholic Church* puts it[147]), the manifestation of which are the theological virtues in the life of the believer. The believer is enabled to be obedient to God through faith, hope, and love, grow in virtue, "joyfully . . . respond to the stirrings and promptings of the Holy Ghost," which advance one's own holi-ness, and exercise the *charismata* for the salvation of others.[148] Needless to say this is all the work of the Holy Spirit but viewed from the perspective of the Christian as the recipient of grace.

In light of this, if one were to pose the question of the priority of purity or power, one could answer as follows. In answer to the question of whether gratuitous grace (*gratiae gratis datae* or "graces freely given," in essence the *charismata*) is nobler than sanctifying grace, Thomas Aquinas answers to the contrary. Quoting Paul on a more excellent way (1 Cor. 12:31), he argues that sanctifying grace orders a person immediately to his last end, whereas gratuitous grace ordains one "to what is preparatory to . . . [that] end."[149] In other words, spiritual gifts or the *charismata* are bestowed in service of those called to be holy. The primary pur-pose of the work of the Holy Spirit, including all the graces and gifts that are part of the inheritance that Christ gives to the church, is that conformity to Christ to which all those who are in Christ are called (Rom. 8:30).

Dunning says as much, without excluding the notion that empowerment to witness regarding the reception and use of the *charismata,* is also a part of the Spirit's ministry in the church today. That empowerment is necessary for both holiness and wit-ness may go some way to avoiding any dilemma over the matter. Even as the church is holy (one of the traditional marks of the church) and exists in mission (therefore, constitutive of the nature of the church), so too, the perfection of the Christian in holiness envisions the orientation of the Christian to the other in love. All of this may be presumed in Dunning's recognition that the work of the Holy Spirit in Wesleyan perspective possesses an intrinsic ecclesiological dimension and that holiness is social as well as per-sonal in nature.

Finally, following Fletcher and others (and not limiting himself to the definitions of the Holiness movement itself), Dunning expands the notion of Spirit baptism to embrace several works of the Spirit—new birth, subsequent infillings, entire sanctification. His concern is never to separate the Christological dimension from the pneumatological one. On the latter point the Catholic tradition is in full agreement, so much so that the *Catechism of the Catholic Church* speaks of the economy of the Son and the Spirit as their joint mission.[150] Whether Spirit baptism may be so broadly considered is open to debate. Norbert Baumert, as essayed in my chapter, might agree, although other Catholics prefer its designation to a specific event in the Christian life.

My own view underscores the ecclesiological dimension of Spirit baptism while simultaneously allowing for specific prayer for a release of the Spirit already given in the sacraments of baptism and confirmation. Empowerment in this instance embraces both the gifts of the Holy Spirit (the traditional seven) for holiness and the *charismata* for witness. However, the nature of the sacramental reception of the Holy Spirit in the new life of baptism and the anointing or strengthening in confirmation also suggests a distinction in the Spirit's work. Pentecost is associated more with the latter, although the term *Spirit baptism* has also been used with respect to the former.[151] In any case, we may both affirm that the coming of the Holy Spirit both imparts new life and anoints with power for holiness and witness. In this respect one can sit well with the intent of Dunning's proposals while allowing for a Wesleyan parsing of the matter that allows for the particular emphasis of that tradition (and therefore its gift to the church catholic) to come to the fore.

Response by Larry Hart

Pentecostals and Charismatics are children of John Wesley, both spiritually and theologically. And more honest Evangelical scholars would be willing to admit that, at least in ethos and missional vision, Evangelicals are also children of Wesley. Dr. Dunning has provided us a window into the best of that tradition with a much-needed, Christ-centered, and holiness-oriented perspective on the work of the Spirit.

It is the *Holy* Spirit we are talking about in our discussions on Spirit baptism. Thus, somewhere in the mix we should be able to discern a *holiness dynamic* in our depiction of this reality. Dr. Dunning's presentation demonstrates the substance and significance of such an emphasis. In addition, Jesus Christ—and Jesus Christ alone—is described in the New Testament as the Baptizer in the Spirit, so our language and thinking in these discussions should be thoroughly Christ-centered as well. Dr. Dunning has ably defended this overall orientation.

One weakness, which, in my view, the Pentecostals and Charismatics inherited from the Wesleyan tradition, however, was the punctiform nature of its conception of spiritual life. This was only exacerbated in American frontier revivalism. Dr. Dunning's argument was more full-orbed, but at the grassroots level problems abound, both spiritually and theologically. An early Pentecostal testimony, for example, might sound something like this: "I've been saved, sanctified, and baptized in the Holy Ghost. Y'all pray for me!" Three punctiliar experiences—salvation, sanctification, and Spirit baptism—are envisioned here, the language and concepts being largely inherited from the Wesleyan-Holiness tradition. Even Wesley himself, however, would emphasize more the *process* involved in our Christian experience. So we Wesleyans, Pentecostals, and Charismatics—all at least spiritual cousins—have our theological homework cut out for us! And the Baptist, Reformed, and Catholic voices heard in this volume could provide many helpful pointers.

Also, more needs to be heard from the Wesleyan tradition on spiritual empowerment for mission and on the Charismatic dimension of the Spirit's work. Wesley himself defended the Charismatic outbreaks that accompanied his revivals. Unfortunately, these themes atrophied over the centuries, perhaps in part because of excesses and abuses. But spiritual fire needs regulation, not extermination, and Wesley exemplified this pastoral wisdom. Thus, in our day it is not enough simply to indicate the sanctification dynamic of Spirit baptism. Christ can only be fully glorified by a Spirit-*empowered* church—a church in continual reformation, revival, and renewal.

Dr. Dunning's presentation sets him apart as a careful Wesleyan scholar who has gone back to the source: John Wesley himself. I empathize with Dr. Dunning's concern. I have more difficulties with some forms of Calvinism than I do Calvin himself. And the same is true with Wesleyanism. The nineteenth century *did* see an evolution and bifurcation in the Wesleyan-Holiness movement with a number of fundamental ramifications—not the least of which being the emergence of the Pentecostal movement in the twentieth century. Wesley's emphasis on the *social* dimension of the Christian life and his Christocentric orientation are a needed corrective today. The balance between justification and sanctification is also exemplary for our times. Dr. Dunning skillfully ferrets out these distinctives and demonstrates their contemporary relevance.

Most amazing and encouraging to me, however, is how Dr. Dunning and I have come to similar conclusions concerning Spirit baptism from completely different backgrounds! The broader view of the various dimensions of the Holy Spirit's work, all of which being subsumed under the rubric of Spirit baptism, is the wave of the future, in my view. And this very volume may be pointing us all in that direction!

As Dr. Dunning has ably expressed, our unity is ultimately in Christ himself, and all blessings, be they regenerational, purifying, or empowering in nature, emanate from that union. Dr. Dunning's presentation should haunt the shallow, materialistic, carnal Charismatic who cares little about holiness. One can just as easily, and more seriously, grieve the Holy Spirit in this manner (indifference toward holiness) as by resisting Charismatic manifestations. And the Wesleyan perspective can also balance out those children of Calvin who, in their celebration of sovereign grace, may have lost sight of their Puritan roots, also shared by Wesley, with the glorious vision of a radical pursuit of holiness. Therefore, one major benefit to be gleaned from Dr. Dunning's informative and insightful presentation is that there is a need to return to the source of much of the vital Christianity we see in our own day, a source too often overlooked—John Wesley himself.

Response by Stanley M. Horton

One Christmas when I was in seminary, my uncle gave me a copy of John Wesley's sermons. When I unwrapped it, my ten-year-old cousin, said, "Now, Stanley, you can *really* preach!" But Wesley was the one who could really preach. I know of no greater preacher in modern times. The Pentecostal movement owes a great deal to him—even though H. Ray Dunning makes clear that Wesley himself did not draw a great deal of attention to Spirit baptism. Wesley prepared the way for the Holiness Movement, and the Holiness Movement did much to prepare the way for the Pentecostal revival of the twentieth century.

Dunning seems to draw a line of division between Wesley's Christological emphasis on Christian life and the pneumatological emphasis developed in the nineteenth century. Both have influenced Pentecostals. My observation of Pentecostal preaching and worship finds that they are primarily Christocentric. Jesus is the center of our attention, our hope, and our life. He is our Savior, Baptizer in the Holy Spirit, Healer, and coming King. But we recognize the Holy Spirit as our Helper in every aspect of our relationship to Jesus.

Dunning gives a great deal of attention to Wesley's view of sanctification and his doctrine of Christian perfection. I was impressed by Wesley's recognition of perfect love or entire sanctification as being perfect only in the sense of being unmixed. This is not the view of entire sanctification as understood by many Pentecostals. The Assemblies of God originally included in their 1916 Statement of Fundamental Truths a section entitled "Entire Sanctification: The Goal for All Believers." It stated, "The Scriptures teach a life of holiness without which no man shall see the Lord. By the power of the Spirit we are able to obey the command, 'Be ye holy for I am holy.' Entire sanctification is the will of God for all believers and should be earnestly pursued by walking in obedience to God's Word." This left questions in the minds of many. The same section in the current Statement is entitled simply, "Sanctification." The last sentence is omitted so that "entire sanctification" is not mentioned—since that has been so often misunderstood as meaning becoming unable to sin—and the following paragraph has been added: "Sanctification is realized in the believer by recognizing his identification with Christ in His death and resurrection and by faith reckoning daily upon the fact of that union, and by offering every faculty continually to the dominion of the Holy Spirit."

That Wesley would agree with James D. G. Dunn that "it was only at Pentecost that the 120 became Christians," seems an over-simplification. Certainly the nineteenth-century revivalistic Holiness movement in America emphasized a "second definite work of grace" and used Pentecostal terminology to define it. It was out of this holiness emphasis on a distinct crisis experience that the early twentieth-century Pentecostals were encouraged to believe that the baptism in the Holy Spirit with the evidence of speaking in other tongues was also a crisis experience. Many Pentecostals today still hold to Spirit baptism as a third experience after a crisis sanctification experience.

I would agree with the importance of seeing Luke's purpose for understanding Acts. His purpose was the same as that of Jesus in Acts 1:8. The empowering of the Spirit is still the key to the spread of the gospel. In view of this I agree also that the best translation of Paraclete is "Helper." He is another Helper who will do for us what Jesus did for the disciples while he was ministering here on earth, and he glorifies Jesus in all that he does.

CHAPTER 5

Spirit Baptism: A Catholic Perspective

RALPH DEL COLLE

Spirit baptism, or the baptism in the Holy Spirit, is a new arrival on the Catholic scene, relatively speaking that is. Mindful that the Catholic Church tends to think in terms of centuries and now millennia—witness Pope John Paul II's preparation for and celebration of the Third Christian Millennium[1]—"Spirit Baptism" has only been a part of the Catholic lexicon since 1967. That was the year when Charismatic renewal, also then known as Catholic Pentecostalism, began in the Catholic Church, spreading first in the United States and then throughout the universal church. The story is well-known and need not be rehearsed except to say that at Duquesne University, the University of Notre Dame, and Michigan State University, prayer meetings and later Charismatic communities formed around Catholics newly baptized in the Holy Spirit. From there it spread to other campuses, parishes, and religious communities with laypeople, priests, and those in consecrated life[2] taking part. Soon it was a burgeoning movement in the Catholic Church with bishops and even cardinals actively involved.[3] This ensured that the movement, unlike its classical Pentecostal predecessors, did not split with the mother church. Which is to say, they were not expelled from the Catholic Church. No doubt this was due to the dedication of its leaders, both lay and clerical, to the bishops and the Apostolic See in Rome, and to the enormous amount of theological work generated from within the movement.

The story of the Catholic Charismatic Renewal is one reminder of how a new renewal movement may be integrated within the life of the larger ecclesial community without schism and at the same time maintaining the vitality of its inspiration in the new life and gifts that the Holy Spirit bestows. As will become apparent later in this essay, the integration of the hierarchical and Charismatic gifts of the Spirit within the church was one of the major promises of the Second Vatican Council. For the moment we must register the provenance of the concept and experience of Spirit baptism for its newly acquired status in Catholic faith and practice. This will prepare for the various explications of its doctrinal and theological significance from a Catholic perspective.

As elucidated throughout this volume, the origin of the doctrine of Spirit baptism as subsequent work of grace to conversion/regeneration should be located within the various streams of the nineteenth-century Holiness movement, beginning in its Wesleyan wing while not excluding some non-Wesleyan permutations. The two interpretations of Spirit baptism differed about its intended purpose. Wesleyan Holiness Spirit baptism primarily effects sanctification—"entire sanctification" as they were wont to say. The non-Wesleyan position argued that Spirit baptism was primarily about the empowerment of the converted Christian for life and witness. Both of these interpretations are distinct from other Evangelical positions that identify Spirit baptism with immersion by the Spirit into the body of Christ at conversion (per 1 Cor. 12:13). It was the specifically Pentecostal interpretation of Spirit baptism as an effusion of power manifested in spiritual gifts that triggered and influenced the Catholic Charismatic renewal.[4]

By all accounts the relationship between classical Pentecostalism and the Catholic Charismatic renewal was rather direct. The impact of Assemblies of God minister David Wilkerson's book *The Cross and the Switchblade,* as well as some association with the Full Gospel Business Men's Fellowship,[5] guaranteed that Catholics would be receptive to the classical Pentecostal doctrine of Spirit baptism rather than other possible Holiness or Evangelical interpretations. It would also be the Pentecostal version of the doctrine that would be subject to critique and theological revision by Catholics.

Before proceeding further, it is important to note that the introduction of Spirit baptism into the Catholic Church via the Charismatic renewal does not necessarily translate into an official Catholic doctrine of the baptism in the Holy Spirit. For example, the *Catechism of the Catholic Church* only makes reference to the baptism in the Holy Spirit but not in reference to its reception in the Charismatic renewal.[6] For the most part those Catholic theologians who have considered the subject have been participants in or sympathetic to the Charismatic renewal. Others have perhaps taken notice, especially of the economy of the Holy Spirit and the *charismata,* but have not directed their theological work to the subject of Spirit baptism itself. In addition to the work of theologians there have also been official and unofficial statements promulgated by the renewal itself and some by the church hierarchy. All of this is to suggest that one must be nuanced in articulating the Catholic position on Spirit baptism.

In this chapter I will then proceed as follows. First, I will examine the theology of Spirit baptism emerging from within the Charismatic renewal itself, both from theologians and from representative groups within the renewal. As will soon be evident, this will embrace a variety of positions on Spirit baptism. Second, official church statements including reports from the international dialogue between the Catholic Church and classical Pentecostals will be queried. Finally, I shall attempt to offer my own constructive theological statement on Spirit baptism as one possible Catholic theological position on the matter.

Spirit Baptism in the Catholic Charismatic Renewal

Without question early Catholic Charismatics were quite convinced that a new outpouring of the Holy Spirit had dawned in their lives. Testimonial literature on the subject flourished as in other Pentecostal and Charismatic movements. Also, from the beginning Catholics were aware of and in contact with other neo-Pentecostals and Charismatics. "Spiritual ecumenism," the practice of shared worship in prayer and praise and even the blending of Christians in covenant communities, was characteristic of the renewal in all of the historic churches as well as among nonde-nominational groups.[7] Regional, national, and even international gatherings of Charismatics from all denominations, not only Catholics, became a staple of the Charismatic movement in the 1970s. This background is important in order to appreciate that Catholic views on Spirit baptism were formed not in isolation but within a context in which many ecclesial and theological perspectives were attempting to assimilate the classical Pentecostal doctrine and experience.

I highlight "doctrine" and "experience" since for all intents and purposes they can and ought to be distinguished. That is to say a Christian may have what many Pentecostals would recognize as a Pentecostal experience without necessarily assenting to or promoting the classical Pentecostal doctrine of baptism in the Holy Spirit. Although a clear definition is required, suffice it to say that a "Pentecostal experience" entails an empowering by the Spirit with some manifestation of the *charismata*. It is this type of Christian experience that has characterized the so-called "third wave" of Charismatic renewal among Evangelicals with no notable shift to the Pentecostal doctrine of Spirit baptism subsequent to regeneration in the *ordo salutis.*

At the least, one must affirm the possibilities of Pentecostal experience without adherence to Pentecostal doctrine, as indeed many Pentecostals would allow. Nevertheless—and it seems to me that the following affirmation must be as strong—there would have been no Charismatic renewal (including a Catholic one) without the Pentecostal doctrine of Spirit baptism as a gift for the already converted Christian. In other words, the classical Pentecostal doctrine of subsequence enabled its reception by Christians within the historic churches. This does not diminish the significance of the long-standing dispute between Evangelicals and Pentecostals over subsequence and its importance relative to a view of Spirit baptism. It is simply to recognize that the Pentecostal teaching on subsequence was able to facilitate the transition of Pentecostal experience into the historic churches. With this in mind we now examine an early reception of Spirit baptism in the Catholic Charismatic renewal. We will also note the elements of Catholic doctrine and Charismatic experience that must be considered for any adequate Catholic view of Spirit baptism.

Early leaders of the Catholic Charismatic renewal combined experience and testimony, study of the Scriptures, Pentecostal witness and doctrine, with Catholic tradition, spirituality, and theology. Not unlike the Pentecostal pioneers, a desire for God and the power of the Holy Spirit led to prayerful investigations of the Scripture and a serious consideration of the Pentecostal witness. One can almost draw a parallel between the small revival at Bethel Bible College in Topeka, Kansas, and the beginnings of the Catholic renewal. When Agnes Ozman was baptized in the Holy Spirit on January 1, 1901, in Topeka, she had already been under the direction of Charles Fox Parham who led her and her fellow students in search of the biblical evidence of the blessing. Which is to say that the experience of Spirit baptism cannot be divorced from its nascent doctrinal articulation. In the same way the students and professors who gathered on the university campuses of Duquesne, Notre Dame, and Michigan State had spent considerable time in prayer and study in their quest for the baptism in the Holy Spirit.

Kevin and Dorothy Ranaghan in their book *Catholic Pentecostals,* an early witness to the movement, begin their account with a narrative of how "several Catholic laymen, all members of the faculty of Duquesne University in Pittsburgh, were drawn together in a period of deep prayer and discussion about the vitality of their faith life."[8] It is very much within the genre of Pentecostal testimony. In the numerous testimonies provided by the Ranaghans, one can note several recurrent themes that were influential for the birth of the movement.

First, a spiritual hunger characterized the pioneers. Despite being men of prayer and sincere Christian faith, they "felt there was something lacking in their individual Christian lives."[9] Although active in the sacramental life of the church, they sought a renewal of "all the graces of their baptism and confirmation."[10] Note that there is no denial of the sacramental graces they received. This is important for the subsequent theological interpretations advanced by the renewal. None of the pioneers envisioned a contradiction of Spirit baptism with their Catholic faith. They did not seek an alternative to their Catholic sacramental practice and their experienced forms of prayer and devotion. Rather, and this would prove the rule in the renewal, the new experience of the Holy Spirit complemented and strengthened that faith with members of the movement, often advocating a return to some traditional Catholic devotions.[11]

Second, there was a strong emphasis on Evangelical renewal. This was not separated from the renewal in the Holy Spirit but was a significant dimension of it. James Cavnar was an early recipient of Spirit baptism at the University of Notre Dame. Before that experience he had undergone a Cursillo, a lay movement in the church that promoted a retreat experience that Cavnar could describe in the following words: "To be a Christian meant having a personal relationship with another person—Christ himself; and it meant living in union with other Christians with Christ; it meant introducing others to Christ."[12] Several early leaders in the renewal came from a Cursillo background, and as one may easily surmise, Evangelicals would be comfortable with this focus.

Third, the baptism in the Holy Spirit was the particular manifestation of the Spirit's work that gave the renewal its own specific definition. In the history of the Catholic Church, there has been a variety of evangelical renewals and in some cases with a pneumatological emphasis or experience. For example, the mendicant renewals of the thirteenth century took up the apostolic way of life, *apostolica vita,* as means by which they sought to follow Jesus and renew the church. Francis of Assisi and Dominic helped inaugurate a new form of consecrated life in the founding of their respective religious orders, the Franciscans and Dominicans. As friars rather than monks, they exemplified and preached the gospel by their holy poverty and willingness to take the faith to new areas. Catholics speak of the formative influence of these founders on their movements as a charism given to the church. This serves to illustrate that renewal usually takes on a Christolological and evangelical dimension—to follow Jesus in a new way—and a pneumatological aspect that the founder's charism informs the spiritual life of his disciples.

The Catholic Charismatic renewal presents an interesting case in this regard. Its pneumatological emphasis harks back to the church's beginnings in the event of Pentecost with the most frequent Christological expression being the confession of Christ's lordship (1 Cor. 12:3). The Pentecostal description is taken from the classical Pentecostal witness to Spirit baptism as that event in the life of the believer that immerses the Christian in the power of the Holy Spirit and is expressed in the manifestation and exercise of the *charismata,* what Catholics traditionally consider to be the extraordinary charisms.

To return to James Cavnar's testimony, he then could go on to describe his baptism in the Holy Spirit as an event subsequent to his Cursillo experience and one that was characterized by the laying on of hands to be "filled with the Holy Spirit"—or "asking the Father for the outpouring of the Spirit promised by his Son"[13]—with the following experiential fruit: assurance of the power of the Holy Spirit, a strong "sense of the presence and love of God," a "real boldness," joyful prayer, deliverance from Satan's power and the gift of tongues.[14] All of these experiential descriptors characterize other testimonies within the renewal as they also do for classical Pentecostals and other denominational and non-denominational sectors of the Charismatic movement. Pertinent to a Catholic understanding of Spirit baptism is how this and the other two themes of the early renewal were integrated theologically.

The Ranaghans use the term "baptism in the Holy Spirit" for the Pentecostal experience that helped define the Catholic Charismatic renewal. As we will later see, this term will be disputed within Catholic renewal circles. Even so, the Ranaghans situate the experience and teaching within a Catholic theological framework. Spirit baptism was taught in catechetical fashion to new inquirers of the renewal in order to prepare them for their own personal reception of this grace and experience. It was not—and this will need to be adjudicated later in this essay—a teaching taught by the rest of the church in its catechetical process.

The Catholic ethos is evident in the Ranaghans' exposition of the doctrine of Spirit baptism. Their initial appeal is to Scripture and tradition. Even for the former they elucidate the Spirit's work within the scope of the New Testament church. Statements such as the "Spirit is clearly the soul of the Church," bespeak the Catholic provenance of their analysis.[15] Originally, it was employed by Augustine in an analogical form to articulate the relationship between the Spirit and the church; later Popes Leo XIII and Pius XII used it in encyclical letters on the Holy Spirit and the mystical body of Christ respectively.[16] Although only one sentence, it usually would not be employed by Protestant theologians, never mind

Pentecostal ones, and therefore can only be adequately considered from the perspective of a distinctly Catholic ecclesiology.[17]

The Ranaghans' point is actually to accentuate the pneumatological dimension of Catholic faith and practice. In so doing they attend to the passages in the Gospels and Acts that speak of Jesus baptizing in the Holy Spirit and conclude that the "Pentecost outpouring, the wellspring of Christian baptism, is a baptism in the Spirit."[18] They go on to say that "at least in these instances [the events in the Acts narrative] the Spirit is always received in the baptismal context in some way,"[19] indeed another Catholic indicator of their way of thinking. The efficacy of the sacraments must be taken into consideration in regards to the grace of the Holy Spirit. In this case the issue is how the impartation of the Holy Spirit in the sacraments of baptism and confirmation relate to the new experience of the Spirit in Spirit baptism. In fact, this is the key theological issue at stake in any Catholic interpretation of Spirit baptism.

By investigating the patristic era, the primary site for any affirmation of tradition as bearer of the Word of God,[20] the Ranaghans recognize the consolidation of the mediation of grace to new converts in the sacraments of initiation (baptism, confirmation or chrismation, eucharist) and the still Charismatic flavor of the ancient church. The former is decisive for sacramental theology, including its pneumatological dimension, while the latter is often the consequence (and justly so) of a Pentecostal hermeneutic of church history and tradition. If on the basis of the continued presence of Charismatic gifts in the ancient church one can affirm their presence today—there is no such thing in Catholic theology of cessation of spiritual gifts after the first century—then the integrated rite of Christian initiation in the ancient church evokes the question if its relationship to the reception of Spirit baptism and Charismatic gifts in today's church as well.[21] The Ranaghans are quick to point out a decline in Charismatic manifestations in the later patristic era[22] and query whether the separation of confirmation from baptism confuses the relationship between sacramental and Charismatic impartations of the Holy Spirit.[23]

All of this continues to highlight important Catholic indicators for the reception of Spirit baptism in a Catholic context. In addition to the need to deal adequately with the nature of the grace of the Holy Spirit in baptism and confirmation relative to each other, the larger question of the relationship of the work of the Holy Spirit to sacramental and nonsacramental modalities must also be adjudicated. Catholic theology and spiritual doctrine, i.e., the theology of the spiritual life, has never confined the Spirit's presence and operation to the sacraments. The infused graces of the mystics, the continued bestowal of the Holy Spirit in new charisms that launch new forms of religious life and lay ecclesial movements—the actual graces by which any believer is strengthened in virtue, witness, and Christian life—are part and parcel of Catholic teaching, even if at times there has been tension between new spiritual movements and the hierarchical and juridical structure of the Catholic Church.

The point, however, is that from a Catholic perspective they are never seen to be in contradiction to each other. For example, the graces one senses in private prayer do not undermine sacramental grace but are understood to flow from it, even if they may be bestowed in a nonsacramental context, e.g., in one's own oratory. Likewise, when a new spiritual movement begins, it will be integrated with the life of the church including its sacramental and hierarchical dimensions. Witness the lives and deeds of the founders of the great religious orders. Two will suffice as examples. Francis of Assisi, already mentioned, and Ignatius Loyola, the founder of the Jesuits, both began their spiritual journeys through a conversion experience. Companions joined them and became the nucleus of a larger movement. In both cases they submitted the approval of their communities to church authority (the current pope for each of them). It would not be too much to say that from a Catholic perspective this submission was not only important for the formal canonical structure of the Franciscans and Jesuits but for their spiritual fruitfulness as well.

The Catholic Charismatic pioneers were confronted by a similar spiritual and ecclesial circumstance. In fact, although they did submit the approval of the renewal to church authority in the ecclesial sense, our concern is with the theological integration of Spirit baptism with Catholic sacramental and spiritual theology. The classical Pentecostal doctrine of Spirit baptism inevitably raised for them this important theological question. The Ranaghans responded by situating Spirit baptism within `the sacramental theology of the Catholic Church. Rather than interpreting Spirit baptism as the reception of a new event of grace, they spoke of it as "renewal and actualization of baptismal initiation."[24] They wanted to be clear that Spirit baptism was "not a sacrament nor a replacement for any sacrament,"[25] yet at the same time it was related to the sacramental initiation undergone by baptized and confirmed Catholics. So one should properly, according to this theological interpretation, be concerned with the existential renewal and actualization of baptismal grace,[26] not the reception of the baptism in the Holy Spirit but its renewal.[27] In other words, Spirit baptism was being identified with the sacramental initiation of Christians, now renewed through faith-filled prayer, a position that would become the dominant one among Catholic Charismatics and to be developed by Kilian McDonnell, whose work we shall examine later.

Other early Catholic Charismatic positions were similar. I shall only review several among the noteworthy pioneers. Stephen B. Clark, cofounder of the Word of God covenant community in Ann Arbor, Michigan, which along with the People of Praise covenant community in South Bend, Indiana (to which the Ranaghans belonged), was the most influential in the Catholic renewal. He advanced a slightly different position on Spirit baptism than the Ranaghans. While similar to the Ranaghans in that he conceived of Spirit baptism as a release of the Spirit given in baptism and confirmation, there is a significant difference. Clark focuses more on the sacrament of confirmation. The Ranaghans' problem with the somewhat ambiguous theology of confirmation led them to stress the integrated event of conversion enacted in the sacraments of initiation. Spirit baptism is to be identified with that event as a whole. They even go so far as to state that "we can be more sure about what it means to be baptized in the Holy Spirit than about what it means to be confirmed."[28]

Clark, on the other hand, is firm about the distinct aspects of Christian initiation represented by baptism and confirmation. In his reading of the Acts of the Apostles as well as his understanding of the distinctive grace of each of the sacraments, Clark argues that one first comes to Christ and that Christ, in turn, bestows the Spirit.[29] This is not to deny that coming to Christ and conversion/baptism is a work of the Holy Spirit for "Christ is at work in us through his Spirit."[30] However, Clark does not equate Spirit baptism with conversion: "Being baptized in the Spirit is not the same as having a conversion to the Lord or a deeper conversion to the Lord."[31] The latter phrase reflects the Catholic spiritual doctrine that one may undergo a series of conversions in one's life,[32] equivalent to a deeper consecration encouraged by some Evangelicals, pietists, or "deeper life" advocates. Therefore, Clark would agree that Spirit baptism properly belongs to Christian initiation and consequently *"should normally not happen at a different time* from coming to Christ."[33] However, in facing the reality that all Catholic Charismatic theologians wrestle with—that many baptized, confirmed, and spiritually minded Catholics experience something new when they are baptized in the Holy Spirit—Clark chooses to associate Spirit baptism with the sacrament of confirmation.

Similar to the Ranaghans, Clark describes Spirit baptism as a release of the Spirit, or being opened to the Spirit,[34] or a renewal effected by the Spirit. But in the latter case he is quite explicit and deserves to be quoted in full.

> If it is true that there can be a difference between being joined to Christ and receiving the Spirit, then it is permissible to talk about baptism in the Spirit as something different than becoming a Christian, and it is permissible to talk about it as a renewal of confirmation (and not just as a renewal of the whole process of initiation). It is also permissible to appropriate different effects in the believer to the union with Christ and the union with the Holy Spirit.[35]

His major premise is the distinction between conversion to Christ and receiving the Spirit (without denial of the presence of the Spirit in conversion/baptism). Clark does admit that if being "joined to Christ and receiving the Spirit normally come together" as in the New Testament then we might speak of one event but with the following parenthetical nuance: "perhaps a two-fold event, but one event nevertheless."[36] In other words, Clark is aware of the complexity of the issue in the New Testament itself,[37] and more to the point, in the different contexts of ecclesial situations of the church as it exists today as compared to the primitive community in the New Testament.[38] Nevertheless, in his own position on Spirit baptism within a Catholic sacramental perspective, he associates it more with the sacrament of confirmation than with all the sacraments of initiation. In a pamphlet entitled *Confirmation and the "Baptism of the Holy Spirit,"* Clark asks the following question. "If a real conversion to Christ can renew the sacrament of baptism in a person's life so that the effect of the sacrament is realized, should there not be a similar renewal of the sacrament of confirmation?"[39] His answer is a resounding yes. "It happens when a person receives what is called 'the baptism of the Holy Spirit.'"[40]

In addition to the interpretation of Spirit baptism as a renewal of the sacraments, Clark and the Ranaghans also share another emphasis that was common in the early Catholic Charismatic renewal. Both highlight the significance of speaking in tongues. Clark is more emphatic by suggesting that tongues is "the *normal* first sign" of Spirit baptism.[41] This is by no means the same as the doctrine of "initial evidence" held by a number of classical Pentecostal denominations.[42] That doctrine holds that there is no evidence that Spirit baptism has occurred unless one speaks in tongues. Clark argues that "inspired praise" is the only initial evidence, whether in one's own language or in tongues.[43] However, the high expectation of speaking in tongues as a consequence of Spirit baptism is not that far removed from the classical Pentecostal ethos.[44]

Clark's early work is also significant because he situates Spirit baptism in comparison with traditional Catholic spirituality. Under the rubric of being "fully in Christ," Clark elucidates "three main categories of things that happen to people when they are 'baptized in the Spirit.'"[45] Spirit baptism may be part and parcel of Christian initiation, conversion to Christ, and reception of the Holy Spirit.[46] It may also mark a transition "from a Christian life lived 'according to doctrine' to a Christian life lived 'according to the Spirit.'"[47] In other words, the experiential dimension of life in the Spirit becomes an existential reality to the believer. Finally, for the spiritually mature, those "who have had some formation in spirituality and have experienced the presence and workings of the Spirit in some kind of way," Spirit baptism may be experienced as a "Charismatic release," bringing a greater freedom of the Spirit and a doorway into "all the normal workings of the Spirit."[48] It is this last category that introduces us to the next pioneer, already a trained theologian and priest, Edward D. O'Connor, CSC.[49]

O'Connor situates the new Pentecostal experience of the Charismatic renewal in light of a Catholic theology of grace. This is important for any Catholic understanding of Spirit baptism. The experiential dimensions of grace already have a long history in Catholic spirituality, and the spiritual life has been the subject of reflection in what has been variously known as spiritual theology, ascetical theology, and mystical theology.[50] The theology of grace is also a locus in dogmatic theology, especially in regard to the doctrine of justification. Both are combined in O'Connor's reflections, although I shall again return to the theology of grace along with sacramental theology in the next section.

O'Connor presents a theology of grace within a pneumatological perspective. In this respect, while the theology of grace is traditional, indeed "classical," with a provenance in the church fathers and especially in the Scholastic tradition, his concern is to expose the dynamic spiritual vitality that underlies it; this in contrast to the somewhat dry form it took in the neo-Scholastic theology of the first half of the twentieth century.[51]

O'Connor investigates the compatibility of the new experience and notion of Spirit baptism among Catholic Charismatics with the traditional Catholic doctrine of grace. When taken up by Protestants, as, for example, by many Charismatics from nonsacramental or Evangelical traditions, the question usually focuses on the *ordo salutis*[52]—whether Spirit baptism is subsequent to conversion/regeneration and (for those in the Wesleyan tradition) sanctification. For Catholics the question is a bit more complicated, not only in regard to sacramental grace but also with respect to the distinctive types of grace that characterize its theological tradition.

The Pauline emphasis on the new creation in Christ (2 Cor. 5:17) is at the heart of the Catholic teaching on grace. The grace that justifies, known as sanctifying or habitual grace, cleanses one of sin. With the remission of sins grace is infused in the believer, thereby making the believer actually righteous with Christ's own righteousness, now the believer's own. It also elevates the person to share in the divine nature (2 Pet. 1:4). As O'Connor notes, this "involves a real transformation of our very being" and is "made dynamic and effective" through the theological virtues of faith, hope, and charity.[53] In other words, the Holy Spirit who comes to indwell the believer in baptism grants the person "grace-given potencies" for "genuine contact with God himself" and "real personal communion with God."[54] These potencies are not transitory but habitual, hence a virtue in the moral sense. They are theological because they relate the believer to God by elevating the faculties of intellect and will and proceed from the core of one's being now made anew in Christ.

There is much that could be added to situate O'Connor's account among the important developments in the Catholic theology of grace in the last half century. One observation is sufficient and will help to underscore the experiential dimension that he emphasizes. The common Scholastic distinction between created grace and uncreated grace gave the impression, especially during the neo-Scholastic era (roughly between Vatican I and Vatican II [1870–1962]), that grace was extrinsic to the believer. This meant that the offer of divine grace was beyond psychological awareness or experiential consciousness.[55] The concern of the extrinsic emphasis was to preserve the supernatural character of grace. However, O'Connor, who argues for intrinsic or interior awareness of grace, is in no danger of compromising its supernatural character. In fact, he desires to restore that dimension as much as possible. However, his tactic is not to make grace experientially accessible by diminishing its supernatural character[56] but to reinvigorate the scholastic categories with their original basis in spiritual experience.

If the indwelling Holy Spirit is the source of all grace—uncreated grace as the font of all created graces, to use the scholastic terminology—then the distinctions in the theology of grace are significant for a rich sense of the Spirit's work in a person. The Holy Spirit is at work in the believer (uncreated grace) and actually transforms the believer (created graces). Even though the believer can think and act out of the created transformations of sanctifying or habitual grace (since one is a new creation in Christ), it also bespeaks a relationship of constant dependence on God. Communion with God, in this sense, embraces the reality of actual graces—continual new influxes of grace that assist and strengthen the believer—and the inspirations of the Holy Spirit that make one docile to the work of God in one's life.

The inspirations of the Holy Spirit in classical spiritual doctrine are treated under the rubric of the gifts of the Holy Spirit. This is not to be confused with the charisms or Charismatic gifts that are distinctive of the Charismatic renewal and Pentecostalism.[57] The gifts of the Holy Spirit are infused supernatural habits that enable the believer to be "receptive and docile to the inspirations and promptings of the Spirit."[58] The traditional number is seven, taken from Isaiah 11:2—wisdom, understanding, counsel, knowledge, fortitude, piety, fear of the Lord.[59] Even though both sanctifying grace and the gifts of the Holy Spirit are supernatural in origin and bespeak human dependence on God, O'Connor distinguishes between the psychological postures that characterize each. Of the former, although one is constantly supplied afresh with energy by the Holy Spirit (especially in regard to actual graces, remembering that sanctifying grace is more of a habitual posture), one is psychologically one's own master acting and perceiving by faith. With the gifts of the Holy Spirit, the Holy Spirit himself takes the initiative in the believer's life with the Christian in a state of receptivity to these inspirations. They are also intended primarily for the sanctification of the believer.[60]

The third dimension of this supernatural (and pneumatological!) organism of grace is the Charismatic operations of the Holy Spirit, what classical Pentecostals usually refer to as the spiritual gifts. In Catholic theology these are known as *gratiae gratis datae* or "graces freely given." They include the list of gifts mentioned by Paul in 1 Corinithians 12:8–10 and other "preternatural gifts of the Holy Spirit."[61] In concert with the tradition he emphasizes that these gifts "do not of themselves sanctify the recipient, even though they are useful aids toward the sanctification of the community."[62] Many Pentecostals would not disagree with this. The spiritual gifts or *charismata* exist for the edification of the community (1 Cor. 12:7).

The three dimensions of the classical spiritual doctrine should be considered as a whole, although they are distinct with respect to how the Holy Spirit is operative in the believer. As presented by O'Connor, the interface of the Catholic theology of grace with the Pentecostal/Charismatic experience already presumes a strong pneumatological aspect to the traditional doctrine. What is the significance of Spirit baptism for this theology of grace?

By highlighting the presence of God, O'Connor parses the emphasis placed by the classical and Pentecostal perspectives on this aspect of the divine self-communication in grace. In his mind he states it bluntly: "The former put the accent on the *practice,* whereas the latter put it on *presence.*"[63] By starting with *presence* Pentecostals and Charismatics may in fact be more aware of the divine presence in their lives than those (especially priests and Catholic religious) who continually recall God's presence to themselves through the various disciplines that characterize the classical doctrine. This lack of the "*actual awareness* of the presence of God" does not rule out the contributions of Pentecostal spirituality for Catholics but calls them to explore their "own authentic tradition" through the grace of the new experience of Spirit baptism.[64] On the other hand, "the cultivation of a constant attention to his presence"[65] is an important exercise in the spiritual life. Along with the wisdom of the classical tradition—that is, infused contemplation in prayer, the discernment of the inspirations of the Holy Spirit, stages of development in the spiritual life, the purification that happens in the dark night of the spirit (from St. John of the Cross) and the subordination of the *charismata* to the grace which sanctifies[66]—attention to God's presence will bring many spiritual benefits to those newly baptized in the Spirit.

Overall, O'Connor brings the wisdom of the Catholic spiritual tradition to his appreciation and reception of Pentecostal spirituality. However, the latter also has much to teach the church in regard to the presence of the Holy Spirit and the charisms, something O'Connor notes was one of the important developments of the Second Vatican Council.[67] As far as Spirit baptism itself is concerned (O'Connor examines the whole spiritual reality of the new movement; hence his use of the term "Pentecostal spirituality"), O'Connor sees that "there is nothing substantially new in what is called baptism in the Spirit, but there is something new in the circumstances and mode of its occurrence."[68] In other words, there is nothing unorthodox about Spirit baptism. Nevertheless, it should not be equated with "any religious experience whatsoever."[69] It possesses its own specificity in relationship to the fruits, inspirations, and gifts of the Holy Spirit and differs from other manifestations of the Spirit's renewing work in the church in that Spirit baptism cannot be associated with any one Charismatic individual. Its experience and continued reception by many happens in the context of prayer communities, oftentimes with specific prayer through the laying on of hands that one might receive it. This is new in the church and corresponds biblically with the primitive church.

If O'Connor served to situate Spirit baptism within the broader framework of the Catholic understanding of grace, two early Catholic Charismatic theologians addressed the nature of Spirit baptism more directly, one with an intended degree of ambiguity and the other more definitely, at least with regard to the use of the term itself. Donald Gelpi, SJ, has emerged as one of the most important and prolific of Catholic Charismatic theologians. Well versed in things Pentecostal, he has written extensively in the area of foundational theology and dogmatics. Our concern is with his early work on the Charismatic movement in order to identify another possible Catholic interpretation of Spirit baptism.

Unlike the Ranaghans and Clark, Gelpi is less concerned about relating Spirit baptism to the sacramental grace of baptism and confirmation as he is to distinguish the experience of Spirit baptism from these sacraments. However, he is more definitive in stating what Spirit baptism is not than what it is. That "it is not a sacrament" is clear for several reasons. It does not require a priestly minister and therefore "does not enjoy the kind of efficacy which attends . . . sacramental prayers." As such, Spirit baptism "does not express as fully as the sacraments the historical, ecclesial, and incarnational aspects of the salvific process."[70] Most Catholic theologians would agree with this statement. But how is Spirit baptism related to sacramental grace?

Gelpi does not give a strict theological definition but chooses to situate the meaning of Spirit baptism within the prayer praxis of those who receive it. In this respect "its precise meaning and purpose are of necessity situationally variable and dependent on the ecclesial and sacramental status of the one who receives it."[71] In other words, Gelpi recognizes that in the contemporary situation (as in the book of Acts) some are baptized in the Spirit prior to water baptism, others after, and in the case of today's different ecclesial affiliations that sacramental practice and understanding will vary.

Spirit baptism is best understood as an expression of docility to the Holy Spirit and "receptivity to whatever Charismatic gifts the Spirit may choose to give."[72] For those baptized and confirmed, Spirit baptism may indeed be a prayer to "ratify and acknowledge . . . previous sacramental confirmation."[73] For others—such as classical Pentecostals—no such sacramental connotation is proffered. The point here is not to belabor the obvious, namely that Pentecostals and Evangelicals are not sacramentalists. It is to suggest that for Catholics the sacramental meaning or connection does not capture the primary meaning of Spirit baptism. Indeed from a Catholic perspective Spirit baptism should deepen the sacramental and ecclesial participation of those so immersed in the Spirit as the Catholic Charismatic renewal seems to have borne out. However, Gelpi's emphasis on the spiritual dynamic of petitionary prayer and God's generosity in answering it in order to deepen life in the Spirit serves to underscore an interpretation of Spirit baptism that is not linked theologically to sacramental grace even though it promotes the integration of charisms and sacraments in the life of the church.[74]

Finally, for this early period, Cardinal Joseph Suenens was a great advocate of the Charismatic renewal and played no small part in fostering its warm reception in Rome. In his book *A New Pentecost?* Suenens introduces two Catholicizing tendencies to the understanding of Spirit baptism, one of which is fairly radical. First, in order to preserve the sacramental integrity of baptism and to avoid confusion, Suenens suggest that it is "better not to speak of 'baptism in the Holy Spirit' but to look for another expression."[75]

The theology behind this statement—he never actually suggests an alternative expression although he notes quite a few[76]— excludes the notion that Spirit baptism is some "sort of super-baptism, or a supplement to baptism which would then become the pivot of the Christian life."[77] The Christian life founded on baptism is determined by both paschal and pentecostal dimensions, that is, the saving death and resurrection of Jesus Christ and the coming of the Holy Spirit. It is fair to say that is something no classical Pentecostal would deny—hence, their doctrine of subsequence in regard to Spirit baptism. But Suenens is concerned to uphold the sacramental fullness of baptism. Or to put it another way, when the Spirit is received in baptism, the Spirit already comes in fullness. All that is subsequent to baptism, including confirmation—which does not supplement baptism but confirms it—is an unfolding of the Spirit's work, who is already present as an abiding gift and an abiding power. It is worth quoting Suenens in full: "When the action of the Holy Spirit becomes more effective in us, it is not that the Spirit has suddenly awakened like some dormant volcano unexpectedly come to life. It is we who are awakened to his presence by a combined movement of his grace, a deeper faith, a more living hope, a more burning love."[78]

The combination of divine action and human response is characteristic of the Catholic theology of grace (as was true for O'Connor and Gelpi as well) and bespeaks the particular interpretation adopted by Suenens. In order to account for a "new sending" of the Spirit leading to a "new state or a new act of grace," Suenens prefers an interpretation of Augustine and Thomas Aquinas that regards this "new sending" as a matter of perception. Such is indeed an experience and may be theologically articulated in a fairly traditional scholastic formula: "The Spirit is sent whenever he is perceived."[79] In summary, Suenens affirms this renewal of the Spirit in a manner that does not diminish the sacramental grace of baptism (hence, his exclusion of the term *Spirit baptism*), and that accentuates the anthropological locus (graced as it is!) of how we might speak of a new work of the Spirit.

This review of early Catholic Charismatic views of Spirit baptism (although by no means a comprehensive review) sets the parameters for how a Catholic understanding of Spirit baptism may proceed. Inevitably one will have to negotiate the relationship of Spirit baptism to the sacraments, though even there the emphasis could vary (the Ranaghans and Clark). One cannot ignore the received tradition of the Catholic theology of grace (O'Connor) and therefore must be able to situate Spirit baptism such that it would be true to Catholic experience. Spirit baptism as a grace not directly linked to the sacraments (Gelpi) must be considered, as well as the possibility that the renewal, but not Spirit baptism as conceived in a classical Pentecostal manner (even if already revised), may be assimilated to Catholic tradition (Suenens). In order to proceed forward, a review of official magisterial responses to the renewal must be examined along with the response (and initiative) of the renewal's leadership.

Official Statements
on Spirit Baptism and Charismatic Renewal

Official responses to the Charismatic renewal on Spirit baptism come from a number of sources. Generally speaking, three types are of particular interest—those from episcopal conferences and commissions, the final reports of the International Catholic/Pentecostal Dialogue (sponsored on the Catholic side by the Pontifical Council for Promoting Christian Unity), and those that are the product of leaders of the renewal. From a Catholic perspective the first are more authoritative since they represent the pastoral teaching authority of the church, its Magisterium. However, even in regard to documents of bishops' conferences, the level of authority attributed to them varies. Not all pronouncements by bishops' conferences are doctrinal declarations. Those that are pastoral in nature cannot in their doctrinal principles violate the universal teaching of the Catholic Church. Although they do not promulgate an official doctrine on Spirit baptism, the pastoral guidance they exercise vis-à-vis the Charismatic renewal implicates those doctrinal principles that are relevant for a Catholic understanding of Spirit baptism.[80]

The episcopal documents tend as a whole to be receptive to the renewal affirming the grace manifest in the movement, its fruit in the revivification of Christian life, and some cautions about possible theological and pastoral extremes. For example, the 1969 *Report of the Committee on Doctrine* of the U.S. Catholic bishops considers that the "most prudent way to judge the validity of the claims of the Pentecostal movement is to observe the effects of those who participate in the prayer meetings."[81] On this basis they note that "[m]any have experienced progress in their spiritual life."[82] Similar sentiments are registered by other episcopal conferences. Canadian bishops from the western province of Quebec in 1974 also judge the renewal by its fruits and rejoice that they "see more desire for personal and community prayer, a greater thirst for the Word of God, [and] a greater openness to the call of the Spirit" among other things.[83] At the same time the bishops from Puerto Rico in 1972, although not reproving the movement, do attempt to correct abuses such as the notion that "the so-called baptism of the Spirit" would lead some to believe that they have the assurance of salvation.[84] Clearly on this point the necessary clarification concerns doctrine, namely, the relationship between Spirit baptism and the Catholic understanding of justification.

Since it is not the case that most classical Pentecostals would identify Spirit baptism with the assurance of salvation, there seems to be some confusion on this point.[85] Similar to the position of many Evangelicals, Pentecostals affirm that the assurance of salvation follows new birth and is based on faith in Jesus Christ and may include the witness of the Holy Spirit (Rom. 8:16) as an experiential assurance that regeneration has taken place.[86] Such assurance was cultivated in the revivalist tradition of Evangelical Protestantism. This is a dimension of Christian life and the doctrine of grace that is alien to the Catholic tradition.

There are several reasons for this. The notion that one may be assured of salvation by the witness of the Spirit is not an operative category in the Catholic doctrine of justification. Since salvation or justification is an ongoing process the language more commonly used by Catholics is whether one is in a state of grace. The *Decree on Justification* of the Council of Trent (Sixth Session, 1547) directly addresses this question. Chapter IX entitled "Against the Vain Confidence of Heretics" states: "For as no pious person ought to doubt the mercy of God, the merit of Christ and the virtue and efficacy of the sacraments, so each one, when he considers himself and his own weakness and indisposition, may have fear and apprehension concerning his own grace, since no one can know with the certainty of faith, which cannot be subject to error, that he has obtained the grace of God."[87]

The decree is even more specific when the context is the doctrine of election; hence, the clarification of Chapter XII of the Decree. "No one . . . ought in regard to the sacred mystery of predestination, . . . presume as to state with absolute certainty that he is among the number of the predestined."[88]

A Catholic, therefore, would not speak in the words of Wesley (and many Pentecostals) of "an assurance that I am now in a state of salvation,"[89] nor describe the newborn Christian as one who "feels . . . [and] is inwardly sensible of, the graces which the Spirit of God works in his heart,"[90] if this be interpreted as a witness to that assurance. When translated into the Catholic version of the query—are you in a state of grace?—the *Catechism of the Catholic Church* invokes the example of St. Joan of Arc when she was asked this question during her trial. She responded: "If I am not, may it please God to put me there; if I am, may it please God to keep me there."[91] The theological reason is also given by the *Catechism*. "Since it belongs to the supernatural order, grace *escapes our experience* and cannot be known except by faith."[92]

With this clarification in mind, we are free to turn to the more relevant issue, that is, the relationship between faith experience and the baptism in the Holy Spirit, a connection not gone unnoticed by Catholic bishops. The statements by the bishops tend to note the various fruits of the renewal as already noted. The bishops of the Antilles in their statement of 1976 gave an impressive list of these: a new attitude to worship, a new love of the Word of God, an appreciation of the value of Christian asceticism, an awareness of the church as the people of God, what it means to have an authentic local church, a new awareness of the church as community, and a genuine desire to have close contact with those who have charge over the church.[93] Nothing could be more Catholic.

Noting similar fruit, including "a special grace characterized by a strong call to conversion, based on an adult acceptance, conscious and free, of Jesus Christ as Lord and Savior of their lives," the Panamanian bishops interpret "these experiences . . . as a return to a life of grace, the infused virtues, gifts, and charismas" that were already received in the sacraments of initiation.[94] The use of the word *experiences* connotes sensitivity to the self-understanding of the renewal itself. It is the German bishops who provide the most comprehensive statement on this matter.

In 1987 the German Episcopal Conference approved a paper, "It is the Spirit that Gives Life," prepared by Theological Commission of Charismatic Community Renewal.[95] It dealt extensively with the notion of experience, Spirit baptism, and Charismatic renewal. The document is important for two reasons. First, it rehabilitates the category of experience for a Catholic theology of grace, a project undertaken by a number of theologians after the demise of neo-scholasticism as the reigning theological method in the late nineteenth and early to mid-twentieth centuries.[96] Second, in direct response to the Charismatic renewal, it provides an experiential framework within which to understand Spirit baptism.

The Spirit Gives Life first defines experience before turning to the Charismatic nature of some experiences of the Spirit. The presupposition of the document is that there are indeed fresh outpourings of the Holy Spirit taking place in the church and that the spiritual and dogmatic traditions of the church offer ample resources for discernment and pastoral guidance. At the same time these new stirrings of grace certainly benefit the life of the church.

Experience is defined as "man's entry into his own inner self."[97] It embraces the emotive dimension of our humanity and can widen the consciousness of the person. Spiritual experience may indeed include "feelings or spiritual emotions," but these are gifts that accompany the experience and do not constitute its core, which is the "integral experience of faith."[98] Testing, suffering, and aridity may characterize spiritual experience as well as "perceptible joy, even jubilation."[99] The document further goes on to describe the ecclesial context of such experience and then offers criteria of the Christian faith and behavioral fruit that can establish the authenticity of such experiences. These also include criteria from the nature of spiritual experience itself in the interplay of consolation and desolation.[100] Why is this so important for interpreting Spirit baptism?

Since Spirit baptism does not possess a doctrinal status in Catholicism—the point of this essay is that there are various Catholic interpretations of Spirit baptism—the privileging of one emphasis will color the theological interpretation. In the case of *The Spirit Gives Life,* the concentration on spiritual experience locates Spirit baptism within a variety of possible experiences of the Spirit, all of them legitimate in the life of grace. In fact, the document advocates the term "experience of the Spirit" as a substitute for "baptism of the Spirit."[101] The reason given is to prevent the notion that all experiences of the Spirit must be "a personal Pentecost experience or a breakthrough experience."[102] This does not discount breakthrough experiences or the full flowering of Charismatic gifts. It is, however, intended not to universalize the experience of the Spirit witnessed to and promoted by the Charismatic renewal. This, by no means, delegitimizes the renewal's witness but contextualizes it within the broader context of the entire church. Several theological reasons are advanced in support of this position.

First, there can be no denial that the Holy Spirit is already received in baptism and confirmation, a universal position held by Catholics and a matter of Catholic doctrine. Second, the "sending forth" of the Spirit is a continuous event and does not exclude new outpourings of the Spirit of God, a position affirmed by Thomas Aquinas and to which we shall return later in this essay.[103] Third, all experiences of the Spirit must be considered in light of "integral conversion," that is, the "conversion of the whole person," by which the Christian becomes more committed to the Lord and more receptive to his Spirit.[104]

The German bishops (in their approval of this document) do not undermine in the least the Charismatic dimension of the renewal or its effect on the church. Charisms are strongly affirmed but not limited to the ones characteristic of the renewal. As in Edward O'Connor's evaluation, the full panoply of the Spirit's working is noted, including the "seven gifts of the Holy Spirit . . . stimulations of the Holy Spirit . . . and the springing up of faith, hope and charity."[105] However, the typical Charismatic gifts such as tongues, prophecy, and healing (as well as others) are attended to and are placed in a fruitful relationship with the sacraments and office in the church. Although charisms are subordinated to office, this is only understood within the dynamic of both order and charisms. "'Sacramental order,' as spiritual authority for the good ordering of the Church, and 'charism' as a gift that is always unique, stand in reference to and are dependent on one another, they are viable with one another. In the interaction between them the Church experiences the pulsation of the Spirit and perceives His guidance."[106]

In sum, *The Spirit Gives Life* provides a Catholic theological justification for the Charismatic experience as a new outpouring of the Spirit integrated into the life of the church. It acknowledges that the renewal has generated its own forms of prayer and catechesis. The latter include "Life in the Spirit courses" that help prepare participants and neophytes in the renewal to request a "new outpouring of the Holy Spirit."[107] However, it drops the terminology of Spirit baptism and envisions the new life in the Spirit as oriented to renewal of parish life and not some separate spiritual association.[108]

The German bishops have provided both the renewal and the church with a careful and spiritually rich assessment of Charismatic renewal. It has recontextualized Spirit baptism as a new outpouring of the Spirit that is oriented to the sacramental life of the church but is not presented as a renewal or release of baptismal grace per se. Certainly the new outpouring is an "outstanding experience"[109] and may be akin to the filling (or multiple fillings of the Spirit) that many Evangelicals promote without a subsequent and distinct baptism in the Holy Spirit as the gateway into the Spirit-filled life.[110] Although it is not identified as a necessary second experience of the Spirit that should be universally appropriated by all Christians, nevertheless, it maintains a strong Charismatic flavor. In this respect the "new outpouring" continues to bear similarities and differences to the classical Pentecostal doctrine of Spirit baptism.

Other bishops' statements do not enter into such detail, but one more serves to highlight the doctrinal issues involved. The Canadian bishops in 1975 state "that 'baptism in the Spirit' administered in Charismatic groups is not a second baptism but a symbolic act signifying a new openness in the believer to the Spirit received at baptism."[111] While this differs from *The Spirit Gives Life* in that it upholds the sacramental connection more clearly, its use of "baptism in the Spirit" is qualified by quotation marks and only indicates that this is the term used by those in the renewal. As with most other statements and Catholic theology in general, it subordinates the manifestation of the Spirit and the purpose of the charisms to the "exercise of charity."[112]

The *Final Reports* of the International Roman Catholic/Pentecostal Dialogues provide another source for official Catholic responses to the Pentecostal doctrine of Spirit baptism. The reports are products of a Roman Curial office—in this case the Pontifical Council for Promoting Christian Unity (formerly known as the Secretariat for Promoting Christian Unity)—but do not possess the same doctrinal status as bishops' statements unless they are formally received by the Curia with the approval of the Pope. Nevertheless, they do express an official Catholic engagement with the issues.

In the *Final Report* of the first round of the dialogue from 1972 to 1976, the subject of Spirit baptism was directly addressed. The report rehearses the Pentecostal understanding but does not really offer a Catholic position except to affirm the presence of the Spirit in Christian initiation.[113] Both sides agree that the Holy Spirit is the agent of regeneration but disagree over the nature and sacramental efficacy of water baptism (including paedobaptism). They also acknowledge that there is no agreement on "whether there is a further imparting of the Spirit with a view to Charismatic ministry, or whether baptism in the Holy Spirit is, rather a kind of release of a certain aspect of the Spirit already given."[114] Perhaps more significantly there is the recognition by both sides that the Charismatic movement in the historic churches does not compete with the larger church, nor does it desire to separate from them. Rather it "is a renewal in the Body of Christ, the Church, and is, therefore, in and of the Church."[115] This will figure significantly in emphasizing the ecclesial context for a Catholic interpretation of Spirit baptism.

The most comprehensive statement of Catholic Charismatic leaders, and one that is comparable to *The Spirit Gives Life* in its comprehensiveness, is the 1974 *Theological and Pastoral Orientations on the Catholic Charismatic Renewal*. Its primary author was Kilian McDonnell, who assembled with a group of pastoral leaders and theologians in Malines, Belgium. It subsequently became known as *Malines Document I*. This document has been the most influential in providing the dominant Catholic view on Spirit baptism from within the Charismatic renewal. "*Malines I* situates Spirit baptism in direct relation to the sacraments of initiation. In sacramental terms, the Charismatic renewal is based on the renewal of that which makes one belong to the Church, that is, a renewal of initiation (Baptism, Confirmation, Eucharist). The Spirit given in initiation is more fully appropriated."[116]

Care is taken to establish the Trinitarian foundations of the renewal in the nature of the church itself. Following the Second Vatican Council, the document envisions the church as the sacrament of Christ (*Lumen Gentium*, 4). In fact, the pneumatological dimensions of the church are accentuated. The church is constituted by the Holy Spirit and "the Holy Spirit makes the Church manifest at Pentecost."[117] The pneumatological dimension of the church, however, cannot be separated from its Christological foundations as well. Christ and the Spirit constitute the church with no temporal priority between them. Rather than conceiving of the church as an extension of the incarnation, as some Catholic ecclesiologies are wont to do, it prefers to speak of the church as an extension of Christ's anointing by the Spirit. The Spirit therefore assures both the unity and distinction between Christ and the church.[118]

The importance of these ecclesiological foundations is to register the Charismatic dimension of the church as a whole. If the "Holy Spirit dwells in the Church as a perpetual Pentecost" including its sacramental order—for example, the ministry of deacon, priest, and bishop being understood as a charism—then there can be "no distinction between the institutional Church and the Charismatic Church."[119] Every Christian then is a Charismatic.[120]

Mindful of the renewal's concentration on experience, *Malines I* explores the various aspects of experience in relation to faith and the doctrine of the Spirit. It is affirmative of the experience of the Holy Spirit including the notion that experience is "something that God does in a human person"[121] while at the same time acknowledging that there can be a "tyranny of subjective experience."[122] The document also takes account of culture, specifically, theological culture in the understanding and integration of Spirit baptism. This means that it must be integrated into Catholic culture without compromising its "distinctive Charismatic characteristics."[123] What is the import of these factors for Spirit baptism?

The document prefers to retain the phrase "baptism in the Spirit," although it is open to possible substitutes. It retains the theological affirmation that "every member of the Church has been baptized in the Spirit because each has received sacramental initiation."[124] Yet it also underscores the experiential appropriation of it in conscious experience. Baptism in the Spirit, or release of the Spirit, is "the power of the Holy Spirit, given in sacramental initiation but hitherto unexperienced, . . . [becoming] . . . a matter of personal conscious experience" with an intentionality "to an ongoing life in Christ through the Spirit."[125]

This review of official Catholic positions on Spirit baptism has not yielded any one definitive theological understanding. Rather a plurality of interpretations has emerged. We turn now to

a theological assessment of the two dominant interpretations proffered by the Charismatic renewal and conclude with a constructive
theological statement as a contribution to the discussion.

Assessment and Proposal

Our review thus far of Catholic reflection on Spirit baptism has
revealed a plurality of theological interpretations for what possesses, at best, a quasi-doctrinal status. In other words, theological
judgments are required for adequate pastoral guidance by both
bishops and renewal leaders regarding the promotion by the
renewal of the experience of Spirit baptism. The retention or not of
the term "baptism in the Holy Spirit" is an issue, but, more importantly, its theological meaning in light of the Catholic doctrine of
grace and the sacraments is required. Although a number of perspectives have emerged, it is safe to say that two major views are
dominant, both by participants in the renewal or those sympathetic
to it. These require review for a theological assessment of their via-
bility and then must be correlated with an overall Catholic evaluation. This latter will be my own, as a Catholic theologian, and
possesses no official status in Catholic doctrine.

One more caveat is needed before proceeding. The theological
judgments rendered are in regard to Spirit baptism as it has been
received and practiced in the Charismatic renewal in the Catholic
Church, hence, the necessity of some sort of theological interpretation precipitated by the pastoral charge. As we have demonstrated, this already Catholic version of Spirit baptism bears a
resemblance to and owes a historical connection to the classical
Pentecostal doctrine of Spirit baptism. The two, however, are not
identical. Therefore, a Catholic constructive proposal on Spirit
baptism will necessarily relate to both expressions of Spirit baptism
but in distinct ways. That will inform my reflections in the final
portion of this essay.

Two Interpretative Streams in the Catholic Charismatic Renewal

The two views largely come to expression in the work of Norbert
Baumert, SJ, and Kilian McDonnell, OSB, whose influences are
paramount in *The Spirit Gives Life* and the *Malines Document I*
respectively. Other theologians have contributed to the discussion

and will be noted when appropriate, but the following assessment will be limited to these two representative positions.

Kilian McDonnell has long been engaged in theological reflection on the Charismatic renewal. *Malines Document I* has been a standard for theological guidance for the movement and was followed by two documents that dealt with the subject of the renewal and ecumenism: *Malines Document II* in 1978 authored by Léon Cardinal Suenens,[126] and *The Charismatic Renewal and Ecumenism* in the same year by McDonnell.[127] Since the Pentecostal/ Charismatic movement has been transconfessional, it has been important to delineate how Spirit baptism (as the representative experience/doctrine of the movement) promotes Christian unity and simultaneously is integrated into the various ecclesial and theological traditions. McDonnell attempts this by positing Pentecost as a *Communion Which Reaches Out,*[128] hence the impulse toward unity (and mission) that the outpouring of the Holy Spirit signifies. At the same time the ecclesial and theological reception of Spirit baptism must be consistent with Catholic faith and practice.

In this respect McDonnell is an advocate of the sacramental interpretation of Spirit baptism originally articulated by many of the early Catholic Charismatic leaders. The logic is clear to McDonnell. The coming of the Spirit constitutes the church and the Christian. In sacramental terms "Christian initiation is the effective sign of the Spirit's bestowal."[129] This requires that Spirit baptism (or by whatever name it is called[130]) is a matter of the power of the Holy Spirit or the graces of Christian initiation emerging into consciousness.[131]

McDonnell further developed this position in a coauthored study entitled *Christian Initiation and Baptism in the Holy Spirit: Evidence from the First Eight Centuries.* As the title suggests, he and George Montague, SM (who covered the New Testament) attempted to demonstrate from the early church that "the 'baptism in the Holy Spirit' refers . . . to the integral event of Christian initiation."[132] For our purposes his thesis was restated in popular form in the pamphlet *Fanning the Flame: What Does Baptism in the Holy Spirit Have to Do with Christian Initiation?*[133] Summarizing the evidence from the New Testament, and Latin, Greek, and Syriac church fathers, McDonnell and Montague propose a programmatic thesis: "Their [the church fathers'] testimony demonstrates that the baptism in the Holy Spirit is not a matter of private piety, but of the official liturgy, and of the church's public life. Historically the baptism in the Holy Spirit is integral to those initiatory sacraments which are constitutive of the church, namely, baptism, confirmation, and eucharist. In this sense, the baptism in the Holy Spirit is normative."[134]

There is no doubt that *Fanning the Flame* entails a pastoral application in the life of the church that is intended to be normative. Baptism in the Holy Spirit ought not to be limited to the Charismatic renewal. The fruit of the renewal is evident in this ecclesialwide recovery of the church's pneumatological foundations with high expectations for the spiritual life of the faithful. "The retrieving of the baptism in the Holy Spirit means a new depth in one's personal relationship to Jesus as Mighty Lord and Savior sent by the Father in the power of the Spirit."[135] More specifically, a doctrinal identity is established between Spirit baptism and the sacraments of initiation. Therefore, the recovery may be described as "the reappropriation of initiation with charisms, which is the baptism in the Holy Spirit," and "all are called to fan into flame the gift of the Holy Spirit received in the sacraments of initiation."[136] There is no intrusion here on the sovereignty of God, who freely gives the Spirit, or on the necessary faith response of those so renewed.[137]

In sum, this stream of interpretation intends to preserve the pneumatological integrity of the sacraments while extending Spirit baptism as the conscious appropriation of the grace communicated in the sacraments. This normative programmatic may or may not be held by others who agree with the basic thesis that Spirit baptism is a release of sacramental grace. McDonnell and Montague do not restrict the operation of the Spirit to one Charismatic model— as if all should speak in tongues—but they do encourage the charismatization of the church, consistent with the ecclesiological vision of the Second Vatican Council.[138]

The other interpretative stream certainly upholds the pneumatological dimension of the church's sacraments and their efficacy. However, it believes that the interpretation of Spirit baptism as a release or retrieval of sacramental grace is not consistent with the biblical, doctrinal, and experiential dimensions of Spirit baptism. Various versions of this position have been proposed. They may be summarized as representing (1) the Thomistic doctrine of the sendings of the Holy Spirit, (2) the eschatological emphasis of Spirit baptism in light of the Parousia, (3) Spirit baptism as a sacramental in the life of the church, (4) Spirit baptism as a distinctive spirituality in the church. This is by no means a comprehensive review of this stream but is intended to highlight the various non-sacramental associations Spirit baptism may have in Catholic understanding.

Francis Sullivan, SJ, early in the history of the renewal, challenged the sacramental interpretation. Sullivan notes that the New Testament term "baptize in the Holy Spirit" is "simply a metaphorical way of saying that he sends or gives the Spirit. To 'be baptized in the Spirit' is to receive an outpouring of the Spirit, or literally, to receive the Spirit."[139] In this respect Spirit baptism along with "ritual baptism" (water baptism) are two moments in Christian initiation.[140] All Christians then have been baptized in the Spirit since they have received the gift of the Spirit.[141] Nevertheless, Sullivan gives credence to the Pentecostal experience without the use of their terminology by proposing an alternative and more Catholic understanding of what happens in the renewal.

Sullivan turns to Thomas Aquinas in question 43 of the first part of the *Summa Theologiae*. Thomas considers the missions of the divine persons, and more specifically the giving and sending of the Holy Spirit. In short, the sending of the Spirit means that the Spirit "becomes present in a new way."[142] Through the Spirit's indwelling (*inhabitatio*) there results "a real *innovatio*—a 'making new' of the creature."[143] This may include "the conferring of a Charismatic gift," and "a more intimate and 'experiential' knowledge of God as present in the soul, a knowledge that 'breaks out' into more ardent love."[144] All of these may characterize what believers experience and mean by Spirit baptism in the Charismatic renewal.

In this version of the nonsacramental interpretation of Spirit baptism, Sullivan suggests that baptized and confirmed Catholics, in whom the Spirit is already present, "are praying for and receiving . . . a 'new sending of the Holy Spirit,' or 'a new outpouring of the Holy Spirit,' for their 'renewal in the Spirit.'"[145] Even if the term "baptism in the Spirit" is still used in the renewal, it should not be understood as a one-time event. There is certainly an initiatory event of the Spirit's coming in baptism and confirmation. However, new comings of the Spirit may be anticipated. For Sullivan this bespeaks the heart of the Christian life. "I am convinced that there will never be a time during our pilgrimage on earth when the Lord could not give us a powerful new gift of his Spirit that would really move us into some new act or new state of grace."[146]

Philippe Larere also builds on Aquinas's notion of the coming of the Spirit in distinction from the reception of the Spirit in the sacraments. The "Charismatic baptism in the Holy Spirit" is a "visitation of the Spirit which has for its effect a transformation of the baptized persons." He proposes that although belonging to the sacramental order it is not a sacrament and should be understood as a sacramental of the Catholic Church.[147] The latter is some pious or devotional practice or prayer in which the faith of the recipient is essential for the offer and reception of grace that is communicated. It differs from a sacrament in which the offer of grace is always communicated, and its reception bears fruit according to the faith and cooperation of the recipient.

Peter Hocken is concerned that the sacramental interpretation, "by collapsing baptism in the Spirit into ritual initiation," undermines the "eruptive-invasive character of Pentecost." The latter bespeaks the heavenly origin of the event and the immediacy of relationship that it evokes.[148] The present Charismatic outpouring of the Spirit heightens eschatological hope, prayerfully anticipates the Parousia, and calls for Christian unity.[149]

Each of these nonsacramental views of Spirit baptism is intended to accentuate the sovereign work of the Spirit for the benefit of the church. In this respect they do not differ from the intentionality of the sacramental view. In both cases the Charismatic renewal is at the service of the entire church by underscoring its Charismatic nature. They want to preserve what is distinctive about the renewal's emphasis on Spirit baptism and the new life in the Spirit it offers without being sectarian. They also intend the revitalization of the church in broader terms than the renewal itself. Similar concerns inform the last position under review, that of Norbert Baumert.

In his article, "'Charism' and 'Spirit-baptism,'"[150] Baumert challenges the Pentecostal notion that the New Testament term "to baptize in the Holy Spirit" is to be strictly identified with the contemporary Pentecostal/Charismatic doctrine of Spirit baptism. The New Testament usage is appropriate for any sending of the Spirit. On the other hand, the substantive "Spirit baptism" ought not to be applied to the release of baptismal grace. This would both undermine the distinctiveness of the event as experienced by Charismatics and require it as normative for all Christians. Rather, one ought to identify different types of experiences of the Spirit.

There is the universal reception of the Spirit by all Christians, and for Catholics this reception is ritualized in the related but distinct sacramental occurrences of the water bath and anointing. Then one may speak of spiritual experiences that are universal and are intended for every human being. This is followed by experiences of the Spirit distinct from experiences of God and Christ. He then specifies the infilling of the Spirit, which in fact may take different forms. The latter would include mystical experience and Spirit baptism as known by Pentecostals and Charismatics. Spirit baptism then emerges as a mark of a particular type of spirituality in the church and is not to be considered normative for all. As is now clear, this more restrictive sense of Spirit baptism does indeed preserve its distinctive Charismatic form but limits its universality and is not proposed as an experience of the Spirit that all Christians should have.

Assessment

As has been evident throughout this essay, the introduction of the experience and teaching of Spirit baptism has had to negotiate the parameters of Catholic faith and practice. This is precisely due to the pastoral acceptance and integration of the Catholic Charismatic renewal in the life of the church. One has only to conjecture that if the renewal was rejected early on there would have been no theological assessment of Spirit baptism, as has indeed taken place in the last several decades. For example, unlike the early Fundamentalist/Evangelical reaction to classical Pentecostalism, there has not been a denouncement of the doctrine of subsequent Spirit baptism as a second or third work of grace in the *ordo salutis* combined with a rejection of the Charismatic gifts manifested in the movement (especially by those who were cessationist in their theology). In fact, the gifts were accepted, including tongues, prophecy, healing, etc.; pastoral caution was exercised against extremes and attempts were made to integrate the Charismatic emphasis with sacramental and liturgical life, traditional spirituality, and the theology of grace. No one accepted the Pentecostal doctrine as is but revised it to better suit a Catholic perspective. In so doing these major streams of interpretation have emerged.

In assessing those two streams, a number of principles emerge for the Catholic theologian and can help form the basis of the constructive statement to follow. In fact, these principles are worthy of consideration precisely because of the disagreement that exists between the two streams. In other words, they are part of the substance of Catholic faith and theology and, therefore, cannot be compromised.

Essential to Catholic faith is the sacramental economy of the church. It cannot be ignored, and neither stream is guilty of doing so. At stake is the ecclesial mediation or embodiment of grace by virtue of Christ's promise and his grace that unites the faithful to him as his ecclesial body. The efficacy of the sacraments is not a matter of the church substituting itself for Christ or restricting the grace of Christ in its offer of salvation to the world. It is a matter of how the presence of the risen Christ is signified and communicated in our human reality. The analogy between the incarnation and the church used by *Lumen Gentium* (Vatican II's *Dogmatic Constitution on the Church*) is exemplary in this regard and is worth quoting in full.

> Christ, the one Mediator, established and continually sustains here on earth His Holy Church, the community of faith, hope and charity, as an entity with visible delineation through which He communicated truth and grace to all. But, the society structured with hierarchical organs and the Mystical Body of Christ, are not to be considered as two realities, nor are the visible assembly and the spiritual community, nor the earthly Church and the Church enriched with heavenly things; rather they form one complex reality which coalesces from a divine and human element. For this reason, by no weak analogy, it is compared to the mystery of the incarnate Word. As the assumed nature inseparably united to Him, serves the

divine Word as a living organ of salvation, so, in a similar way, does the visible social structure of the Church serve the Spirit of Christ, who vivifies it, in the building up of the body.

It is on this basis that the church is understood to be "like a sacrament or as a sign and instrument both of a very closely knit union with God and of the unity of the whole human race" (LG 1). Christ's Spirit vivifies the church and is communicated through its sacramental order. However, this does not restrict the bestowal of grace within the church and in the lives of Christians. Extra-sacramental grace, or grace that is bestowed in sacramentals, or according to the freedom of God's Spirit in the lives of Christians is witnessed to abundantly in the church. These include actual grace, the grace of infused contemplation and no doubt Charismatic graces and gifts as well. The accurate observation that Spirit baptism and the Charismatic gifts are more often than not bestowed in prayer meetings rather than within the liturgical celebration of the sacraments does not violate the principle of sacramental order in the church. Such, in fact, is to be expected in new movements of the Spirit wherein new charisms emerge in the life of the church often with new spiritualities that arise as the fruit of them, e.g., Ignatian spirituality that arises from the charism of St. Ignatius Loyola as embodied in his *Spiritual Exercises.*

The theological issue under dispute has arisen, though not in regard to the Charismatic gifts per se. *Lumen Gentium* acknowledges even the extraordinary gifts among the charisms.[151] The theological and doctrinal issue concerns the status of Spirit baptism as the gateway into the reception and exercise of the Charismatic gifts. This is not dissimilar from some so-called "Third Wave" Evangelicals who emphasize the power of the Spirit and his gifts but prefer not to be identified as Pentecostals or Charismatics. They have not changed their doctrinal understanding of the coincidence of baptism of the Spirit with regeneration and conversion. However, there is a significant issue of ecclesial practice that has forced the issue among Catholics.

With the initial acceptance of the term *Spirit baptism* at the beginning of the renewal, and despite the numerous suggestions for alternative terminology, Catholics prayed for a new coming of the Spirit in Spirit baptism with the expectation of Charismatic gifts in evidence. This took place both formally and informally at prayer meetings and in covenant communities. The Life in the Spirit Seminars were a quasi-catechetical institutionalization of this. Baptized and confirmed Catholics followed a several-week preparation before making an evangelical commitment to the lordship of Jesus and then praying to be baptized in the Holy Spirit.[152] The Pentecostal nature of the event is undisputed, hence, the question of the relationship between this "Pentecostal" grace and the sacraments of initiation.

We are then left with two valid principles in the order of grace that respectively represent the two interpretative theological streams. They are the Pentecostal basis of the church and the sacraments of initiation that constitute believers as members of Christ and the church, and the ongoing work of the Holy Spirit in which new charisms and graces continually arise in the life of the church. Where is one to locate Spirit baptism? Considered as a prayer of petition, is one praying for the Pentecostal grace of that which constitutes the church and Christians as members of the body of Christ, or is one praying for a new outpouring or coming of the Spirit, which because of its Charismatic manifestations, also possesses a Pentecostal signification? And one can also query both positions as to their universal applicability. Should all Christians be renewed in the Pentecostal foundations of their sacramental initiation or seek this particular coming of the Spirit in their ongoing discipleship of the risen Christ? Finally, should the appropriation of this grace bear the same Charismatic effusion (and type of spirituality) that characterizes the Charismatic renewal? Answering these questions moves us into our constructive proposal.

Constructive Proposal

It needs to be repeated at this juncture that this proposal, as was true for the others reviewed in this essay, represents an informed theological attempt to account for what the Pentecostal/ Charismatic movement has called "Spirit baptism" in an ecclesial and theological tradition in which *Spirit baptism* is not doctrinally defined.[153] The theological imperative is a consequence of the pastoral acceptance of the grace of the Charismatic renewal in the Catholic Church.

First and foremost in the Catholic reception of Spirit baptism (and here I remind the reader of the Catholic Charismatic revision of the classical Pentecostal doctrine) is the ecclesial contextualization of it. As the Eucharistic preface for the Solemnity of Pentecost demonstrates, the coming of the Spirit at Pentecost is associated with the beginning of the church. "Today you sent the Holy Spirit on those marked out to be your children by sharing the life of your only Son, and so you brought the paschal mystery to its completion. Today we celebrate the great beginning of your Church when the Holy Spirit made known to all peoples the one true God, and created from the many languages of humanity one voice to profess one faith" (P28).[154]

The church exists within the missions of the Son and the Holy Spirit sent by the Father for the salvation of the world. In fact, the *Catechism of the Catholic Church* prefers to speak of the "Joint Mission of the Son and the Spirit" since the "Son and the Spirit are distinct but inseparable" (689). The mission of the Spirit is decisive for all aspects of the Christological mystery from the incarnation (Matt. 1:20), to the ministry of Jesus (Acts 10:38), his self-offering on the cross (Heb. 9:14), and his resurrection from the dead (Rom. 1:4). Jesus who bore the Spirit without measure (John 3:34) is the one from whom the Spirit is poured forth (John 7:38–39). In the language of the scholastic theology of grace, the habitual grace of Christ (the grace by which he is holy) is identical with the capital grace given to the church.[155] Or, as the *Malines Document I* stated, "the Church is the extension to us of Christ's anointing by the Spirit."[156]

All of this is dependent on the Pentecostal outpouring of the Holy Spirit who brings "the paschal mystery to its completion," as the Pentecost preface proclaims before God. That Jesus' promise to baptize in the Holy Spirit is fulfilled in the Pentecostal outpouring of the Holy Spirit is the stuff of the Lukan narrative in the Acts of the Apostles (Acts 1:5, 2:1–21). The sacraments of initiation are grounded in this Pentecostal outpouring since they are means by which the grace of God is communicated and offered in the joint mission of the Son and Spirit. They "lay the *foundation* of every Christian life."[157] Indeed, the "faithful are born anew by Baptism, strengthened by the sacrament of Confirmation, and receive in the Eucharist the food of eternal life."[158]

The pneumatological dimensions of both baptism and confirmation are also clear. "Holy Baptism is the basis of the whole Christian life, the gateway to life in the Spirit (*vitae spiritualis ianua*), and the door which gives access to the other sacraments."[159] Confirmation, which is "necessary for the completion of baptismal grace" also "in a certain way perpetuates the grace of Pentecost in the Church."[160] This latter quote of Pope Paul VI, now incorporated in the catechism, combined with the prior notion that baptism is the "gateway to life in the Spirit," embraces the Pentecostal effusion of grace in the life of the church. Since confirmation "brings an increase and deepening of baptismal grace,"[161] and its effect is understood as "the special outpouring of the Holy Spirit as once granted the apostles on the Day of Pentecost,"[162] it is nothing less than the Pentecostal outpouring of the Holy Spirit, or Jesus' baptizing in the Spirit, as offered in the sacraments of initiation.[163] Therefore, from a Catholic perspective the properly ecclesial gateway into the fullness of the Spirit are the sacraments of initiation.[164]

This affirmation confirms the emphasis of the first interpretative stream reviewed above. However, it does not exclude new and continual outpourings of the Holy Spirit in the ongoing life of the church (Acts 4:31), nor prayer for a "new Pentecost" as Pope John XXIII prayed for the success of the Second Vatican Council.[165] Scripture suggests that new outpourings of the Spirit will take place as a harbinger of eschatological fulfillment (Acts 3:19–21). Hence, the emphasis of the second interpretative stream is not misplaced. It looks not only to Pentecost but ahead to the Parousia as well.

In light of the Spirit's presence and action through the sacraments, in sovereign freedom and in response to prayer, we may reconsider the transconfessional nature of the Pentecostal/ Charismatic movement. This outpouring of the Spirit is not confined to the Catholic Church, nor did it even begin there. Catholic ecclesiology does not exclude the working of grace and ecclesial elements being present in other churches and ecclesial communities.[166] Hence, a new outpouring of the Spirit with Pentecostal signification such as glossolalia and other Charismatic gifts could indeed take place both within and outside the Catholic Church.

Such an outpouring would not be unrelated to the sacramental order of the church. The sacraments signify this same grace in its full ecclesial context, that is, all grace and gifts are oriented to the building up of the body of Christ. The sacramental expression of Pentecostal grace portends its universal scope—it extends to all the baptized and confirmed Christians—and yet is responsive to the faith and prayer of all the people of God. The epicletic posture of the church, liturgically enacted in the sacraments, may also be taken up by the faithful following their sacramental reception or by those outside of sacramental communion. In this respect prayer for a "new Pentecost" or a "personal Pentecost" is entirely justified. The perpetuation of Pentecost is a matter of both the sacramental economy of the church and an unceasing epiclesis for the coming of the Spirit.

What is Spirit baptism? Spirit baptism signifies the fullness of grace and gifts. The effusion of the Spirit's life and power embraces holiness and mission, life and power, grace and gifts; in other words, the full spectrum of life as an ecclesial person. It is no accident that the language of Spirit baptism has been used by both the Wesleyan-Holiness and Pentecostal traditions with their respective emphases on holiness of life and power for witness.

In the Catholic tradition the explicitly Charismatic effusion that Spirit baptism signifies in the renewal is enriched by the full scope of pneumatic agency in graces, gifts of the Holy Spirit, and *charismata*. It elicits discernment of the Spirit's present work and recognition of the many new charisms that the Spirit bestows. The practice of Spirit baptism as an epicletic event signifies the fullness of the Spirit in which the church is baptized. It likewise calls all the baptized to their full inheritance in Christ. Since its manifestation lies within the realms of signs, namely the Charismatic gifts that are manifested, its scope need not be as universal as the sacramental economy of the church. The signs are not to be rejected or coveted for their own sake (1 Cor. 12:31–14:1). They are to be gratefully received as the Lord gives, calling the Christian and the church to live its baptism and to be sent forth in mission as the Spirit leads.

Responses to Ralph Del Colle's Catholic Perspective

Response by H. Ray Dunning

My knowledge of Roman Catholic theology is largely derived from the history of Christian thought rather than a careful study of contemporary developments. Thus, my remarks in response to this enlightening essay will be marked by considerable diffidence.

The thing that strikes me first is a remarkable similarity to my own tradition in that there are diversities of views held within the context of a unifying commitment. Within the Wesleyan tradition that unifying commitment is to the centrality of the holy life as articulated in Scripture commonly referred to as sanctification, whereas the Catholic commitment is to the primary authority of the church. This is clearly stated in Del Colle's essay: "One cannot ignore the received tradition of the Catholic theology of grace and therefore must be able to situate Spirit baptism such that it would be true to Catholic experience." This clearly highlights a contrast of theological methodologies. For the Catholic, the arbiter of theological adequacy is the (institutional) church shaped by tradition, whereas for the Wesleyan, like all classical Protestantism, it is Scripture. As Del Colle says, "First and foremost in the Catholic reception of Spirit baptism . . . is the ecclesial contextualization of it."

Unless I misread his report, this results in the church somewhat uncritically incorporating the Pentecostal theology of "Spirit baptism" into its ecclesial structures. This observation is suggested early in the essay: "The story of the Catholic Charismatic renewal is one reminder of how a new renewal movement may be integrated within the life of the larger ecclesial community without schism and at the same time maintaining the vitality of its inspiration in the new life and gifts that the Holy Spirit bestows." His brief definition that a "Pentecostal experience entails an empowering by the Spirit with some manifestation of the *charismata*" reinforces this impression since there is little suggestion in this chapter that this interpretation has been subjected to content criticism. This broad inclusivism is only possible in a situation where the ecclesiastical structure is sufficiently flexible to accommodate a variety of understandings of Christianity.

Nevertheless, the Wesleyan shares the sense of the importance of the church as a safeguard against individual, subjective vagaries. We recognize the only authentic context for the practice of the Christian life to be the body of Christ. The difference is in the way the church is defined. John Wesley identified the one essential mark of the church as "living faith," which may be present when ecclesiastical structures are absent; on the contrary such structures may be present when "living faith" is absent. But such faith is always corporate in nature.

In similar fashion, the Catholic emphasis on the importance of the sacraments is a strong element in their approach. The sacraments tend to keep the believer in contact with the historical events that constitute the core of the gospel and stand sentinel against the tendency toward a type of Gnosticism to which individualistic Charismatic experience is susceptible. In a letter to his brother, John Wesley confessed: "I think the rock on which I had the nearest made shipwreck of the faith was the writings of the Mystics; under which term I comprehend all, and only those, who slight any of the means of grace."[167] However here, also, there is a significant contrast between Catholic and Wesleyan spirituality. The latter holds to the importance of the sacraments (Baptism and Eucharist) as means of grace to the believers who participate in faith. At least in the theology of medieval Catholic thought, the sacraments were understood to function *ex opere operato,* and when grace is "infused" into the soul, it does not occur as a conscious experience (this language is used on p. 21). This issue appears in Del Colle's report about the work of O'Connor who, he says, seeks to emphasize the "interior awareness of grace." This was one of Martin Luther's problems with the piety of his day, and if that understanding informed the participant's sacramental piety, one might surmise that this lack of existential experience could have been a catalyst for the emergence of Charismatic movements within the church.

The distinction Del Colle refers to between "created grace" and "uncreated grace" is significant. It has been my understanding that the former is dominant in the Western Church while the latter is emphasized in the Eastern Church. If we are on the same page,

O'Connor's emphasis on "uncreated grace" is clearly supportive of what is here termed "Pentecostal experience" since this understanding of grace is relational in nature. Classical Wesleyan theology would be in full sympathy with this way of conceptualizing grace but would demur on the nature of the relationship and the concomitant outcomes.

Two closely related points come to expression when he discusses the matter of "assurance of salvation" and its relation to justification. Here, the Wesleyan tradition would be much closer to the Pentecostal tradition, as explained in Del Colle's discussion, than the Catholic, primarily because of the contrasting views of justification. If one defines justification, following St. Augustine, as "making holy," the logical consequence is the impossibility of any reality to the doctrine of "assurance," since there is always a question as to whether one has enough love, as St. Thomas put it.

This was the view of "justification" challenged by Luther occasioned by his discovery of the biblical meaning of the term through his study of Romans. However, his basic premise remained the same with the Western Church regarding "merit" as the basis of salvation with the result that he transferred the locus of the holiness that is requisite to final salvation from the believer to Christ. But the corollary of unconditional predestination vitiated the possibility of assurance in this context. With St. Paul, Wesley defined "justification" as a relative change that transformed, not the believer, but the sinner from a relationship of alienation to one of reconciliation. Wesleyans, following Wesley, teach that the moment of justification is accompanied chronologically by a transformation of the believer, but this was a qualitatively different activity of grace and (1) would be best described as initial sanctification (not Wesley's term), and (2) that one's acceptance by God was on the basis of justification, not this transformation. Since Wesleyans are further committed to a universal provision in the atonement, the work of Christ becomes the objective basis of assurance, not merely a subjective feeling.

In the context of this discussion, Del Colle somewhat misrepresents Wesley's view of "assurance." In the letter to his brother, Samuel, to which he refers (dated April 4, 1738), John is distinguishing between two understandings of assurance and does use the term "assurance of salvation" but rejects it in a letter to Arthur

Bedford on August 4, 1738. He clarifies his own studied position by using a different terminology, calling his own view the "assurance of faith." He wrote: "That assurance of which alone I speak, I should not choose to call an assurance of salvation, but rather (with the Scriptures) the assurance of faith. . . . I think the Scriptural words are always the best."[168]

This is far more than a semantic squabble. Both Bedford and Wesley understood that the term "assurance of salvation" meant a knowledge that we would *persevere* in a state of salvation, whereas Wesley was only willing to claim that we had the witness of the Spirit that we are *now* in a state of salvation.[169]

It is understandable that one should confuse classical Wesleyan theology with Pentecostal theology since as my own essay in this volume demonstrates, Wesleyan theology underwent a significant transformation in the American Holiness movement, which spawned the "Pentecostal" phenomenon, including making one's entire sanctification the basis of final salvation and, therefore, of assurance.

Response by Larry Hart

Even a cursory reading of Dr. Del Colle's presentation would demonstrate that, in general, the Roman Catholic Church far excelled the other ecclesial communities in providing sound theological guidance on the Pentecostal/Charismatic question. Early on, leading Catholic scholars were touched by the renewal and tapped for theological guidance—not the least of which was Léon Joseph Cardinal Suenens of Belgium, one of the four moderators of the Second Vatican Council! My background is Southern Baptist. When Charismatic outpourings began in our midst in the 1970s, we were notoriously unsophisticated in our response. I was completely intrigued by the irony of the ease in which the high church traditions assimilated the renewal in contrast to the chaos among us Baptists. A volume such as this one is long overdue!

Dr. Del Colle's presentation aids us Protestants in another way. Evidently, because we have been so fearful of sacramentalism at times, we have been unnecessarily blinded to the gracious workings of God's Spirit in the events of baptism and communion. Too often these rites have become rote—a shallow legalism rather than a vital declaration of faith and experience of the Spirit. This is all the more evidence for the value of the kind of cross-pollination that can take place in such a volume as this one.

Therefore, I am even further amazed at the fact that having been involved in the renewal for some thirty-eight years, I, a Southern Baptist, find myself in almost exact theological agreement with Dr. Del Colle, a Roman Catholic. In our own distinctive ways, we have each come to use the term *Spirit baptism* in a much more comprehensive, dynamic sense, referring to the total eschatological, soteriological work of the Spirit. This is the direction I believe the Lord is pointing his church at present. It literally is "what the Spirit is saying to the churches"!

It allows each of us to guard the distinctives of our particular traditions, while being able to communicate across theological lines regarding the Holy Spirit's work in our own time. It is bridge-building. And it is biblical, as I have argued in my own presentation. But its ecumenical implications are disturbing. If we were able to find this much common ground theologically across ecclesial lines, would we be able to affirm "the unity of the Spirit in the bond of peace" (Eph. 4:3 ESV) to the extent that functionally we could evangelize the world together? And what about in our own particular communions? Could a local Southern Baptist congregation, for example, given this bridge-building theological perspective, enjoy authentic spiritual unity among both traditionalists and renewalists in the worship, witness, and work of the church?

I am not a sacramentalist, and I have serious questions related to Roman Catholic theology. But I have found over the years a kinship with those I have encountered in the renewal from the Catholic tradition. Once I found myself enthusiastically and sincerely blurting out, "Oh, Brother Father, great to see you!" to a Catholic priest at a Charismatic prayer service. Can such an "ecumenical" dynamic also be evident *within* a given tradition? What most disturbs me at present is the massive division among Southern Baptists in my home state of Texas. Might not a mighty Pentecostal outpouring do more to break down barriers and shed light on doctrinal differences than all our political maneuverings?

When I came to Southern Baptist Theological Seminary in 1970, I could love almost anyone but a liberal. Then I saw, first-hand, liberals being filled with the Spirit and being transformed both personally and theologically. Now they were able to accept the inspiration of the Scriptures and the miracles in the Bible! Now I am convinced that the theological extremes, both Fundamentalist and liberal, are uncomfortable bedfellows. Both are narrowly rationalistic, and both are mortally afraid of religious experience. Perhaps Southern Baptists could learn a lesson in maturity from Roman Catholics, many of whom have welcomed the winds of the Spirit.

Perhaps if more of us Protestant Evangelicals would reverence the Lord's Supper as sincerely as do our Catholic counterparts, we would search our souls more honestly before going to the table, and we would open our lives more fully than ever before to the Lord and to one another. Creedal identity is noble and necessary. Spiritual humility and hunger are just as crucial. The former without the latter is dead orthodoxy. The latter without the former can degenerate into a shallow, superior triumphalism. Both reformation and renewal are needed, and Dr. Del Colle's presentation provides helpful pointers in that ongoing pilgrimage.

It may be that the most helpful overview of the theology of Catholic Charismatic renewal and the church's considered response to it is to be found right here in Dr. Del Colle's thorough, fair, and informative analysis. He may be opening up whole new worlds for some Protestant readers! And he certainly nudges all of us further down the path of respectful and receptive dialogue. The Holy Spirit still has much to teach us.

Response by Stanley M. Horton

Before there was an outpouring of the baptism in the Holy Spirit at Duquesne University or the University of Notre Dame, a number were filled at a monastery in the neighborhood of Ava, Missouri. I was awakened one morning at two by one of my students who had gone to the monastery seeking to find a quiet place for a time. Eight of the brothers and the abbot told him about their interest in the Holy Spirit. Study of the Scriptures had convinced them that the Holy Spirit is the mediator of Christ to us. My student wanted me to go the next day to meet with them, but I was already committed to go elsewhere. So he found a professor at Evangel University who did go. As a result, all eight were baptized in the Spirit, speaking in other tongues. I talked to one of the brothers later, and he said he was glad this happened before the outpourings at the Catholic universities because it made him see that the spread of Spirit baptism among Catholics was not by their influence but by the Holy Spirit's power.

Later, when teaching at our Bible college in Brussels, Belgium, I had an appointment to see Léon Joseph Cardinal Suenens. He was called away in an emergency, but he left an autographed copy of his *A New Pentecost?* for me. His secretary, also Spirit filled, was cordial, and we had a long talk. One of my close friends has been a member of the Catholic-Pentecostal dialogue at the Vatican in Rome. For several years now I have also taken part in an unofficial dialogue with the last three bishops of the Springfield-Cape Girardeau diocese and with some of their staff along with some Pentecostal pastors and teachers. We have learned that both the Pentecostals and the Catholics have had misconceptions of each other. The Catholics in the dialogue have been gracious and call us "separated brethren."

Many Pentecostals wondered about the outpouring among Catholics. This was especially true of former Catholics who were baptized in the Holy Spirit years ago and left the Catholic Church to join a Pentecostal church. They could not forget how their families and former friends persecuted them. One of my friends, however, spent time with a Catholic prayer group in St. Louis and came back thoroughly convinced of the reality of the Holy Spirit's outpouring. In the dialogue also we went over the major premises of the Second Vatican Council. We also had as guests a number of Catholics prominent in the Catholic Charismatic renewal. I have also listened to Catholics who spoke at the Society for Pentecostal Studies. Thus, I am happy that a Roman Catholic view is included here.

Ralph Del Colle is right in recognizing that there would have been no Charismatic renewal (including the Catholic one) without the Pentecostal doctrine of Spirit baptism as a gift for the already converted Christian. But like all the Catholic Charismatics I had heard, he emphasizes that their desire is to keep their experience and teaching within a Catholic framework. More of them followed the interpretation of Clark that Spirit baptism is a renewal of the sacrament of confirmation than that of the Ranaghans. O'Conner's teaching on grace, constant dependence on God—except for the fact we accept as scriptural only the ordinances of water baptism and the Lord's Supper. We do not accept the Catholic sacramental system. However, his statement that gifts of the Spirit "do not of themselves sanctify the recipient, even though they are useful aids toward the sanctification of the community," as Del Colle recognizes, are not foreign to much Pentecostal thinking.

The two streams of interpretation that Del Colle recognizes are important. Since most of the Catholic Charismatics I have heard give a sacramental interpretation, I found it interesting that Sullivan gives a nonsacramental version. I am surprised that he agrees with Dunn—a view that Pentecostals cannot accept.

It is important that Del Colle recognizes that "prayer for a 'new Pentecost' or a 'personal Pentecost' is entirely justified and that Spirit baptism signifies the fullness of grace and gifts." As Pentecostals some of us were at first hesitant to recognize what God was doing in the Charismatic movement. Most of us now recognize the sovereign working of God the Holy Spirit.

Response by Walter C. Kaiser Jr.

"Spirit baptism," we are told, has only been part of the Catholic vocabulary since 1967. It is a thrilling story of the grace of God working in Charismatic renewal. For those who enjoyed this renewal in its earliest days, it was a combination of experience, testimony, study of the Scriptures, Pentecostal witness, along with Catholic tradition, spirituality, and theology. As presented here, there is a theological integration of Spirit baptism with a Catholic sacramental and spiritual theology.

In the Catholic view, Spirit baptism is not to be considered a new sacrament, nor was it a replacement for any of the sacraments, even though it has been related either to a sacramental initiation experienced in baptism or in confirmation. Accordingly, Catholic Charismatics do not talk about "receiving" the baptism in the Holy Spirit, but being renewed thereby. It was a releasing of the Spirit given in the sacraments of baptism and confirmation.

For Catholic theologians in general, being baptized in the Spirit is not the same as being converted or with receiving a second or third blessing as meant in their technical senses. This is because for many Catholics one may undergo a series of conversions in a lifetime. It is more accurately linked for many Catholics perhaps with the sacrament of confirmation. It is an opening up to the Spirit. Normally being joined to Christ and receiving the Holy Spirit should come together, as the New Testament depicts them, but perhaps we can speak of one event with a twofold aspect, according to some Catholic theologians.

How to make this square with 1 Corinthians 12:13, however, where Paul links baptism in the Holy Spirit with our being joined together in one body and made to partake jointly of one drink is difficult to say. It is this lack of common ground in appealing to the Scriptures on this doctrine of Spirit baptism that makes it difficult to dialogue properly with Catholics.

Added to the above discussion is the matter of speaking in tongues. Some Catholic Charismatics accept speaking in tongues as the *normal* sign of Spirit baptism, but this is not the same as the doctrine of Pentecostals of "initial physical evidence." Instead, at least one Catholic writer has described "'inspired praise' as the only initial evidence, whether it is in one's own language or in tongues."

It is more difficult to evaluate a Catholic position of Spirit baptism or tongues as the initial sign thereof since there are various Catholic interpretations of Spirit baptism. Therefore, we must look for those majority opinions among Catholics in order to express some type of assessment. One universal seems to be that the Holy Spirit has already been received in the sacraments of baptism and confirmation. Another universal is that the Holy Spirit is continuously sent forth, so numerous new outpourings of the Spirit are not unwelcomed but are what we are witnessing in the renewal movement in the Catholic Church. These new outpourings are viewed in some Catholic quarters in a way that is akin to the multiple infillings of the Holy Spirit that Evangelicals approve of having.

The result of such thinking resulted in the Canadian Catholic bishops defining Spirit baptism in 1975 as "a symbolic act signifying an openness in the believer to the Spirit received at baptism." However, Catholics must be careful not to imply or teach that a second baptism has taken place. That would violate Catholic teaching.

Catholic teaching on Spirit baptism, as Del Colle has noted, "has had to negotiate the parameters of Catholic faith and practice." There is no statement that all Catholics adhere to that claims Spirit baptism takes place at one's conversion (an impossible position for Catholic doctrine), or as a second or third work of grace. Even our doctrines of grace in justification and sanctification are difficult to bridge since the Reformation. But when the teaching role of the church is also added to the normative role of Scripture Protestant Evangelicals hold to so strongly, the tensions rise even higher.

To be sure, the doctrine of the church separates Evangelicals and Catholics from linking Paul's interpretation of Spirit baptism in 1 Corinthians 12:13 with the organic unity of the body of Christ. This is one place where the discussion must ultimately go for Evangelicals.

Where, then, can Catholic Charismatics locate Spirit baptism? It is not something that can be doctrinally defined; instead, it is more the result of pastoral acceptance of a spirit of renewal that exists in the Catholic Church. For the pastoral guidance and sensitivities to the desire of the Holy Spirit to do a new work among Catholics, as he is doing among Evangelicals and Pentecostals, is beautiful to behold and much to be desired and encouraged.

But the full joining of a discussion of the critical biblical passages with Catholic theologians does not seem to have come to fruition as yet except in a selective and small way. We would encourage the dialogue to continue but with greater engagement with the relevant Scriptures.

Notes

Introduction: The Holy Spirit and Spirit Baptism in Today's Church

1. Clement of Rome *Corinthians* 13.3 in *The Ante-Nicene Fathers,* vol. 2, trans. F. Crombie, ed., Alexander Roberts, James Donaldson, and A. Cleveland Coxe (Grand Rapids: Eerdmans, n.d.).

2. B. B. Warfield, *Counterfeit Miracles* (Edinburgh: Banner of Truth, 1972), 6. This work was first published in 1918.

3. Since Pentecostalism was in its nascent stages and was considered to be little more than an aberration of the Holiness movement, its claims do not receive treatment in Warfield's analysis. On the theological problems in Holiness thought, see also idem, *Perfectionism,* ed. Samuel G. Craig (Philadelphia: Presbyterian and Reformed Publishing Co., 1958), 3–65.

4. Warfield, *Counterfeit Miracles,* 35–230 and *passim.*

5. Adherents to this view include Abraham Kuyper, *The Work of the Holy Spirit,* Introduction by Benjamin Breckenridge Warfield, trans. Henri De Vries (New York: Funk and Wagnall, 1900), 184–9; John Walvoord, *The Holy Spirit* (Grand Rapids: Zondervan, 1954), 167; W. A. Criswell, *The Holy Spirit in Today's World* (Grand Rapids: Zondervan, 1966), 178–226; Robert G. Gromacki, *The Modern Tongues Movement* (Philadelphia: Presbyterian and Reformed, 1967), 5–30; Norman Geisler, *Signs and Wonders* (Wheaton: Tyndale, 1988), 127–46. Some of these are not directly dependent on Warfield (notably, Kuyper) but are in the same tradition. It is also worth noting that this list spans the barriers between Dispensational and Covenant theologians.

6. A modification of Warfield's biblical argument which does not discard it completely is found in D. A. Carson, "The Purpose of Signs and Wonders in the New Testament," *in Power Religion: The Selling Out of the Evangelical Church?* ed. Michael Scott Horton (Chicago: Moody, 1992), 89–118, esp. 91–110.

7. William DeArteaga attempts to debunk the whole Warfieldian historical argument. DeArteaga, *Quenching the Spirit: Examining Centuries of Opposition to the Moving of the Holy Spirit* (Lake Mary, FL: Creation House, 1992), esp. 59–102. See also Jon

Ruthven, *On the Cessation of the Charismata: The Protestant Polemic on Postbiblical Miracles* (Sheffield: Sheffield Academic Press, 1993).

8. "Watch out, you Evangelicals—the young Pentecostal scholars are coming!" Clark H. Pinnock, Foreword to Roger Stronstad, *The Charismatic Theology of St. Luke* (Peabody, MA: Hendrickson, 1984), vii. In 1970, advocates of Penetecostal/Charismatic renewal founded the Society for Pentecostal Studies and published the inaugural issue of the semiannual journal *Pneuma.* This society helped spur a remarkable advance in "Pentecostal scholarship," particularly in institutions such as Asbury Theological Seminary, Regent University, Oral Roberts University, and Evangel College and Seminary. The academic renewal has expanded beyond the traditional Pentecostal schools, however. Individual scholars in this tradition are also teaching at institutions not specifically identified with Pentecostal/Charismatic renewal. These institutions include Drew University (Donald Dayton), Southwest Missouri State University (Stanley Burgess), University of Notre Dame (Morton Kelsey, Josephine Massyngberde Ford, and Edward O'Connor), Fuller Theological Seminary (C. Peter Wagner, Cecil M. Robeck, and Russell P. Spittler), Regent College (Gordon Fee), McMaster University (Clark H. Pinnock), University of Birmingham (Walter Hollenweger), The Jesuit School of Theology in Berkeley (Donald Gelpi), Gregorian University in Rome (Francis Sullivan), and St. John's University (Kilian McDonnell). For an analysis of this young Pentecostal scholarship, see Russell P. Spittler, "Maintaining Distinctives: The Future of Pentecostalism," in *Pentecostals from the Inside Out,* ed. Harold B. Smith with a Foreword by David Edwin Harrell Jr. (Wheaton: Victor, 1990), 126–28.

9. The biblical question is, of course, the most important question. But in this Introduction I am merely assessing the historical evidence through the fourth century as a foil for the debate that ensues in this volume.

10. Warfield attempts no definition of "miracle." One may, however, deduce from his discussion that miracles involve an invasion by God of the natural order (construed, no doubt, in terms of some sort of Newtonian physics), and a public interference with normal biological, meteorological, or astrological functions for some divine purpose. "Miracle," thus, is distinct from providence, as well as from the active presence of God in the life of an individual or a congregation in such matters as personal spiritual sustenance, salvation, or in the exercise of sacraments and spiritual gifts (such as preaching). These all involve the personal presence and activity of God but are not viewed as "miracle."

11. Glossolalia could be considered a special case since there is some question as to whether it should be considered paranormal in all its manifestations. The experience on the day of Pentecost was clearly miraculous since it involved communication in unlearned languages. There is some question, however, whether the Corinthian experience was the same. See Donald Burdick, *Tongues: To Speak or Not to Speak* (Chicago: Moody, 1969), 48–58; Gordon D. Fee, *The First Epistle to the Corinthians,* New International Commentary on the New Testament, gen. ed. F. F. Bruce (Grand Rapids: Eerdmans, 1987), 569–75. As to "speaking in tongues" in later Christian (or even non-Christian) experience, there is an enormous body of literature which argues for psychological and emotional explanations of the phenomenon. One of the best examples is Vern S. Poythress, "Linguistic and Sociological Analyses of Modern Tongues-Speaking: Their Contributions and Limitations," in *Speaking in Tongues: A Guide to Research on Glossolalia,* ed. Watson E. Mills (Grand Rapids: Eerdmans, 1986), 469–91.

12. The disclaimer placed on glossolalia also applies to prophecy. Some manifestations of this "charism" may be considered miraculous, and others may not.

13. Morton Kelsey, *Healing and Christianity in Ancient Thought and Modern Times* (New York: Harper and Row, 1973), 131.

14. This is the translation as rendered by Kydd. Ronald A. N. Kydd, *Charismatic Gifts in the Early Church* (Peabody, MA: Hendrickson, 1984), 15. *The Ante-Nicene Fathers* translation reads, "And as respects those that are not seen, pray that [God] would reveal them unto thee, in order that thou mayest be wanting in nothing, but mayest abound in

every gift." Ignatius *Epistle to Polycarp* 2., trans. Marcus Dods, ed. Alexander Roberts, James Donaldson, and A. Cleveland Coxe (Grand Rapids: Eerdmans, n.d.). There is a footnote in this text at the words, "not seen," which indicates that some authorities refer this to the mysteries of God. See also R. Leonard Carroll, "Glossolalia: Apostles to the Reformation," in Wade Horton, ed., *The Glossolalia Phenomenon* (Cleveland, TN: Pathway Press, 1966), 78–82.

15. Ignatius *Epistle to the Philadelphians* 7.2. This passage indicates Ignatius's understanding of the immediacy of the Spirit's revelatory activity.

16. *The Pastor of Hermas* in *The Ante-Nicene Fathers,* vol. 2, trans. F. Crombie, ed. Alexander Roberts, James Donaldson,, and A. Cleveland Coxe (Grand Rapids: Eerdmans, n.d.), Vision 1.1., Vision 2.1.,4., Vision 3.10., Vision 4.1, Vision 5.

17. From the translation by G. F. Snyder, *The Shepherd of Hermas, The Apostolic Fathers: A New Translation and Commentary,* ed. R. M. Grant (Camden, NJ: Thomas Nelson, 1968), 87. In the traditional numbering system employed in *The Ante-Nicene Fathers, Hermas* Commandment 11.

18. Snyder, *Shepherd,* 88; *Hermas* Commandment 11. See also Louis Boyer, "Some Charismatic Movements in the History of the Church," in Edward D. O'Connor, SSC, ed., *Perspectives on Charismatic Renewal* (Notre Dame: University of Notre Dame Press, 1975), 113–31.

19. "[Some] are also receiving gifts, each as he is worthy, illumined through the name of this Christ. For one receives the spirit of understanding, another of counsel, another of strength, another of healing, another of foreknowledge, another of teaching, and another of the fear of God." Justin Martyr *Dialogue with Trypho, a Jew* 39, *The Ante-Nicene Fathers,* vol. 1, trans. Marcus Dods, ed. James Donaldson,, Alexander Roberts and A. Cleveland Coxe (Grand Rapids: Eerdmans, n.d.).

20. Justin Martyr *Dialogue* 82. He goes on, "And hence you ought to understand that [the gifts] formerly among your nation have now been transferred to us. And just as there were false prophets contemporaneous with your holy prophets, so are there now many false teachers amongst us, . . . so that in no respect are we deficient . . ." (ibid.).

21. Justin Martyr *The Second Apology of Justin* 6, *The Ante-Nicene Fathers,* vol. 1, trans. Marcus Dods, ed. James Donaldson,, Alexander Roberts and A. Cleveland Coxe (Grand Rapids: Eerdmans, n.d.). The text reads, "For numberless demoniacs throughout the whole world, and in your city, many of our Christian men exorcising them in the name of Jesus Christ, . . . have healed and do heal, rendering helpless and driving the possessing devils out of the men, though they could not be cured by all the other exorcists, and those who used incantations and drugs." See also George Hunston Williams and Edith Waldvogel, "A History of Speaking in Tongues and Related Gifts," in Michael P. Hamilton, ed., *The Charismatic Movement* (Grand Rapids: Eerdmans, 1975), 61–113.

22. Evelyn Frost, in her monumental study on healing in the early church, writes: "The Church regard[ed] it as a great sin not to heal sufferers. (Failure to heal, not failure to try to heal, was the sin)" (*Christian Healing: A Consideration of the Place of Spiritual Healing in the Church of Today in the Light of the Doctrine and Practice of the Ante-Nicene Church,* Foreword by T. W. Crafer [London: Mowbray, 1949], 19). She adduces for evidence these lines from *Hermas* (which she cites in the Wake translation): "I would that all men should be delivered from the inconveniences they lie under. For he that wants, and suffers inconsistencies in his daily life, is in great torment and necessity. Whosoever, therefore, delivers such a soul from necessity, gets great joy unto himself . . . and many upon the account of such calamities, being not able to bear them, have chosen to destroy themselves. He, therefore, that knows the calamity of such a man, and does not free him from it, commits a great sin, and is guilty of his blood." (The passage is from *Hermas* Similitude 10.4. It is quoted thus in Frost, *Healing,* 103.) Her interpretation of this text has been adopted uncritically by Kelsey, *Healing and Christianity,* 148–9. But this interpretation appears to be seriously flawed. The term, *calamity,* is a translation of the Latin *calamitas.* (This portion [Similitude 10] of the otherwise Greek *Hermas* is extant only in

Latin translation.) The use of this word to indicate physical malady is certainly a possibility. But more determinative is the word rendered "necessity," *incommodum*. This term normally refers to an "inconvenience" or a "misfortune"; only rarely is it a reference to an ailment. P. G. W. Glare, ed., *Oxford Latin Dictionary* (Oxford: Clarendon Press, 1982), s.v. "incommodum." In the context, it seems preferable to interpret this as referring to some sort of misfortune, rather than miraculous healing. See J. Reiling, *Hermas and Christian Prophecy* (Leiden: E. J. Brill, 1973), 22–4.

23. The exact date of the founding of Montanism is uncertain. Eusebius quotes an anonymous opponent to the effect that Montanus began to prophesy when Gratus (probably Quadratus) was proconsul in Asia. A Quadratus was proconsul in Asia Minor in AD 155 and another in 166. The same writer indicates that fourteen years had passed since the death of the Montanist prophetess Maximilla. Eusebius *Church History* 5.167.; 5.7.4, *The Nicene and Post-Nicene Fathers, Second Series,* vol.1, trans. Arthur C. McGiffert, ed. Philip Schaff and Henry Wace (Grand Rapids: Eerdmans, n.d.). Montanus probably began his work between AD 155 and 166, and Maximilla's death was likely in 178 or 179. Frederick C. Klawter, "The Role of Martyrdom and Persecution in Developing the Priestly Authority of Women in Early Christianity: A Case Study of Montanism," *Church History* 49 (September 1980) 3:252–5.

24. The early Fathers were not in agreement on this matter. Jerome considered them Sabellian, as did Dydimus the Blind, while Hippolytus regarded them to be orthodox in regards to the Father and the Son. David F. Wright, "Why Were the Montanists Condemned?" *Themelios* 2 (1975): 16; Jaroslav Pelikan, *The Emergence of the Orthodox Tradition (100–600): The Christian Tradition, Volume 1* (Chicago: University of Chicago Press, 1971), 100. None considered the Montanists orthodox in regard to the Spirit, with the likely exception of Tertullian. It is questionable, however, whether Tertullian accepted the theology of the movement as a whole. See Gerald Lewis Bray, *Holiness and the Will of God: Perspectives on the Theology of Tertullian,* New Foundations Theological Library (Atlanta: John Knox, 1979), 54–63.

25. Maurice Barnett, *The Living Flame: Being a Study of the Gift of the Spirit in the New Testament, with Special Reference to Prophecy, Glossolalia, Montanism and Perfection* (London: Epworth Press, 1953), 114.

26. Tertullian complained that the bishop of Rome had at first accepted the validity of the Montanist gifts, but later, at the insistence of Praxeas, had enforced ecclesiastical pressure on the Phrygians. Tertullian *Against Praxeas* 1, *The Ante-Nicene Fathers,* vol. 3, trans. Peter Holmes and S. Thelwell, ed. Alexander Roberts, James Donaldson, and A. Cleveland Coxe (Grand Rapids: Eerdmans, n.d.).

27. Ibid., 115. One of the primary concerns of Montanus was the remarriage of widows. He was opposed to all such marriages, and his words were echoed by Tertullian, who wrote, referring to the teachings of the second century ecstatic and his female associates, "[The *psychichi*] marry more often than they fast." Tertullian *On Fasting. In Opposition to the Psychics* 1., *The Ante-Nicene Fathers,* vol. 4, trans. S. Thelwall, ed. Alexander Roberts, James Donaldson, and A. Cleveland Coxe (Grand Rapids: Eerdmans, n.d.).

28. Maximilla had predicted "war and anarchy" (Eusebius *Church History* 5.16.18).

29. Ibid., 5.16.13.

30. Frederick Dale Bruner, *A Theology of the Holy Spirit* (Grand Rapids: Eerdmans, 1970), 36; Ronald Knox, *Enthusiasm: A Chapter in the History of Religion* (Oxford: Oxford University Press, 1950), 34–6.

31. Eusebius indicated that Montanus was "beside himself, and suddenly in a sort of frenzy and ecstasy, he raved, and began to babble and utter strange things (*cenofevin*), prophesying in a manner contrary to the custom of the church handed down by tradition from the beginning" (Eusebius *Church History* 5.16.7). Harold Hunter, a Pentecostal scholar, contends that it is not certain that this text is a reference to glossolalia ("Tongues-Speech: A Patristic Analysis," *Journal of the Evangelical Theological Society* 23 [June 1980] 2: 129).

32. On Irenaeus's reaction to Montanism, see Eusebius *Church History* 5.3.4.–5.4.3.

33. Irenaeus *Against Heresies* 4.33.6., *The Ante-Nicene Fathers,* vol. 1, trans. A. Cleveland Coxe, ed. Alexander Roberts, James Donaldson, and A. Cleveland Coxe (Grand Rapids: Eerdmans, n.d.).

34. Speaking of Marcus and his devotees, "he says to her, 'Open thy mouth, speak whatsoever occurs to thee, and thou shalt prophesy.' She then vainly puffed up and elated by these words, and greatly excited in soul by the expectation that it is herself who is to prophesy, her heart beating violently reaches the requisite pitch of audacity, and idly as well as impudently utters some nonsense as it happens to occur to her. . . . Henceforth she reckons herself a prophetess, and expresses her thanks to Marcus for having imparted to her of his own Charis" (Irenaeus *Against Heresies* 1.13.3).

35. Ibid., 4.33.6.

36. Ibid., 2.32.4. "Wherefore, also, those who are in truth His disciples, receiving grace from Him, do in His name perform [miracles], so as to promote the welfare of other men, according to the gift each one has received from Him."

37. Ibid., 5.7.2.–5.8.1. See Cecil M. Robeck, "Irenaeus and the 'Prophetic Gifts,'" in *Essays on Apostolic Themes: Studies in Honor of Howard M. Ervin,* ed. Paul Elbert (Peabody, MA: Hendrickson, 1985), 111.

38. He writes, "In like manner we do also hear many brethren in the Church, who possess prophetic gifts, and who through the Spirit of God do speak in all languages, as he used Himself also to speak . . . and bring to light for the general benefit the hidden things of men, and declare the mysteries of God" (Irenaeus *Against Heresies* 5.6.1).

39. Ibid., 3.32.4. He goes on to say, "Nor does she perform anything by means of angelic incantations . . . but, directing her prayers to the Lord, who made all things . . . she has been accustomed to work miracles for the advantage of mankind. . . . If, therefore, the name of our Lord Jesus even now confers benefits, and cures thoroughly and effectively all who anywhere believe on Him . . ." (ibid., 3.32.5).

40. Kelsey goes beyond the evidence, however, when he writes, "There is no indication that Irenaeus viewed any disease as incurable or any healing as against God's will. Indeed the whole attitude he voiced was that healing is a natural activity of Christians as they express the creative power of God, given them as members of Christ" (Kelsey, *Healing and Christianity,* 151).

41. Hippolytus *The Apostolic Tradition* 15.1., trans. Gregory Dix (London: S. P. C. K., 1937). "If anyone among the laity appears to have received a gift of healing by a revelation, hands shall not be laid upon him, because the matter is manifest." There is some question about whether this document should be ascribed to Hippolytus. The question is not particularly relevant to this discussion, but Dix is of the opinion that it is the work of the Roman Father and that it represents the mind of the whole Catholic Church in the second century (ibid., xliv).

42. Kydd, *Charismatic Gifts in the Early Church,* 59.

43. Origen *Against Celsus* 3.24., *The Ante-Nicene Fathers,* vol. 4, trans. Frederick Crombie, ed. Alexander Roberts, James Donaldson, and A. Cleveland Coxe (Grand Rapids: Eerdmans, n.d.). It is not altogether clear what he intends by "history." It may have been an appeal to his "historical sojourn as God incarnate" (Cecil M. Robeck, "Origen's Treatment of the Charismata," in *Charismatic Experiences in History,* ed. Cecil M. Robeck [Peabody, MA: Hendrickson, 1985], 115).

44. ". . . and those who have earned advancement to this grade by the sanctification of the Holy Spirit, will nevertheless obtain the gift of wisdom according to the power and working of the Spirit of God" (Origen *De Principiis* 1.3.8., *The Ante-Nicene Fathers,* vol. 4, trans. Frederick Crombie, ed. Alexander Roberts, James Donaldson, and A. Cleveland Coxe (Grand Rapids: Eerdmans, n.d.)

45. "[Even unlettered persons do this,] making manifest the grace which is in the word of Christ, and the despicable weakness of demons, which, in order to be overcome and driven out of their bodies and souls of men, do not require the power and wisdom of

those who are mighty in argument, and most learned in matters of faith" (Origen *Against Celsus* 7.4).

46. Ibid., 7.3.

47. Gregory Nazianzen *Oration XLIII, The Panegyric on St. Basil* 54., *The Nicene and Post-Nicene Fathers,* Second Series, vol. 7, trans. Charles Gordon Browne and James Edward Swallow, ed. Philip Schaff and Henry Wace (Grand Rapids: Eerdmans, n.d.).

48. Ibid., *Oration VII, On His Sister Gorgonia* 15.

49. Wayne Grudem shifted the debate somewhat in his treatment of NT prophecy as being distinct from OT prophecy. In that case, prophecy does not take on the character of "miracle," but only of charism. See Wayne Grudem, *The Gift of Prophecy in the New Testament and Today,* rev. ed. (Wheaton: Crossway, 2001). His views have been thoroughly critiqued by O. Palmer Robertson, *The Final Word* (Edinburgh: Banner of Truth, 1993).

50. Donald Bloesch, *A Theology of Word and Spirit* (Downers Grove: InterVarsity Press, 1990), 67.

51. Quoted in John Garvey, "Truth Flashes," *Commonweal* 113 (1986) 22:677.

52. In analogical predication, "what we do not know exceeds by far what we are able to glean even from the resources of faith and tradition" (Donald Bloesch, *God the Almighty* [Downers Grove: InterVarsity Press, 1992], 35).

53. Bloesch, *A Theology of Word and Spirit,* 68.

54. Ibid.

55. Paul Tillich, *The Courage to Be* (New Haven: Yale University Press, 1958), 186. See also idem, "The Religious Symbol," *Journal of Liberal Religion* 2 (1940) 1:13–33. Language used of God is extremely problematic due to his nature of being-as-such. "When applied to God, superlatives become diminutives" (Paul Tillich, *Systematic Theology* [Chicago: University of Chicago Press, 1951], 1:235). Further, "In mysticism one can talk about God only in metaphors and similes. He remains basically unknowable, though he can be experienced" (Bloesch, *God the Almighty,* 47–48; idem, *Essentials of Evangelical Theology,* 1:44).

56. Bloesch, *A Theology of Word and Spirit,* 69. See also idem, *Battle for the Trinity* (Ann Arbor: Servant, 1985), 14–28; idem, *God the Almighty,* 43; Leon J. Podler, *The Church Impotent: The Feminization of Christianity* (Dallas: Spence, 1999), 102–38. This is precisely what Ruether does. Rosemary Radford Ruether, *Sexism and God-Talk: Toward a Feminist Theology,* second edition (Boston: Beacon Press, 1993), 61–67.

57. Sallie McFague, *Metaphorical Theology: Models of God in Religious Language* (Philadelphia: Fortress, 1982), 4–6.

58. McFague, *Models of God,* 97. Since God is unknowable it is "important to listen to women's experiences to discover the spiritual dynamics of this revolution and to speak these dynamics in our own lives and words" (Mary Daly, "Why Speak about God?" in *Womanspirit Rising,* 216).

59. Letty Russell, "Liberation Theology in a Feminist Perspective," in *Liberation, Revolution and Freedom,* ed. Thomas McFadden (New York: Seabury, 1975), 89–95.

60. Pannenberg argues that both language and the meaningfulness of life toward which it points await a future vindication. See Wolfhart Pannenberg, *Metaphysics and the Idea of God,* trans. Philip Clayton (Grand Rapids: Eerdmans, 1990), 164–70.

61. Karl Barth, *The Humanity of God* (Philadelphia: Westminster, 1972), 33–45.

62. T. F. Torrance, *Theological Science* (Oxford: Oxford University Press, 1969), 150.

63. Quoted in Bloesch, *A Theology of Word and Spirit,* 70. A. W. Tozer is someone Bloesch normally quotes with approval, but Tozer seems to take a different approach on this point, finding a barrier to knowledge of God due to God's ineffability, an attribute which places a "great strain on both thought and language in the Holy Scriptures" (A. W. Tozer, *The Knowledge of the Holy* [New York: Harper & Brothers, 1961], 14). Bloesch nowhere notes his disagreement with Tozer on this matter, but he does take a different approach, affirming that God makes himself knowable through a miracle of grace.

64. T. F. Torrance, *Transformation and Convergence in the Frame of Knowledge* (Grand Rapids: Eerdmans, 1984), 317. Though Bloesch generally favors Torrance's approach, the language here sounds curiously like the approach of the Evangelical rationalists Bloesch so often critiques. There are apparently similarities between them in exposition, though decided differences in approaches to apologetics. See also Donald G. Bloesch, *Essentials of Evangelical Theology* (San Francisco: Harper & Row, 1979), 2:275. Mysticism, on the other hand, accepted the idea of reality being "unordered in any objective way that man's mind can discern" (Huston Smith, "Revolution in Western Thought," *The Saturday Evening Post,* 26 August 1961, 61).

65. Hans J. Hillerbrand, "Thomas Muentzer," in *Reformers in Profile,* ed. B. A. Garrish (Philadelphia: Fortress, 1967), 220–23.

66. Quoted in George Hunston Williams, *The Radical Reformation,* 3rd ed. (Philadelphia: Westminster, 1962), 1249.

67. Meic Pearse, *The Great Restoration: The Religious Radicals of the 16th and 17th Centuries* (Carlisle, Cambria: Paternoster, 1998), 41.

68. Williams, *The Radical Reformation,* 1250.

69. Kenneth Scott Latourette, *A History of Christianity, Volume 2: Reformation to the Present* (San Francisco: HarperSanFranciso, 1975), 789.

70. See, for instance, along with previous literature cited, Paul Christianson, *Reformers and Babylon: English Apocalyptic Visions from the Reformation to the Eve of the Civil War* (Toronto: University of Toronto Press, 1978); Hillel Schwarz, *The French Prophets: History of a Millenarian Group in Eighteenth-Century England* (Berkeley: University of California Press, 1980); Rene Weis, *The Yellow Cross: The Story of the Last Cathars* (New York: Knopf, 2001).

71. On the KJV-only controversy, see James R. White, *The King James Version Only Controversy* (Minneapolis: Bethany, 1996). On the Manifested Sons, see Richard M. Riss, *A Survey of 20th-Century Revival Movements* (Peabody, MA: Hendrickson, 1988), 105–24. On Word/Faith, see Robert M. Bowman Jr., *The Word-Faith Controversy: Understanding the Health and Wealth Gospel* (Grand Rapids: Baker, 2001).

72. Eduard Schweizer, "pneuma," *Theological Dictionary of the New Testament,* ed. Rudolf Kittel, trans. Geoffrey Bromiley (Grand Rapids: Eerdmans, 1964), 6.396. Of course, it also needs to be recognized that the Spirit was a theme of doctrine as far back as the fourth century when Basil the Great wrote a treatise on the Spirit in opposition to the Pneumatomachians.

73. L. S. Thornton, *Confirmation: Its Place in the Baptismal Mystery* (London: A. and C. Black, 1954), 13–9. See also Ralph Del Colle's discussion of the matter in this book.

74. *Shepherd of Hermas* 9.16.4.

75. Thomas Goodwin, *The Works of Thomas Goodwin,* ed. J. C. Miller (Edinburgh: James Nicol, 1861), 1:231–62.

76. D. Martyn Lloyd-Jones, *God's Ultimate Purpose: An Exposition of Ephesians 1:1–23* (Grand Rapids: Baker, 1978), 243–311.

77. John Fletcher, *The Works of the Reverend John Fletcher* (New York, 1851), 2:632–9, 4:230–2. See for further discussion, Donald W. Dayton, *Theological Roots of Pentecostalism* (Metuchen, NJ: Scarecrow Press, 1987), 149–53; George H. Williams and Edith Waldvogel, "A History of Speaking in Tongues and Related Gifts," in *The Charismatic Movement,* ed. Michael P. Hamilton (Grand Rapids: Eerdmans, 1975), 81.

78. Williams and Waldvogel, "A History of Speaking in Tongues," 81.

79. In 1894 Phineas Bresee preached a sermon on the "Baptism with the Holy Ghost" to open his national camp meeting, in which he proclaimed that the dispensation of the Holy Spirit was ushered in soon after the ascension of Jesus (Dayton, *Theological Roots of Pentecostalism,* 93). A. B. Simpson saw Spirit baptism as a "second conversion" which was purifying (Charles W. Nienkirchen, *A. B. Simpson and the Pentecostal Movement* [Peabody, MA: Hendrickson, 1992], 6–11). Benjamin Irwin, founder of the Fire-Baptized Holiness Church, articulated a threefold scheme of salvation, sanctification, and

fire-baptism, the latter of which entailed power for Christian living (Joseph E. Campbell, *The Pentecostal Holiness Church, 1898–1948* [Franklin Springs, GA: Pentecostal Holiness Church, 1951], 194–9). On Asa Mahan, see Edward H. Madden and James E. Hamilton, *Freedom and Grace: The Life of Asa Mahan* (Metuchen, NJ: Scarecrow Press, 1982).

80. John L. Gresham Jr., *Charles G. Finney's Doctrine of the Baptism of the Holy Spirit* (Peabody, MA: Hendrickson, 1987); Charles Edwin White, *Beauty of Holiness: Phoebe Palmer as Theologian, Revivalist, Feminist and Humanitarian* (Grand Rapids: Zondervan, 1986).

81. For a history of the early Keswick movement, see Steven Barabas, *So Great Salvation: The History and Message of the Keswick Convention* (London: Marshall, Morgan, and Scott, 1952).

82. H. C. G. Moule, *Epistle to the Romans,* 5th ed. (New York: Armstrong, 1902).

83. Representative works include F. B. Meyer, *Way into the Holiest* (Fort Washington, PA: Christian Literature Crusade, 1982); Andrew Murray, *Absolute Surrender* (Chicago: Moody Press, 1988); R. A. Torrey, *The Baptism and Fullness of the Holy Spirit* (Old Tappan, NJ: Revell, 1957); Hannah Whitall Smith, *The Christian's Secret to a Happy Life* (New York: Whittaker House, 1988); A. J. Gordon, *The Two-Fold Life* (Fort Washington, PA: Christian Literature Crusade, 1977); D. L. Moody, *Power from on High* (Chicago: Moody Press, 1971).

84. Watchman Nee, *The Spiritual Man* (Fort Washington, PA: Christian Literature Crusade, 1965); idem, *The Normal Christian Life* (Fort Washington, PA: Christian Literature Crusade, 1972); Ian Thomas, *The Saving Life of Christ* (Grand Rapids: Zondervan, 1989); Alan Redpath, *Victorious Christian Living: Studies in the Book of Joshua* (Old Tappan, NJ: Revell, 1993).

85. J. I. Packer, *Keep in Step with the Spirit* (Old Tappan, NJ: Revell, 1984), 161.

86. Ibid. Packer contends that this theology essentially holds to a passive understanding of faith.

87. Robert Owens, "The Azusa Street Revival: The Pentecostal Movement Begins in America," in *The Century of the Holy Spirit: 100 Years of Pentecostal and Charismatic Renewal,* ed. Vinson Synan (Nashville: Thomas Nelson, 2001), 43. For careful examination of all historical aspects of the Topeka situation, see Robert Mapes Anderson, *Vision of the Disinherited: The Making of American Pentecostalism* (Oxford: Oxford University Press, 1979).

88. Gary B. McGee, "Early Pentecostal Hermeneutics: Tongues as Evidence in the Book of Acts," in *Initial Evidence: Historical and Biblical Perspectives on the Pentecostal Doctrine of Spirit Baptism,* ed. Gary B. McGee (Peabody, MA: Hendrickson, 1991), 96–118; Howard M. Ervin, *These Are Not Drunken as Ye Suppose* (Plainfield, NJ: Logos, 1968), 56–61.

89. Dayton, *Theological Roots of Pentecostalism,* 96.

90. Roger Stronstad, *The Charismatic Theology of St. Luke* (Peabody, MA: Hendrickson, 1984); William W. and Robert P. Menzies, *Spirit and Power: Foundations of Pentecostal Experience* (Grand Rapids: Zondervan, 2000).

91. Dennis and Rita Bennett, *Nine O'clock in the Morning* (Plainfield, NJ: Bridge, 1970).

92. Richard Quebedeaux, *The New Charismatics II: How a Christian Renewal Movement Became Part of the American Religious Mainstream* (San Francisco: Harper & Row, 1983), 62–4.

93. Henry I. Lederle, "Initial Evidence and the Charismatic Movement: An Ecumenical Appraisal," in *Initial Evidence: Historical and Biblical Perspectives on the Pentecostal Doctrine of Spirit Baptism,* ed. Gary B. McGee (Peabody, MA: Hendrickson, 1991), 131–41.

94. Max Turner, *The Holy Spirit and Spiritual Gifts* (Peabody, MA: Hendrickson, 1996), 150–68.

95. Lederle, "Initial Evidence and the Charismatic Movement," 138–41.

96. John R. W. Stott, *The Baptism and Fullness of the Holy Spirit* (Leicester: InterVarsity Press, 1964); James D. G. Dunn, *Baptism in the Holy Spirit* (Philadelphia: Westminster, 1970); Frederick Dale Bruner, *A Theology of the Holy Spirit* (Grand Rapids: Eerdmans, 1970); Richard B. Gaffin, *Perspectives on Pentecost: Studies in New Testament Teachings on the Gifts of the Holy Spirit* (Phillipsburg, PA: Presbyterian and Reformed Publishing Company, 1979).

97. Gaffin, *Perspectives on Pentecost*, 27–8; Dunn, *Baptism in the Holy Spirit*, 4.

Chapter 1, The Baptism in the Holy Spirit as the Promise of the Father: A Reformed Perspective

1. John R. W. Stott. *The Baptism and Fullness of the Holy Spirit* (Chicago: InterVarsity Press, 1964), 3–4.

2. Ibid., 4–22.

3. James D. G. Dunn, *Baptism in the Holy Spirit: A Re-examination of the New Testament Teaching on the Gift of the Spirit in Relation to Pentecostalism Today* (London: SCM Press, 1970), 7. Dunn preferred to use the term *conversion-initiation* consistently to signal the "total event of becoming a Christian."

4. Ibid., 3.

5. James D. G. Dunn, "Baptism and the Unity of the Church in the New Testament," in *Baptism and the Unity of the Church,* ed. Michael Root and Risto Saarinen (Grand Rapids: Eerdmans, 1998), 78–103, especially p. 84.

6. Dunn, "Baptism and the Unity of the Church," 83.

7. For a popular development of this promise-plan thesis, see Walter C. Kaiser Jr., *The Christian and the "Old" Testament* (Pasadena, Calif.: William Carey Library, 1998). Also stated in an earlier but more scholarly fashion, idem. *Toward an Old Testament Theology* (Grand Rapids: Zondervan, 1978).

8. While four different dates have been proposed for the writing of Joel, see Walter C. Kaiser Jr., *A History of Israel: From the Bronze Age through the Jewish Wars* (Nashville: Broadman & Holman, 1998), 336–37. Tentatively the date we argue for is c. 845 BC.

9. For a fuller discussion of this Joel 2:28–32 passage, see Walter C. Kaiser Jr., "Participating In and Expecting the Day of the Lord—Joel 2:28–32," in my book, *Uses of the Old Testament in the New* (Chicago: Moody Press, 1985), 89–100 (now reprinted in Eugene, Oreg.: Wipf and Stock Publishers, 2001). This article originally appeared under the title, "The Promise of God and the Outpouring of the Holy Spirit," in *The Living and Active Word of God,* ed. Morris Inch and Ronald Youngblood (Winona Lake, Ind.: Eisenbrauns, 1983), 109–22.

10. See the clear discussion of Willis Judson Beecher, *The Prophets and the Promise* (Grand Rapids: Baker, 1975), 263–88, chapter 12, "Messianic Terms: The Servant."

11. Walter C. Kaiser Jr., "The Holy Spirit in the Old Testament," in *Pentecostalism in Context: Essays Presented to William W. Menzies on the Occasion of His Sixty-Fifth Birthday,* JPT Supplemental Series, 11, ed. Wonsuk Ma and Robert Menzies (Sheffield: Sheffield Academic Press, 1997), 38–47.

12. Beecher, *The Prophets and the Promise,* 191, emphasis mine.

13. Modern English translations have persisted in rendering 1 Cor. 12:13 baptism "*by* the Holy Spirit." However, to be baptized "*by*" someone in the New Testament is always expressed by the Greek preposition *hypo* followed by the genitive noun; e.g., Matt. 3:6; Mark 1:5; Luke 3:7. As Wayne Grudem described it in *Systematic Theology: An Introduction to Biblical Doctrine* (Grand Rapids: Zondervan, 1994), 768, n. 11, "Therefore, if Paul had wanted to say that the Corinthians had all been baptized *by* the Holy Spirit he would have used *hypo* plus the genitive, not *en* plus the dative. . . . Further support for the view that 1 Cor. 12:13 means 'in (or with) one Spirit' is found in M. J. Harris, 'Prepositions and Theology in the Greek New Testament,' in *NIDNTT*, 3:1210."

14. Matt. 3:11–12; Mark 1:8; Luke 3:16–17; John 1:33; Acts 1:5; 11:16.

15. Though not discussed here, the "baptism of fire," mentioned by John the Baptist in Matt. 3:11 and Luke 3:16 is most naturally connected with judgment since "fire" is often represented in the Old Testament as judgment (Gen. 19:24; 2 Kings 1:10; Amos 1:4–7). Some prefer to connect "fire" with the fiery tongues that came on those who were baptized in the Holy Spirit at Pentecost. Craig Blomberg, in his article on "Baptism of Fire," in *Evangelical Dictionary of Biblical Theology,* ed. Walter A. Elwell (Grand Rapids: Baker, 1996), 48–49, disagrees, saying, "But the grammatical construction in Greek (the use of one preposition to govern two objects) is most naturally taken as referring to only one baptism that involves both blessing and judgment (cf. esp. Isa. 4:4). Pentecost may well represent the firstfruits of purgation for believers, but the baptism is not complete until all people experience final judgment."

16. Stott, *The Baptism and Fullness of the Holy Spirit,* 5–6.

17. Whether one chooses to translate Greek *en* as *in* or *with* most likely depends on whether one considers water baptism to be administered by immersion or by affusion. Baptists and Pentecostals who practice immersion prefer *in* the Holy Spirit, while Anglicans prefer *with* the Holy Spirit. The former point to those texts that speak of much water being present while the latter group notes that the Holy Spirit was "poured out."

18. See note 13.

19. Stott, *The Baptism and the Fullness of the Holy Spirit,* 15.

20. James D. G. Dunn, *Unity and Diversity in the New Testament,* 2nd ed. (Philadelphia: Trinity Press International, 1990).

21. This point is made by Clark Pinnock in his foreword to R. Stronstad, *The Charismatic Theology of St. Luke* (Peabody, Mass.: Hendrickson Press, 1984), vii. Pinnock said, "Ironically, at this point at least, there is greater diversity in the New Testament than even Jimmy Dunn is prepared to grant! St. Luke speaks of a baptism of power for service which is not oriented to the soteriological work of the Spirit, which Paul often addresses."

22. See especially H. D. Hunter, *Spirit-Baptism: A Pentecostal Alternative* (Lantham, Md.: University Press of America, 1983); H. Ervin, *The Charismatic Theology of St. Luke* (Peabody, Mass.: Hendrickson, 1984); R. Stronstad, *The Charismatic Theology of St. Luke* (Peabody, Mass.: Hendrickson, 1984); J. B. Shelton, *Mighty in Word and Deed: The Role of the Holy Spirit in Luke-Acts* (Peabody, Mass.: Hendrickson, 1991); and R. P. Menzies, *The Development of Early Christian Pneumatology with Special Reference to Luke-Acts* (JSNT Sup, 54; Sheffield, JSOT Press, 1991).

23. Stronstad, *Charismatic Theology,* 12.

24. William W. and Robert P. Menzies, *Spirit and Power: Foundations of Pentecostal Experience* (Grand Rapids: Zondervan, 2000), 50–52.

25. R. P. Menzies, *The Development of Early Christian Pneumatology with Special Reference to Luke-Acts* (JSNT Sup, 54; Sheffield: JSOT Press, 1991), 275.

26. J. B. Shelton, *Mighty in Word and Deed: The Role of the Holy Spirit in Luke-Acts* (Peabody, Mass.: Hendrickson, 1991), 127.

27. James D. G. Dunn, "Baptism in the Spirit: A Response to Pentecostal Scholarship on Luke-Acts," *Journal of Pentecostal Theology* 3 (1993): 3–27, especially 11–16.

28. Ibid., 12.

29. Ibid., 15, further notes that in Acts 15:8–9, both aorist participles "must indicate the same time as their principal verb. That is to say, the parallel form of the clauses prevents us from understanding the cleansing of the heart as antecedent to God's making no distinction, since the parallelism would then mean that the giving of the Spirit was antecedent to God's bearing witness."

30. Stott, *The Baptism and the Fullness of the Holy Spirit,* 7.

31. See for example, Bernard Ramm, *Protestant Biblical Interpretation,* 3rd ed. (Grand Rapids: Baker, 1970), 107. This was similar to his first edition published in 1956.

32. Gordon D. Fee and Douglas Stuart, *How to Read the Bible for All Its Worth* (Grand Rapids: Zondervan, 1981), 97, his emphasis. In the second edition of 1993, Fee qualified

this statement by adding "unless it can be demonstrated on other grounds that the author intended it to function in this way."

33. Grant R. Osborne, *The Hermeneutical Spiral: A Comprehensive Introduction to Biblical Interpretation* (Downers Grove: InterVarsity Press, 1991), 172.

34. William W. Klein, Craig L. Blomberg, and Robert L. Hubbard, *Introduction to Biblical Interpretation* (Dallas: Word, 1993), 349–50.

35. Gordon Fee, *Gospel and Spirit: Issues in New Testament Hermeneutics* (Peabody, Mass.: Hendrickson, 1991), 92.

36. I. Howard Marshall, *Luke: Historian and Theologian* (Grand Rapids: Zondervan, 1970).

37. William W. and Robert P. Menzies, *Spirit and Power: Foundations of Pentecostal Experience* (Grand Rapids: Zondervan, 2000), especially 37–45, chapter 2, "Hermeneutics: The Quiet Revolution," which traces the same material I have just presented.

38. Stronstad, *The Charismatic Theology of St. Luke,* 12.

39. It is becoming common to divide the history of twentieth-century Pentecostalism into three waves: the first wave is traced to the beginning of the twentieth century with Agnes Ozman and the Azusa Street revival in 1906; the second wave is the "Charismatic renewal" of the 1960s; and the "third wave," so named by missions professor C. Peter Wagner at Fuller Seminary, as the renewal movement that began in the 1980s. Those who belong to this third wave are Evangelicals who view the work of the Holy Spirit positively in divine healing, receiving of new prophecies, and casting out of demons. They deny, however, the teaching of a "second blessing" and teach that believers are baptized in the Holy Spirit at the time of their conversion! They also are not strong in the insistence that public glossolalia must be present, usually playing this feature down, contrary to the normal Pentecostal practice.

40. See William W. and Robert P. Menzies, *Spirit and Power,* 51.

41. I. Howard Marshall, "An Evangelical Approach to 'Theological Criticism,'" *Themelios* 13 (1988): 83.

42. Gordon L. Anderson, "Baptism in the Holy Spirit, Initial Evidence, and a New Model," *Paraclete* 27 (1993), 2.

43. This list came from William W. and Robert P. Menzies, *Spirit and Power,* 56.

44. On "The Analogy of Faith," see Walter C. Kaiser Jr., "Hermeneutics and the Theological Task," *Trinity Journal* 12 NS (1990): 3–14.

45. Glen Menzies, "Tongues as 'The Initial Physical Sign' of Spirit Baptism in the Thought of D. W. Kerr," *Pneuma* 20 (1998): 175. Also see "Glossolalia as 'Initial Evidence'" in *Pentecostal Theology and the Christian Spiritual Tradition.* Journal of Pentecostal Theology: Supplement Series, eds. John Christopher Thomas, Richie Moore, and Steven J. Land, vol. 21 (Sheffield: Sheffield Academic Press, 2000): 40–72.

46. Larry W. Hurtado, "Normal, but Not a Norm: Initial Evidence and the New Testament," in *Initial Evidence,* ed. G. McGee (Peabody, Mass.: Hendrickson Press, 1991), 191.

47. Donald A. Carson, *Showing the Spirit: A Theological Exposition of 1 Corinthians 12–14* (Grand Rapids: Baker, 1987).

48. Carson, ibid., 160.

49. Craig S. Keener, *Gift Giver: The Holy Spirit for Today* (Grand Rapids: Baker, 2001), 155.

50. See my essay, "The Holy Spirit's Ministry in Personal Spiritual Development: Ephesians 5:15–21," in *The Spirit and Spirituality: Essays in Honor of Russell P. Spittler,* eds. Wonsuk Ma and Robert P. Menzies (Edinburgh: T. & T. Clark, forthcoming).

51. I am beholden to William Atkinson's discussion of this point in "Pentecostal Responses to Dunn's Baptism in the Holy Spirit: Luke-Acts," *Journal of Pentecostal Studies* 6 (1995): 106, as Atkinson interacted favorably with the views of David Petts, "The Baptism of the Holy Spirit in Relation to Christian Initiation" (M.Th. dissertation, Nottingham University, 1987), 74.

52. William W. and Robert P. Menzies. *Spirit and Power,* 202 citing *The Full Life Study Bible-New Testament,* ed. Donald Stamps (Grand Rapids: Zondervan, 1990), 244.

53. Ibid., 205.

54. Ibid.

55. Ibid., 202.

56. Chicago: Moody Press, 1974, 7–19.

57. Ibid., 10.

58. The book by Craig Keener, which Dr. Kaiser also mentions, provides a solid basis for greater unity on these issues: *Gift and Giver: The Holy Spirit for Today* (Grand Rapids: Baker, 2001).

Chapter 2, Spirit Baptism: A Pentecostal Perspective

1. The word *baptism* "is used figuratively to describe immersion in the energizing power of the Divine Spirit." Myer Pearlman, *Know the Doctrines of the Bible* (Springfield, Mo.: Gospel Publishing House, 1937), 310.

2. Simon Chan, "The Language Game of Glossolalia, or Making Sense of the 'Initial Evidence'" in Wonsuk Ma and Robert P. Menzies, eds., *Pentecostalism in Context: Essays in Honor of William W. Menzies* (Sheffield, England: Sheffield Academic Press, 1997), 84.

3. Stanley Howard Frodsham, *With Signs Following: The Story of the Pentecostal Revival in the Twentieth Century* (Springfield, Mo., Gospel Publishing House, rev. ed. 1941), 253–62; Kilian McDonnell and George T. Montague, *Christian Initiation and Baptism in the Holy Spirit: Evidence from the First Eight Centuries* (Collegeville, Minn.: The Liturgical Press, 2d rev. ed., 1994); George H. Williams and Edith Waldvogel, "A History of Speaking in Tongues and Related Gifts," in *The Charismatic Movement,* ed. Michael P. Hamilton (Grand Rapids: Eerdmans, 1975), 61–113; Klaude Kendrick, "Pentecostal Phenomena in Church History" in Gwen Jones, ed., *Conference on the Holy Spirit Digest* (Springfield, Mo.: Gospel Publishing House, 1983), I, 124–128; Stanley M. Burgess, *The Spirit and the Church: Antiquity* (Peabody, Mass., Hendrickson Pub., 1984); Ronald A. Kydd, *Charismatic Gifts in the Early Church* (Peabody, Mass., Hendrickson Pub., 1984).

4. I often heard her tell this.

5. See Matthew S. Clark, "Initial Evidence: A Southern African Perspective" in *Asian Journal of Pentecostal Studies,* 1 (July 1998) 2:215–16.

6. See Anthony D. Palma, *The Holy Spirit: A Pentecostal Perspective* (Springfield, Mo.: Logion Press, Gospel Publishing House, 2001), 137–40.

7. Stanley Horton, *Reflections of an Early American Pentecostal* (Baguio City, Philippines: Asia Pacific Theological Seminary Press, 2001), 2–3.

8. W. I. Evans, *This River Must Flow* (Springfield, Mo.: Gospel Publishing House, 1954), 9.

9. See Frank D. Macchia, "Groans Too Deep for Words: Towards a Theology of Tongues as Initial Evidence," *Asian Journal of Pentecostal Studies,* 1 (July 1998) 2:160.

10. Torrey, however, did not accept tongues as valid today.

11. Frodsham, *With Signs Following,* 19.

12. Edith L. Blumhofer, *The Assemblies of God* (Springfield, Mo.: Gospel Publishing House, 1989), 1:83.

13. Roger Stronstad, *Spirit, Scripture and Theology: A Pentecostal Perspective* (Baguio City: Asia Pacific Theological Seminary Press, 1995), 11–12. He discusses Parham's contributions of a "pragmatic" hermeneutic on pp. 12–14.

14. Blumhofer, *Assemblies,* 1:98.

15. Douglas J. Nelson, "The Black Face of Church Renewal: The meaning of a Charismatic Explosion, 1901–1985," in Paul Elbert, ed., *Faces of Renewal: Studies in Honor of Stanley M. Horton* (Peabody, Mass.: Hendrickson Publishers, 1988), 175.

16. Roger Stronstad, "The Prophethood of All Believers: A Study in Luke's Charismatic Theology" in Wonsuk Ma and Robert P. Menzies, eds., *Pentecostalism in Context: Essays in Honor of William W. Menzies,* 75.

17. Blumhofer, *Assemblies,* 1:99.

18. In a New Testament Introduction class taught by the Baptist professor Merrill C. Tenney at Gordon Divinity School in 1942, I heard him point out that Simon had already heard the Word, he had already seen miracles, prophecy would not have been distinguishable as supernatural, and the only recognizable sign that would have caught his attention was speaking in tongues.

19. "The Bridegroom's Messenger," June 15, 1909, 2. For somewhat later Pentecostal apologies, see Robert Chandler Dalton, *Tongues like as of Fire: A Critical Study of Modern Tongue Movements in the Light of Apostolic and Patristic Times* (Springfield, Mo.: Gospel Publishing House, 1945) and Carl Brumback, *What Meaneth This? . . . A Pentecostal Answer to a Pentecostal Question* (Springfield, Mo.: Gospel Publishing House, 1947).

20. Hardy W. Steinberg, "Initial Evidence of the Baptism in the Holy Spirit" in Gwen Jones, ed., *Conference on the Holy Spirit Digest* (Springfield, Mo.: Gospel Publishing House, 1983), I, 37.

21. Blumhofer, *Assemblies,* 1:117.

22. For an early account of the rapid spread of the Pentecostal Revival, see Stanley Howard Frodsham, *With Signs Following: The Story of the Pentecostal Revival in the Twentieth Century* (Springfield, Mo.: Gospel Publishing House, rev. ed., 1941), 7–228.

23. D. B. Barrett, T. M. Johnson, "Global Statistics," in Stanley M. Burgess, ed., *The New International Dictionary of Pentecostal and Charismatic Movements,* rev. and expanded ed. (Grand Rapids: Zondervan, 2002), 293–94.

24. William W. Menzies and Stanley M. Horton, *Bible Doctrines: A Pentecostal Perspective* (Springfield, Mo.: Logion Press, 1994), 263–64.

25. Ibid., 122.

26. Ibid., 134.

27. I. Howard Marshall, *Luke Historian and Theologian* (Grand Rapids: Academie Books, Zondervan, enlarged ed., 1989), 69.

28. Stanley M. Horton, *Acts* (Springfield, Mo.: Logion Press, 2001), 18–19.

29. Marshall, *Luke Historian and Theologian,* 32.

30. Horton, *Acts,* 19.

31. C. Peter Wagner, *Spreading the Fire* (Ventura, Calif.: Regal Books, Gospel Light, 1994), 20.

32. Stronstad, *Spirit, Scripture and Theology,* 59.

33. See Stanley M. Horton, *What the Bible Says about the Holy Spirit* (Springfield, Mo.: Gospel Publishing House, 1976) for some defense of the Pentecostal position against Fredrick Dale Bruner and James D. G. Dunn. See also Roger Stronstad, *The Charismatic Theology of St. Luke* (Peabody, Mass.: Hendrickson Publishers, 1984) for a more formidable defense or apology.

34. Benny C. Aker and Edgar R. Lee, "Naturally Supernatural" in Benny C. Aker and Gary B. McGee, *Signs and Wonders in Ministry Today* (Springfield, Mo.: Gospel Publishing House, 1996), 90.

35. Ben Aker, "New Directions in Lucan Theology: Reflections on Luke 3:21–22 and Some Implications," in Paul Elbert, ed., *Faces of Renewal* (Peabody, Mass.: Hendrickson Publishers, 1988), 119.

36. Horton, *Acts,* 55.

37. Ibid., 56–57.

38. Stronstad, "The Prophethood of All Believers," 63.

39. Howard Clark Kee, *To Every Nation under Heaven: The Acts of the Apostles* (Harrisburg, Pa.: Trinity Press International, 1997), 43–44, 49.

40. Horton, *Acts,* 57.

41. Stronstad suggests that Luke was purposefully ambiguous here, "for the inspiration of the Spirit may have resulted in both worship and proclamation." See Stronstad, *Spirit, Scripture and Theology,* 129.

42. Palma, *The Holy Spirit,* 116.

43. *Charismatic* is a word coined from "a Greek word frequently used to designate a special impartation of spiritual power." Myer Pearlman, *Knowing the Doctrines,* 312.

44. Don W. Basham, *A Handbook on Holy Spirit Baptism* (Monroeville, Pa.: Whitaker Books, 5th ed., 1972), 17.

45. Wagner, *Spreading the Fire,* 68.

46. Horton, *What the Bible Says about the Holy Spirit,* 153–54.

47. Palma, *The Holy Spirit,* 120.

48. See James B. Shelton, "'Filled with the Holy Spirit' and 'Full of the Holy Spirit': Lucan Redactional Phrases" in Paul Elbert, ed. *Faces of Renewal* (Peabody, Mass.: Hendrickson Publishers, 1988), 88.

49. See Palma, *Baptism in the Holy Spirit,* 121.

50. See further discussion of the aorist participle in connection with the Ephesian disciples below.

51. Horton, *What the Bible Says,* 158.

52. See French Arrington, *The Acts of the Apostles* (Peabody, Mass.: Hendrickson Publishers, 1988), 112–13.

53. I. Howard Marshall, *Luke Historian and Theologian* (Grand Rapids: Academie Press, Zondervan, enlarged ed., 1989), 199.

54. Acts 9:25 is not an exception since it identifies them as Paul's followers. See Anthony D. Palma, *Baptism in the Holy Spirit* (Springfield, Mo., Gospel Publishing House, 1999), 27–28.

55. See William W. Menzies and Robert P. Menzies, *Spirit and Power: Foundations of Pentecostal Experience* (Grand Rapids: Zondervan, 2000), 74.

56. See E. M. Blaiklock, *Acts: The Birth of the Church* (Old Tappan, N.J.: Fleming H. Revell, 1980), 183.

57. Stanley M. Horton, *Acts: A Logion Press Commentary* (Springfield, Mo.: Gospel Publishing House, 2001), 316–17.

58. James D. G. Dunn, *Baptism in the Holy Spirit* (London: SCM Press, 1970), 86, 158–59.

59. Horton, *What the Bible Says,* 159–60.

60. "Including Codex Bezae (D), p38 (a papyrus from the third or fourth century A.D.), p46, plus the Syriac and Sahidic versions originating in the second and third centuries A.D."

61. Horton, *Acts,* 317–19.

62. Horton, *What the Bible Says,* 237.

63. Ibid., 237–38.

64. Ibid., 238.

65. Ibid., 239.

66. Ibid., 239, literally, "upward"; it was a continuing, growing experience.

67. Ibid., 118.

68. Stanley M. Horton, *I and II Corinthians: A Logion Press Commentary* (Springfield, Mo.: Gospel Publishing House, 1999), 118–19.

69. Palma, *The Holy Spirit,* 103. He also shows why it is correct to translate "baptize in the Spirit" rather than "baptize with the Spirit," 101.

70. Horton, *Acts,* 102.

71. Ibid., 237.

72. Hardy W. Steinberg, "Initial Evidence of the Manifestation of the Holy Spirit" in *Conference on the Holy Spirit Digest,* ed. Gwen Jones (Springfield, Mo.: Gospel Publishing House, 1983), 1:39.

73. Max Turner, *Power from on High: The Spirit in Israel's Restoration and Witness in Luke-Acts* (Sheffield, England: Sheffield Academic Press, 1996), 357.

74. William G. MacDonald, *Glossolalia in the New Testament* (Springfield, Mo.: n.d.), 4.

75. Ibid., 4.

76. Anthony D. Palma, *The Holy Spirit: A Pentecostal Perspective* (Springfield, Mo.: Logion Press, Gospel Publishing House, 2001), 143.

77. Stanley Horton, "Inside the Bible," in *Today's Pentecostal Evangel,* June 8, 2003, 30.

78. Horton, *What the Bible Says,* 278.

79. Palma, *The Holy Spirit,* 149.

80. Ernest Swing Williams, *Systematic Theology* (Springfield, Mo.: Gospel Publishing House, 1953), 3:49–50.

81. William W. Menzies and Stanley M. Horton, *Bible Doctrines, A Pentecostal Perspective* (Springfield, Mo.: Logion Press, 1994), 129.

82. MacDonald, *Glossolalia in the New Testament,* 7.

83. Robert P. Menzies, "Evidential Tongues: An Essay on Theological Method" in *Asian Journal of Pentecostal Studies,* I (July 1998), 2:115

84. F. F. Bruce, *Commentary on the Book of Acts* (Grand Rapids: Wm. B. Eerdmans, 1954), 201.

85. Horton, *Acts,* 183.

86. Horton, *I and II Corinthians,* 123.

87. See Palma, *The Holy Spirit,* 150–51.

88. MacDonald, *Glossolalia,* 9.

89. Palma, *The Holy Spirit,* 156–57.

90. Randy Hurst, "Power for Purpose" in *Today's Pentecostal Evangel,* June 8, 2003, 13.

91. Melvin L. Hodges, *The Indigenous Church* (Springfield, Mo.: Gospel Publishing House, 1953, 1976; also published by Moody Press).

92. *Today's Pentecostal Evangel,* June 1, 2003, 30–31.

93. Everett A. Wilson, *Strategy of the Spirit* (Carlisle, Cumbria: Paternoster Press, 1997), 3.

94. Dan Kersten, "Christian Web Site Draws Record Traffic" in *Today's Pentecostal Evangel,* June 1, 2003, 7.

95. Horton, *Reflections,* 74–75.

96. Léon Joseph Cardinal Suenens, *A New Pentecost?* tr. Frances Martin (London: Darton, Longman & Todd, 1976), 23.

97. See Howard M. Ervin, *"These Are Not Drunken as Ye Suppose"* (Plainfield, N.J.: Logos, 1968), 218–21.

98. Ibid., 37–39.

99. A. C. George, *Dimensions of Spirituality* (Chennai, India: Bethesda Communications, 1997), 27.

100. D. B. Barrett; T. M. Johnson, "Global Statistics" in Stanley M. Burgess, ed. *The New International Dictionary of Pentecostal and Charismatic Movements,* rev. and expanded ed. (Grand Rapids: Zondervan, 2002), 285–87. Burgess includes articles about Pentecostal leaders and articles about the development of the Pentecostal Revival in specific places and countries all over the world.

101. Del Tarr, "The Church and the Spirit's Power" in Benny C. Aker and Gary B. McGee, *Signs and Wonders in Ministry Today* (Springfield, Mo.: Gospel Publishing House, 1996), 9–10.

102. Macchia, "Groans Too Deep for Words," 164.

103. Shelton, "Filled," 85.

104. Hurst, "Power for Purpose," 15.

105. Horton, *I and II Corinthians,* 33.

106. Ibid., 35.

107. John V. York, *Missions in the Age of the Spirit* (Springfield, Mo.: Logion Press, 2000), 149.

108. Horton, *I and II Corinthians,* 37.

109. Ibid., 38.

110. Ibid., 39.

111. See Donald Gee, *The Fruit of the Spirit* (Springfield, Mo.: Gospel Publishing House, 1934) for a Pentecostal study of the fruit.

112. Hurst, "Power for Purpose," 15.

113. Ibid., 15–16, 18.

114. Palma, *The Holy Spirit,* 166.

115. Horton, *I and II Corinthians,* 137–38.

116. Palma, *The Holy Spirit,* 168.

117. Because Paul is speaking to the Corinthians who were overusing and failing to interpret tongues in the public worship, he does not mean he was a better linguist, nor does he mean that he spoke in more languages than the other apostles. See Ervin, *"These Are Not Drunken,"* 170–74.

118. Evans, *This River Must Flow,* 39.

119. Robert P. Menzies, *Evidential Tongues,* 120.

120. See my commentary, *Isaiah: A Logion Press Commentary* (Springfield, Mo.: Logion Press, Gospel Publishing House, 2000), 26, 32–33, 36, 137–45, 152, 180–82, 195, 289–81, 350–51, 358.

121. See Mahesh Chavda, *The Hidden Power of Speaking in Tongues* (Shippensburg, Pa.: Destiny Image Publishers, 2003) for several examples of the benefits and blessings of speaking in tongues. See also Arthur Wallis, *Pray in the Spirit* (Eastbourne, England: Victory Press, 1977, 1st American ed.).

122. Jean Héring, *La Premiére Épitre de Saint Paul oux Corinthiens,* 2d ed. (Neuchatel: Éditions Delachaux & Nestlé, 1959), 126.

123. Harold Horton, *The Gifts of the Spirit* (Nottingham, England: Assemblies of God Publishing House, 1934), 134.

124. See David Lim, *Charismata: A Fresh Look* (Clayburn, B.C.: Western Pentecostal Bible College, n.d.), 79–80.

125. Jack Hayford, *The Beauty of Spiritual Language: A Journey to the Heart of God* (Dallas: Word Publishing, 1992), 9.

126. Ibid., 157.

127. This was said also by Dennis Bennett at a meeting of the Society for Pentecostal Studies in Vancouver, B.C., 1979. His views were much like that of classical Pentecostals. See Vinson Synan, "The Role of Tongues as Initial Evidence" in Mark W. Wilson, ed., *Spirit and Renewal: Essays in Honor of J. Rodman Williams* (Sheffield, England: Sheffield Academic Press, 1994), 67–68.

128. Myer Pearlman and Frank M. Boyd, *Pentecostal Truth* (Springfield, Mo.: Gospel Publishing House, 1968), 72–73, 77.

129. Sam McGraner, "Baptism in the Holy Spirit" in Homer G. Rhea, compiler, *The Holy Spirit in Action* (Cleveland, Tn.: Pathway Press, 1996), 62.

130. For another recent defense of the Pentecostal position, see Donald Johns, "Some New Directions in the Hermeneutics of Classical Pentecostalism's Doctrine of Initial Evidence" in Gary B. McGee, ed., *Initial Evidence: Historical and Biblical Perspectives on the Pentecostal Doctrine of Spirit Baptism* (1991).

131. Robert H. Spence, "The Holy Spirit Outpouring in Acts" in *Conference on the Holy Spirit Digest* (Springfield, Mo.: Gospel Publishing House, 1963), I: 81.

132. South Plainfield, N.J.: Bridge Publishing, 1985.

133. Monroeville, Pa.: Whitaker Books, 1969.

134. Dennis and Rita Bennett, *The Holy Spirit and You Teaching Manual* (Plainfield, N.J.: Logos International, 1973), 25. See also Dennis and Rita Bennett, *The Holy Spirit and You* (Plainfield, N.J.: Logos International), 56–77.

135. James D. G. Dunn, *Baptism in the Holy Spirit* (London: SCM Press, 1970), preface.

136. Roger Stronstad, *Spirit, Scripture, and Theology: A Pentecostal Perspective* (Baguio City, Philippines: Asia Pacific Theological Seminary Press, 1995), 59 (italics mine).

137. Robert P. Menzies, "Evidential Tongues: An Essay on Theological Method," *Asian Journal of Pentecostal Studies* 1 (July 1998): 115 (italics mine).

138. *Plain Account of Christian Perfection as Believed and Taught by the Reverend Mr. John Wesley from the Year 1725 to the Year 1777* (London: Wesleyan Conference Office, 1872; reprint, Kansas City: Beacon Hill Press of Kansas City, 1966), 67.

139. Cf. W. M. Greathouse, *Wholeness in Christ* (Kansas City: Beacon Hill Press of Kansas City, 1998), 60. Greathouse is one of the most articulate spokesmen for the Wesleyan position in the Holiness movement.

140. F. F. Bruce, *Commentary on the Book of Acts* in the *New International Commentary on the Old Testament* (Grand Rapids: Wm. B. Eerdmans Pub. Co., 1975), 57; he cites Deut. 18:22; 13:1ff and outside the canon *Didache,* chs. 11–12.

141. *The Christian Faith* (Edinburgh: T. & T. Clark, 1960), 576.

142. *Catechism of the Catholic Church,* #1288, (New York: Doubleday, 1994), 359.

143. *Catechism of the Catholic Church,* #1262, Doubleday edition, 353.

144. *Catechism of the Catholic Church,* #1302, Doubleday edition, 363.

145. *Catechism of the Catholic Church,* #1266, Doubleday edition, 354.

Chapter 3, Spirit Baptism: A Dimensional Charismatic Perspective

1. Larry Douglas Hart, "A Critique of American Pentecostal Theology," Unpublished PhD Dissertation, The Southern Baptist Theological Seminary, Louisville, Kentucky, 1978, 16–90.

2. See Vinson Synan, *The Holiness-Pentecostal Tradition* (Grand Rapids: Eerdmans, 1997); Vinson Synan, *The Century of the Holy Spirit* (Nashville: Thomas Nelson, 2001).

3. John Pollock, *Billy Graham: The Authorized Biography* (New York: McGraw-Hill, 1966), 39.

4. See Henry I. Lederle, *Treasures Old and New: Interpretations of "Spirit Baptism" in the Charismatic Renewal Movement* (Peabody, Mass.: Hendrickson, 1988).

5. Donald G. Bloesch, *The Holy Spirit* (Downers Grove: InterVarsity Press, 2000), 200.

6. Luke 3:2.

7. Paul Barnett, *Jesus and the Rise of Early Christianity* (Downers Grove: InterVarsity Press, 1999), 121.

8. Ben Witherington III, *New Testament History* (Grand Rapids: Baker, 2001), 99.

9. Ibid., 104.

10. On this interpretation of "Spirit-and-fire baptism" see: James D. G. Dunn, *Baptism in the Holy Spirit* (London: SCM Press, 1970), 8–22; James D. G. Dunn, "Spirit and Fire Baptism," *Novum Testamentum* 14 (1972), 81–92; Max Turner, *The Holy Spirit and Spiritual Gifts* (Peabody, Mass.: Hendrickson, 1996), 25–27.

11. Turner, *The Holy Spirit and Spiritual Gifts,* 27.

12. (Grand Rapids: Baker, 2001). On the above points concerning the words of John the Baptist, see esp. pp. 143–46, 151, 159. Keener exemplifies sound scholarship, spiritual sensitivity, practical wisdom, and a gracious spirit.

13. Matthew 3:13.

14. Dunn, *Baptism in the Holy Spirit,* 36.

15. See Witherington, *New Testament History,* 118; Turner, *The Holy Spirit and Spiritual Gifts,* 28–29.

16. Roger Stronstad, *The Charismatic Theology of St. Luke* (Peabody, Mass.: Hendrickson, 1984), 40. Stronstad, however, mistakenly denies Jesus' *visionary* experience altogether.

17. See James B. Shelton, *Mighty in Word and Deed: The Role of the Holy Spirit in Luke-Acts* (Peabody, Mass.: Hendrickson, 1991), 49.

18. On John's account here, see the extremely insightful comments of Gary M. Burge and Leon Morris: Burge, *The Anointed Community: The Holy Spirit in the Johannine Tradition* (Grand Rapids: Eerdmans, 1987), 50–62; Morris, *Reflections on the Gospel of John,* vol. 1 (Grand Rapids: Baker, 1986), 27–34.

19. (Peabody, Mass.: Hendrickson, 1984), 5–14.

20. Dunn, *Baptism in the Holy Spirit,* 24. Dunn would even allow for an *imitatio Christi* dynamic here!

21. Acts 2:1.

22. I had the privilege of attending the opening night of the Greater Louisville Billy Graham Crusade in the summer of 2001. I noted that Dr. Graham actually did use Pentecostal language, leading the inquirers in a prayer that mentioned receiving the Holy Spirit. I wondered if any of the believers seated in the stadium were uncomfortable with the evangelist's language. Dr. Graham himself certainly was not!

23. Ken Hemphill, *The Antioch Effect* (Nashville: Broadman & Holman, 1994), 27–28.

24. I have written more fully on these questions in my systematic theology: *Truth Aflame: A Balanced Theology for Evangelicals and Charismatics* (Nashville: Thomas Nelson, 1999), 326–57.

25. Ervin, *Conversion-Initiation and the Baptism in the Holy Spirit,* 15–16.

26. Ibid., viii.

27. Howard M. Ervin, *Spirit Baptism: A Biblical Investigation* (Peabody, Mass.: Hendrickson, 1987), 38.

28. Acts 8:17.

29. See Roger Stronstad, *The Prophethood of All Believers: A Study in Luke's Charismatic Theology* (*Journal of Pentecostal Theology,* Supplement Series, 16; Sheffield: Sheffield Academic Press, 1999).

30. See Robert P. Menzies, *Empowered for Witness: The Spirit in Luke-Acts* (*Journal of Pentecostal Theology,* Supplement Series, 6; Sheffield: Sheffield Academic Press, 1994). Compare also Craig S. Keener, *The Spirit in the Gospels and Acts* (Peabody, Mass.: Hendrickson, 1997).

31. See footnote 16.

32. Acts 2:4.

33. Acts 2:4 ESV.

34. See Ervin, *Spirit Baptism,* 14–21.

35. Dunn ends up resorting to a "defective faith" defense, which many on both sides of the debate find inadequate: Dunn, *Baptism in the Holy Spirit,* 55–72.

36. Progress in human understanding often takes this root. And one can acknowledge this fact without surrendering to Hegelian relativism.

37. Thomas R. Schreiner and Ardel B. Caneday have masterfully applied this eschatological principle to the Christian discussion on perseverance and assurance in *The Race Set Before Us* (Downers Grove: InterVarsity Press, 2001).

38. D. A. Carson, *Showing the Spirit* (Grand Rapids: Baker, 1987), 160. Keener, who cites Carson here, adds: "Some of us have lost count!" (Keener, *Gift and Giver,* 222, fn. 14).

39. See his endorsement of Keener's *Gift and Giver* on the back cover.

40. 1 Corinthians 12:13 ESV.

41. Thomas R. Schreiner, *Paul, Apostle of God's Glory in Christ: A Pauline Theology* (Downers Grove: InterVarsity Press, 2001), 373.

42. Gordon D. Fee, *God's Empowering Presence: The Holy Spirit in the Letters of Paul* (Peabody, Mass.: Hendrickson, 1994), 178.

43. Ervin, *Conversion-Initiation and the Baptism in the Holy Spirit,* 98–102; Ervin, *Spirit Baptism,* 28–37.

44. Fee, *God's Empowering Presence,* 180.

45. See Fee, *God's Empowering Presence,* 181.

46. James D. G. Dunn, *The Theology of Paul the Apostle* (Grand Rapids: Eerdmans, 1998), 429–30.

47. Acts 2:38; 10:45.

48. Compare also the accusative/adverbial use of this term: *dorean* in Rom. 3:24.

49. J. Rodman Williams, *The Gift of the Holy Spirit Today* (Plainfield, N.J.: Logos International, 1980).

50. David du Plessis, *A Man Called Mr. Pentecost* (Plainfield, N.J.: Logos International, 1977), 181–89.

51. I have presented the following material in another form in: Hart, *Truth Aflame,* 343–57.

52. Timothy L. Smith, "The Cross Demands, the Spirit Enables," *Christianity Today,* 16 February 1979, 22–26. I have introduced the term *dialect* here.

53. Burge, *The Anointed Community,* 95.

54. Ibid., 96.

55. Ibid., 95–96; I owe the felicitous phrase "water of the Spirit" (John 3:5) to Craig Keener, *Gift and Giver,* 139.

56. See also the footnote on v. 6 in the CEV.

57. John 3:8.

58. Keener, *Gift and Giver,* 141.

59. I am indebted to my mentor, the late Dale Moody, for this analysis of John 7: Dale Moody, *Spirit of the Living God* (Philadelphia: Westminster, 1968), 161–64.

60. John 20:22.

61. Hart, *Truth Aflame,* 101; Moody, *Spirit of the Living God,* 164–75.

62. John also refers to Jesus as our Paraclete with the Father in 1 John 2:1–2.

63. Burge, *The Anointed Community,* 149.

64. Fee, *God's Empowering Presence,* 127–32.

65. Ibid., 50–53.

66. Richard Lovelace's *Dynamics of Spiritual Life* remains a classic treatment of these fundamental issues (Downers Grove: InterVarsity Press, 1979).

67. See C. E. B. Cranfield, *The Epistle to Romans,* vol. 2, International Critical Commentary (Edinburgh: T. & T. Clark, 1979), 830–33, upon which the following comments are based.

68. Hart, *Truth Aflame,* 347.

69. Ibid., 351.

70. See I. Howard Marshall, *Luke: Historian and Theologian* (Grand Rapids: Zondervan, 1970), and Ben Witherington III, *The Acts of the Apostles: A Socio-Rhetorical Commentary* (Grand Rapids: Eerdmans, 1998), 68–72.

71. Witherington, *The Acts of the Apostles,* 70.

72. See Stronstad, *The Charismatic Theology of St. Luke,* 17–22; Menzies, *Empowered for Witness*; Keener, *The Spirit in the Gospels and Acts,* 190–201; Turner, *The Holy Spirit and Spiritual Gifts,* 36–56; *Power from on High* (*Journal of Pentecostal Theology,* Supplement Series, 9; Sheffield: Sheffield Academic Press, 1996); "The 'Spirit of Prophecy' as the Power of Israel's Restoration and Witness" in I. Howard Marshall and David Peterson, eds., *Witness to the Gospel: The Theology of Acts* (Grand Rapids: Eerdmans, 1998), 327–48.

73. *Oral Roberts University Catalogue,* volume 21, No. 1, 2000–2002, Oral Roberts University, Tulsa, Oklahoma, 15.

74. D. Martyn Lloyd-Jones, *Revival* (Wheaton: Crossway Books, 1987), 54.

75. D. Martyn Lloyd-Jones, *Joy Unspeakable: Power and Renewal in the Holy Spirit,* ed. Christopher Catherwood (Wheaton: Harold Shaw, 1984), 280.

76. John V. Taylor, *The Go-Between God: The Holy Spirit and the Christian Mission* (London: SCM Press, 1972), 3.

77. Hart, "A Critique of American Pentecostal Theology," 59; Sydney E. Ahlstrom, *A Religious History of the American People,* vol. I (Garden City, New York: Doubleday, 1975), 170–78.

78. See Norman Pettit, *The Heart Prepared: Grace and Conversion in Puritan Spiritual Life,* Yale Publications in American Studies, no. 11 (New Haven: Yale University Press, 1966).

79. Martin E. Marty, "Pentecostalism in the Context of American Piety and Practice" in *Aspects of Pentecostal-Charismatic Origins,* ed. Vinson Synan (Plainfield, N.J.: Logos International, 1975), 223.

80. F. Ernest Stoeffler, *The Rise of Evangelical Pietism* (Leiden: E. J. Brill, 1965); idem, *German Pietism during the Eighteenth Century* (Leiden: E. J. Brill, 1973).

81. Stoeffler, *The Rise of Evangelical Pietism,* 13–23.

82. See Philipp Jakob Spener, *Pia Desideria,* trans. and ed. Theodore G. Tappert (Philadelphia: Fortress Press, 1964).

83. F. Ernest Stoeffler, "Pietism, the Wesleys, and Methodist Beginnings in America," in *Continental Pietism and Early American Christianity,* ed. F. Ernest Stoeffler (Grand Rapids: Eerdmans, 1976), 218.

84. Dunn, *Baptism in the Holy Spirit,* 1.

85. Keener, *Gift & Giver,* 151.

86. Prudencio Damboriena, *Tongues as of Fire: Pentecostalism in Contemporary Christianity* (Washington, DC: Corpus Books, 1969), 15.

87. More recent outpourings, such as in Toronto or Pensacola, can be seen as tributaries of the wider Pentecostal river.

88. Harvey Cox, *Fire from Heaven* (New York: Addison-Wesley, 1995), 119.

89. See Richard J. Foster's engaging portrait of Seymour in *Streams of Living Water: Celebrating the Great Traditions of Christian Faith* (San Francisco: HarperSanFrancisco, 1998), 112–25.

90. Minneapolis: Bethany Fellowship, 1968.

91. Christenson, *Speaking in Tongues,* 108.

92. Larry Christenson, *The Charismatic Renewal among Lutherans: A Pastoral and Theological Perspective* (Minneapolis: Bethany Fellowship, 1972), 9, 11.

93. Christenson, *The Charismatic Renewal,* 11, 37–38, 117–28. See also J. D. Douglas, ed., *Let the Earth Hear His Voice: International Congress on World Evangelization, Lausanne, Switzerland* (Minneapolis: World Wide Publications, 1975), 1150–53 (a study group on Charismatic renewal chaired by Christenson).

94. Christenson, *The Charismatic Renewal,* 50–51.

95. Larry Christenson, *A Message to the Charismatic Movement* (Minneapolis: Bethany Fellowship, 1972), 70–71.

96. Larry Christenson, *Ride the River* (Minneapolis: Bethany House Publishers, 2000). See especially Appendix Two for his discussion on "receiving the Holy Spirit."

97. See, e.g., J. Rodman Williams, *The Era of the Spirit* (Plainfield, N.J.: Logos International, 1971); *The Pentecostal Reality* (Plainfield, N.J.: Logos International, 1972).

98. See *The Gift of the Holy Spirit Today* (1980).

99. Thomas Smail, *Reflected Glory: The Spirit in Christ and Christians* (Grand Rapids: Eerdmans, 1975), 48–49.

100. Ibid., 143.

101. See, e.g., Kevin and Dorothy Ranaghan, *Catholic Pentecostals* (New York: Paulist Press, 1969).

102. See, e.g., Léon Joseph Cardinal Suenens, *A New Pentecost?* (New York: Seabury, 1974), 132–33.

103. Ibid., 111.

104. Second rev. ed. (Collegeville, Minn.: The Liturgical Press, 1994).

105. McDonnell and Montague, *Christian Initiation,* 89.

106. Space does not permit an exploration of Eastern Orthodox contributions, but, unsurprisingly, they are similar to those of Roman Catholicism, being of a sacramental nature.

107. See Rick Warren, *The Purpose-Driven Church* (Grand Rapids: Zondervan, 1995).

108. Bob Russell, *When God Builds a Church* (West Monroe, La.: Howard Publishing, 2000).

109. Larry Hart, "Models for Ministry in the 21st Century," *Ministries Today,* November/December 2001, 55–59.

110. James D. G. Dunn, "Spirit-Baptism and Pentecostalism," *Scottish Journal of Theology,* XXIII (November 1970): 406.

111. See Hart, *Truth Aflame,* 497–98.

112. On the presentation to follow see ibid., 160–61.

113. See George T. Montague, *The Holy Spirit: Growth of a Biblical Tradition* (New York: Paulist Press, 1976), 258–60.

114. McDonnell and Montague, *Christian Initiation,* 40.

115. Ibid., 40–41.

116. Wayne Grudem, *The Gift of Prophecy in the New Testament and Today* (Westchester, Ill.: Crossway Books, 1988).

117. Charles E. Hummel, *Fire in the Fireplace* (Downers Grove: InterVarsity Press, 1993); Jack Deere, *Surprised by the Power of the Spirit* (Grand Rapids: Zondervan, 1993); Doug Banister, *The Word and Power Church* (Grand Rapids: Zondervan, 1999).

118. James L. Simmons, "Renewing a Discipleship Program at the Memorial Baptist Church," Unpublished DMin Applied Research Project Report, School of Theology and Missions, Oral Roberts University, Tulsa, Oklahoma, May 2002.

119. Paul Basden, *The Worship Maze* (Downers Grove: InterVarsity Press, 1999); Sally Morgenthaler, *Worship Evangelism* (Grand Rapids: Zondervan, 1995).

120. Ninian Smart, *The Religious Experience of Mankind,* 2d ed. (New York: Charles Scribner's Sons, 1976), 10–12.

121. James D. G. Dunn, *Jesus and the Spirit: A Study of the Religious and Charismatic Experience of Jesus and the First Christians as Reflected in the New Testament* (London: SCM Press, 1975), 360.

122. Keener, *Gift and Giver,* 167.

123. Millard J. Erickson, *Truth or Consequences: The Promise and Perils of Postmodernism* (Downers Grove: InterVarsity Press, 2001), 301–2.

124. Leonard Sweet, *Soul Tsunami* (Grand Rapids: Zondervan, 1999), 34.

125. Henry T. Blackaby and Claude V. King, *Experiencing God* (Nashville: Broadman & Holman, 1994), 5.

126. *De Ecclesia Constitution on the Church* (Washington, D.C.: United States Catholic Conference, 1964) #3, p. 3.

127. Cf. Paul Tillich, *Biblical Religion and the Search for Ultimate Reality* (Chicago: University of Chicago Press, 1963) for a demonstration of the inevitable use of philosophical language and concepts in theology.

128. Cf. Alister McGrath, *Christian Theology: An Introduction* (Malden, Mass.: Blackwell, 1997), 304–5. McGrath suggests that this depersonalizes the Spirit but to me it implies differently.

129. This seems to be the implication of Paul's word in 1 Corinthians 12:13: "For by one Spirit we were all baptized into one body . . . and have all been made to drink into one Spirit" (NKJV).

130. Timothy L. Smith, *Speaking the Truth* (Kansas City: Beacon Hill Press of Kansas City, 1977), 38–40.

Chapter 4, A Wesleyan Perspective on Spirit Baptism

1. Portions of this essay are taken from the author's systematic theology, *Grace, Faith and Holiness* (Kansas City: Beacon Hill Press, 1988) and are used by the kind permission of Beacon Hill.

2. Donald Dayton, "Pneumatological Issues in the Holiness Movement," in *The Spirit and the New Age*, ed. Alex R. G. Deasley and R. Larry Shelton (Anderson, Ind.: Warner Press, 1986), 250, makes the same point and goes further to note that "there is a fundamental ambiguity in the Holiness movement [itself] that makes it difficult to determine what might constitute its normative expression."

3. John Wesley, *Standard Sermons*, ed. by E. H. Sugden (London: The Epworth Press, 1921), 1:381–82.

4. See Robert Chiles, *Theological Transition in American Methodism: 1790–1925* (New York: Abingdon Press, 1965) for a discussion of several areas in which Wesley's followers moved in a different (often liberalizing) direction.

5. The Church of the Nazarene is the largest; others include the Church of God (Anderson), The Wesleyan Church (result of later unions), the Salvation Army, and a number of smaller denominations, most of which are loosely connected by way of the Christian Holiness Association (now Partnership).

6. A radically different version may be found in a "systematic theology," also published by Beacon Hill Press of Kansas City (imprint of the Nazarene Publishing House) by J. Kenneth Grider, titled *A Wesleyan-Holiness Theology* (Kansas City: Beacon Hill Press, 1994). In chapter 17, "The Second Work of Grace: Christ's Spirit Baptism," Grider develops the same exegetical arguments used by the popular apologies extensively published in the late nineteenth and early twentieth century, taking exception to his scholarly peers who have been formative in this essay. Grider's thesis is that his denomination is the child of the nineteenth-century Holiness movement and therefore not under any commitment to be true to Wesley himself. My systematic theology referred to in footnote 1 and Dr. Grider's (my good friend) reflect rather sharply the bifurcation present in the Holiness movement on what might be the Wesleyan view.

7. This transformation has been the subject of intensive research by scholars in the Wesleyan tradition, most of whom have worked in the context of the Wesleyan Theological Society. Donald Dayton has done some of the most definitive research on this matter. In the essay noted above, he agrees that Wesley's "treatments (of the Holy Spirit) are buried in larger discussions, and are, at least according to my reading, very Christocentric in character," 253.

8. *Wesley's Christology: An Interpretation* (Dallas: Southern Methodist University Press, 1960).

9. *The Works of John Wesley*, 3rd ed. 14 vols. (London: Wesleyan Methodist Book Room, 1872; reprint, Kansas City: Beacon Hill Press, 1978), 7:205.

10. *The Rediscovery of John Wesley* (New York: Henry Holt and Co., 1935).

11. "The Place of Wesley in the Christian Tradition," in *The Place of Wesley in the Christian Tradition*, ed. Kenneth E. Rowe (Metuchen, N.J.: Scarecrow Press, 1976).

12. *Works*, 1:98.

13. Ibid., 1:100.

14. Ibid., 1:93, 95, 97.

15. *Works*, 5:57.

16. John Wesley, *The Journal of the Rev. John Wesley, A. M.* edited by Nehemiah Curnock, 8 vols. (London: Epworth Press, 1938), 2:467.

17. "On the Holy Spirit" *(Works,* 7:508–20) and "On Grieving the Holy Spirit" (*Works,* 7:485–92).

18. *Responsible Grace* (Nashville: Kingswood Books, 1994), 312, n. 1 and n. 2. Maddox mistakenly cites the letter to the bishop as found in 11:467.

19. *Works*, 5:141. This passage also reveals one of the major ambiguities in Wesley's thought. As a result of not doing a systematic analysis of the Atonement, he continued to

use the legal language of the prevailing satisfaction theories such as referring to the "meritorious" work of Christ. This is in contradiction to the understanding of grace as stated in the quote since, as P. T. Forsyth once said, "Procured grace is a contradiction in terms."

20. *Responsible Grace,* 120–121.

21. *Steele's Answers* (Chicago: Christian Witness Co., 1912), 130–31.

22. Frank John McNulty, "The Moral Teaching of John Wesley" (unpublished Ph.D. dissertation, The Catholic University of America, 1961), 53.

23. Albert C. Outler, *John Wesley* (New York: Oxford University Press, 1964), 27.

24. Wesley, *Works,* 8:494–95.

25. Allen Lamar Cooper, "John Wesley: A Study in Theological and Social Ethics" (unpublished Ph.D. dissertation, Columbia University, 1962), 28.

26. The accounts of this disagreement are found in Wesley's *Journal* between November 1, 1739, and September 3, 1741. In stating the results of the Moravian *stillness,* i.e., ceasing from outward works until one had received perfect faith, he says: "Many who were beginning to build holiness and good works on the true foundation of faith in Jesus, being now wholly unsettled and lost in vain reasonings and doubtful disputations. . . . And many being grounded on a faith which is without works, so that they who were right before are wrong now" (*Journal,* 2:331). Albert Outler says that "at the heart of the conflict lay Wesley's genuine abhorrence . . . of any notion of Christian ethics that allows in the believer a passive attitude toward either the means of grace or the demand of the gospel for *actual righteousness." John Wesley,* 347.

27. John L. Peters, *Christian Perfection and American Methodism* (New York: Abingdon Press, 1956), 38.

28. Cooper, "John Wesley," 48.

29. "Remarks on the Life and Character of John Wesley" by the late Alexander Knox, Esq. in Robert Southy, *The Life of Wesley* (New York: Harper & Bros., 1847), 2:345.

30. Outler, *John Wesley,* 27.

31. From "A Plain Account of Christian Perfection," *Works,* 11:387.

32. Wesley, *Standard Sermons,* 1:299–300.

33. *Works,* 11:402.

34. *Standard Sermons,* 1:342–43.

35. Ibid., 2:156.

36. *Works,* 5:37–38.

37. Ibid., 6:71.

38. Ibid., 6:488.

39. Ibid., 488–89.

40. "Plain Account," *Works,* 11:402.

41. Harald Lindström, *Wesley and Sanctification* (Wilmore, Ky.: Francis Asbury Publishing Co., n.d.), 120–22.

42. *StS,* 2:240.

43. E. C. Blackman, "Sanctification," *Interpreter's Dictionary of the Bible,* vol. 4, ed. by George Buttrick (New York: Abingdon Press, 1962).

44. Peters, *Christian Perfection,* 52.

45. In their *Compend of Wesley's Theology,* Burtner and Chiles categorize sanctification under soteriology and Christian perfection under "The Moral Ideal."

46. *Notes on the New Testament* (London: Epworth Press, 1954), 392.

47. This should not be taken to imply that the experience of the Holy Spirit was not personal, but that it is different from individualistic.

48. *Works,* 1:279.

49. *Responsible Grace,* 177.

50. "The Current Wesleyan Debate on the Baptism with the Holy Spirit," (March 1979), 3.

51. *Works,* 8:104, 106.

52. John Wesley, *Letters of the Reverend John Wesley,* edited by John Telford, 8 vols. (London: Epworth Press, 1931), 5:214–15.

53. Ibid., 215.

54. Ibid., 5:228.

55. Ibid., 6:146.

56. James D. G. Dunn, *Baptism in the Holy Spirit* (Philadelphia: Westminster Press, 1970), 53.

57. *Responsible Grace,* 337, n. 116.

58. David Cubie, "Perfection in Wesley and Fletcher: Inaugural or Teleological?" *Wesleyan Theological Journal* (Spring 1976); Staples, "The Current Debate on the Baptism with the Holy Spirit," March 1979, unpublished paper.

59. *Works of John Fletcher,* 4 vols. (Salem, Ohio: Schmul Publishers, 1974), 2:627–29. John Wesley built his belief in the possibility of perfection in this life on four foundation stones: promises of perfection, commands (precepts), prayers for perfection, and examples of perfection. The latter three are what he called "covered promises," and the presupposition was that what God promises he will perform.

60. Ibid., 631.

61. Ibid.

62. Ibid., 632. Wesley frequently used this "family" language from 1 John to describe stages in Christian maturation, with the "father" having reached the stage of Christian perfection.

63. Ibid., 633.

64. "Perfection in Wesley and Fletcher," 25.

65. This is the term used by John A. Knight in his Ph.D. dissertation on Fletcher and which he argued, came to pervade Wesley's thought late in his career. John Allen Knight, "The Theology of John Fletcher," Vanderbilt University, 1966.

66. *Works,* 7:195.

67. "The Gift of the Spirit," *Westminster Theological Journal* 13 (November 1950), 1:2, 6.

68. Charles W. Carter, *The Person and Ministry of the Holy Spirit: A Wesleyan Perspective* (Grand Rapids: Baker Book House, 1974).

69. Ibid., 188–89.

70. Ibid., 20. Cf. H. Orton Wiley, *Christian Theology,* 3 vols. (Kansas City: Beacon Hill Press, 1947), 2:329ff. This theology was the quasi-official theology of the Church of the Nazarene for many years and has served a similar function for many other Holiness groups. The whole section referenced here is a sustained argument for the corporate nature of the Christian experience of the Holy Spirit based on the identification of Pentecost as the birthday of the church.

71. "Foreword" to H. Ray Dunning, *A Layman's Guide to Sanctification* (Kansas City: Beacon Hill Press, 1991), 10.

72. "Theological Roots of the Wesleyan Understanding of the Holy Spirit," *Wesleyan Theological Journal* 14 (Spring 1979), 1:77–78. Wynkoop's *magnum opus, A Theology of Love* (Kansas City: Beacon Hill Press, 1972) was the climax of her lifelong effort to restore what she called "the whole Wesley" to the Holiness movement.

73. I have in my own files a list of forty-eight doctoral dissertations on various aspects of Wesley's theology, and this is doubtless incomplete.

74. Leo George Cox, *John Wesley's Concept of Perfection* (Kansas City: Beacon Hill Press, 1964).

75. Ibid., 149.

76. The most complete report and analysis of this debate was a paper written by Rob Staples, professor of theology at Nazarene Theological Seminary (now retired) in 1979. This analysis was updated in an addendum written a few years later. I have relied heavily on Staples's excellent research and insights in this discussion.

77. The majority of attempts during the nineteenth century to provide exegetical support for these two aspects of sanctification reflect extremely poor knowledge of proper biblical interpretation. Heavy reliance upon the aorist tense, fostered by Daniel Steele, who should have known better, has turned out to be a broken reed. (Cf. Randy Maddox, "The Use of the Aorist Tense in Holiness Exegesis," *Wesleyan Theological Journal* 16 [fall 1981], 2:119–18.)

78. *Theological Roots of Pentecostalism* (Metuchen, N.J.: The Scarecrow Press, 1987), 108.

79. At the 1919 General Assembly, the Pentecostal Church of the Nazarene opted to drop the term "Pentecostal" from its name for the ostensive reason that it made the name too long. But no one recognizes that as the real reason.

80. "The Doctrine of the Sanctifying Spirit: Charles G. Finney's Synthesis of Wesleyan and Covenant Theology," *Wesleyan Theological Journal* (Spring 1978). Note how Smith understands Fletcher to equate entire sanctification with the baptism with the Holy Spirit, a popular misconception. Influenced by Smith's research on Finney's doctrine of Spirit baptism, John L. Gresham Jr. did an MA thesis on Finney's teaching that was published in 1989: *Charles G. Finney's Doctrine of the Baptism of the Holy Spirit* (Peabody, Mass.: Hendrickson Publishers, 1989). Gresham's conclusions reflect a significantly different version of Finney's view than the popular one, as we will note below.

81. *Christianity Today*, 16 February 1979, 22–26.

82. Cf. *Works*, 5:56.

83. Cf. Randy Maddox, "John Wesley and Eastern Orthodoxy: Influences, Convergences and Differences," *The Asbury Theological Journal* 45(1990): 2.

84. Dayton, *Theological Roots of Pentecostalism*, 93.

85. *Holiness and Power* (Cincinnati: M. W. Knapp, 1897), and *Pentecost Rejected* (Cincinnati: Office of God's Revivalist, 1902).

86. *Foundations of Wesleyan Arminian Theology* (Kansas City: Beacon Hill Press, 1967), 112.

87. Cf. Alister E. McGrath, *Christian Theology: An Introduction* (Malden, Mass.: Blackwell, 1997), 6ff.

88. John Bright, *The Authority of the Old Testament* (Grand Rapids: Baker Book House, 1975), 41.

89. Ibid., 42.

90. This is not intended to imply that there is the possibility of an approach to Scripture that is completely free of presuppositions but rather an honest attempt to hear the text in its original intention minimizes the text meaning what it means to me as read through my own cultural, dogmatic, or otherwise biased lenses.

91. Walther Eichrodt, *Theology of the Old Testament*, 3 vols. (Philadelphia: Westminster Press, 1961), 1:310ff., discusses the role of the sacred dance in this phenomenon.

92. Charles D. Isbell, "The Origins of Prophetic Frenzy and Ecstatic Utterances in the Old Testament World," *Wesleyan Theological Journal* 11 (Spring 1976), 62ff.

93. *Theology*, 292.

94. *Promise of the Spirit* (Philadelphia: Westminster Press, 1960), 14.

95. An extensive contrast between the ecstatic and literary prophets is drawn by Abraham J. Heschel, *The Prophets* (New York: Harper and Row Publishers, 1962), 2:131–46. Cf. also Isbell, "Origins."

96. *The Kingdom of God* (New York: Abingdon Press, 1953), 31ff.

97. This observation reflects an almost universal phenomenon as to how the New Testament transcends the literal or intended message of the Old Testament, thus making a one-to-one correlation between prophecy and fulfillment impossible.

98. David Hill, *Greek Words and Hebrew Meanings* (Cambridge: Cambridge University Press, 1967), 211.

99. See Ibid., 213; George S. Hendry, *The Holy Spirit in Christian Theology* (Philadelphia: Westminster Press, 1965), 18.

100. It should be kept in mind that these two figures are not identified either in the Old Testament or post-Old Testament Judaism but are only merged in the person of Jesus Christ.

101. Hill, *Greek Words*, 227.

102. Ibid., 232–33.

103. Ibid., 240.

104. Dunn reflects this methodological principle by noting that "the common error into which too many [systematic theologians] fall is to treat the New Testament as a homogeneous whole, from any part of which texts can be drawn on a chosen subject and fitted into a framework and system which is often basically extrabiblical. . . . The method of [biblical theologian and exegete] is to take each author and book separately and to (attempt to) outline his or its particular theological emphases." *Baptism in the Holy Spirit*, 39.

105. Robert W. Lyon, "Baptism and Spirit Baptism in the New Testament," *Wesleyan Theological Journal* 14 (Spring 1979), 1:14–26. I have basically summarized the extensive exegesis of this material by Lyon rather than "reinventing the wheel."

106. J. H. E. Hull, *The Holy Spirit in the Acts of the Apostles* (Cleveland: World Publishing Co., 1968); W. F. Lofthouse, "The Holy Spirit in the Acts and the Fourth Gospel," *Expository Times* 52 (1940–41) 9:334ff.; G. W. H. Lampe, "The Holy Spirit in the Writings of St. Luke," in *Studies in the Gospels*, ed. D. E. Nineham (Oxford: Blackwell, 1955); H. B. Swete, *The Holy Spirit in the New Testament* (Grand Rapids: Baker Book House, 1964); Frederick Dale Bruner, *A Theology of the Holy Spirit* (Grand Rapids: Wm. B. Eerdmans Publishing Co., 1970); Dunn, *Baptism in the Holy Spirit*.

107. Gordon D. Fee and Douglas Stuart, *How to Read the Bible for All Its Worth* (Grand Rapids: Zondervan Publishing House, 1982), 88–89, points out the diversity of interpretations that occur when people approach the text of Acts with different expectations and/or interests.

108. Fee and Stuart present a structural overview of the book, demonstrating how each major segment of the history is deliberately presented to reinforce the way in which this universalizing movement develops in stages. Ibid., 90–91.

109. Acts, New Testament, vol. 5 in *Search the Scriptures* (Kansas City: Beacon Hill Press, 1954), 6.

110. "Entire Sanctification and the Baptism with the Holy Spirit: Perspectives on the Biblical View of the Relationship," *Wesleyan Theological Journal* 14 (Spring 1979): 1.

111. *How to Read the Bible*, 92.

112. *Steele's Answers*.

113. Hull, *The Holy Spirit in the Acts of the Apostles*, 68.

114. "Entire Sanctification and the Baptism with the Holy Spirit," 27ff.

115. "The Holy Spirit in the Acts and the Fourth Gospel," *Expository Times* 52 (1940–41): 9.

116. I am initially indebted to Dale Moody, *Spirit of the Living God* (Philadelphia: Westminster Press, 1968) for calling attention to this structure.

117. See George Eldon Ladd, *A Theology of the New Testament*, rev. ed. (Grand Rapids: Wm. B. Eerdmans Publishing Co., 1993), 259–68.

118. Moody, *Spirit of the Living God*, 159.

119. Hill, *Greek Words and Hebrew Meanings*, 288–89.

120. So Otto Piper, "Truth," *Interpreter's Dictionary of the Bible*, 4 vols., ed. George Buttrick (New York: Abingdon Press, 1962), 4:716.

121. *Theology of the New Testament*, 291.

122. The term *filioque* refers to the double procession of the Holy Spirit, that is "from the Father and the Son," which the Eastern Church rejected in favor of the theory that

the Spirit proceeded "from the Father only." This dispute became the ostensive basis for the split between Eastern and Western Christendom in 1054.

123. *The Gospel According to John 1–12,* vol. 29 of the *Anchor Bible,* ed. William Foxwell Albright and David Noel Freedman (Garden City, N.Y.: Doubleday and Co., 1966).

124. *Promise of the Spirit,* 32.

125. *The Way to Power and Poise* (New York: Abingdon-Cokesbury Press, 1949), 42, 47, 55.

126. Swete, *The Holy Spirit in the New Testament,* 148.

127. This identification furthermore implies a soteriological motif since "truth" in John carries the connotation of "faithfulness" (Heb, *emeth*) in relation of salvation promises. See footnote 119 above.

128. Quoted by W. T. Purkiser, source unknown.

129. *An Introduction to the Theology of the New Testament* (New York: Harper & Bros. Publishers, 1958), 112–24.

130. Hill, *Greek Words,* 287.

131. *Theology,* 289.

132. Ibid.

133. It has been suggested with considerable credibility that if the Pentecost experiences are paradigmatic for contemporary experience, it is the 3,000 and not the 120 who provide the pattern.

134. See Paul M. Bassett and William M. Greathouse, *Exploring Christian Holiness,* vol. 2, *The Historical Development* (Kansas City: Beacon Hill Press of Kansas City, 1985).

135. "Entire Sanctification," 39. Cf. Bassett and Greathouse, *Exploring Christian Holiness,* vol. 2, to see how baptism as understood and preached in the early church bore these same multiple connotations.

136. *Christian Theology,* 2:323–24.

137. Gresham, *Finney,* 86.

138. W. T. Conner, *The Work of the Holy Spirit* (Nashville: Broadman Press, 1949), 92. Unfortunately, Conner disparages the sanctifying work of the Spirit in his exposition.

139. *A Man in Christ* (New York: Harper and Row Publishers, n.d.), 308.

140. See E. Earle Ellis, "Christ and Spirit in 1 Corinthians," in *Christ and Spirit in the New Testament,* ed. Barnabas Lindars and Stephen S. Smalley (Cambridge: Cambridge University Press, 1973).

141. Stewart, *A Man in Christ,* 310.

142. C. H. Dodd, *The Epistle of Paul to the Romans* (London: Collier, 1959), 140.

143. *Summa Theologiae* IIae. 113.4. From *St. Thomas Aquinas Summa Theologica Volume Two,* Translated by Fathers of the English Dominican Province (New York: Benzinger Brothers, 1948; reprinted Westminster, Md.: Christian Classics, 1981), 1147.

144. "Decree Concerning Justification," chapter 7 in *Canons and Decrees of the Council of Trent,* translated by H. J. Schroeder, O.P. (Rockford, Ill.: Tan, 1978), 33.

145. For a typical scholastic account of the all the nuances in the Catholic doctrine of grace, see Ludwig Ott, *Fundamentals of Catholic Dogma,* edited by James Canon Bastible (St. Louis: Herder, 1958), 219–69.

146. Ott, *Fundamentals of Catholic Dogma,* 259–61.

147. *Catechism of the Catholic Church,* 1991 (New York: Doubleday, 1995), 536.

148. Ott, *Fundamentals of Catholic Dogma,* 261.

149. *Summa Theologiae* IIae. 112.5. From *St. Thomas Aquinas Summa Theologica Volume Two,* 1140.

150. *Catechism of the Catholic Church,* 689 (New York: Doubleday, 1994), 198.

151. As in the following quote from the *Catechism of the Catholic Church:* "Finally, with John the Baptist, the Holy Spirit begins the restoration to man of 'divine likeness,' prefiguring what he would achieve with and in Christ. John's baptism was for repentance; baptism in water and the Spirit will be a new birth" (720).

Chapter 5, Spirit Baptism: A Catholic Perspective

1. He prepared the church for the turn of the millennium in his Apostolic Letter *Tertio Millennio Advenientei* (1994) and its celebration of the Jubilee of the year 2000. Following that, the pope exhorted the church to enter more deeply into the mystery of Christ in another Apostolic Letter, *Novo Millennio Ineunte* (2001). In both cases the call to holiness is extended to all believers as an invitation to move forward in hope.

2. Catholic priests, brothers, nuns, and sisters who live the evangelical counsels of poverty, chastity, and obedience in a religious community.

3. Cardinal Léon Joseph Suenens of Brussels-Malines, one of the four moderators of the Second Vatican Council, was the most significant. He soon functioned as the Holy See's liaison to the International Charismatic Renewal.

4. Wesleyan-Holiness Pentecostals located Spirit baptism as a third event in the *ordo salutis*. It followed conversion/regeneration and the second blessing, the latter being the gift of entire sanctification. Non-Pentecostal Wesleyan-Holiness churches often refer to this as the baptism with the Holy Spirit, not to be confused with its Pentecostal signification.

5. For some informative early accounts of the Catholic Charismatic movement by participants, see Edward D. O'Connor, CSC, *The Pentecostal Movement in the Catholic Church* (Notre Dame, Ind.: Ave Maria, 1971) and Kevin and Dorothy Ranaghan, *Catholic Pentecostals* (New York: Paulist, 1969).

6. The reference is to the new birth as in John 3:5. The exact quote is: "Finally, with John the Baptist, the Holy Spirit begins the restoration to man of 'divine likeness,' prefiguring what he would achieve with and in Christ. John's baptism was for repentance; baptism in water and the Spirit will be a new birth" (720). However, the notion of baptism in the Holy Spirit as associated with new birth—a position held by many Evangelicals—is not developed.

7. For Catholics this would, however, exclude shared Eucharists with non-Catholics.

8. Ranaghan, *Catholic Pentecostals,* 6.

9. Ibid., 7.

10. Ibid., 8.

11. A personal anecdote can illustrate this. I attended a meeting on World Evangelization and the Holy Spirit in Orlando, Florida in 1995. Different segments of the Pentecostal/Charismatic movement ran their own tracks during the day while assembling together in the evening for plenary sessions of worship and preaching. In the Catholic track a room was set aside for adoration of the exposed Blessed Sacrament, a traditional Catholic devotion but one that has waned in practice in many Catholic parishes.

12. Ranaghan, *Catholic Pentecostals,* 60.

13. Ibid., 63.

14. Ibid., 63–65.

15. Ibid., 122.

16. Leo XIII in *Divinum Illud* quotes Augustine directly but does not keep to the latter's analogical sense. "Let it suffice to state that, as Christ is the Head of the Church, so is the Holy Ghost her soul. 'What the soul is in our body, that is the Holy Ghost in Christ's body, the Church.'" The quote is from Augustine's *Serm. 187, de Temp. The Great Encyclical Letters of Pope Leo XIII* (New York: Benziger, 1903), 430. Pius XII in turn quotes Leo XIII in *Mystici Corporis Christi* 57.

17. The closest a Protestant might come to this would be the statement by Friedrich Schleiermacher that the Holy Spirit is the spirit of the community or church. The fact that this conceptuality comes under criticism by Karl Barth and other Protestant theologians who reacted against the liberal theology that Schleiermacher represented only confirms that a truly Protestant perspective overturns the anthropological basis of so much nineteenth-century neo-Protestantism in Germany at the time. Schleiermacher's statement is § 123 of *The Christian Faith* ET of Second German Edition translated and edited by H. R. Mackintosh and J. S. Stewart (Edinburgh: T & T Clark, 1928; reprinted

Philadelphia: Fortress, 1976), 569: "The Holy Spirit is the union of the Divine Essence with human nature in the form of the common Spirit animating the life in common of believers."

18. Ranaghan, *Catholic Pentecostals,* 127.

19. Ibid.

20. The *Catechism of the Catholic Church* identifies the Word of God as mediated to the church by Scripture and tradition (#s 74–83). Tradition, of course, is not confined to the patristic era, but the Fathers of the church along with the ancient ecumenical councils have always had a privileged position in teaching the Word of God. Subsequent tradition is valid as well, including magisterial decrees and teaching (from councils, the college of bishops and pope) and especially the liturgical rites of the church.

21. Ranaghan, *Catholic Pentecostals,* 129–34.

22. Ibid., 134–36.

23. Ibid., 136–40.

24. Ibid., 150.

25. Ibid.

26. Ibid., 147.

27. Ibid., 151. Their exact words are: "If we were to be more precise we would not talk of receiving the baptism in the Holy Spirit but of renewing the baptism in the Spirit." Does this mean that baptism in the Spirit is identical with the reception of the Spirit in baptism and simply requires existential renewal? If so, then Spirit baptism takes on a rather strong sacramental meaning. Baptism or the sacraments of initiation are in effect the baptism in the Holy Spirit for all who receive them.

28. Ibid., 140.

29. "First of all, being baptized in the Spirit *can be* different from coming to Christ. This is true in the scriptures; and it is true in the early church." Steve Clark, *Baptized in the Spirit and Spiritual Gifts: A Basic Explanation of the Key Concepts and Experiences of the Charismatic Renewal* (Pecos, N.M.: Dove, also Ann Arbor, Mich.: Word of Life, 1976), 68.

30. Ibid., 79.

31. Ibid., 40. This is the first of a list of clarifications of what Spirit baptism is not. They also include the following: Spirit baptism is not "a new realization of the doctrine of the Holy Spirit in us." Rather it is "a change in people's relationship with God" (p. 42). Spirit baptism also is not "a greater devotion to the Holy Spirit," (p. 43) nor "a sign of spiritual maturity or holiness" (p. 44) or "everything we need" (p. 48). All of these may be present before Spirit baptism and will flourish all the more with Spirit baptism. His "simple definition" (not a particularly doctrinal one) is: "To be baptized in the Spirit means that we have a change in our relationship with God such that we can begin to experience in our lives all the things which God promised that the Holy Spirit would do for believers" (p. 65).

32. See, for example, Reginald Garrigou-Lagrange, *The Three Ways of the Spiritual Life* (Westminster, Md., Newman Press, 1950), where three conversions are correlated with the traditional stages of spiritual growth: the purgative, illuminative, and unitive.

33. Clark, *Baptized in the Spirit and Spiritual Gifts,* 74.

34. Ibid., 65.

35. Ibid., 78.

36. Ibid.

37. Ibid. For example, in Titus 3:5–7 he does in fact see a distinction between the "cleansing water of rebirth" and "renewing us with the Holy Spirit" (p. 72) but also admits that they are presented in terms of one result, as "part of justification by grace, the new birth" (p. 78).

38. Clark is astute in delineating the different ecclesial and theological contexts for those who take a position on Spirit baptism including Evangelicals, Pentecostals, as well as Catholics. Ibid., 79–87.

39. Stephen B. Clark, *Confirmation and the "Baptism of the Holy Spirit"* (Pecos, N.M.: Dove, 1969), 11.

40. Ibid.

41. Clark, *Baptized in the Spirit and Spiritual Gifts,* 36. The Ranaghans use the phrase "a concrete, tangible sign." *Catholic Pentecostals,* 197.

42. See, for example, the Statement of Fundamental Truths of the (General Council of the) Assemblies of God #8: "THE EVIDENCE OF THE BAPTISM IN THE HOLY GHOST The Baptism of believers in the Holy Ghost is witnessed by the initial physical sign of speaking with other tongues as the Spirit of God gives them utterance (Acts 2:4). The speaking in tongues in this instance is the same in essence as the gift of tongues (1 Cor. 12:4–10, 28), but different in purpose and use." *The Encyclopedia American Religions: Religious Creeds, First Edition,* ed. J. Gordon Melton (Detroit: Gale Research Company, 1988), 359.

43. Clark, *Baptized in the Spirit and Spiritual Gifts,* 36.

44. Clark says of tongues: "The scriptures do not say that every Christian must speak in tongues. . . . My own personal experience is that it can be for everyone." Ibid., 35. The Ranaghans' position is not much different: "Glossolalia, the gift of tongues, the gift of prayer and praise is in fact meant to be, we believe, a normal experience for all Christians." *Catholic Pentecostals,* 206.

45. Clark, *Baptized in the Spirit and Spiritual Gifts,* 96.

46. Ibid., 96–97.

47. Ibid., 97.

48. Ibid., 97–98.

49. The Ranaghans and Clark are laypeople who had completed theological studies at the masters level. Kevin Ranaghan was in doctoral studies when the renewal began. O'Connor, on the other hand, was already on the theology faculty of the University of Notre Dame at the time.

50. Ascetical theology and mystical theology are usually considered as disciplines within spiritual theology. O'Connor refers to the classical spiritual theology or "classical doctrine" of the church drawn from a long list of Fathers, theologians, and spiritual doctors of the church. *The Pentecostal Movement in the Catholic Church,* 183, n. 2.

51. The critique exercised against the so-called neo-Scholastic "manual tradition" is nearly universal among Catholic theologians after the Second Vatican Council (1962–1965).

52. Order of salvation—a term originating in Reformed dogmatics denoting the different aspects of salvation bestowed through the grace of Christ, e.g., justification, regeneration, adoption, etc.

53. O'Connor, *The Pentecostal Movement in the Catholic Church,* 185.

54. Ibid.

55. Other aspects of the theology of grace also were implicated by the extrinsic emphasis.

56. O'Connor is really charting a course between the Charybdis of a static ontological account of grace, i.e., grace is only a state of being, and the Syclla of "naturalistic psychology" or "a Spirit-less humanism." Ibid., 191. O'Connor implicitly accuses other Catholic theologians of this tendency. Whom he has in mind are never named and whether he is accurate in his reading is another matter. Nevertheless, the tendency is present at both the theological and pastoral levels, therefore rendering his corrective as relevant now as when it was first written.

57. O'Connor uses charisms in the technical sense for the *charismata* or Charismatic gifts, although oftentimes it has a wider theological usage.

58. O'Connor, *The Pentecostal Movement in the Catholic Church,* 187.

59. These are considered to be all of a piece. In fact, they are classically referred to as the "sevenfold gift" or the *sacrum septenarium* and constitute "an organic whole with habitual or sanctifying grace." R. Garrigou-Lagrange, *Christian Perfection and*

Contemplation according to St. Thomas Aquinas and St. John of the Cross (New York: Herder, 1939), 275.

60. A debate ensued in spiritual theology over whether the gifts of the Holy Spirit are necessary for salvation. Although O'Connor does not address this, Garrigou-Lagrange did and answered in the affirmative. O'Connor states that the "seven gifts" "have come to be regarded as mere ornaments of the life of grace, or perhaps as prerogatives of exceptional saints, but their relevance to the everyday conduct of the ordinary Christian has been forgotten." O'Connor, *The Pentecostal Movement in the Catholic Church,* 191. Garrigou-Lagrange, on the other hand, associates them with the mystical grace of infused contemplation as well. What needs to be kept in mind is that while always present with sanctifying grace—Thomas Aquinas refers to sanctifying grace as "the grace of the virtues and gifts" (*Summa Theologiae* IIIa.q.62,a.2, quoted in *Christian Perfection and Contemplation,* 275)—the extent of their manifestation and exercise will vary according to the maturity and consecration of the believer. According to the *Catechism of the Catholic Church* the gifts of the Holy Spirit are imparted in baptism (1266) and increased in confirmation (1302).

61. O'Connor, *The Pentecostal Movement in the Catholic Church,* 189.

62. Ibid.

63. Ibid., 197.

64. Ibid., 198.

65. Ibid., 196.

66. The list is worth repeating: "namely, sanctifying grace, actual grace, the infused virtues [the theological virtues of faith, hope, and love, and the moral virtues of prudence, fortitude, justice, temperance, etc.] and the seven traditional 'gifts of the Holy Spirit.'" Ibid., 209.

67. Ibid., 213.

68. Ibid., 216.

69. Ibid.

70. Donald L. Gelpi, SJ, *Pentecostalism: A Theological Viewpoint* (New York: Paulist, 1971), 183.

71. Ibid., 178.

72. Ibid., 184.

73. Ibid., 181.

74. A subject Gelpi explored more directly in a subsequent book, *Charism and Sacrament: A Theology of Christian Conversion* (New York: Paulist, 1976).

75. Léon Joseph Cardinal Suenens, *A New Pentecost?* (New York: Seabury, 1975), 83.

76. Ibid., 84. They include: "the grace of actualizing gifts already received, a release of the Spirit, a manifestation of baptism, a coming to life of the gift of the Spirit received at confirmation, profound receptivity or docility to the Holy Spirit." In any case, he does not deny that the experience is "a very special grace . . . [and] a renewal of . . . spiritual life."

77. Ibid., 82.

78. Ibid., 87.

79. Ibid., 88.

80. The role and function of Episcopal conferences is a recent development in the Catholic Church. Although particular councils (as distinguished from ecumenical councils), both plenary and provincial, were held in the ancient church, the Catholic Church only formed national and territorial episcopal conferences in the modern era with the Second Vatican Council explicitly laying down norms for them. Particular councils often debated doctrinal issues and even produced creedal symbols, e.g., Toledo (675), or doctrinal condemnations, e.g., Orange (529). These are to be distinguished from synodal structures that have continued in the Eastern churches. According to the present structure of the Catholic Church, plenary councils are called by the episcopal conference and provincial councils by the ecclesiastical province, a grouping of dioceses presided over by a metropolitan who is archbishop in his own diocese. Episcopal conferences are limited

in the scope of their doctrinal pronouncements. The 1998 Apostolic Letter of Pope John Paul II *Apostolos Suos* (*On the Theological and Juridical Nature of Episcopal Conferences*) states that an episcopal conference "must take special care to follow the magisterium of the universal Church" and may only act on "doctrinal declarations" when "new questions" arise "from changes in society." However, "these pronouncements do not have the characteristics of the universal magisterium," i.e., of the College of Bishops (the bishops worldwide) in union with the pope (21–22).

81. Printed in *Presence, Power, Praise: Documents on the Charismatic Renewal Volume I—Continental, National and Regional Documents Numbers 1 to 37, 1960–1974*, ed. Kilian McDonnell (Collegeville, Minn.: The Liturgical Press, 1980), 210.

82. Ibid.

83. "Message of the Bishops of the Western Province of Quebec on the Catholic Charismatic Renewal," *Presence, Power, Praise: Documents on the Charismatic Renewal Volume I*, 583.

84. Ibid., 367.

85. Oneness Pentecostals do indeed consider Spirit baptism as integral to salvation along with repentance and water baptism in the name of Jesus. The salvation event embraces the three aspects of Acts 2:38: "Repent and be baptized, every one of you, in the name of Jesus Christ for the forgiveness of sins. And you will receive the gift of the Holy Spirit." Oneness theologians debate whether regeneration takes place through conversion and confession of faith in Jesus Christ or through the integral event of water baptism and Spirit baptism with glossolalia as evidence. See "Oneness Pentecostalism," D. A. Reed in *The New International Dictionary of Pentecostal and Charismatic Movements Revised and Expanded Edition,* Stanley M. Burgess, ed, Eduard M. Van Der Maas, assoc. ed. (Grand Rapids, Mich.: Zondervan, 2002), 943–44.

86. The classic case for this position was argued by John Wesley in his two sermons "The Witness of the Spirit." In his second sermon on the matter, *The Witness of the Spirit, II,* Wesley defines it as follows: "The testimony of the Spirit is an inward impression on the souls of believers, whereby the Spirit of God directly testifies to their spirit that they are children of God." *The Sermons of John Wesley, Sermons I, 1–33,* edited by Albert C. Outler (Nashville: Abingdon, 1984), 296.

87. *The Canons and Decrees of the Council of Trent.* Tr. H. J. Schroeder, OP (Rockford, Ill.: Tan, 1941, 1978), 35.

88. *The Canons and Decrees of the Council of Trent,* 38.

89. *Letters*: "To His Brother Samuel" (I, 290) quoted in *John Wesley's Theology: A Collection from His Works,* edited by Robert W. Burtner and Robert E. Chiles (Nashville, Abingdon, 1954, 1982), 98.

90. *Sermons*: "The New Birth," II, 4 (S, II, 232–34), quoted in *John Wesley's Theology,* 169.

91. *Catechism of the Catholic Church* (New York: Doubleday, 1995), 540 (2005).

92. Ibid. The italics are those of the Catechism. One should also note that as Thomas Aquinas points out in the *Summa theologiae* that one cannot know if one is in a state of grace with certainty, but an imperfect knowledge may be obtained by conjecture such that one, for example, draws this conclusion because one delights in God, despises worldly things and is not conscious of mortal sin (ST I–II q.112, a.5).

93. "Statement on the Catholic Charismatic Renewal," by the Antilles Episcopal Conference, in *Presence, Power, Praise: Documents on the Charismatic Renewal, Volume II—Continental, National and Regional Documents Numbers 38 to 80, 1975–1979,* ed. Kilian McDonnell (Collegeville, Minn.: The Liturgical Press, 1980), 259–60.

94. "A Collective Letter from the Episcopacy of Panama concerning the Movement of Renewal in the Spirit, directed to Priests, Religious, and Lay People who work in Apostolic Movements," *Presence, Power, Praise: Documents on the Charismatic Renewal, Volume II,* 101.

95. Published in English as *"The Spirit Gives Life," Charismatic Community Renewal in the Catholic Church in the Federal Republic of Germany: A Theological Guide* (Vatican City: International Catholic Charismatic Renewal Office, n.d.).

96. One only has to go as far as Karl Rahner and Hans Urs von Balthasar to register how they use the category of experience in their work. A good case can be made that they are the two most significant Catholic theologians of the last century.

97. *The Spirit Gives Life*, 17.

98. Ibid., 22.

99. Ibid.

100. Ibid. 31.

101. Ibid., 37.

102. Ibid.

103. *Summa theologiae* I. q. 43 a.6 is quoted where Thomas affirms that through these new outpourings a Christian "is enabled to perform some action of grace or is placed in a new state of grace." Ibid., 36. Francis Sullivan, SJ, and Norbert Baumert, SJ, are the primary architects of a position on Spirit baptism based upon this passage. Baumert is the primary drafter of this document.

104. Ibid., 38–41.

105. Ibid., 42.

106. Ibid., 15.

107. Ibid., 56.

108. Ibid., 57–58.

109. Ibid., 37.

110. Charles C. Ryrie, Lewis Sperry Chafer, and John R. W. Stott are representative of this position. They both identify various works of the Spirit, some of which are unrepeatable. These include the regenerating work of the Spirit, his indwelling, sealing, and the baptizing work (as into the body of Christ ala 1 Cor. 12:12). All are simultaneous with conversion. The filling of the Spirit is meant to be continuous, not dependent on a gateway experience or work of grace subsequent to conversion, and enhances the quality of the Christian life in conformity to Christ. See Ryrie's *The Holy Spirit* (Chicago: Moody 1965), 93–103; and Chafer's *He That Is Spiritual: A Classic Study of the Biblical Doctrine of Spirituality,* rev. ed. (Grand Rapids: Zondervan, 1967), 40–69; and Stott's *Baptism and Fullness: The Work of the Holy Spirit Today,* 2d ed. (Downers Grove, Ill.: InterVarsity Press, 1975), 47–75.

111. "Charismatic Renewal: Message of the Canadian Bishops Addressed to all Canadian Catholics," *Presence, Power, Praise: Documents on the Charismatic Renewal, Volume II,* 89. A similar statement appears on the Web site of the United States Conference of Catholic Bishops (http://www.usccb.org/liturgy/q&a/general/baspir.htm). While it affirms that many people may experience "baptism in the Holy Spirit" as a "Charismatic milestone" in their ongoing faith life, it warns that the use of the term may imply that a second baptism has taken place. This would clearly violate Catholic teaching.

112. Ibid., 90.

113. *Final Report* of the International Roman Catholic/Pentecostal Dialogue (1972–1976), in *Pneuma: The Journal of the Society for Pentecostal Studies,* 12:2 (Fall 1990). The report states that the expressions "baptism in the Holy Spirit," "being filled with the Holy Spirit," and "receiving the Holy Spirit," "should not be used to exclude traditional understandings of the experience and faith in the reality of Christian initiation," 87–88. This seems to be an attempt at a common statement that would not exclude the Catholic position on baptism and confirmation.

114. Ibid., 89.

115. Ibid., 91.

116. "Theological and Pastoral Orientations on the Catholic Charismatic Renewal: Malines Document I," *Presence, Power, Praise: Documents on the Charismatic Renewal,*

Volume III—International Documents Numbers 1 to 11, 1973–1980, ed. Kilian McDonnell (Collegeville, Minn.: The Liturgical Press, 1980), 18.

117. Ibid., 22.

118. Ibid., 23.

119. Ibid., 25.

120. Ibid., 24.

121. Ibid., 33.

122. Ibid., 36.

123. Ibid., 38.

124. Ibid., 39.

125. Ibid., 42.

126. "Ecumenism and Charismatic Renewal: Theological and Pastoral Orientations: Malines Document II," *Presence, Power, Praise: Documents on the Charismatic Renewal, Volume III,* 82–174.

127. "The Charismatic Renewal and Ecumenism," *Presence, Power, Praise: Documents on the Charismatic Renewal, Volume III,* 175–279.

128. Ibid., 219. Emphases his.

129. From the 1973 "Statement of the Theological Basis of the Catholic Charismatic Renewal," *Presence, Power, Praise: Documents on the Charismatic Renewal, Volume III,* 5, authored by McDonnell at the request of Cardinal Suenens.

130. Alternatives listed in the *Statement of the Theological Basis of the Catholic Charismatic Renewal* include "release of the Spirit," "renewal of the sacraments of initiation," "a release of the power to witness to the faith," "actualization of gifts already received in potency," "manifestation of baptism whereby the hidden grace given in baptism breaks through into conscious experience," "reviviscence of the sacraments of initiation." Ibid., 8.

131. Ibid.

132. Kilian McDonnell and George T. Montague, *Christian Initiation and Baptism in the Holy Spirit: Evidence from the First Eight Centuries,* rev. ed. (Collegeville, Minn.: The Liturgical Press, 1994), xii.

133. Kilian McDonnell and George T. Montague, ed., *Fanning the Flame: What Does Baptism in the Holy Spirit Have to Do with Christian Initiation?* (Collegeville, Minn.: The Liturgical Press, 1991). The document emerged from "The Heart of the Church Consultation" of theologians and pastoral leaders that met in Techny, Illinois, from May 6–11, 1990.

134. Ibid., 16.

135. Ibid., 26.

136. Ibid., 27.

137. "God freely gives this grace, but it requires a personal response of ongoing conversion to the Lordship of Jesus Christ and openness to the transforming presence and power of the Holy Spirit." Ibid.

138. See *Lumen Gentium,* 4, 12 where the charisms are noted including the "extraordinary gifts." Another eloquent and thorough statement of this position is offered by Francis Martin, *Baptism in the Holy Spirit: Reflections on a Contemporary Grace in the Light of the Catholic Tradition* (Petersham, Mass.: St. Bede's, 1998). Note his summary statement on p. 37: "Thus it can be said that baptism in the Holy Spirit, as a grace of intensified faith or revelation, brings to awareness that which was given to us in Baptism, enables understanding of the preaching of the Church and gives empowerment to commit our lives to Christ. In this regard we can see that the grace of baptism in the Holy Spirit forms part of that 'calling down of the Holy Spirit' (*epiclesis*) upon the baptized believer that characterizes the sacrament of Confirmation. It may be said as well that baptism in the Holy Spirit, because it revivifies and intensifies the conscious faith of the baptized person, makes participation in the Eucharist more fruitful. This is because the grace of Baptism, which is the absolutely necessary work of the Holy Spirit enabling

us to receive the other sacraments, has come alive in a new way: the faith by which we believe has been quickened and made more efficacious."

139. Francis A. Sullivan, SJ, "Baptism in the Holy Spirit: A Catholic Interpretation of the Pentecostal Experience," *Gregorianum* 55 (1974), 59. He also explores the same theme in his later book, *Charisms and Charismatic Renewal: A Biblical and Theological Study* (Ann Arbor, Mich.: Servant Books, 1982). See especially chapter 5.

140. Ibid.

141. Ibid., 60. Here he registers his agreement with James D. G. Dunn, *Baptism in the Holy Spirit* (London: SCM Press, 1970), in the latter's critique of the Pentecostal doctrine. First, one cannot separate Spirit baptism from conversion/initiation and, second, the *charismata* and the power to witness (the classical Pentecostal emphasis) are corollaries to the main purpose of that gift, namely (in Dunn's words quoted by Sullivan), "the gift of saving grace by which one enters into Christian experience and life, into the new covenant, into the Church."

142. Ibid., 64.

143. Ibid.

144. Ibid., 66.

145. Ibid.

146. Sullivan, *Charisms and Charismatic Renewal: A Biblical and Theological Study*, 75.

147. Philippe Larere, *Baptism in Water and Baptism in the Spirit: A Biblical, Liturgical and Theological Exposition* (Collegeville, Minn.: The Liturgical Press, 1993), 82.

148. Peter Hocken, *The Glory and the Shame: Reflections on the 20th Century Outpouring of the Holy Spirit* (Guildford, Surrey: Eagle, 1994), 59.

149. Ibid., 62–75.

150. Forthcoming in the *Journal of Pentecostal Theology*. A more comprehensive study is published in two volumes, *Charisma—Taufe—Geisttaufe*, Band 1 & 2 (Würzburg: Echter, 2000).

151. See 12. "It is not only through the sacraments and the ministries of the Church that the Holy Spirit sanctifies and leads the people of God and enriches it with virtues, but allotting His gifts to everyone according as He will, He distributes special graces among the faithful of every rank. By these gifts he makes them fit and ready to undertake the various tasks and offices which contribute toward the renewal and building up of the Church, according to the words of the Apostle: 'The manifestation of the Spirit is given to everyone for profit.' These charisms, whether they be the more outstanding or the more simple and widely diffused, are to be received with thanksgiving and consolation for they are perfectly suited to and useful for the needs of the Church. Extraordinary gifts are not to be sought after, nor are the fruits of apostolic labor to be presumptuously expected from their use; but judgment as to their genuinity and proper use belongs to those who are appointed leaders in the Church, to whose special competence it belongs, not indeed to extinguish the Spirit, but to test all things and hold fast to that which is good." *Second Vatican Council, De Ecclesia November 21, 1964, Constitution on the Church,* Washington, DC, United States Catholic Conference, n.d., 14.

152. The original version of the guidebook for the Life in the Spirit Seminar entitled *Finding New Life in the Spirit* (Notre Dame, Ind.: Charismatic Renewal Services, 1972), 23, culminates in the following prayer by the person making the seminar. After renouncing Satan, confessing faith in Christ who died for our sins, and affirming that he or she will follow Jesus as Lord, one prays: "Lord Jesus Christ, I want to belong to you from now on. I want to be freed from the dominion of darkness and the rule of Satan, and I want to enter into your kingdom and be part of your people. I will turn away from all wrongdoing, and I will avoid everything that leads me to wrongdoing. I ask you to forgive all the sins that I have committed. I offer my life to you, and I promise to obey you as my Lord. I ask you to baptize me in the Holy Spirit and give me the gift of tongues." The similarity

to the typical sinner's prayer of Evangelicals and to the Rite of Christian Initiation of Adults (RCIA) in the Catholic Church is interesting.

153. It should be said that this is the situation of many of the historic churches that have been impacted by the Charismatic movement. Spirit baptism occupies a doctrinal place in Pentecostal and some Holiness churches. What is proposed here is, at best, from a Catholic perspective an unofficial theologoumenon.

154. *Daily Roman Missal,* ed. Fr. James Socias (Chicago: Scepter Publishers & Midwest Theological Forum, 1993), 617.

155. Thus Thomas Aquinas states in the *Summa theologiae* IIIae. q.8 a.5: "Hence the personal grace, whereby the soul of Christ is justified, is essentially the same as His grace, as He is the Head of the Church, and justifies others; but there is a distinction of reason between them." From *St. Thomas Aquinas Summa Theologica, Volume IV,* translated by Fathers of the English Dominican Province 1911 (Westminster, Md.: Christian Classics, 1981), 2073.

156. *Presence, Power, Praise Volume III,* 23.

157. *Catechism of the Catholic Church,* 1212.

158. Ibid.

159. Ibid., 1213.

160. Ibid., 1285, 1288.

161. Ibid., 1303.

162. Ibid., 1302. The deepening and increase of baptismal grace includes divine filiation, union with Christ, the gifts of the Holy Spirit, the bond with the church and strength to witness.

163. See also the prayer in the RCIA for confirmation of the newly baptized. "Let us pray, dear friends, to God, the all-powerful Father, that he will pour out the Holy Spirit on these newly baptized to strengthen them with his abundant gifts and anoint them to be more like Christ his Son." As the neophyte is anointed with the chrism the following is said: "N., be sealed with the Gift of the Holy Spirit." *The Rites of the Catholic Church* (New York: Pueblo, 1976), 103–4.

164. One must also note in this regard that baptism and confirmation cannot be repeated as sacraments and imprint an indelible spiritual mark or character on the soul.

165. See *The Documents of Vatican II,* ed. Walter M. Abbott, SJ, (New York: Guild, 1966), 793. One should also note that Pope John Paul II has anticipated a "new springtime of Christian life" in his Apostolic Letter *Tertio Millennio Adveniente* 18, which celebrated the Great Jubilee of the third Christian millennium.

166. See *Lumen Gentium,* 8. "This Church constituted and organized in the world as a society, subsists in the Catholic Church, which is governed by the successor of Peter and by the Bishops in communion with him, although many elements of sanctification and of truth are found outside of its visible structure. These elements, as gifts belonging to the Church of Christ, are forces impelling toward catholic unity." *Second Vatican Council, De Ecclesia,* 8.

167. *The Works of John Wesley,* 3rd ed. 14 vols. (London: Wesleyan Methodist Book Room, 1872, reprint Kansas City: Nazarene Publishing House, 1978), 12–27.

168. John Wesley, *Letters of the Reverend John Wesley,* ed. by John Telford, 8 vols. (London: Epworth Press, 1931), 1:255

169. A. S. Yates, *The Doctrine of Assurance* (London: Epworth Press, 1952), 61, 133–34.

Scripture Index

Name Index

Subject Index

direct revelation to individuals, 8
in John, 219–222
in Luke/Acts, 22–24
in relation to confirmation, 10
in relation to Scripture, 7
in relation to the church, 170
in the New Testament, 19–21,
 212–219
in the Old Testament, 208–212
power of, 175
Inner witness of the Spirit, 8
Jesus' baptism, 112–115
Johannine Pentecost, 132–133
Justification, 183–201
Keswick theology, 11
Language
 as used by Barth, 8
 role of, 7
Magisterium, 43
Malines Document I, 266–267
Miracles
 and B.B. Warfield, 2, 6
 and the church fathers, 3
 cessation, 2, 6
 in the early church, 2
Montanism, 4
Oberlin Theology, 230
Ordo Salutis, 43, 171
Paraclete, 134–135, 223–229
Pentecostal revival, 49–56
Pentecostalism
 and the Spirit, 12
Pietism, 143–144
Pontifical Council for Promoting
 Christian Unity, 265
Postmodernism, 168
Prayer, 158–161
Purifying work of the Holy Spirit,
 135–139
Puritans, 10, 142–143
Q source, 111
Reformation theologians, 13
Revival, 141
Revivalism, 145–147
Sacramental theology, 248–252, 281
Samaritan Pentecost, 123
Sanctification, 183–201
Septuagint, 121
Spiritual hermeneutic, 98
Spiritual gifts, 255
Subsequence, 61, 145, 149, 150, 244
Tongues (Glossalalia)
 as a psychological condition, 71
 as a second blessing, 122
 as an evidence of the Holy Spirit,

 29–31, 151
 as nonsensical language, 73
 as the language of angels, 72
 edifying, 89–90
 in the post-apostolic age, 4
 on the day of Pentecost, 71–75
 pastoral wisdom regarding, 165–167
 Paul, 76
Unity among believers, 125
Wesleyanism
and the Spirit, 10, 144-145
Wesleyan hermeneutic, 99
Wesleyan Quadrilateral, 207, 230
Wesley Theological Society, 230
Wind
 as divine manifestation, 57